MARINA TSVETAYEVA

Marina Tsvetayeva: Paris, 1925

MARIA RAZUMOVSKY

MARINA TSVETAYEVA

A CRITICAL BIOGRAPHY

TRANSLATED BY
Aleksey Gibson

BLOODAXE BOOKS

Copyright © Maria Razumovsky 1981, 1983, 1994
Translation © Aleksey Gibson 1994

ISBN: 1 85224 045 8

First English edition published 1994 by
Bloodaxe Books Ltd,
P.O. Box 1SN,
Newcastle upon Tyne NE99 1SN.

Bloodaxe Books Ltd acknowledges
the financial assistance of Northern Arts.

Jacket printing by J. Thomson Colour Printers Ltd, Glasgow.

Printed in Great Britain by
Cromwell Press Ltd, Broughton Gifford, Melksham, Wiltshire.

*To the memory of my mother, to whom
I owe my knowledge of Russian culture*

ACKNOWLEDGEMENTS

The original edition of this biography was first published in German in 1981 by Age d'Homme-Karolinger, Vienna, as *Marina Zwetajewa 1892-1941: Mythos und Wahrheit*. A revised edition translated into Russian by E.N. Sayn-Wittgenstein as *Marina Tsvetaeva: Mif i dejstvitelnost'* was published by Overseas Publications Interchange Ltd, London, in 1983. This first English edition was translated by Aleksey Gibson from the Russian edition, incorporating additional material from later French (1988) and German (1989) editions of the book, and working with Maria Razumovsky to incorporate important additional material.

Quotations from Marina Tsvetaeva's poetry are mostly taken from two editions: *Selected Poems*, translated by David McDuff (Bloodaxe Books, 1987), or from *The Demesne of the Swans*, translated by Robin Kemball (Ardis, Ann Arbor, 1980); unattributed quotations are translated by Aleksey Gibson. The short quotations from Rilke's 'Elegy for Marina' are translated by Walter Arndt, taken from *Boris Pasternak, Marina Tsvetaeva, Rainer Maria Rilke: Letters, Summer 1926* (Harcourt Brace Jovanovich, Inc, 1985).

The photographs are from the collection of Mikhail A. Baltsvinik (1931-80), reproduced from *Tsvetaeva: A Pictorial Biography*, edited by Ellendea Proffer (Ardis, Ann Arbor, 1980).

Contents

List of Illustrations

MARINA TSVETAYEVA

Introduction

In 1974 when Solzhenitsyn mentioned Marina Tsvetayeva, during an interview for Swiss television, as a major Russian poet of the twentieth century (along with Pasternak and Akhmatova), only a small group of specialists in Russian literature had ever heard of this name or vaguely knew that it was the name of a woman poet who had lived abroad as a Russian émigré after the revolution of 1917 and who finally returned to the Soviet Union shortly before the outbreak of World War II. At that time information about her was accessible only to English speaking specialists who could find it in Simon Karlinsky's book *Marina Cvetaeva: Her Life and Art* published in 1966. This was the first attempt at a biography of the writer and a scholarly interpretation of her poetic legacy. With this volume Karlinsky became the pioneer of research on Tsvetayeva, and all subsequent explorers of her work, including the author of this book, are highly indebted to him.

Marina Tsvetayeva was not only an outstanding poet and prose writer, who opened new paths for Russian poetry and the Russian language, she also had to face the problems of life and death which befell the entire Russian population of her generation. Coming from a well situated, highly intellectual Moscow family, she had to endure first the dangers and hardships of 1917, then the hungry years which followed in Moscow during the period of "War Communism". After spending seventeen years in emigration she returned to the Soviet Union in 1939, where, at the age of forty-eight, she took her own life in August 1941. Tsvetayeva has thus become a symbol of the fate of her generation and of a tragedy that in many cases was systematically and intentionally overlooked and deliberately suppressed by Western intellectuals who found it was so much easier to dream about the happy future of mankind and the "birth of a new man", that was going on in the new workers' paradise, than to concentrate on reality and take notice of the real situation of living men and – still more – women in Russia and in the countries where they had taken refuge.

When I began, as early as 1970, to try to find out more about Marina Tsvetayeva as a poet and human being, many details of her life and many of her poems were unknown. Although unofficially loved by her public, she was still officially banned in her native country; in Western countries, however, most of her friends had already given their testimony. Since then, she has also become known to non-Russian readers in the West. Translations of her works have been published in different languages, more and more scholars have taken an interest in her work and many articles have been written about it. A Tsvetayeva symposium was even held in Lausanne in 1982. But the task of writing a comprehensive biography is still not an easy one.

We are well informed about Marina Tsvetayeva's childhood and youth by her sister Anastasia, whose very detailed memoirs were published in three editions between 1971 and 1984. Ariadna Efron has also left us her recollections of her mother, but they cover only a short span of time. Over the last few years various contributions by Russian scholars to a more comprehensive portrait of the poet have appeared in the Soviet Union and elsewhere.

Another important source for biographical details are Tsvetayeva's own autobiographical writings, as well as many of her poems which reflect, as in a mirror, her moods and feelings. Because of their subjective point of view, however, they must sometimes be used with caution. Finally, Tsvetayeva's letters to friends and acquaintances, which have been published "there" and "here" (often on the basis of *samizdat* texts) provide a great deal of significant literary and biographical information.

The "new era" in Russia has also promoted official recognition of Marina Tsvetayeva as a great poet. Books and articles by Anna Saakyants, Maria Belkina, and Irma Kudrova published in Moscow since 1986 offer, not only new possibilities for understanding and identifying facts, persons, and poems connected with Tsvetayeva, but also the truth about what happened to the Efron family after their return to the Soviet Union. An attempt has been made to include in this book the most recent information about Tsvetayeva and her contemporaries.

Some Western sources are still not available to lovers of

Tsvetayeva's poetry. Her letters to Nikolay Gronsky and Salomea Andronikova-Halpern, which undoubtedly contain interesting details about her life, have not been published, while other letters have been published, but in an abridged form. Nevertheless, we can remain reasonably certain that the idea we have of Tsvetayeva's personality will not be overthrown by them. This is mostly to the credit of Karlinsky, whose second book on Tsvetayeva, published in 1985, not only gives a description of the character, work and problems of the poet, but also provides a picture of life in pre-Revolutionary Russia and in the Russian emigration. We should also mention here another biography in English which has recently been written by the first translator of Tsvetayeva's poetry into English, Elaine Feinstein.

Finally, as a further development of the Tsvetayeva revival, a great number of scholarly articles analysing her work have appeared lately in English, French and German, as well as Russian. They all represent different ways of approaching an artist, to whom Maksimilian Voloshin once said: 'There is enough material in you for ten poets, and all of them remarkable.' But there are also so many different aspects to Marina Tsvetayeva as a human being that more than one book is necessary to find the right clues to understanding her personality.

An important part of this book is the bibliography. It will help interested readers to form their own opinion of Tsvetayeva on the basis of primary sources. As recent Western literature can easily be found, special attention has been given to Soviet publications which are more difficult to trace.

Nearly all the friends and acquaintances of Marina Tsvetayeva who gave me their precious help and advice are now dead, but I would still like to express my deep gratitude to the specialists of the younger generation who continue to do so. I would also like to offer my warmest thanks to Aleksey Gibson for his excellent translation of this book and to Professor Robin Kemball and David McDuff for permission to include in this edition their translations of poems by Marina Tsvetayeva.

Due to circumstances beyond my control, the publication of this book was delayed for several years. The reader will forgive me if some of the details of Marina Tsvetayeva's life are now seen, not differently, but with more focus.

MARIA RAZUMOVSKY

Translator's Note

In the interests of both the general reader and the scholar I have used in this translation two systems of transliteration as recommended by Professor J. Thomas Shaw in his *The Transliteration of Modern Russian for English-Language Publications* (Madison, Milwaukee, and London, 1967). In the main body of the text and in the expository sections of the notes I have used, with a few modifications, Shaw's 'System I' for rendering names of persons, places and periodicals; titles of books, plays and cycles of poems, and the occasional Russian word. In all citations of bibliographical material and in the 'Notes on Persons Mentioned in the Text' I have used the more precise international scholarly system of transliteration (Shaw's 'System III').

With regard to the translation itself I would like to thank both Maria Razumovsky and the publisher's reader Irina Kuzminsky for their painstaking reading of the entire manuscript and for their invaluable suggestions and comments on it.

ALEKSEY GIBSON

PART ONE

Childhood

Childhood is the time of blind truth, youth, – of seeing mistakes and illusions. According to their youth no one should be judged...The history of my truths – is my childhood. The history of my mistakes – my youth. Both are precious, the first as the story of God and myself, the second as the story of myself and the world. If you seek the Goncharova of today, go to her childhood, and if you can – to her infancy. There are the roots...

from 'Natalya Goncharova'

CHAPTER 1

Moscow – Tarusa – Early Childhood
1892 – 1900

Russia at the end of the nineteenth century was a fantastic world, which differs so much from the present-day country that it has already become a myth, and has vanished like the legendary city of Kitezh.

The contrasts were as enormous as the country: next to the peaceful hospitable world of the landowners, whose lives, and those of their households and servants, were regulated only by the succession of seasons and church festivals, there was also the restless life of the political idealists, who, as if driven by the Furies, devoted themselves to change and reform, and who would not stop even at murder in order to realise what they considered to be a just society. Next to the reigning house, which was guided by the best intentions, and which concerned itself with the preservation of the inheritance of the past, but which had become insecure and susceptible to destructive influences, lived the community of artists and intellectuals, who entertained a visionary idea of the future and who wanted to create new moral standards for the decades to come. This was a world in which a hare cost five *kopeks* (five pence), but in which people also died of hunger and tuberculosis; a world which accommodated Christian virtues in their purest form, as well as the most brutal vices; which assimilated thousands of foreigners, while tolerating Jewish pogroms; which opened the way to success for the hard working, and which looked after their salvation, by prohibiting the publication of dangerous books. All of this was nineteenth-century Russia, and all of this helped to form the soul and personality of Marina Tsvetayeva.

Ivan Vladimirovich Tsvetayev, the father of Marina Tsvetayeva, was a native of the village of Talitsy in the province of Vladimir. Born in 1846 he was the third son of a poor and simple, but deeply

Marina's father, Ivan Vladimirovich Tsvetayev, 1900s

respected priest. His mother died at the age of thirty-five soon after the birth of her fourth son, and the children grew up without a mother. During his childhood Ivan possessed only one pair of shoes which he wore when he went into town. By ceaseless work the two younger sons made a way for themselves and managed to go to university. Dmitry Tsvetayev specialised in Russian history and became a well-known scholar, while Ivan had already become, at the age of twenty-nine, a professor of the history of art.

> He began his academic career with a dissertation in Latin on the ancient Italic people, the Oscans, for which he travelled all over Italy, crawling on his hands and knees in the earth around ancient monuments and graves, copying, collating, deciphering and interpreting the archaic inscriptions. This work made him famous throughout Europe.[1]

In 1888 Ivan Tsvetayev was invited to take the chair of the History of Art at the university of Moscow; along with this he was made a departmental curator, then director, of the Rumyantsev Museum. He put a great deal of energy into the creation of the Alexander III Museum of Fine Arts, whose opening in 1912 was the summit of his career. Both of his daughters praise his inexhaustible love of work, his modesty, goodness and benevolence to the people around him. Aleksandra Chernakova-Nikolayeva describes him as a man with a soft gentle soul, and as someone who could also be perfectly naive at times. Marina Tsvetayeva says of her father:

> Our Tsvetayev family is from the village of Talitsy, near the town of Shuya; a family of priests. From here comes the Alexander III Museum on the Volkhonka...from here come my poems of 2000 lines and the rough drafts for them of 20,000 lines, from here comes my son's head which will not fit into any kind of head-covering...From here comes that which is better and greater than poetry (poetry itself comes from my mother, like all the rest of my misfortunes) – *the will* to poetry, to it and to everything else – from a four line stanza to a four *pood* sack [(36 lb × 4),] which one has to – lift up, there! and carry. From here comes my heart, not an allegorical one, but an anatomical...the heart not of a poet, but of a walker.[2]

Ivan Tsvetayev was married twice. His first wife was Varvara Dmitrievna Ilovaiskaya, the daughter of the famous historian. She, the 'first love, the eternal love, eternal grief of my father' died of tuberculosis soon after the birth of her children Valeria (1882–1966) and Andrey (1890–1933). In order to provide his young orphaned children with a mother the forty-four year old Ivan married again in 1891. His second wife, Maria Aleksandrovna Meyn, was then twenty-two; she was a cultured and well-educated

Marina's mother, Maria Aleksandrovna Tsvetayeva, 1903

young woman who differed as much from her husband in background as in age.

The Meyn family originated in Germany, but we do not know when they settled in Russia. The father of Maria, Aleksandr Danilovich Meyn, was a typical Baltic German, fair-haired and very proper. He was evidently a man of considerable wealth. Although it is stated in Soviet sources that he worked in a bank, Marina writes that he edited a newspaper. He married a twenty-year-old girl who came from a noble Polish family; her mother, or grandmother, was a Countess Ledochowska. Soon after the birth of her only daughter this woman died at the age of twenty-eight. A portrait of her, this 'youthful grandmother', hung in the Tsvetayevs' drawing-room and stirred Marina's imagination from childhood:

> An oblong and severe oval,
> The bell-shaped folds of the black dress...
> Youthful grandmother! Who dared to kiss
> Your proud lips?
>
> A dark, direct and exacting look,
> A look ready to defend itself.
> Young women do not look at one like that.
> Youthful grandmother, who are you?
>
> . . . .
>
> The day was innocent, and the wind was fresh
> The dark stars grew dim.
> Grandmother! – This cruel mutiny
> In my heart – is it not from you?...[3]

From the age of seven Maria Aleksandrovna was a half-orphan, as Marina Tsvetayeva recalls:

> My mother's life was passed between my grandfather and a Swiss governess, – a closed-in, fantastic, unhealthy, unchildlike, bookish life. By the age of seven she knew world history and mythology, she dreamt of heroes and learnt to play magnificently on the piano. There were hardly any other children around her...My mother's youth was like her childhood, lonely, unhealthy, rebellious, deeply secretive. Her heroes: Wallenstein, Possart, Ludwig of Bavaria. A moonlit trip on the lake where he drowned. From her hand slips a ring – the waters receive it – a betrothal with the dead king...The whole atmosphere of her education was German. Intoxication with music, along with a tremendous talent...A gift for languages, a brilliant memory, a splendid style, verses in Russian and German, painting; pride often mistaken for aridity, shyness, self-control, lack of affectionateness (on the surface) passion for music, longing. At the age of twelve she met a young man...he was twenty. They went riding together on moonlit nights. At sixteen she understood, and he understood, that they loved each other. But he was now married. My grandfather considered that divorce was a sin, and my

mother loved my grandfather too well...Seryozha E. left for somewhere
far away. For six years my mother pined for him...When she was twenty-
two she married my father with the express purpose of becoming a
mother for his orphaned children...Her tormented soul lives on in us –
only we reveal openly what she had kept hidden. Her rebelliousness, her
frenzy, her thirst have reached the point of crying out in us...[4]

In this way the characteristics of three nations were combined in
Marina Tsvetayeva: from her father she inherited a strong will,
assiduity, and a love for the Russian language and the Russian past;
from her mother, romanticism and an enthusiasm for everything
German; and from her grandmother a feeling of honour and a
sense of her own worth, 'Polish pride'.

'Do not be mistaken, there is very little Russian in me,'
Tsvetayeva writes to Yury Ivask, 'even by blood I am a real mixture:
from my mother's side there is no trace of Russia in me, but on my
father's Russia is present in its entirety. And thus it is with *me*:
either Russia is completely there, or not at all. Spiritually as well I
am a half-breed.'[5]

For our understanding of Marina Tsvetayeva's childhood and
youth we have at our disposal three main sources. The first is her
poetry, which she began to write from childhood and in which she
directly expresses everything she feels. The second are the
autobiographical episodes which appear in many of her late works
and which provide a picture of the poet's spiritual growth and
"psyche"; they do not however, have much in common with
everyday reality, which the poet treats rather freely at times,
proceeding from what has already been recalled or from the
immediate facts of the poetic text. The third source is particularly
valuable, for in it historical truth is conveyed with all its details;
these are the memoirs of Marina's sister, Anastasia Ivanovna,
which were written many years later. At times they diverge from
Marina's account and certain accents are placed differently.
Anastasia herself makes a comparison between the stormy moun-
tainous river of Marina's memoirs and her own, which flow
smoothly. In particular Anastasia disagrees with Marina's belief
that she was loved less than her younger sister. They are
unanimous, however, in their appreciation of their mother; they
both emphasise that she was a very remarkable and rare person:

> She arrived as a second wife in a house which was still pervaded by the
> atmosphere of death. She miscalculated her strength in relation to the
> eldest of the children and could not deal successfully with either the
> reserved nature of this girl, or with her own tempestuous one; she left
> with her step-daughter poor memories of herself forever. Perhaps she

underestimated her strengths as a woman and as a mother...Perhaps she did not entirely succeed in her attempt to immerse herself in her books, diaries and piano-playing; maybe she did make many mistakes in the house in which she entered.[6]

My mother and father were people completely unlike each other. Each carried in their hearts a particular wound. With mother it was associated with music, poetry, longing; with father, learning. They lived their lives along side each other, without merging them. But they still loved each other very much.[7]

Marina was the eldest and was born on 26 September 1892; Anastasia (Asya) was born on 14 September 1894. Maria Aleksandrovna was at first disappointed: she passionately wanted to have sons ('Because of this I became a poet, not a poetess')

When instead of the desired, predicted, almost commanded son, Aleksandr, only I was born, my mother proudly swallowed a sigh and said, 'At least she will be a musician.' When my first distinct, though clearly meaningless, word spoken before the age of one turned out to be *gamma* [scale] my mother only confirmed it by saying 'I knew it', and immediately began to teach me music, humming ceaselessly the same scale: '*Do*, Musya, *do*, and this is *re*, *do-re*...' When two years later, after Aleksandr-me, the undoubted Kirill-Asya was born, my mother, once again corrected, said: 'Well, so what, there will be a second musician.' But when the first intelligible word of Asya, whose foot had become entangled in the blue netting of her bed was heard as "*ranga*" (*noga*) [i.e. foot – A.G.] my mother was not only distressed but indignant: 'Foot? What does that mean – a ballerina? I have a ballerina for a daughter? Grandfather has a ballerina for a granddaughter? Thank God no one in our family has ever been a dancer!'[8]

In her memoirs Anastasia recalls a photograph which was taken when she was two and Marina four:

The large forehead and round face of the elder...the adult-like look on the child's face, already somewhat proud despite the lost expression of inborn short-sightedness...What was my first memory of Marina? There isn't any, for it is preceded by a feeling of her presence around me, which begins in that mist where all memories are born. For as long as I can recall there was always a feeling of plurality with us, a "twosomeness" like a single breath, which was full of her, of "Musya's" qualities, her seniority, self-will, strength, superiority, disdain for my immaturity, clumsiness, and jealousy for my mother's love. Our "threesomeness", – including my mother, was full of my mother's pride in her first-born, her strong spirit and character. This was accompanied, also, by love and pity for the younger child who was often ill.[9]

Eighty years later Anastasia returns to the same theme: 'Our perception of things was not so much identical as inter-connected, as though we were twins. For example, our voices could not be distinguished from each other...Along with an *astonishing* similarity in the mental sphere, there was a *profound* difference of characters and aspirations..."[10]

A 'unity' which was 'like a single breath' was hardly conducive to their growing apart. One wonders if Asya perceived accurately her adored elder sister, whom she admired but also feared on account of her tyranny and her strength. Could she, in spite of this intimacy, see her clearly, understand her and enter into the complicated impulses of her soul? All her life Marina felt that her mother, whose worship was the great motif of her childhood, whose favour she sought to win, her mother, who served as an unattainable standard for measuring her own strengths, preferred her demanding and often crying sister to herself.

The personal impressions of Mark Slonim add to this picture:

> Maria Aleksandrovna treated her daughter somewhat cooly, responded to her adoration with restraint and always tried to control Marina's imagination and to impose limits on her stormy temperament...The traces of her mother's strict, slightly prim, upbringing remained on Marina her entire life; it was evident from her manners in society that she had been a young lady brought up in a rather old-fashioned environment, and I think that she lacked a mother's affection and love, which explains why she sought the friendship of women; for example in her rather older Czech friend Anna Tesková she especially valued this maternal warmth and care...[11]

Anastasia does not agree with this version. She stresses that their mother loved them both equally and that Marina's reproach is unjust. In her article 'Roots and Fruits' she describes more clearly than her sister the exceptional personality of Maria Aleksandrovna, who had a perfect command of several European languages, as well as a remarkable musical talent, and who became a close assistant to her husband.

Maria Aleksandrovna could not establish any real contact with the children from her husband's first marriage; the relations between her and Valeria were especially bad. She sought in the education of her own children compensation for her own unrealised youth and her own unjustified aspirations, at least her children could become what she was not: free artists. Despite the fact that French governesses and German "Fräuleins" were continuously employed in the household, as well as servants of all kinds, their mother supervised herself the education of her daughters and established the moral and ethical standards of their spiritual development.

> We did not receive any religious education (as is often described in memoirs of childhood with diligent attendance at church, the learning

of traditions and prayers). Although we celebrated Christmas and Easter, and fasted during Lent, a custom to which my parents adhered, as did other professors' families and the schools of that period, a fast in the strict sense of the word was not observed; we were not made to go to church early in the morning; in general everything was made easier. But to make up for this the ethical principle, the question of good and evil, was instilled in us by my mother zealously, perhaps more zealously than is necessary for children; ardently, wrathfully, at every misdeed, sometimes provoking in us a certain annoyance at having to hear the same thing time and again, as well as a secret protest.[12]

Maria Aleksandrovna's world-view included a particular Spartan disdain for an easy life. From their earliest years she cultivated in her children a suspicious attitude to the concepts of "money" and "fame": 'From childhood we were taught: money is filth.' Marina's 'organic aversion to satiety and self-satisfaction', about which Slonim speaks later, apparently derives from this source.

It was also considered perfectly impossible to ask for the fulfilment of any wish. ('It was not given to me because it was so much desired, such as the sausage which we had only to look at for it to be refused. The right to request something did not exist in our house, even the request of the eyes.')[13]

Although she noticed that Marina was particularly interested in words and rhymes ('My four-year-old Marusya walks around me and makes up rhyming words – perhaps she will be a poet?' she wrote in her diary), Maria Aleksandrovna wanted her daughter to become a pianist. She took away the paper on which Marina liked to write so much and sat the five-year-old girl, in whom a musical talent was evident, at the piano with an iron persistence.

Playing on the piano was associated with Marina's earliest memories:

> From the darkest depths a round, five-year-old, inquisitive face, without any sort of smile is looking at me; a face which is pink, even through the blackness, like a black person plunged in the dawn, or roses – in a pond of ink. The grand piano was my first looking-glass, and my first awareness of my own face was through this blackness, which was turning my face itself into blackness as though it were translating it into a dark but intelligible language. Thus, throughout my whole life in order to understand the simplest thing it has been necessary for me to plunge it into verse, to recognise it *from there*.[14]

Marina made such progress at the piano that she was enrolled at the age of five in the Zograf-Plaksina School of Music. In the following year she appeared in public at a student recital, playing a composition for four hands with Valeria Yakovlevna Bryusov, the sister of the poet Valery Bryusov. Anastasia recounts this episode with all the delight and admiration of a younger sister.

According to their mother, however, more important than success was a conscious aspiration for it:

> My mother rejoiced at my sense of hearing and involuntarily praised it, but then, after each 'well done' which broke loose, she coldly added: 'But of course, you have nothing to do with it. A good ear comes from God.' This has always remained with me, that I have nothing to do with it, that a good ear comes from God. This has saved me both from self-importance and from self-doubt, and especially in art from false pride; for once you understand that hearing is from God, you know that the only thing you have is the striving, because every divine gift can be ruined, as my mother used to say above my four-year-old head, which obviously did not understand anything and which because of this remembered it so well that later nothing could knock it out of me...Oh, how my mother rushed through life with her musical notes and alphabets, her Undines, and her Jane Eyres...as if she knew she would not manage in life, she would not manage, no matter what, to do everything; she would not manage, no matter what, to do anything; and so, if only this could be done, and then perhaps that, and then still something else? So that there might be something to be remembered by! In order that we be fed at once – for our whole life! Thus from the first minute to the last she gave – and even pressed! not allowing herself to lie down, to be trodden down (and us to calm down) pouring and forcing on us from above impression upon impression, and memory upon memory, as if into a trunk which is full to bursting (but which all the same proved to be bottomless); was all this by accident or on purpose?...And what good fortune that all this was not book-learning but Lyricism, that of which there is always little, twice too little...that of which there can never be *too much*, because it is itself – *too much*...My mother did not educate – she put one to the test, against one's powers of resistance: would the rib-cage collapse? No, it would not collapse, but it expanded so much that later – now – no matter what you feed it you will not fill it. After such a mother there only remained one thing for me to do, to become a poet. In order to free myself from her gift – to me, which would have stifled me or forced me to transgress all human laws.[15]

Marina and Asya grew up together, sharing everything between them and resembling each other very much in gestures and in their manner of speaking. From an early age, however, there was something extraordinary about Marina; it was as if her soul, her "psyche" were of an order different from that of her sister or other children. She possessed a vast imagination and a great sensitivity; she was easily offended. Marina was often unhappy, she wanted to join the gypsies or run away to an Old Believer monastery because she felt she was not loved enough. Or she would be suddenly convinced that she was possessed by the devil, who was waiting for her in Valeria's room. She says herself about her early childhood:

'Fear and pity (and anger, and longing and defensiveness) were the principal passions of my childhood, and where there was no food for them, I was not to be found.'[16]

To Marina's self-portrait Anastasia adds a few interesting details based on her own impressions:

> There was from the earliest years a feeling, a passion for words, in the literal sense, for the letters which composed them; the sound of words, full to the extremes with meaning, afforded a purely physical joy...The precious existence of words, as a source of light, awoke in us such a response, which even at the age of six or seven brought with it the torment and happiness of mastery. For some years the writing of a first line of poetry or a first sentence in prose seemed to be a much desired means of liberation from being over-satiated by the feeling of words...
>
> From childhood Marina had a flawed attitude to good and evil. With her generally passionate nature and inordinate pride she easily and frequently did wrong. After all it is not so easy to be carried away by good! She would mock and deny any judgement over her. But then when she had begun to repent she would consume her guilt with her heavy but scarcely visible tears. I have remembered my whole life her face on such days and hours, it was radiant with eyes which shone more brightly than usual on account of her tears and her tormented shyness. There was also an expression of aloofness and distance in front of those from whom she was seeking pardon. It was as though she were listening to something only she could hear, to something which had an immutable message for her alone.
>
> Musya's special character, which was by no means like my own, revealed itself to me with difficulty. The desire to separate her joys from those of other people's, the domineering hunger to discover and love everything on her own; her penetrating knowledge that all this belonged to her alone, to her, her, her, more than to everyone else; her jealousy of the fact that someone else (especially me who resembled her) might love trees, meadows, a country lane or the spring as much as she did, all formed a shadow of hostility which fell from her possessiveness of books, music, and nature onto those (such as me) who felt in the same way. She was driven by an impulse to antagonise and to eclipse others, to possess indiscriminately, not to share anything with anyone, to be the first and only one – in everything![17]

Marina herself confirms the last point. She speaks of her 'innate jealousy' and about her 'complete inability of loving something together with someone else': 'No, the gods forgot to bestow the gift of collective love on me in my cradle' she adds.[18]

In comparison with the domineering personality of their mother, the other members of the family played a secondary role in the lives of the girls. Their beloved, benevolent and absent-minded father spent night and day in his study and rarely appeared in their daily lives. Valeria, who was called Lyora by her family, was much older than they and was not often at home as she attended a boarding school. She was fond of both her half-sisters and protected them from the severity of their mother. As a child Marina was very attached to her, but later an irreparable rift occurred between them. Andrey was a good-looking boy, but lazy; he had no imagination and was as Marina said, 'not of their spirit', so that quarrels often broke out between them.

Although the various German "Fräuleins", French governesses, housekeepers, as well as Andrey's tutor and Asya's nurse (which Marina did not have), must have added something to the development of the girls' personalities, they did not have a great influence on them. An important role, however, was played by the older generation of the family, such as their grandfather Aleksandr Meyn and his second wife, a Swiss woman who had been the governess of their mother. She survived her husband by many years; even so she never learnt to speak Russian properly. Both sisters describe her as 'an amusing old lady' whom they called 'Tio'. A great impression was made on the children by the grandfather of Andrey and Valeria, Professor Dimitry Ilovaisky, who was an extremely conservative historian and also violently anti-Semitic. Marina Tsvetayeva immortalises him in her memoir 'The House at Old Pimen'. In it she remarks on the fact that Ilovaisky was on good terms with her mother although she had a particular love for Jews and sought their company, a side of her personality which was explained:

> ...neither by birth (half-Polish), nor by her social circle (very right-wing) – but *only* by Heinrich Heine, *only* by Rubinstein, *only* by the Jewish genius and her own feminine inspiration, *only* by her Reason, *only* by her conscience...The leitmotif of all *her* life and of *my* life – has been a Tolstoyan 'against the current' – even if of one's own blood, and against the stasis of every environment, of every pool of stagnant water.[19]

It is possible that this early influence of her mother contributed to the fact that later on Marina also sought the society and friendship of Jews, and that she married a man who was half-Jewish.

Tsvetayeva considered her childhood to be the most important period of life. In a short autobiographical piece written after her return to the Soviet Union in 1939 she maintained that at the age of forty-seven it seemed as though everything she was destined to know, she knew before she was seven, and that it took her the remaining forty years to understand this.[20]

Those familiar with the memoirs of Anastasia Tsvetayeva know the important part the Tsvetayevas' house, No. 8 Trekhprudny

Lane [i.e. 'Three Ponds Lane'], played in the lives of the two sisters. It was a spacious old Moscow style house painted a chocolate brown colour with a courtyard and trees around it, which Anastasia describes with affectionate detail. One also finds many descriptions of the house in the works of Marina: her father's study with its statue of Zeus, the cold "hall", where the grand piano stood and where family gatherings took place, and the comfortable children's rooms on the mezzanine with the various pictures on the walls. One of these, depicting Pushkin's death after his duel, exerted a particularly strong influence on Marina's imagination:

> The first thing that I knew about Pushkin was – that they killed him. Then I learnt that Pushkin was – a poet, and that d'Anthès was a Frenchman. D'Anthès hated Pushkin because he himself could not write poetry. A duel in black and white, without a single patch of colour; a black deed being carried out on the whiteness of the snow: the eternally black deed of the murder of the poet – by the mob. Pushkin was my first poet – and they killed my first poet. Since that time, yes, since that time, when they killed Pushkin before my eyes in Naumov's painting, daily, hourly, ceaselessly, they have been killing my infancy, my childhood, my youth – I have divided the world into the poet and all the rest, and I have chosen – the poet to take under my protection: to defend the poet – from all the others, how ever all these may be dressed or called.[21]

If in the memoirs of Anastasia their life in Moscow is presented as a succession of happy days, then their summer months spent in Tarusa are described as an earthly paradise. For many years the family rented a *dacha* not far from the town which stood on a steep hill above the Oka, a simple grey house in a large over-grown garden. 'A richer, happier childhood than ours in Tarusa I have never heard of, and cannot imagine...' writes Anastasia; and Marina recalls with nostalgia in 1934:

> I would like to be buried in the Old Believers' cemetery in Tarusa beneath an elder bush, in one of those graves with a silver dove on it, where the reddest and largest strawberries in these parts grow. But if this is not possible, if this cemetery no longer exists and it is not only me who cannot be buried there, then I should like for a stone from the Tarusa quarry to be placed on one of those hills, over which the "Kirillovnas" [women of the flagellant sect – A.G.] would come to see us at Pesochnoye, and over which we would go to visit them in Tarusa with the inscription:
>
> Here wished to lie
MARINA TSVETAYEVA[22]

Tsvetayeva's best memorial to Tarusa, however, was already written in 1909:

The clear morning is cool
And you run easily through the meadow.
Slowly down the Oka
Crawls a wooden barge.

A few words rise against one's will
And you repeat them on end.
Somewhere in the field horse-bells
Are faintly ringing.

Are they ringing in the fields? Are they
Riding to the meadow? To the threshing?
Little eyes for a moment
Glimpsed into someone's fate.

The blue distance between the pines
The conversation and humming on the threshing floor...
And the autumn smiles
At our spring.

Life revealed for us new forces, but all the same...
Ah, golden days!
God, how far away they are!
Lord, how far away![23]

CHAPTER 2

Travel Abroad

1901 – 1905

Marina and Asya attended neither a private nor a public preparatory school, as Maria Aleksandrovna herself took charge of their education. From early childhood the girls spoke Russian and German, and from the age of seven Marina spoke French as well. They soon were familiar with all the children's books and fairy tales of world literature. Anastasia Ivanovna cannot recall when and from whom she learnt to read.

Proper regular schooling began for Marina in the autumn of 1901 when she was nine years old. She entered the first year of the Fourth *gymnasium* on Sadovy Street. From the very beginning she was a brilliant pupil, although she did not, in fact, like going to school. Among the girls of her own age she had no friends.

In the afternoon Asya would come with a governess to collect Marina. On one occasion there was no one at the front of the school to take her home, so an older girl from the eighth year, who also lived on Trekhprudny Lane, took her by the hand and led her home. This girl was called Natalia Goncharova, like Pushkin's wife, and when they met for the next time in a café in Paris, Goncharova was a famous artist.

Anastasia Ivanovna also tells of another event which apparently belongs to the same year; Andrey did not go to school, but studied with a tutor at home. This teacher was a student from Siberia who would often laugh loudly. As she says, this student 'affected Marina's imagination'; in other words, Marina had fallen in love with him. Marina thought she knew exactly what love was since the time she had seen a scene from *Yevgeny Onegin* at the music school:

> A bench. On the bench – Tatyana. Then Onegin enters, but does not sit down and *she* stands up. They are both standing. And only

> he speaks, the whole time, a long time, and she does not speak a
> word. And then I understand...that this is love: when there is a
> bench, and she is on the bench and then he enters and speaks the
> whole time, and she does not utter a word.[1]

When Tatyana falls in love she writes a letter to Onegin. Marina
followed her example and also wrote a letter to this student, in
which she declared her love. She did not yet suspect that letters of
this sort would subsequently play an important part in her life and
art. She also did not know that the fate of this, her first letter,
anticipated the fate of much of her future correspondence: it was
misunderstood. The perfidious tutor had a good laugh and
underlined the mistakes in her spelling with a red pencil. This
event stirred up her family a great deal; Marina cried and felt her
pride to be deeply offended. On this occasion, however, fate
appeared to be just and struck at the offender himself; the tutor fell
in love with Valeria and wanted to marry her, but Valeria spurned
him and her parents moved the teacher to a distant wing of the
house.

We can recognise a reference to this story in a description by
Marina of the family table:

> A round table. The family circle. On the blue serving dish pastries from
> Bartels. One each. Children! Help yourselves! I want a *baiser* and take
> an éclair. Embarrassed by the clear-sighted look of my mother I lower
> my eyes and completely close them while reciting:
>
> > Fly my ardent horse
> > Across the fields and meadows.
> > And shaking your mane
> > Carry me away!
>
> But where is away? They are laughing: my mother (triumphantly I will
> never become a poet!), my father (good humouredly), my brother's
> tutor, a student from the Urals (ho-ho-ho!), my brother, who is two
> years older begins to laugh (following his tutor) and my sister, who is
> two years younger (following my mother); only my elder sister is not
> laughing, the seventeen-year-old schoolgirl Valeria, to the pique of her
> stepmother (my mother). And me – I am red like a peony, and am
> deafened and blinded by the rushing and pounding of blood in my
> temples. Through the boiling but not yet flowing tears (at first I had
> been silent) I cry Away – far away! Away – Away![2]

In the summer of 1902, during their first real holidays since
Marina had successfully completed her year at school, the family,
as always, went to Tarusa. Marina was captivated by Pushkin,
whom she was reading secretly from her mother; and with a special
love she would declaim his poem 'To the Sea'. The word sea
became transformed for her into a concept of a distant fabled

world, into the object of her yearning.

In September the girls were aged eight and ten. The family moved back to town and as soon as they began to get ready for the winter it seemed as though thunder had roared in a clear sky: a slight illness of their mother's, which had been taken for influenza, turned out to be tuberculosis of the lungs. The doctor's order was categoric: Maria Aleksandrovna had to leave the cold of Moscow immediately and move to a southern climate. It was decided that the entire family, with the exception of Andrey, would accompany her to Italy.

Both sisters describe the traumatic moment when they learn of their mother's serious illness and about the long journey to come. Anastasia writes:

> How special the house became from that minute, when we knew that we had to leave it! Every run up and down the staircase, every room, every corner, every moment which flew past – all became dearer a hundred fold. And the terrible parting which had begun was so bitter that later, in that enormous *later*, after everything which had begun and continued, there was nothing new in any other parting, even with a person, whom one loved incurably, and from whom one was separated by trains, wars, revolutions or another person; in spite of whatever force these partings might have had, only that first 'farewell', which rang out in the house during the days and weeks of the preparations to leave, was remembered. Perhaps because of this we later became generous to the strangest of all thieves – to life itself! – and we secretly knew: we will survive, having *already* survived...[3]

Marina reacted completely differently. She was touched neither by her mother's serious illness, nor by the departure at hand. She understood only one thing: we are going to the sea, to Pushkin's 'sea of liberty'.

> In November 1902 when mother said: 'to the sea' while coming into our nursery she did not suspect that she was uttering the magic word, that she was declaring 'To the Sea', in other words, giving a promise which she could not keep. From that minute I was going to the sea, during that entire interminable month before our departure, which was without school or any activity, I was continuously, and alone, on my way to the sea.[4]

At the end of November or in the beginning of December 1902 the Tsvetayevs set out on their journey, leaving in Moscow only Andryusha with his Ilovaisky grandfather. In Vienna the trip was interrupted for several days as Maria Aleksandrovna's health suffered a complete breakdown.

The trip through the Tyrol and the arrival in Italy enraptured Marina and Asya. But after this followed the inevitable disappointment: the harbour of Genoa did not correspond to Marina's conception of the sea. The myth of the "free element" was dispersed; only a salty after-taste remained.

> Such a sea – my sea – the sea of Pushkin's and my 'To the Sea' could only exist on a sheet of paper – and within...Pushkin's sea was – a sea of farewell. One does not meet seas and people in such a way. One can only bid farewell in this manner...[5]

The family arrived in Nervi and settled in several rooms of the Pension Russe, which was situated directly above the sea. This *pension* belonged to a German, a widower. His eleven-year-old son Volodya played a great role in the life of Marina and Asya. While their sick mother was incapable of leaving her bed and their father was preparing for a scholarly trip through Italy, the children were allowed to play in the garden under the supervision of Volodya. In fact they spent their time climbing on the cliffs, wading in the sea, grilling fish on an open fire and eating Italian sweets. They even learnt to smoke from their protector. At home it would never have entered their minds even to dream of such a life. Later, Marina Tsvetayeva dedicated three poems to Volodya, her 'first knight'.[6]

Their stay in Nervi widened the horizons of the girls. They became acquainted with a different way of life and met people who did not belong to their closely knit domestic circle. On the top floor of the Pension Russe lived a young book-keeper from Berlin who

Anastasia and Marina with V. A. Kobylyansky: Italy, 1903

was seriously ill with tuberculosis and who died during the time of the Tsvetayev family's stay. When the girls went to visit him he lit a cigarette paper above a kerosene lamp and the ashes dispersed into the air: 'Look, the soul flies!' ('*Seht, die Seele fliegt!*') He wrote in Marina's album a line, which she considered to be quintessentially German: '*Tout passe, tout casse, tout lasse, excepté la satisfaction d'avoir fait son devoir.*'

Tsvetayeva writes in her journal of 1919: 'The soul is duty. The duty of the soul – is flight. Duty is the soul of flight – I fly, because I must. In a word, one way or another: *Die Seele fliegt.*'[7]

At one stage Aleksandra Ilovaiskaya, the second wife of Andrey's grandfather, appeared with her two children, Seryozha and Nadya. The handsome young people were also ill with tuberculosis. However, as a tender romance began to develop between Nadya and a poor student, Marina and Asya helping from time to time with their letters, their angry mother, without thinking, sent both invalids back to Russia, even though their health had only just begun to improve. Not two years passed before they both died in the same month.

Nadya Ilovaiskaya, 'the rose on the graves of Nervi', made a great impression on Marina.

> We were not friends – and not because of the difference in age – that is nonsense! but because of my shyness before her beauty, with which I could not cope in my poetry...More simply, we were not friends, because I loved her. And then – less than two years later, her death...Nadya Ilovaiskaya means to me ten years of the ABYSS. Since that time I have done what?...Learnt to write and unlearnt to love...[8]

A group of Russian anarchists which settled at the Pension Russe created an even greater stir. Their head, Vladislav Kobylyansky, especially impressed Marina and Asya, who gave him the nickname of 'Tiger'. While their father travelled around Italy in the company of Valeria, there arose between Maria Aleksandrovna and the revolutionaries a close friendship. In the evenings they gathered in the Tsvetayevs' drawing-room. They argued fiercely about politics and the situation in Russia, and sang revolutionary songs to the accompaniment of Maria's guitar. The children were allowed to be present.

> As for Marusya, she has become an entirely new person, as though she were an adult...They speak to Marusya as if to an equal. They are interested in her poetry: she writes poems about them, the enemies of the Tsar, and she is full of a new passion, which her heart can sense in this captivating atmosphere: hatred for the Tsar-tyrant. The sharp, loud, sarcastic Herb does not provoke Marusya like the others. He

respects her...Something unites all of them with this remarkable girl, who writes poetry and keeps a journal, who plays difficult pieces of music, and who possesses such a talented, intelligent, haughty mother. They feel instinctively that Musya's mother is on guard against them. Does she fear for her daughter? And they are glad and proud that Musya is already theirs.[9]

Kobylyansky's influence was growing all the time:

...Like mother we knew that this encounter was shaking the foundations of our life. The derision alone with which he regarded the way of life which formed our family's existence was a disruption of it, a call to something different. It seemed he rejected everything by which we lived, our family structure, society...It was the first time that my mother and we had met such a man. For the first time we heard everything amongst which we lived repudiated – even God. On the last point mama did not agree with him and his companions. But we soon surrendered in the question about God, quickly and heedlessly...How intelligently, patiently, convincingly did Koshechka speak about the errors of religion; fastening on us her large dark-blue eyes she led us away from God and prayers quite easily, so easily perhaps because religion was in fact quite distant from us. We had no kind of grandmother or nanny to bring us up; we went with mama to church because papa, who had grown up in a priest's family, went. Mama was a believer in general, but after her own fashion.[10]

Not only were the young girls attracted by 'Tiger', but also their gravely ill romantic mother. She even considered abandoning her family and going with him to Zurich. Anastasia Ivanovna relates how one evening during a strong storm, while Maria Aleksandrovna and Kobylyansky were walking by the shore of the sea, Marina slipped on a wet staircase and fell, severely hurting her head. Like a *deus ex machina* this unexpected event forced their mother to return to the needs of the family and to look after the invalid.

Marina Tsvetayeva never mentioned one word about this incident. But the theme of the conflict of the mother, who does not know whether she should remain with her children or follow the thief who has killed her husband ('...indeed she had loved him earlier, but was married like Tatyana...') appears in a story written decades later, 'The Tale of the Mother'.

The freedom on the cliffs of Nervi lasted only a few more weeks. The doctors advised Maria Aleksandrovna to remain another year in Italy, so they decided to send the girls to a Swiss boarding school. 'Tio' came to Nervi from Russia in order to take the children to her own country. Marina and Asya had to stay with their aunt at an elegant hotel, and to learn again how to wear hats and gloves and to go for drives in a smart carriage instead of climbing barefoot over cliffs.

From the spring of 1903 to the summer holidays of 1904 fate cast Marina and Asya on the shores of Lake Geneva. In the school of the Lacaze sisters at No. 3, Boulevard de Grancy in Lausanne they spent a happy time, where a good climate reigned. The pupils and teachers were affable and far more emphasis was placed on praising good results than on punishing bad ones. Excursions in the environs or trips by steamers on Lake Geneva were often arranged.

Unexpected friction arose between Marina and her surroundings only on the grounds of religious questions. Both elderly Lacaze sisters were fervent Catholics and they educated the girls entrusted to them in the same spirit. They were helped in this by an intelligent, experienced Abbé. When Marina began to spread her atheistic convictions brought from Nervi among her new friends a profound disturbance was felt in the school. Monsieur l'Abbé summoned Marina for conversations many times and entered into long discussions with her. Judging by the fact that the views of Marina and Asya changed fundamentally in the course of this year, he was an expert "fisher of souls". They turned into little *devotes* who diligently attended all the Catholic services, prayed at length in the evenings on their knees by their beds, and by their letters threw their parents into the greatest confusion. In Lausanne Marina made her 'first and only confession' to a Catholic priest. Although Tsvetayeva never mentions a single word about this religious impulse, we know from her herself that she was only attracted by the devil, this religious mood is clearly reflected in a poem without a date from *Evening Album* (*Vecherny al'bom*), 'The Lady in Blue'.

Not long before the summer holidays of 1904 Maria Aleksandrovna came to Lausanne to visit her daughters. She stayed in a hotel not far from the school and the girls were permitted to spend all their free time with their mother. Anastasia Ivanovna describes in detail the arrival of her mother, and Marina's poem 'In Ouchy' is based on it. The state of their mother's health had improved significantly, but when Marina asked, if she really intended to move to Zurich, she evaded further conversation on this subject.

For the summer holidays the entire school moved to neighbouring France. At first they stayed in Chamonix and then in Argentière, from where they made excursions with a guide into the glacier regions.

The doctors advised Maria Aleksandrovna to spend another year in central Europe in order to acclimatise her gradually again to

colder weather. For this purpose Freiburg-im-Breisgau was chosen
as the place of residence. For Marina and Asya a new period in life
began – Germany.

Before the beginning of the school term the family stayed in the
Schwarzwald at the hotel Zum Engel in the village of Langackern,
where they could enjoy the large forests, recalling Tarusa, the
swift-flowing river and the heavenly peace of the comfortable
Gasthaus which smelled of trees and cleanliness. The girls felt
happy in Langackern and made friends with the children of the
proprietors. In the garden their mother read to them Hauff 's
Lichtenstein and the legends of the Black Forest. Marina and Asya
sometimes played for hours alone in the forest.

> We are both fairies, good neighbours,
> Our rule divides the dark forest in two.
> We lie in the grass and through the branches watch
> How a small cloud turns white in the heights of heaven.
>
> We are both fairies, but the large ones (strangely)
> See in us only two wild girls.
> But it is clear to us, everything is dim for them:
> As for everything else one needs special sight to see a fairy.
>
> . . . .
>
> But the day passed, and again the fairies were children,
> Whom they are awaiting and whose step is silent...
> Ah! how can my still immature verse
> Convey the peace and joy of being on this earth?[11]

The next stage (during the school year of 1904-5) was the
boarding school of the Brink sisters in Freiburg, at No. 10,
Wallstrasse. This school differed sharply from the one in Lausanne: the spirit of Prussian barracks reigned here. At half past six in
the morning the headmistress rang a bell in the corridor and when
she entered the dormitory the children had to be already on their
feet. Only a few minutes was allowed for washing in ice-cold water,
after which they went, two by two, into the dining-room for a
meagre breakfast, which lasted only eight minutes. After their
morning lessons and a lunch, which was so modest that the pupils
were always hungry and spoke of nothing but food, they were taken
every day in pairs to the Schlossberg. The road there led through
the 'Schwabentor'. Every day Marina looked at the heroically
romantic portrayal of St George with his sword raised high, which
had only been painted the year before in 1903. Ten years later we
meet this St George from Freiburg's 'Schwabentor' in the poem
'Germany'.

Asya hated the German school.

> In Marusya's case the severity of the school aroused her bitterness,
> which was growing all the time. She withdrew into herself; in her eyes
> were concealed protest and disdain. On some days she even distanced
> herself from me as well. I, who was softer than she, fell into an
> inconsolable sadness.[12]

She did not know, however, why Marina was so detached from
everyone around her and why she withdrew even from herself.
Marina was thrown into despair, not by the Brinks' school, but by
the news of the death of her beloved Nadya Ilovaiskaya. She took to
playing the piano, seeking salvation in that one quiet corner; she
played but she only heard one word, one name: 'Nadya, Nadya...'

> I then gave free, complete rein to my feelings; for two years I loved,
> without ceasing, in advance (and *dreamt in advance* – these dreams I still
> remember!) – and I do not know why I did not die then (or did not
> break down afterwards). You are the first to whom I am telling this –
> strangely enough! I hid this love in myself to – yes, to the present hour!
> and carried it through all of 1905. It eclipsed in me even my mother's
> death.[13]

At the beginning, when their mother could rent a room not far
from the school at No. 2, Marienstrasse, everything was easier to
bear. The children could visit her and spend the night with her in
turns from Saturday to Sunday. Their mother would make tea for
them on a spirit lamp and tell them news from home, such as about
the fall of the fortress at Port Arthur and the terrible, bloody
massacre carried out during the peaceful demonstration of 9
January in front of the Winter Palace.

In February 1905 the actor Emil Possart arrived in Freiburg. He
was looking for singers to reinforce his choir. Maria Aleksandrovna
wanted to take part and saw how near the realisation was of her
dream of appearing on stage. During a rehearsal, however, she
caught cold. Pleurisy set in and her tuberculosis flared up with
renewed vigour. Professor Tsvetayev was summoned. While he sat
by the bed of his wife, who was delirious and unconscious by turns,
a fire broke out in his uncompleted museum of fine arts, which
destroyed a great number of priceless works of art. Maria
Aleksandrovna was taken to hospital and after this to the
sanatorium of Sankt-Blasien.

At Easter all the children at the school went home; only Marina
and Asya remained there alone. The Brink sisters had pity on them
and took them to have tea with Princess Marie von Thurn-und-
Taxis. This trip, which was so different from the grey daily
boredom in Freiburg remained in Marina's memory as a great

event. She recalled this day when she received as a gift from Rilke a copy of his *Duino Elegies* and wrote about this in one of her memoirs.[14]

Not long before the end of the school year both Russian pupils were practically expelled and only after the intervention of their father were they allowed to stay until 25 July 1905, the beginning of the summer holidays. After this their father freed them from the hated school and took them to Sankt-Blasien, where their mother was still being treated at the sanatorium. He settled them in a small hotel. The girls were left almost entirely to themselves and took walks along the dusty roads under the protection of a Newfoundlander, who belonged to the proprietor of the hotel. Occasionally their father spent some time with them and they undertook long excursions on foot. Ivan Vladimirovich passionately loved long walks and found this summer a worthy companion in the person of Marina.

After three years of a nomadic life and visits to the famous doctors of Europe, Maria Aleksandrovna's health had not improved, but had, to the contrary become worse. And so, as the doctors wanted to get rid of this hopelessly sick woman, they recommended that she return to her native land and settle in the Crimea. Ivan Vladimirovich, who had lost hope of her recovery, had no other option but to return to Russia with his family in the autumn of 1905.

Their return route led through Munich and the Austrian border station of Podwoloczyska in Galicia. On the other side of the river Zbrus was the town of Volochisk, the gate to the Russian Empire. Here was the border control and the place where one changed to the wide gauge Russian train carriages. It was forbidden to bring live flowers into Russia and travellers usually gave them to the curious barefooted children who came every day to the station in order to look at the elegant people of the *grand monde*. In her book Elizabeth Poretsky relates how among these children were several friends who subsequently made careers in the G.P.U., and how, already having premonitions that they would themselves soon become its victims, they would recall these flowers from Podwoloczyska after all other themes of conversation had become too dangerous. Could Marina Tsvetayeva have then suspected that she had perhaps looked into the eyes of the person who many years later would become known under the false name of 'Ignaz Reiss' and who would, in such a tragic way, influence her fate?[15]

CHAPTER 3

Yalta – Death of Mother
1905 – 1906

In her memoirs Anastasia Ivanovna does not give an exact date for the family's return to Russia; this was probably at the end of August or at the beginning of September of 1905.

Their first stop on their way home was Sebastopol; they were forced to stay here for several days as Maria Aleksandrovna was feeling very unwell. It smelled of the sea in the town and Asya was happy to find herself in an atmosphere which recalled Nervi. In the company of their father they became acquainted with the sights of the city: 'the Count's Harbour' with its white marble staircase decorated with columns and the 'Panorama of the defences of Sebastopol' from the time of the Crimean war. The girls immersed themselves rapturously in memories of the heroic past of the city. Having only come from abroad, however, they also did not suspect what was going on in the country, such as the fact that after the disastrous war with Japan their homeland was on the brink of revolution and that where they were standing much blood would soon flow again. In Sebastopol an incident with a motley-coloured book, which her father had bought for her at her request, made a great impression on Asya. Her mother and sister regarded this purchase with disdain.

As there was no railway between Sebastopol and Yalta, where the Tsvetayevs planned to spend the winter, they had to travel by sea or cross the mountains in a carriage. The Tsvetayevs chose the steamer and Marina, who would be sick even during the trip from Tarusa to the station at Pesochnoye, suffered from seasickness for the entire journey.

We also do not know the exact date of the family's arrival in Yalta: 'It was autumn, the winds were blowing.' At first the mother

and daughters took a floor in the hotel 'Quisisana' in Zareche, a
suburb of Yalta. The hotel belonged to an old doctor, whose eldest
daughter Vera Marina especially liked. A serious dark-eyed girl she
considered herself, unlike the rest of her family, to be a
revolutionary. While her parents were beginning to accustom
themselves to life in the strange city and were busy seeing doctors,
which left no time to spend with their daughters, and while Asya
was playing with the doctor's younger children, Marina would often
vanish into Vera's room where various suspicious persons sometimes made their appearance. Anastasia Ivanovna thinks that the
sudden end to their stay in the *pension* Quisisana is explained by this
new friendship of Marina's, which was too dangerous in those
uneasy days.

Their new flat was on Darsanovsky hill, high above the city and
the sea. The house belonged to S. Ya. Yelpatievsky, a relation of
Ivan Vladimirovich who himself lived at some distance in a new
summer house on the coast, while renting out the rooms of his
empty house. The site of this house, however, was not suitable for
sick people; it stood on a rocky knoll without the slightest
protection from the cruel icy winds which blew that stormy autumn
from all directions. On the top floor lived the Nikonov family, about
whom it was said that they organised illegal gatherings. Marina was
forbidden to go to the top floor. When Ivan Vladimirovich returned
to Moscow all the residents of the lower floors began to gather at a
common dining-table to discuss political questions and the exciting
events of the day. Marina Tsvetayeva lived and suffered through
the revolutionary winter of 1905–06 in these surroundings.

At the time that Maria Aleksandrovna and her daughters were
staying in the Yelpatievsky villa, the tense atmosphere reached its
peak in Yalta, as in the rest of Russia. In different parts of the
country riots broke out; at first there was a printers' strike, which
meant no newspapers were available, and then a general strike. The
railwaymen stopped working immediately after Ivan Vladimirovich
left for Moscow and communications were cut off. In Petersburg
the first workers' council was formed; in Sebastopol an uprising
began under the leadership of Lieutenant Schmidt, an officer on
the battleship *Potyomkin*. Much blood was shed, the mutiny was
suppressed and Schmidt was executed on 6 March 1906.

On 17 October the Tsar issued a manifesto granting a
constitution: it guaranteed the right to hold meetings and the
freedom of the press. But on 8 December street-fighting broke out
in Moscow, which lasted until 2 January 1906. Next to the

Tsvetayevs' house on Trekhprudny Lane barricades were set up. On the barricades at Presnaya, Ye. P. Efron, a mother with numerous children, was found fighting. She was exiled from the country after the suppression of the uprising. In Yalta, aside from a few demonstrations, it was quiet; a cruel 'Black-Hundreds' commandant whom everyone feared ruled here. Many inhabitants of the city were arrested, among them the young Nikonov. On the evening before this, Marina was with the family despite her parents' prohibition.

During this winter the thirteen-year-old Marina lived through the first serious crisis in her life, taking a passionate part in everything that went on around her. As if in a moment she lost interest in the children's games of her sister. She fully shared the views of the young people who were fighting for national freedom. She thought only about the heroism of Lieutenant Schmidt and the selflessness of Maria Spiridonova. She was deeply affected by the failure of the revolutionary movement, for whose sake she wanted so much to give her own blood.

> Marusya walked among us children like a wounded animal. She would look about her while lurking around. The events of the past winter...pierced her like wounds. Biting her lip with that "reserve", to say the least, which she adopted in times of enthusiasm or suffering, she shunned everyone with the gesture of someone who is being harassed. Angrily and disgustedly she suspected everyone, especially those who were close to her, mama, myself and those who sat with us at table, of interfering with her torments about heroes and idols, with her passion for revolution, for its future...After the news about the trial of Lieutenant Schmidt and his execution Marusya withdrew into herself and hid from her elders her soul which was stunned with grief. This was a wound which she did not permit anyone to touch.[1]

Marina's misfortune consisted in the fact that at this difficult period in her life, between childhood and adolescence, she had no one to whom she could open up her soul. Lyora, who could have played this important role and helped her, was far away, and serious disagreements between mother and daughter were beginning to arise. Maria Aleksandrovna adhered to completely different views; she was a supporter of the 'Cadets' and rejoiced at the establishment of a constitutional monarchy.

> Marusya only pressed her now unkind lips even tighter together, and in their corners a shadow of mockery was hidden. There – upstairs they spoke differently!

Their mother's health worsened to such an extent that she could no longer go out. She felt that her life was coming to an end, and she simply could no longer enter into her daughter's problems. She forbade her every form of communication with such people as the Nikonovs and failed to notice that Marina was no longer a child and that it was not possible to treat her like one. The aggression towards her mother which is so clearly found in Tsvetayeva's later works and in her declaration that her mother persecuted and neglected her, have their roots, without a doubt, in the experiences of the revolutionary winter in Yalta.

Marina also hid from the members of the household her lofty, fiery poems dedicated to the heroes of the revolution of 1905. These poems were never published and in all likelihood have disappeared forever. Only one poem of this period is quoted from memory by Anastasia Ivanovna in her book. It is still not yet 'first-rate poetry', but all the same it is 'first-rate Tsvetayeva':[2]

> Do not mock the younger generation!
> You will never understand how it is
> Possible to live by aspiration alone,
> By the thirst alone for liberty and the good.
>
> You will not understand, how the chest
> Of the fighter burns with martial bravery,
> How religiously the adolescent dies,
> Loyal to the motto to the end!
>
> . . . .
>
> Thus, do not summon them home,
> And do not hinder their striving,
> For every one of the fighters – is a hero!
> Be proud of the younger generation![3]

Everything which was happening around her made much less of an impression on Asya. She was really still a child and played at first with the Nikonov children and later with the offspring of the new occupants of the top floor, Maksim and Katya Peshkov, the children of Maksim Gorky. Yekaterina Pavlovna Peshkova moved to Yalta after her famous husband had left her for the actress and beauty Andreyeva. But from time to time he came to Yalta to visit his family. The acquaintance with Gorky which took place this winter later had great significance for both sisters: Gorky later regarded Marina's art with disdain and refused to help her, but to his very death he did everything he could to defend Anastasia from attacks of all kinds, and without any doubt she owed him a great deal. The strong personality of Yekaterina Pavlovna, who later became the head of the 'Political Red Cross', made a deep impression on Marina and Asya.

Lessons and studies appeared in the lives of the girls as a ray of

light and as a welcome diversion from anxiety about their mother's
health and the future of the country. Their parents managed to find
a talented teacher who prepared them at home for examinations
which would allow them to enter the fourth and second years of the
gymnasium. The girls studied willingly and were very attached to
their short hunchbacked teacher.

In March Maria Aleksandrovna had the kind of haemorrhage
which she feared so much.

> An illness entered our rooms and settled there, but it was not like the
> one which had lived there until then! Until this time the doctors had
> made a distinction between mama and other invalids. From that night
> she took to the other road, which everyone must take...[4]

From now on Maria Aleksandrovna had no illusions regarding
her condition. All the same, the girls remained in their sick
mother's room, the only change being that the table at which they
prepared their lessons was moved from the side of her bed to the
middle of the room. An additional sorrow for their mother was the
fact that because of her illness and her daughter's studies Marina
almost ceased to play the piano.

At the beginning of the summer Marina and Asya passed their
exams brilliantly at the women's *gymnasium* in Yalta.

When Ivan Vladimirovich saw his family for the first time in June
1906, after all the events which had taken place, he was presented
with a difficult task: he had to arrange moving his dying wife to
Tarusa. It was already out of the question to take Maria
Aleksandrovna by ship, so they had to travel to Sebastopol by horse,
a distance of 70 *versts* [46 miles] then by train, then by horse again.

Both sisters describe the arrival in Tarusa:

> Mother had to be carried all the way from Yalta to Tarusa from one car
> to another ('I left as a passenger, and I am returning as baggage,' she
> joked.) She had to be carried on their arms and be placed in the
> carriage, but she would not allow herself to be carried into the house.
> She stood up and, declining any assistance, made her way on her own
> past us, who were frozen by these few steps, from the porch to the piano,
> unrecognisable and enormous, after several months lying horizontal, in
> a beige travelling cape, which she had ordered to be left as a large cloak
> so as not to be bothered with having sleeves made for it...Well, let's see
> what I am still fit enough for? She said, obviously to herself, smiling.
> She sat down. Everyone else was standing. And then from her hands
> which were already out of practice...This was her last performance.[5]

> She proudly entered the house, as she had left it almost four years
> before: on her own, without any help, not deigning to take notice of
> illness. She waved everyone aside – and entered.[6]

Their meeting with Valeria and Andrey, now almost grown up,

and with the servants, together with the beautiful colours of their childhood paradise could not divert them from the awareness that their mother's life was coming to an end. Within a few days of their arrival Maria Aleksandrovna came down with pneumonia. On 4 July she summoned her daughters for the last time in order to take leave of them:

> Mother's look met us at the very door. Someone said: 'Go to her!' We went to her. First on Marusya's head, then on mine, she placed her hand. Papa, who was standing at the foot of the bed, was sobbing. His face was puffy. Turning to him mama tried to comfort him. Then to us: 'Live *by the truth* children! – she said – You must live *by the truth*...[7]

They learnt of her death in the forest. In order to distract them Valeria had taken them into the woods to collect nuts. Maria Aleksandrovna died on 5 July 1906. She was thirty-seven years old.

The passion of her youth made itself felt even after her death. During the funeral a bearded gentleman with dark eyes came up to the carriage in which Marina and Asya were sitting and asked in a warm low voice, 'The daughters of Manya?' He looked at them as though he wanted to remember them his whole life. The girls understood that this gentleman was the very same whom their mother had loved so much with her first youthful love.

Later on Tsvetayeva often returned to the theme of her conflict with her mother. Without saying this openly she reproached her for a lack of affection and warmth. In her memoirs several traits of her mother's character took on forms which, as Anastasia proves in detail, she did not in fact have. The image of her mother which Marina depicts in *Evening Album* is probably much closer to the truth than the one which will appear in later works:

> In an old waltz by Strauss
> we first heard your quiet call,
> and from that moment all living things have been foreign
> to us, and joyful has been the quick flight of hours.
>
> We, like you, greet the setting of the sun,
> intoxicated by the nearness of the end.
> Everything by which the finest evening enriches us
> Was lodged in our hearts by you.
>
> Bending your head tirelessly over our childhood dreams
> (when you had gone only the moon looked on them!)
> you led your daughters past
> the affairs and designs of bitter life.
>
> From our earliest years, what was sad was near to us:
> laughter we found boring and alien the domestic roof...
> Our ship did not cast off at an auspicious moment
> And it sails at the will of every wind!

The azure island of childhood seems paler and paler,
We stand alone on the deck.
As your inheritance to your daughters
You have obviously left your sorrow![8]

Anastasia Ivanovna also testifies:

She always remained for us Mother with a capital letter, without a
shadow of reproach on her side. Adored, she stood above everyone else
by her heroism and the honour with which she came out of the battle
with herself, out of the struggle between happiness and duty, in which
she lost the strength to fight against her illness. She gave up the man she
loved and did not destroy the life of her husband, our good already
ageing father. These qualities led us by the hand decades later in our
battle with life. What a joy to be born of such a strong and pure man,
who lived his life unselfishly, as did our father, and of such a tragic
woman as our mother, who lived so valiantly! No one wishes tragedy for
themselves; one is born with it. Gratitude and peace to their ashes![9]

Marina with her father, 1906-07

CHAPTER 4

Moscow
1906

Their mother's death formed a great turning point in the lives of
Marina and Asya, making a sudden unexpected transition from a
pleasant cloudless childhood to the "freedom" and alienation of
adulthood. It threw Marina into a state of shock from which she
could never really recover. In 1936 she wrote to Anna Tesková
about her 'orphanhood'.

> I grew up without a mother, that is, I was knocked about at every angle.
> (The *angularity* of all those who have grown up without a mother has
> remained within me, rather in an inner sense. And *orphanhood*.)

The very thought of returning to their beloved family home in
Moscow after the three year absence and not finding there her
mother was apparently so unbearable for Marina that she requested
to be sent to the strict boarding school of the conservative Von
Derviz *gymnasium*. Asya remained at home; she was less hardy than
her stronger elder sister and her father feared for her health. The
loss of her mother also brought with it her first separation from
Marina. At first she stayed alone with her father in Tarusa. Before
her eyes he suffered a stroke and he had to spend many months in
hospital.

At home on Trekhprudny Lane Asya felt very lonely. Her half-
brother was an eccentric: he would sit the whole time in his room
playing the guitar. Valeria was a teacher, she 'worked for the
people' and received visits from her revolutionary friends. She had
neither the time nor inclination to take an interest in her little sister.
When Marina was at home she sometimes joined Valeria's circle.

Asya studied at home with a tutor. Her father, who was not a very
fine psychologist, began to look for a maternal substitute for her
and summoned the teacher from Yalta, whom Marina and Asya

had loved so much the year before. This plan, however, ended in complete failure. After her an energetic German woman from the Baltic region settled in the house, who thoroughly ruined any form of domestic comfort. Marina eloquently describes the situation at home in her poem 'The Dining Room':

> Four times a day the dining-room reconciles
> For a moment those who have nothing in common.
> The conversation is only about the most mundane concerns
> And whoever is too lazy to answer remains silent.
>
> Everything is unstable, unfriendly, brittle,
> The clatter of dishes. The clipped exchange of words:
> 'Does she want to come back from skating at seven?'
> 'No, at nine' – answers the house-keeper.
>
> The bell. 'We are not at home, tell them we have gone away!'
> 'Today we shall dine without a lamp'...
> Silence again, without expecting a response.
> The knives carry on a conversation with the forks.
>
> 'Has everyone finished? Anyuta, the plates!'
> The hostile tone in low voices,
> And everyone watches as the hands
> On the wall-clock catch up with each other.
>
> They drop their chairs. The footsteps hasten,
> Farewell, oh peace, for the sake of a plate of soup!
> They give thanks for the meagre meal
> And separate again – enemies until supper.[1]

Asya did not remain alone for long, however; in the spring of 1907 Professor Tsvetayev was asked to take Marina from school. They could not keep there a pupil who was trying to incite revolutionary fervour in the others. Anastasia Ivanovna includes in her memoirs several reminiscences of Marina's former class-mates:

> The administration feared her influence on her fellow students; they considered her to be forward. She was undesirable in the *gymnasium* on account of her revolutionary tendencies. From her enthusiasm for adolescent heroes she immediately passed to revolutionary literature; she simply breathed revolution. The administration rejoiced when they got rid of her. [S. I. Liperovskaya]

Valya Generozova, another class-mate and a friend of Marina's writes:

> Worshipping the heroes of the revolution, she dreamt of taking part herself in the struggle for freedom and the radiant future of mankind. Marina tried to acquaint me with the revolutionary movement, supplying me with books which were forbidden at that time. In the atmosphere which reigned in our school Marina was considered to be

(politically) 'unreliable', and they were afraid of her influence. They said that she was ordered to leave us for 'free-thinking'. Marina was certain that in her future personal life she would be free from the fetters of ordinary family life, and would give herself entirely to a revolutionary and literary career.[2]

The names of Anya Lanina and Valya Generozova are familiar to us from *Evening Album*. Two poems are dedicated to them. As it seems unlikely that Marina wrote these poems just after she left the school, it follows that they date to the beginning of 1907 and can therefore be considered the first creative works of the young Tsvetayeva. With this Marina begins her 'lyrical journal', from which she does not part to the end of her days. Thus from 1907 we have at our disposal a direct source of biographical information. This, as well as the image of the inner world of the young Tsvetayeva, which can be gleaned from these early verses, offers extremely important material for the biographer.

Marina also wrote her first prose work at the Von Derviz school. Anastasia Ivanovna recalls that she read her story 'The Fourth' over a weekend, but she does not know what happened to it. During the same spring Asya sat her entrance examination for the third year of the Pototsky *gymnasium*.

The school year of 1907–08 brought important changes with it for both sisters. Marina lived at home again and went to the Alferov *gymnasium*. On the top floor in the former nursery they arranged two rooms for themselves and furnished them according to their taste. They were now aged fifteen and thirteen; Marina was almost an adult and had already put her hair up. Since Asya was completely under the influence of her elder sister she was finally treated by Marina as an equal. The estrangement which began in 1905 came to an end and they became inseparable. They started to read Marina's poetry together with one voice, with identical gestures and with the same elevated feeling.

At this age Marina was especially unbalanced, everywhere and in everything her mother's absence was felt. She suffered a great deal from her appearance: she considered herself to be too heavy and too red-cheeked; she was too vain to wear glasses, although she was very near-sighted. Visits to relations and acquaintances were particularly unpleasant for her.

> The torture of shyness was almost unbearable: to enter someone's drawing-room, where there were people gathered, into the net of crossed glances, under the mercilessly bright glare of lamps and to move between the despicable silk-upholstered armchairs, screens and tables covered with velvet cloths was really beyond one's powers. Petrified,

ready to tear herself to pieces for having blushed again to the roots of
her hair, she walked as though to her execution (with a motionless – no,
not a single muscle! – face); having lowered her eyes she was almost
beautiful during these moments! And they watched her, observing her.
Ah, if she had only raised her eyes! In them was something resembling
the gaze of the ancient Medusa. The white-hot scorch of disdain![3]

Tsvetayeva herself describes this later in the following way:

Pride and shyness, close sisters –
Stood as friends above my cradle.

'Raise your forehead!' pride ordered,
'Cast down your eyes!' shyness whispered.
Thus I pass through, with eyes downcast
And forehead raised – Pride and shyness.[4]

In her kingdom on the top floor Marina saved herself from all
these annoyances. She read and wrote deep into the night. She now
read all the books which her mother had not given her: all of
Pushkin, Goethe, Schiller, Jean-Paul Richter, and many other
authors. Since she was bored at school she began, without any
pangs of conscience, to miss lessons. She hid herself in the attic,
shivering from the cold, until her father left for the Rumyantsev
Museum, of which he was the director. Then the happiest hours of
the day began. When Marina left her room, however, her face bore
an expression of remoteness; she answered all the questions of the
servants with a contemptuous silence; more than anything else she
wanted to sever her ties with everything of the external world and to
live only with her books. After her mother's death she no longer
touched the keys of the piano. All these traits in her character can
be explained by her fear of becoming an adult and of the future
which seemed terrifying to her. Her lost childhood was turned into
an earthly paradise.

They ring, and sing, disturbing my obliviousness,
These words in my soul: Age fifteen!
Oh, why have I grown up?
There is no salvation.

Even yesterday among the green birches
I ran away, free from the morning.
Even yesterday I could play with my hair down,
Even yesterday!

The springtime peal from the distant belfries
Said to me: 'Run and lie down!'
And every cry was permitted to the naughty child,
And every step!

And what is ahead? What kind of disaster?
Deceit is in everything; and ah, on everything lies a ban!
Thus, weeping I bid farewell to my dear childhood,
At age fifteen.[5]

More and more Asya was becoming Marina's only link with the outside world. She was more cheerful than her sister and was completely happy at her school.

Two friends of Asya's, Anya Kalina and Galya Dyakonova, often came to visit her in the evening. Then Marina herself would appear and would talk with the girls, telling them about books and distant countries and would read her poetry to them. Anya and Galya were her first sympathetic audience. From Marina's poem 'The Elf in the Hall' we can conclude that Anya played the piano very well; Galya, however, whom Asya particularly liked, subsequently made a not entirely ordinary career for herself. While she was still ill in Switzerland she met the young French poet Paul Éluard, whom she married during the war. She became famous throughout the world later thanks to the countless portraits which her second husband, Salvador Dali, painted of her. The celebrated Gala Dali died in 1981.

Their family and relations criticised the 'savages' who were growing up without a mother, but no one wanted to take charge of their education. Only one friend of the family, the physician and dentist Lidia A. Tamburer, took an interest in them and became something of a maternal adviser for Marina and Asya. In her essay 'A Living Word About a Living Man' Tsvetayeva speaks of her as a 'unique friend, twenty years older'. She dedicated several poems to her, which were published in *Evening Album* and *The Magic Lantern* (*Volshebny fonar'*).

In the autumn of 1908 Marina was seized by a new passion which forced her to forget her enthusiasm for the revolutionary movement. She read Edmond Rostand's *L'Aiglon* and fell in love with Napoleon and his unfortunate son, the Duke of Reichstadt. During the entire winter of 1908–09 she worked on a verse translation of *L'Aiglon*.

> Which of these did she love more deeply, the powerful father, the conqueror of so many countries, or the son, the dreamer, the prisoner of Austria, who perished in his youth? Marina's love for them was like a wound from which blood flowed. She hated the daytime with its routine, people and obligations. She lived only in portraits and books...Marina's absorption in Napoleon's fate was so deep that she simply did not live her own life. Locked for half the day in her humble little room, which was hung with engravings and portraits, and surrounded by French

books she escaped mentally into another epoch and lived among different names...Not one of Napoleon's wives, nor the mother of his son, perhaps, could have mourned for both of them with such passionate grief as Marina did at the age of sixteen.[6]

Her enthusiasm for Napoleon went to such an extreme that she re-decorated her room in the Napoleonic style, with a dark-red ceiling strewn with small gold stars. 'I wanted to do this with Napoleonic bees, but as such things were not to be found in Moscow I had to reconcile myself to stars...'[7] She then hung the walls with portraits of Napoleon. A stormy scene passed between her father and herself when he remarked on the fact that Marina had hung a portrait of her favourite hero in the icon-case, in place of an icon. Indignant at such interference Marina turned pale and grabbed a candlestick from the table.

> This was a gesture of despair. The self-defence of a wild animal when it is removed from its den. For Marina her whole cult of Napoleon, and all her other cults, of Nadya Ilovaiskaya and Lieutenant Schmidt, was such a den. In her veneration of them her soul was hidden, as in its last refuge, according to her boundless pride, which had not found for itself any recognition or occupation and which forgot itself, as much as it could, in her magical rhythmic gift.[8]

Marina, then, shut herself up in her lair and lived in the realm of the shades of the French Empire. She was not interested in the fact that immediately beyond her doorstep, in contemporary Moscow and Petersburg, there was seething the kind of cultural and intellectual life which falls to man's lot only during his zenith hours. Although she had heard of the struggle of the new "decadent" world of the Symbolists against the Classical literature, and was acquainted with the names of Balmont and Bryusov, they had no influence on her and did not serve as an example. All of her youthful poems are perfectly free from any kind of literary trend. Her idols remained Pushkin and Rostand; the themes of her creations were the heroes of Rostand or simple everyday incidents, described by a child or a very young girl. Tsvetayeva was not familiar with the rules of prosody and was writing according to her ear and her heart. Her caprices and melancholy were the signs of her development and the growth of her artistic world. From the very beginning Marina Tsvetayeva followed her own creative and personal path.

CHAPTER 5

Moscow
1909 – 1910

In the beginning of 1909 a blow of another kind struck Ivan Vladimirovich Tsvetayev, professor at the Imperial University of Moscow and privy councillor. On 25 January it was discovered that a considerable number of valuable engravings had disappeared from the department of engravings at the Rumyantsev Museum. The culprit turned out to be one of the privileged visitors to this department and a protegé of Professor Tsvetayev himself.

In our day it is unlikely that one would hold the director of a library or museum responsible if books or engravings were stolen in similar conditions. Before this incident Professor Tsvetayev had repeatedly made reports about the impossible working conditions on the premises and in the book stacks, and also about the lack of personnel in his institute. The Rumyantsev Museum is the largest public library in the city of Moscow. (After the revolution of 1917 it became the country's national library under the name of the Lenin Library.) In 1909 it had around 12,500 registered readers and about 230,000 volumes, which could be used only in the reading-rooms. The staff consisted of only nine librarians, including the director, and thirty-eight voluntary assistants, on whom fell the responsibility of carrying out all the work in the library and museum.[1] When the theft of the engravings was discovered the Minister of Education, A. N. Shvarts, sent an investigating commission, on several occasions, not in order to improve working conditions, but to damage the reputation of his former university class-mate and present personal enemy, I. V. Tsvetayev. His first action was to obtain the dismissal of the head of the department.

At approximately the same time Marina was making her first steps in the literary world. At the home of a family friend, Lidia

Aleksandrovna Tamburer, she met the poet L. L. Kobylinsky, who was known by his pseudonym of Ellis. He was a thin thirty-year-old man in a black coat, who had a shining bald patch and thin black hair, an oval face with green eyes and a very red mouth. He resembled a sorcerer from some medieval legend. Ellis was a colleague and best friend of Andrey Bely, and several people considered him to be the ideologue of the younger generation of Symbolists.

This first meeting with a real poet made a great impression on Marina. To begin with she was shy, but from the time that Ellis paid a visit to the Tsvetayevs and made more and more frequent appearances at Trekhprudny Lane, Marina thawed out and began to read him her poems: 'Ellis respected Marina's creative gift, he listened to her poetry and praised her translation of L'Aiglon (he himself being a well-known translator).'[2]

Ellis was not well off and lived from day to day, having meals at friends' homes. He began to visit the Tsvetayev sisters often and stayed for dinner, entertaining Marina and Asya with stories of distant countries and events in the Moscow literary world. Together with Andrey Bely and Sergey Mikhailovich Solovyov (the nephew of the philosopher Vladimir Solovyov) he belonged to the group of the philosophical-literary movement, the 'Argonauts'. At this time they were preparing to organise a new publishing house, Musaget, in order to defend themselves from the omnipotent poet and *maître* Valery Bryusov, who played the leading role in the publishing house Vesy. Soon Marina and Asya could not imagine how they could spend an evening without Ellis.

> He flies to us like a bird,
> And enters himself into our net.
> And immediately one is set spinning,
> Wanting to shout and to sing.[3]

Ellis, however, was opposed to introducing the Tsvetayev sisters to the famous Andrey Bely. At the home of their friends from Tarusa, the Vinogradovs, Marina and Aysa met other members of this circle: Seryozha Solovyov and Vladimir Nilender, a specialist in ancient philology. Anastasia Tsvetayeva warmly remembers the gentle smile of Nilender and his sympathetic ability of laughing at himself and others.

From Anatoly Vinogradov Marina heard some bad news: someone had already translated Rostand's L'Aiglon into Russian.

> Marina was very distressed, then shrugged her shoulders...Fate! The thought of providing a new translation, apparently, did not enter

Marina's mind, or soul...I never heard any more about Marina's translation of *L'Aiglon*.[4]

During the summer holidays of 1909 Marina took her first independent step: as a sixteen-year-old girl she went to Paris and enrolled in a course for foreigners at the Alliance Française. She lived in Paris immersed in her dreams. The strongest impression she received from her stay in Paris was a performance of *L'Aiglon* in which Sarah Bernhardt played the title role.

Many years later Marina wrote to A.V. Bakhrakh:

> I was in Paris for the first time at the age of sixteen, alone; I was grown-up, independent, severe. I stayed on rue Bonaparte out of love for the Emperor, and aside from the letter 'N' (the solemn 'Non' to everything which was not him) I saw nothing else in Paris. This was enough...Go in my name to rue Bonaparte and remember me, at sixteen. Only do not be touched. I was not in the least touching, I was heroic: that is, inhuman...[5]

Under the influence of this stay in France, Marina wrote a whole series of poems which were particularly romantic: about Napoleon, the Duke of Reichstadt, Countess Camerata and the "little" Sarah Bernhardt. This cycle of poems reaches its culmination in the poem 'The Separation' in which Marina compares the fate of Napoleon's son with Christ's, and calls the Palace of Schönbrunn Golgotha. From another work, however, which she sent to Asya in Tarusa, one can see that Marina was not very happy in Paris:

IN PARIS

The houses rise to the stars, but the sky itself
Descends to the earth through the smoke.
In vast and joyful Paris
There is all the same a secret sadness.

The evening boulevards are noisy,
The last rays of the sunset have been extinguished,
And everywhere, everywhere, are couples, couples,
The trembling of lips and the audacity of eyes.

I am here alone. How good it is
To lean my head against a chestnut tree!
And in my heart a line from Rostand
Sobs just as it did in abandoned Moscow.

At night Paris is alien and pitiful to me,
Dearer to the heart is its earlier fever!
I go home to find the sorrow of the violets
And someone's beloved portrait.

There on the wall is the sadly fraternal look
And there the tender profile.
Rostand and the martyr of Reichstadt
And Sarah – all will come to me in a dream!

In vast and joyful Paris
I dream of fields and clouds,
And further is laughter, and closer shades,
And the pain is as deep as before.[6]

At this time Asya was spending a happy summer in Tarusa removed from her elder sister's tyranny.

When they were already beginning to stoke the stoves at Tarusa and everyone was getting ready to leave, Marina finally appeared. For a certain time she remained alone there, in order to rest. This period of solitude and reflection acquired a special significance for the young Tsvetayeva. Her stay in Paris had put many things in their place, and her creativity reached its first apogee, as the poem 'The Prayer' shows, which was written on her seventeenth birthday:

Christ and God! I thirst for a miracle
Now, at this hour, at the beginning of the day!
Oh, let me die, while
All of life is still a book to me.

You are wise, You will not say sternly:
'Endure, your time is not yet finished.'
You Yourself have given me – too much!
I thirst, at once, for all roads!

I desire everything: with the soul of a gypsy
To commit robberies accompanied by songs.
To suffer for everyone under the sound of the organ
And to rush into battle as an amazon;

To read the stars in a black tower,
To lead children ahead, through the shadows...
That yesterday be a legend
That every day be madness!

I love the cross, and silk and helmets
My soul is the trail of moments...
You gave me my childhood – better than a legend
And so give me death – at seventeen![7]

During this autumn in Tarusa, Marina finally grew up completely. She began to realise that she could not live continuously in the realm of shades, that she also had to associate with living people. She suddenly remembered her friend Ellis and wrote a letter to him:

Dear Lev Lvovich! I have put your letters under my pillow today and I dreamt about Napoleon and mama...Dear magician, come without fail to Tarusa, I have much, very much to tell you.[8]

This is expressed still stronger in a poem:

THE NEW MOON

The new moon has risen above the meadow
Above the dewy border.
Dear one, distant and strange,
Come, you will be a friend.

During the day I hide, during the day I am silent.
Moon in the sky – I cannot bear it!
During these moonlit nights
I long for a beloved shoulder.

I will not ask: 'Who is he?'
Your lips will tell all!
Only during the day are embraces crude,
Only during the day is emotion absurd.[9]

One might suppose that a great romantic love was starting here; in fact, however, everything turned out otherwise; instead of a bitter-sweet drama, it became a farce. At the time that Marina was beginning to dream of her hero, he himself fell into an unpleasant situation which upset everything: as if on purpose, it was Ellis, a friend of the Tsvetayev family, who was caught tearing pages out of books in the Rumyantsev Museum in order to use them for his own work. In the annual report of the Museum for the year 1909 the director, I. V. Tsvetayev wrote:

> Instead of copying out the texts he needed Kobylinsky tore them out of books belonging to the Museums and glued them in his manuscript. He did this with two books. Caught with the third he candidly confessed to his action and the same day presented new copies to replace the ones he had cut up, as well as money for their binding. In this way he completely made up for the damage incurred by him to the Museums. The Museums, however, cannot leave unpunished such treatment of their property, if only as a matter of principle. The insufficiency of assistants has made the supervision of readers difficult in the highest degree. Besides, it is well known how little respect we have for books. On the force of this the Museums informed the public prosecutor of the circuit court about Kobylinsky's action. The public prosecutor deemed the affair to be within the jurisdiction of the justice of the peace, who investigated it on 27 October. Since the Museums did not seek from Kobylinsky compensation for damages and instituted legal proceedings against him only in the interests of society, they did not appear at the examination of the case, believing also that the judge was not entitled to leave him without examination. When the judge, in view of the non-appearance of the representatives of the Museums, suspended the case at the request of the accused, the Museums were forced to lodge an appeal, and the metropolitan conference of justices of the peace, respecting the arguments of the Museums, transferred the case to a court investigator. With this transfer of the case to the investigating authority the part of the Museums in the case was finished.[10]

The 'Ellis Affair', the name under which it appeared in the press, created a terrible storm. During several weeks the newspapers carried long articles about the depravity of the decadents under large headlines, and communicated with pleasure all the new unpleasant details about them. Although everyone understood that Ellis turned out to be a thief only because of his genial absent-mindedness, and had no bad intentions, his reputation was ruined. He could no longer appear at the Tsvetayevs'. Only Marina took his side, as it was necessary to defend a poet who was being persecuted. She sent him this poem:

TO THE FORMER ENCHANTER

Anguish is tearing your heart, sowing doubt in goodness.
'Cast the stone, do not show mercy! I am waiting, bite more fiercely!'
No, hateful to me is the arrogance of the pharisee,
I love sinners and I have only pity for you.

Let us not be separated by walls of dark words,
Which grow in the dusk! To the locks we shall find keys
And bravely we will exchange mysterious signals
With each other, when everything dreams at night.

Free and alone, far from narrow limits
You will once again return to us with a rich ship-load,
And out of the ethereal lines will arise a well-proportioned castle,
And the one who dares to judge a poet will stand in awe!

'It is all very well to forgive small errors, but this one
Impossible: culture, honour, order – oh no!'
Let them all say that. I will not judge a poet,
And one can forgive everything for a sonnet which weeps![11]

It is not surprising that the ridiculed and outraged Ellis understood this poem of Marina's differently than Marina herself. He quickly wrote her a letter in which he confessed his love for her and asked her to become his wife. He sent his best friend, Vladimir Ottonovich Nilender, with this letter to Marina.

The story became more and more confused: Nilender found Marina in the semi-darkness of the Tsvetayevs' drawing-room, where Asya soon joined them as well. A conversation started and Nilender stayed for dinner. Later, sitting in Marina's small room the three told each other about their lives. Just as day was breaking in the window Nilender grasped his head: 'Marina! He is waiting! What am I to say to him?' All three had completely forgotten Ellis. Marina and Asya had both fallen in love with Nilender, and he with Marina.

That day we bought an album bound in dark-blue with a gilded edge, we called it 'Evening Album' and wrote down everything in it which we remembered about our evening, from what was said by him or by us, and from our conversation after he left. We inscribed the album to him. Later we also wrote in it Marina's new poem 'The Sisters'.[12]

Marina and Asya were in seventh heaven and believed that they had found a new brother. Marina, however, was disturbed by Ellis's proposal: how could she be the wife of the 'Enchanter'? How could such an absurd idea enter his head? For her refusal she found an appropriate form:

When you grasp a snow-flake with your hand
Which airily flies, skimming past
Like a falling star, it melts like a tear
And its etheriality cannot be returned.

When we touch by the caprice of our hands
A jellyfish, fascinated by its transparency,
Like a prisoner, held by its chains,
It suddenly turns pale and suddenly dies.

When we want to see in wandering butterflies
Not a dream but an earthly fact
Where is their attraction? On our fingertips only dust
Remains from them, painted by the dawn!

Leave flight to snowflakes and butterflies
And do not kill the jellyfish on the sands!
It is impossible to grasp a dream with your hands,
It is impossible to hold a dream in your hands!

It is impossible to say to that which was
A tender sorrow: 'Be passion! Rave with grief, burn!
Your love was such a mistake
But without love, Enchanter, we perish![13]

The dream about a new brother lasted for only a few days. On 30 December Marina and Asya again met Nilender, but this day was marked by a fatal star: Asya was the first to understand what was happening here; the brother, who so poorly fulfilled the mission of his friend, quite simply wanted to take his place. He now wanted to marry Marina.

'I understand,' Asya said, and stood up.

'But I do not understand...I did not imagine it would be at all like this,' Marina answered.

Asya knew what the outcome of this tête-à-tête would be. The idea of marriage was completely foreign to Marina; she admitted only a feeling of friendship and respect. It was perfectly clear that she could only reject Nilender's proposal.

Marina rejected Nilender, although she loved him. She 'made her sacrifice', which she learnt from her teacher, Pushkin's

Tatyana. After this 'sacrifice', however, her love only began to flare up for real. That her feelings had nothing to do with a real person, the translator of Heraclitus, who had a very real, that is, another idea of love, and that Marina transformed him into a romantic myth and endowed him with the traits of an unreal hero, are typical phenomena when a girl falls in love for the first time. In distinction from "ordinary" romantic girls, however, the young Tsvetayeva was able to convey the torments of her first love in lyrics, which strike one by their perfection. Before the autumn of 1910 she wrote a whole series of poems, the majority of which she later included in *Evening Album* and *The Magic Lantern*:

> How many radiant possibilities you destroyed without knowing!
> There were more of these in the heart than stars in the heavens.
> I awaited the resplendent day after so many torments,
> I received only a cross.

> What was burning in me? Shall I call this feeling love,
> Or a dream, if you wish, only do not conceal the truth from the heart:
> I could have managed, my friend, to stay by your bed
> As a careful sister.

> I would not touch your idols, brashly and brazenly,
> Nor your favourite names, nor your madly-mourned books.
> Like a sick child I would lull you to sleep
> At an inconsolable hour.

> How many bright possibilities, dear one, and how much confusion!
> There were more of them in the heart than stars in the heavens:
> But in your name I am speechless – shades are my witnesses
> I take up my cross.[14]

Asya did not regard the 'winter's tale' so tragically. She went skating and enjoyed herself in Tarusa. Marina was in complete despair. She began to smoke and even, as Anastasia Ivanovna hints, thought of suicide:

> Only thirty-four year later, already after Marina's death, did I learn about those days. But she had said with hints that a revolver had misfired. She had wanted to do this in the theatre at a performance of Rostand's *L'Aiglon*, as acted by Sarah Bernhardt. In 1943, after Marina's death, they sent me her suicide and farewell letter to me of 1909.[15]

In March 1910 Marina had what seemed to be an insignificant adventure. In Wolf's bookshop on Kuznetsky Bridge she saw and recognised the poet Valery Bryusov and heard him say to the bookseller behind the counter: 'Give me a copy of *Chanteclair*, although I do not admire Rostand.' For Marina these words were like the stab of a dagger: the spirit of protest was immediately

aroused within her and returning home she wrote the famous
maître the following letter:

> Much respected Valery Yakovlevich. At Wolf's you have just now said
> '...although I am not an admirer of Rostand.' There and then I wanted
> to ask you – why? Why do you not love Rostand? Is it possible that you
> see in him only a 'brilliant phrase-monger'? Is it possible that his infinite
> nobility has escaped you, and his love for heroism and purity? This is
> not an idle question. For me Rostand is part of my soul, a very great
> part. He consoles me and gives me the strength to live alone. I think that
> no one, no one can know him, love him as much as I do. Your fleeting
> phrase saddened me very much...[16]

Bryusov probably liked this letter and the great *maître* condescended to sending Marina a kind letter at the address of the
Rumyantsev Museum. He did not love Rostand simply because he
was 'not destined to love him', because 'love is by chance'. He
expressed his wish to become acquainted with the young enthusiast
or to continue corresponding with her. '...To this letter I naturally
(for I so passionately wanted to!) did not reply. For love – is by
chance.'[17]

In the spring of 1910 the minister Shvarts sent his enemy
Tsvetayev two new commissions about the museum. They had to
inspect once more the case of the theft of the engravings. In spite of
this Ivan Vladimirovich left in June on official business for
Germany and took his daughters with him. He had a great deal of
travelling to do and was carrying on negotiations about his new
museum. For this time he sent Marina and Asya to the spa of
Weisser Hirsch in Loschwitz near Dresden, where they stayed with
the family of a rather eccentric pastor who was a passionate lover of
music. Once again they had the opportunity of improving their
German and of perfecting their knowledge of the domestic arts.

Although Marina could not forget her beloved here, which is
apparent in her poems, a new world was revealed to her, with which
she was still not familiar, the works of the German poets: Heine,
Novalis, Bettina von Arnim, and, of course Goethe, who became
her guiding star throughout her life, 'loved immeasurably more
than Tolstoy' (from a letter to Ivask, 12 May 1934). Her love and
enthusiasm for Germany ('...My passion, my homeland, the cradle
of my soul...') was strengthened definitively during this summer.

Bad news arrived from Moscow: on 13 June, within only a few
days of his departure from Russia, Professor Tsvetayev was retired
from his position as director of the Rumyantsev Museum. Minister
Shvarts had triumphed. Ivan Vladimirovich did not break off his
journey through Germany. He completed the programme he had

arranged and then, later, found a room in a quiet village where he wrote his defence which consisted of two works published in Germany in 1910 and 1911.[18] Tsvetayev was deeply struck by the injustice of having been made an official scapegoat for the mistakes and connivances of his superiors. In spite of the fact that soon after the end of 1910 he was not only completely vindicated, but even made an honorary member of the Museum, he never recovered from this disaster.

The summer was approaching its end. Asya did not want to leave her father alone and delayed her departure from Germany. Marina had to return to Moscow for the beginning of the school year. On 17 August she arrived at her empty rooms which had been abandoned for the summer. She was alone: her relations had not yet returned and her beloved was distant and could not be reached. On this day, 17 August, she wrote a poem 'Vitam impendere vero', which concludes the chapter 'Love' in *Evening Album:*

> The weary world sighed from confusion
> The rosy evening shed its oblivion...
> We are separated not by people, but by shadows,
> My boy, my heart!

> Walls rise up, clothed in mist,
> The sun, without strength, broke the lance...
> In the world of dusk I am cold. Where are you?
> My boy, my heart?

> You do not hear. The walls draw near,
> Everything dies out and merges together...
> There was, is and shall be no other,
> My boy, my heart!

Suddenly, an unexpected decision was taken, which was the only possible way of removing the obstacles standing between Marina and Nilender; since she could not send him her poems, she had them printed.

> My first book, *Evening Album*, was published when I was seventeen (including poems from the ages of fifteen and sixteen). I had it published for reasons extraneous to literature, but related to poetry: it was in place of a letter to a person, with whom I was otherwise deprived of the possibility of communicating.[19]

She chose from among the poems she had already written, omitting the most intimate love poems, and took them to the printing press of Mamontov on Trekhprudny Lane and ordered at her expense five hundred copies. She turned over all the copies to one bookshop, Spiridonov and Mikhailov, and did nothing more. After this she "calmed down" and continued to attend the *gymnasium.*

She said not a word about this to her family.

One can suppose that the final editing of *Evening Album* was completed in September, at about the time of Marina's eighteenth birthday. The poem, 'A Further Prayer', which concludes Tsvetayeva's first collection is dated 'Moscow, Autumn 1910', and echoes the one written on her previous birthday:

And again I bend my knees before you
Seeing in the distance your evening crown.
Let me understand, Christ, that not everything is a shadow.
Let me embrace not a shadow, at last!

I am tormented by these long days
Without cares, without purpose, always in semi-obscurity...
One can love shadows, but can one live
With them for eighteen years on earth?

Indeed they sing and write that happiness is at the beginning!
If only the whole soul would blossom, rejoicing, the whole soul!
But is it not true: that there is no happiness outside sorrow?
That aside from the dead there are no friends?

Indeed, from centuries past, did not those who burned with a different
        faith
Withdraw from the world into the uninhabited deserts?
No, I have no need of smiles, procured at the price
Of the desecration of higher sacred things.

I do not need bliss at the price of degradation,
I do not need love. I grieve – but not for it.
Let me give my soul, Saviour, only to a shadow
In the silent realm of beloved shades.[20]

CHAPTER 6

Moscow – 'Evening Album'

1910 – 1911

Evening Album was only one of the many first attempts by young aspiring authors around 1910. It is now difficult to imagine the extent and intensity of Russia's cultural life during the first decade of the twentieth century, and it is no accident that it has been called the 'Silver Age' of Russian poetry. It was particularly important and beneficial that there were two capitals of cultural life. The rivalry between Petersburg and Moscow helped to guarantee that there would be great successes in every sphere of the arts, including poetry, music and the fine arts. In both Petersburg and Moscow there were private patrons and prominent social figures who collected around them writers, musicians, artists and theatrical agents. Publishing houses were financed from private sources and in literary circles one could discuss and argue about the new ideas which were being born.

The 'Religious-Philosophical Society' of Dmitry Merezhkovsky and Zinaida Hippius, the meetings at Vyacheslav Ivanov's 'Tower' and the editorial offices of the journals *The World of Art* (*Mir iskusstva*) and *Apollon* were the centres of Petersburg's literary and cultural life; in Moscow they were Andrey Bely's circle, the Argonauts, and the publishing house Vesy, where Bryusov presided. Among the poets of Petersburg, the most famous were Aleksandr Blok, Nikolay Gumilyov and Mikhail Kuzmin.

Johannes von Guenther, a young poet and native of the Baltic regions, who participated in Petersburg's literary life, describes in his memoirs written in German, *Ein Leben im Ostwind*, how in the autumn of 1910 a new young poetess 'of the first rank' was 'discovered' in Petersburg. This took place in Vyacheslav Ivanov's 'Tower'; when the host went up to her and ceremoniously kissed her hand, after she had read her poetry, she was officially received into the Olympian circle of *Apollon*, (to the great vexation, incidentally, of Zinaida Hippius). The young poetess was the wife of Gumilyov and her literary pseudonym was Anna Akhmatova.[1]

Tsvetayeva's first appearance in the world of literature was rather less noticeable. She had no one she could turn to, if only for some advice on how to conduct herself, and what it was necessary to do 'as a poetess'. She even did not know that it was the usual practice to send a copy of one's book to the editors of a newspaper. It is surprising that the thin volume by an unknown author reached, all the same, the desks of influential people and was commented on in detail. Bryusov reviewed it for the literary section of *Russian Thought* (*Russkaya mysl'*), comparing it with the first work of another young poet, Ilya Ehrenburg:

> The poetry of Marina Tsvetayeva, by contrast [to that of Ehrenburg's], is always derived from some real fact, from some kind of experience which has been lived through. Not afraid of introducing everyday life into her poetry, she directly accepts life's characteristic elements, which gives her poems a terrible intimacy. When you read her volume you feel at certain moments ill at ease, as though you had looked immodestly through a half-closed window into a stranger's room and witnessed a scene which outsiders must not see. This immediacy which is attractive in the more successful poems on many pages of this large collection turns into a certain "domesticity". The results of this are not so much poetic creations (whether good or bad is another question), but simply pages of a personal diary, pages which are insipid besides. The last point can be explained by the youth of the author, who on several occasions indicates her age...
>
> If in Miss Tsvetayeva's subsequent volumes the same favourite heroes appear, mama, Volodya, Seryozha...we hope that they will become synthetic images, symbols of the universally human, and not simply fleeting portraits of relations and friends and reminiscences of her rooms. We will also look forward to the time when the poet will find in her soul feelings which are sharper than the dear trifles which occupy so much space in *Evening Album*, and thoughts which are more requisite than the old truth: 'the arrogance of the pharisee is despicable'. The undoubtedly talented Marina Tsvetayeva can give us the real poetry of intimate life and can also, with that ease, with which she appears to write poetry, squander her talent on unnecessary, though elegant trifles.[2]

Bryusov, who surveyed and analysed new lyrical poetry from the height of his greatness, probably considered that his criticism was very benevolent. We know, however, from Anastasia Ivanovna, that Bryusov probably assumed that the lines 'the despicable lie of the pharisee', which referred to the Ellis affair, and the poem 'Misunderstanding', were directed against him.[3] Tsvetayeva herself

says in her essay 'The Hero of Labour' that this criticism angered
her very much: she saw in it only what was not favourable. Not
retreating she wrote a reply in verse and could find nothing better
than to publish it, with its full dedication, in her next volume:

TO V. YA. BRYUSOV

Smile into my 'window'
Or count me amongst the fools –
All the same, you will not change me!
'Sharp feelings' and 'requisite thoughts'
Were not given to me by God.

It is necessary to sing that everything is dark,
That dreams hang above the earth...
– Thus it is now ordained. –
These feelings and these thoughts
Were not given to me by God![4]

Gumilyov reviewed this new volume by a young author
completely differently. In Petersburg he was pleased by exactly
what Bryusov had so censured in Moscow. In May 1911 he wrote
in *Apollon:*

Marina Tsvetayeva (her book is *Evening Album*) is inherently talented,
inherently original. Even if her book is dedicated to the 'radiant memory
of Maria Bashkirtseva' the epigraph is from Rostand, and the word
'mama' hardly ever leaves the pages. All of this leads one to think only of
the poetess' youth, which is confirmed by her own lines of confessions.
There is much which is novel in this volume: the daring (sometimes
excessively) intimacy, the themes, for example, that of childhood love,
and an immediate, mad love of life's trifles. And finally, as it would
appear that she has divined all the major laws of poetry, we can say that
this book includes not only gentle girlish confessions, but also some
splendid poems.[5]

In 1977, in the journal *Novy Mir*, Irma Kudrova reprinted a
review of *Evening Album* which influenced most of all the future
career of the young Tsvetayeva. This review was written by
Maksimilian Voloshin and was originally published in *The Morning
of Russia (Utro Rossii)*:

Evening Album is a very youthful and inexperienced book...Many poems,
if they were opened in the middle of the book by hazard, would call forth
a smile. One must read them all the way through, like a journal, and
then each line will be understood correctly. She is just on the border
between the last days of childhood and the first of youth. If one adds
that its author has a mastery not only of verse, but also of the precise
outward manifestation of internal observation, that is, the impression-
ist's ability to make fast the fleeting moment, then one can indicate what
documental significance this volume presents, which is a product of
those years when the word is usually insufficiently obedient to convey
faithfully observations and feelings.[6]

With these words Voloshin expressed that which still captivates us so much even after all the years since the publication of Tsvetayeva's first two collections. At that time, however, no one understood this, least of all Marina herself. She continued to attend the seventh year class at the Bryukhonenko *gymnasium*, which Asya also entered in the autumn. But neither the students nor teachers uttered a word about Marina's book; at home they were also silent about it. Ivan Vladimirovich was preoccupied with other matters: he was now concentrating all his energies on the final stages of his creation – the Alexander III Museum of Fine Arts. It is possible that he did not, in fact, know anything about the literary activity of his daughter. Moreover, Tolstoy's departure from Yasnaya Polyana on 28 October and his death on 7 (20) November at the railway station at Astapovo supplanted all other literary sensations in everyone's mind. Marina and Asya, like many others, wanted to bid farewell to the great deceased writer; at night, in the dark and mist, they ran away from home and contrived, with great adventures, to reach Yasnaya Polyana and to be present at Tolstoy's funeral.

One fine evening in December, however, something unexpected occurred: one of the leading representatives of literary Moscow made a call at Trekhprudny Lane. Tsvetayeva describes this in detail in her essay 'A Living Word About a Living Man':

> The bell. I open. On the threshold a top-hat. From underneath the top-hat a vast face mounted in a short curling beard. An ingratiating voice: 'Could I see Marina Tsvetayeva?' 'That is me.' 'And I am Maks Voloshin. Is it possible to visit?' 'Very!' We went upstairs to the children's rooms. 'Have you read my article about you?' 'No.' 'I thought as much and so I have brought it for you. It has already been out for a month...'

The strange guest did not remove the penetrating look of his nearly white eyes from Marina, he took off her glasses and the cap she wore in order to see her better, and breathing heavily (he was very stout) he followed her into her room with the ceiling covered with stars, where he made the acquaintance of Asya as well. They carried on a conversation for many hours about Napoleon and Edmond Rostand and Marina read some of her poetry. Before leaving Voloshin promised to return soon. On the following day Marina received from him a poem which ended with the lines:

> ...Your book is news from whence
> Comes the blessed news of morning.
> I have long ago not believed in miracles,
> But how sweet to see: there is a miracle!

On 23 December Marina answered politely as a well-bred young woman should:

> Moscow, 23 December 1910
>
> Much respected Maksimilian Aleksandrovich.
>
> Please accept my sincere gratitude for your sincere words about my book. You have approached it like life, and have forgiven in life what they do not forgive in literature.
>
> I thank you for your poem.
>
> If you are not afraid of freezing to death, come to the old house with shutters. Only please give notice in advance.
>
> Greetings.
>
> Marina Tsvetayeva[7]

Thus began the friendship between Tsvetayeva and Maksimilian Voloshin, although he was many years older than she. In 'A Living Word About a Living Man' Marina describes this friendship movingly.

Among the many originals of that time Voloshin occupied a conspicuous place; memoirs of all his contemporaries speak of him. In his youth Voloshin had spent several years in Paris and always remained an admirer of French culture. Returning to Russia he became a contributor to *Apollon*. For the most part he lived with his mother in his house in Koktebel. He wrote poetry, translated contemporary French literature and also painted. He was always and boundlessly ready to help people, especially poetesses. In the cultural spheres of Russia he was acquainted with everybody and his influence was enormous.

One of Voloshin's great services was that he appreciated the talent of the young Tsvetayeva and decided to assist its development. With great patience, although unsuccessfully, he tried to tear her away from Rostand and Napoleon and to introduce her to Baudelaire, Rimbaud and Claudel. In the end he began to give her books by George Sand and Victor Hugo, which corresponded more to her taste. In order to overcome Marina's 'shyness and wildness' he turned for help to the writer Adelaida Gertsyk. She and her sister Yevgenia became close friends of both the Tsvetayev sisters. Voloshin also took Marina to the publishing house Musaget and in this way removed her from her solitude in the 'silent realm of beloved shades.'

Musaget was something of a cross between a publishing house, a literary *salon* and a university seminar. It distinguished itself from the publishing house Vesy, which was under the influence of French culture, by adopting a more German orientation. In 1911 a triumvirate of Emil Medtner, Bely and Ellis, directed it. This did not last for long, however. Vladimir Nilender played an important part in it as well. All its authors had the right to vote and the meetings of the editorial board, which were characterised by endless tea drinking, often lasted throughout the night. The principal author of Musaget and the person who set the tone was Andrey Bely. In 1910 both he and Ellis were wholly under the influence of Rudolf Steiner and they spread with great success the teachings of anthroposophy among the intellectuals of Moscow.

From time to time Musaget organised evenings at which the crisis of European culture was discussed in depth. These evenings were highly popular.

One of the most active contributors to Musaget was the young philosopher Fyodor Stepun, who had studied at the university of Heidelberg. Together with S.I. Gessen he published at Musaget the philosophical journal *Logos*. We are grateful to Stepun for his colourful account of Musaget and its collaborators and of the young Tsvetayeva, whom he met there:

> Marina was dressed coquettishly, but carelessly: she wore rings with coloured stones on all her fingers, but her hands were not well-groomed. These rings were not a woman's adornment, but rather talismans, or simply a kind of beauty, which it was pleasant to have before one's eyes. We spoke about romantic poetry, about Goethe, Mme de Staël, Hölderlin, Novalis, and Bettina von Arnim. I am listening and I do not know what amazes me more: that purely feminine intimacy with which Tsvetayeva lives among the shades which are close to her spirit, as among contemporaries, or her perfectly exceptional mind with its aphoristic flights and its steely masculine muscularity. There was something else, however, in Marina's manner of feeling, thinking and speaking, which was not entirely pleasant: the indestructible egocentrism of her spiritual impulses. And never saying anything about her life, she always spoke about herself. It was as if she had, as a girl, somehow, sat on Pushkin's knees, and had wound his disobedient locks around her fingers; as if Zhukovsky had brought to her, and not only to Pushkin, Goethe's goose-quill from Weimar, or as if she had only yesterday walked with Novalis at sunset through a park, which perhaps does not exist in the world, but in which she knows and loves every tree.[8]

Everything which Marina saw at Musaget interested her greatly, but also called forth her feeling of shyness, especially Andrey Bely, who during his courses of 'eurhythmy' had danced before the busts of Goethe and Steiner 'as David before the Ark'. Marina understood nothing in the conversations about gnosticism and gnoseology: she felt the 'superiority of everyone above her' and remained silent 'from continuously wounded pride',[9] although they welcomed her affably at Musaget and requested her to provide

several poems for a collection of contemporary poetry which Ellis
was preparing for publication at Musaget. On 12 December she
wrote:

> Dear Ellis...It was very nice at Musaget. I even dreamt about it...How
> unaccustomed I have become to people and conversations! At the
> slightest disagreement with my interlocutor I wanted to leave, I felt so
> badly! There are many kind people at Musaget who are sympathetic to
> me. I am pleased that I am there, however...[10]

Among the number of kind and sympathetic people Vladimir
Nilender, her passionate love of the previous year, probably
occupied the first place. Their relations, which were strained at
first, turned into a strong, true, friendship. Marina speaks of him as
her 'would-be husband':

> I know that if I were to enter his philological lair, his grotto of Orpheus,
> his Sibyl's cave, so many years later, after ten years, or after twenty
> years, he would push aside, with his right hand, his young wife, and
> would knock over onto my head, with his left, a stack of books piled to
> the ceiling and would rush up to me, opening his arms, which would
> have turned into wings.[11]

But more than all the literary men at Musaget, Marina's
attention was attracted by the charming Asya Turgeneva, the great-
niece of the famous writer. She was the fiancée of Andrey Bely, and
from time to time would attend the *soirées* held by the publishing
house. Marina quite simply fell in love with her and sought her
friendship with all her strength. This greatly irritated her sister
Asya, who was a student in the same class of the *gymnasium* as the
younger of the Turgenev sisters, Tanya.

> I secretly knew that in the friendship between Marina and Asya
> Turgeneva the person suffering was Marina and the one who was
> unappreciative – Asya. In Asya's proud face, in her 'permission to adore
> me' I found Marina's role to be unpleasant.[12]

Anastasia Ivanovna's memoirs of the winter of 1910–11 are less
detailed. She knew nothing about Marina's new friends and about
the time she was spending at Musaget. One can guess that Asya
now had other interests of her own. In the autumn of 1910 she had
turned sixteen and met, while skating, a charming young man,
Boris Trukhachov. The extraneous world began to disappear for
her. Slowly and almost imperceptibly the ways of the sisters began
to part.

CHAPTER 7

Koktebel – Sergey Efron – 'The Magic Lantern' – Marriage
MAY – DECEMBER 1911

One of the most interesting of the publications by the short-lived Musaget was the collection of contemporary Russian lyric poetry which appeared in June 1911 under the modest title of 'anthology'. This collection contains, in alphabetical order, the works of thirty authors. The names of several of them have become, most likely deservedly, forgotten. At the end of the alphabetical list, immediately before Ellis (the editor of the collection) one can find two novices in literature: Vladislav Khodasevich, a friend of Bely's and Nilender's since 1904, and Marina Tsvetayeva. In the collection two of her poems are included.

Evidently the anthology was Ellis' last literary work in Russia, as he disappeared from Moscow sometime during 1911. It was assumed that he had left in order to visit Rudolf Steiner, but Andrey Bely says that the reason for his departure was the scandal about the books from the Rumyantsev Museum, which Ellis could not forget. He never returned to Russia. In April 1913 he lived in Berlin, on Motzstrasse, not far from Steiner. Afterwards he vanished almost without a trace. In the thirties he published in German several works about Russian literature under the name Doktor Leo Kobilinski. In a study of Pushkin published in Switzerland in 1948 it is noted on the dustcover that the author '...lived in Locarno-Montini and died on 17 November 1947'.

One wonders if it was the appearance in the anthology and her new literary profession which finally forced Marina to carry out her longed for desire of escaping to freedom. Not long before her last examination she left school and voluntarily refused an official

Marina Tsvetayeva: Koktebel, 1911

school-leaving certificate. It seemed to her that attendance at the hated *gymnasium* was only a waste of time for a recognised poetess. We do not know how her father reacted to this.

While Asya was preparing for her exams and was going boating with Boris, Marina spent the month of April alone in Gurzuf on the Black Sea. She intended to meet Asya later at Koktebel, where both sisters had been invited by Voloshin's mother to spend the summer.

This 'whole wonderful month of solitude' proved to be for the young Tsvetayeva a time of introspection, contemplation and reflection, which preceded a decisive turning point in her destiny. She was reading George Sand and Dumas, and under Pushkin's cypress tree meditated on the poet she idolised. She also sought solitude in order to analyse her relations with Nilender: 'I then went away from him to Koktebel, not in order "to love another" but not to love him.'[1]

In recalling this time it seemed to Marina that she was happy at Gurzuf, but her letters, which she sent to Voloshin from here, sound a different note:

> I am looking at the sea, from afar and close up – but all of this is not me, and I am not it. One cannot dissolve in it and merge with it. To become a wave? To remain human (or a half-human, it's all the same), is to pine eternally, to remain eternally on the threshold. A closer *ineinander* [mingling] must, must exist. But I do not know of it...
>
> I have mentally experienced everything, tried everything. My imagination always runs ahead. I tear open flowers which have not yet blossomed, I crudely touch the most gentle things and I do this unintentionally, I cannot not do this! Does this mean I cannot be happy? I do not want to forget myself artificially. I have an aversion to such experiments...There only remains the feeling of complete solitude, which has no cure. The body of another person is a wall which prevents one from seeing the soul. Oh, how I hate this wall! And I do not want paradise where everything is ethereal and blissful – I love so much faces, gestures, the rhythm of daily life. But life itself I do not want, where everything is clear, simple and crude – crude...I am tormented and can find no place for myself: from the cliffs to the sea, from the shore to my room, from my room to the shop, from the shop to the park, from the park back to the Genoan fortress, and thus the entire day...[2]

Marina did not suspect that this solitude would soon end. On 5 May she arrived at Koktebel and found herself in an environment the like of which she had never seen elsewhere.

Many amusing stories have been preserved about Voloshin's artistic colony in Koktebel, not far from Feodosia, and about his strange eccentric mother. Yelena Ottobaldovna, who was German by origin and who was known by the name 'Pra' [a contraction of 'ancestress' – A.G.], owned several small *dachas* directly on the sea at the foot of the Kara-Dag mountain, which she let to artists and writers. Maks lived in a tower, where he spent his time painting and where he kept his large valuable library. A merry company gathered in Koktebel: everyone would come together at the dinner table and they would arrange together excursions in the district. For the most part, however, witnesses describe the clothes which the mother and son both wore: Greek *chitons* and sandals on bare feet. This was so unusual that the young Yury Terapiano undertook the journey to Koktebel on bicycle in order to look at this strange company. While he was there they pointed out to him two young girls in white dresses: 'the daughters of Professor Tsvetayev from Moscow'.[3]

Immediately after she arrived from Gurzuf Marina went walking by the sea, along the vast unpopulated shore known as the 'cornelian bay'...Marina began to look for beautiful stones. Suddenly she saw that a handsome melancholy young man was sitting alone on a bench, against the background of the infinite horizon of the sea. He asked permission to help her, and she, enchanted by his splendid blue eyes, agreed. With this she vowed to herself that if he guessed which stone she liked most of all and brought it to her, then she would marry him.

Tsvetayeva recalls later:

> And with the pebble – it came true; as S.Ya Efron, whom I had married within six months, waiting until he was eighteen, discovered on nearly the first day of our acquaintance, – the greatest rarity! a Genoan cornelian, which he handed to me and which is still with me to this day.[4]

> In the Crimea, where I was the guest of Maks Voloshin, I met my future husband, Sergey Efron. We were aged seventeen and eighteen. I promised myself that *whatever happened* I would *never* part from him.[5]

She made good this promise in 1939 in Moscow when her husband was already in prison. The fatal cornelian survived all these events and by 1973 was in the hands of Ariadna Sergeyevna Efron.

One can imagine the kind of shock Asya had when she arrived in Koktebel to meet a completely different and transformed Marina: radiant, and sunburnt, and wearing short trousers and sandals on her bare feet. Only somewhat later did she realise that all of this was connected with this Seryozha, whom Marina introduced at first as the famous poet Igor Severyanin. Seryozha had come to the Crimea with his sisters in order to regain his strength after falling ill with tuberculosis. But Asya was more frightened by the fact that as

Marina said, Seryozha could not tolerate the climate of the Crimea and that they would both soon leave Koktebel. Asya began to understand that there was no longer a 'we', meaning the indissoluble friendship with her sister, which had existed since she could remember herself; Marina's new 'we' excluded Asya. But did Asya have the right to be jealous of her sister?

> Marina was happy; her happiness even passed over to me. I felt joy for her, who was never happy, even in childhood. She was always alone, always longing for something, always dreaming.[6]

Marina's conscience in regard to her sister was, apparently, not very clear. She gave her the strange advice of inviting Boris Trukhachov to Koktebel and of going away with him somewhere, as she herself was planning on going with Seryozha to Ufa. At this time their father was taking a cure at Bad-Nauheim and would not notice anything. Maks could forward to them the money he sent. The sixteen-year-old Asya followed her elder sister's advice and Boris came to Koktebel. The plans which Marina had thought up would be realised.

It turned out that the future brothers-in-law met only on the day of their departures. The young people walked back and forth along the platform of the railway station in Feodosia; from here the two couples would travel in different directions. The moment of separation between the two inseparable sisters was also imminent. And suddenly at the station in Feodosia Marina suggested that they recite a few poems in unison for the last time:

> On the faces of Seryozha and Boris now appeared the expression of amazement and absorption, which people have when they are present at some kind of miraculous occurrence: two voices coming, apparently, from different sides! But this is *one* voice, *one* intonation, from the right, and from the left, some kind of voice which has branched into two...But they – these – both – are *not* on the platform! Where are they? In which dimension?[7]

The trains then arrived and they had to part from each other for real, in opposite directions...Marina says about this break:

TO THE INSEPARABLE ONE UPON DEPARTURE

You stand by the door with your travelling-case,
What sadness is on your face!
While it is not too late let us recite
Some poems together for the last time.

Let the one voice repeat
The words which have been shared until now,
But the heart is broken in two
And the common path has divided.

Sergey and Marina, December 1911

Before it is too late, as in the old days
Above the piano, let us lower our heads
And sing with twin smiles and sorrows
The final farewell.

It is time! The boxes are tied up
The rug has long ago been tightened by the straps...
May the Lord preserve your ringing voice
And your wise mind at sixteen!

When above the forest and above the fields
All the heavens sink into the stars,
Two inseparables will rush
In different trains to different fates.[8]

Marina and Seryozha proceeded to the Uzen-Ivanovsky horse farm in the province of Ufa, where Seryozha had to drink mare's milk and to put on weight. The letters which Marina wrote from there sound differently from those from Gurzuf:

Dear Maks,
    If only you knew how well disposed I feel towards you! You are so amazingly kind, affectionate, careful and attentive. I loved you so much during those evenings in Stary Krym...and for your eternal readiness to help people. I am terribly grateful for Koktebel – (*pays de rédemption*, as Adelaida Kazimirovna calls it) and in general for everything you have given me. How can I repay you?...

And later:

It is strange, Maks, to feel oneself to be suddenly entirely independent. For me this is a surprise, as it had always seemed to me that someone else was organising my life. Now I will act in everything as I did with the printing of the collection of poems. I will go and do. Will you encourage me? Then, I used to think it was stupid to be so happy, even gauche! It is stupid and gauche to think that – this is me today.[9]

In the autumn of 1911 both couples returned to Moscow: Marina and Seryozha from the steppes of Ufa, Asya and Boris from Finland.[10] The first thing that Asya heard was that their father was severely ill with angina pectoris (one could suggest that this illness had some connection with the behaviour of his daughters), and was recovering abroad at a spa for patients with heart trouble. Although she anticipated harsh words, Marina settled Seryozha at home on Trekhprudny Lane, while Boris returned to his relations. Anastasia Ivanovna hints that from the first moment, while the "older" couple found happiness, the "younger" did not. Soon after this, Marina and Seryozha went to live in a flat at no.19, Sivtsev Vrazhek, from where the letter of 28 October 1911 to Voloshin was written. Lilya and Vera Efron moved here also, as well as Pra, who came from Koktebel as a chaperon.[11]

Seryozha, who was a year younger than Marina, still attended the *gymnasium* and was writing his book *Childhood*, in which he provides a portrait of Marina, who at this time was preparing her second collection of poems, *The Magic Lantern*, for publication. She made a warning in advance:

> Maks, I am certain that you will not like my second collection. You have said that it must be better than the first, or it will turn out badly.

Asya Turgeneva was supposed to design the cover for this collection. This joint effort brought them together, but the real collaboration and friendship which Marina dreamt about, did not occur. Asya soon left with Andrey Bely for Italy. This departure deeply shook Marina and she felt it for a long time; she described this event in verse and later, during her own wedding trip to Paris and Sicily she followed step by step the trail of Bely and Asya.

Marina now took an active part in Moscow's literary life. At Musaget she was her own person; she attended the lectures of the sculptor Krakht, visited Aleksey Tolstoy and met Nikolay Berdyayev, which is demonstrated by one of the photographs in the memoirs of Yevgenia Gertsyk.[12]

Another event in the literary world of Moscow, for which we have two accounts, also took place in the autumn of 1911. Bryusov organised a literary evening for his 'Society of Free Aesthetics' at the home of Vorstyakov and invited the newly discovered young poetess to participate. Marina was accompanied to the stage by Asya in order to recite, as they had done previously, some poems together. Anastasia Ivanovna recalls how with their appearance on the stage the audience seemed to be both welcoming and excited:

> We recited a few poems. Of them I remember 'At Age Fifteen' and 'December Tale'...There was a moment of silence after our final word, then the applause crashed through the hall, like spring thunder in the garden! Applause, which was forbidden in this house! We stood, confused (and bowing clumsily?) – and trying to take our leave, retreating and hurrying to go, we were pursued by tempestuous applause...Afterwards they told us it had been a 'triumph'. This was the first evening of Marina's incipient fame.[13]

Another witness, Boris Zaitsev recalls:

> Two young ladies, slender and attractive, wearing identical dresses, recited their poems in unison from the stage. One was Marina, the other Asya, daughters of Professor Tsvetayev. The young ladies recite their sharp, biting poems chirping, at right angles, somewhat breaking them up. Not only is their recitation in unison, but also their smiles, and the twitching of their nervous faces. There was no serenity or stability about them, but this seemed suitable at the time; one sensed their talent.[14]

During the same evening, 3 November 1911, Vladimir Mayakovsky also made his first appearance.

At Christmas 1911 Marina celebrated another literary triumph: on Christmas Eve she learnt from Seryozha that Bryusov had opened a competition on the theme of Pushkin's lines: 'But Jenny will not forsake Edmond even in heaven...' The deadline of the competition was that very day. Without thinking she chose one of her best love poems to Nilender from the still unpublished collection *The Magic Lantern* and sent it to Bryusov, anonymously, as the conditions of the competition required. To her great satisfaction, her enemy was obliged to acknowledge her victory. Bryusov, however, was unwilling to admit to defeat: Marina did not receive the first prize, but 'on account of her age', only one of the two second prizes. The other was given to another newly discovered and promising talent: Vladislav Khodasevich.

Not long before their wedding Marina and Seryozha had their first and only quarrel with Maks Voloshin. Marina was offended because, having received an announcement of their marriage, Voloshin did not congratulate them, but wrote, rather, a letter of condolence. Marina wrote to him without mentioning his name:

> Your letter – was a great mistake. There are certain spheres, where a joke is out of place, and things about which it is necessary to speak with respect, or be completely silent, if there is a lack of the appropriate feeling...Thank you for the lesson![15]

With this, their disagreement ended. Marina and Seryozha telegraphed to Paris: *'Ta patte, cher ours unique!'* All the same, however, Voloshin did not attend the wedding.

One can assume that he was not the only one absent from the quiet wedding ceremony of 27 January 1912, which took place at the Palashevsky Church. It is more than likely that the strained relations between Marina and her half-sister Valeria, and several other members of her family, were further aggravated by this unequal marriage: the Jewish origins and revolutionary tendencies of the Efrons could not have been to the taste of the conservative monarchist families of the Tsvetayevs and Ilovaiskys.

One thing, however, was clear: Marina was happy. The proof of this is the poem 'For Joy' which is dedicated to 'S.E.'. In fact, among all the poems of *The Magic Lantern*, only this one sounds joyous:

> Dusty roads await us,
> Thatched huts, for an hour,
> And the dens of wild animals,

And ancient royal dwellings...
Dear one, dear one, we are like gods:
The whole world is for us!

Everywhere on the earth we have homes,
Calling everything ours.
In the huts, where nets are hung,
On the glistening parquetry...
Dear one, dear one, we are like children:
We have divided the world in two!

The sun burns – from the south on the north
And on the moon!
Let others have the hearth and burden of the plough
We have the space and green of the meadow...
Dear one, dear one, we will always
Be captives to each other.[16]

Asya's fate turned out worse. When she and Boris Trukhachov
set out for their Finnish adventure, she was sixteen and he
seventeen; they were both children, who could not manage adult
relations. From the first moment there was no complete harmony
between them. When it became clear in the autumn that Asya was
pregnant, she had to leave Russia in order to hide her condition
from her father. There was no question of a wedding. Boris
travelled with her for a time, through Italy and France, then
returned to Moscow. Only a certain time later did she receive a
telegram from Boris, asking her to come back in order to get
married; 'he added that later it would be possible to separate, if I
wished...' The wedding took place after Easter in 1912; in the
summer Anastasia Ivanovna gave birth to a son, Andrey.[17]

PART TWO

Youth

*Between 1912 and 1920 I wrote ceaselessly, but I did not
publish...a single book. I lived, the books lay...*

Letter to Ivask, 4 April 1933

CHAPTER 8

Moscow – Feodosia – The Efrons – Birth of Ariadna – 'Poems of Youth'
1912 – 1914

One can best judge how great the distance was between the Tsvetayevs and the Efrons by reading the memoirs of Ariadna Sergeyevna Efron, the daughter of Sergey Yakovlevich and Marina Tsvetayeva. In these she describes in detail her background on her father's side.[1]

Sergey Yakovlevich's great-grandfather was a deeply respected rabbi. His grandson, Yakov Konstantinovich (Sergey's father), belonged, most likely under the influence of the Jewish pogroms, to the revolutionary organisation 'Land and Freedom'. Ariadna Sergeyevna mentions that her grandfather took an active part in the 'execution' of a secret police agent.

One evening at a rally of revolutionaries at Petrovsko-Razumovskoye Yakov Efron saw a beautiful young woman wearing a ball-gown, who had come directly to this demonstration from a ball at the Club of the Nobility. This was Yelizaveta Petrovna Durnovo, the daughter of a former aide-de-camp to the Emperor Nicholas I. She belonged whole-heartedly to this organisation, motivated by the sincere desire to help all the underprivileged. Soon Yakov Efron and Yelizaveta Durnovo were working together on conspiratorial activities. In 1880 the young aristocrat was arrested for the transportation of illegal literature. She was imprisoned in the Peter and Paul Fortress. Her parents, who suspected nothing, obtained her release on bail, but Yelizaveta fled abroad. Soon after, Yakov Konstantinovich followed her. They were married and their first three children were born. The family lived in great need. After seven years they were allowed to return to their mother country. Yakov Konstantinovich, however, was under police supervision and could work, with its permission, only in the most insignificant positions: he ended up as an insurance agent. By this time, six more children had been born; several of whom died. Yelizaveta Petrovna and her eldest children continued their work as conspirators; they organised secret gatherings, hid people and kept material for explosives.

Seryozha (the next to last child) was twelve when the events of 1905 began. He was supposed to continue going to school, while his mother and older brothers and sisters took part in the street fighting. After the suppression of the disorders a storm burst over the Efron family: Yelizaveta Petrovna and her eldest son Pyotr were sent into exile abroad. She was allowed to take with her only her youngest child, Konstantin, of whom Seryozha was especially fond. In 1909 his father died in Paris. In 1910 the fourteen-year-old Kotik hanged himself, without leaving a note, and the following day, his mother, who could not bear this blow, also killed herself.

Seryozha, who adored his mother, contracted tuberculosis. He was restored to health only through the care of his sisters Lilya and Vera. His trip to Koktebel in the spring of 1911 was meant for his health.

By 1912 the revolutionary activities of the Efron family had become a thing of the past. One of Sergey Yakovlevich's sisters became an actress, the other a director.

Those who were acquainted with Sergey Efron describe him as a very handsome, but also very weak man, who could not live without support and help. Boris Zaitsev speaks of him as being 'an elegant young man with truly enchanting eyes...'; Nikolay Yelenev describes him as 'a tall brown-haired man, with sorrowfully knit eyebrows, grey eyes, bluish clean-shaven cheeks and a heavy ape-like jaw...' Mark Slonim adds: 'He was a tall, fine man with a narrow face, slow movements and an almost muffled voice.' Marcel Orbec, a French schoolfriend who studied with him at the Polivanov *gymnasium*, recalls his vanity and his desire to stand out amongst others. On Nikolay Yelenev, however, Sergey made the impression of being a shy person, who was constantly in need of the support and encouragement of his wife, to whom he submitted himself: 'He felt himself to be an outcast in life. There was nowhere, no kind of setting, where Efron could overcome the ghetto of his "I".'[2]

The opinions of his relations sound differently. Anastasia Ivanovna held her 'gentle, affable, charming' brother-in-law in high regard, and emphasises how Marina and Sergey loved each other and how their 'intimacy grew with every day'. With Ariadna

Sergeyevna one feels that her only desire is to defend her beloved father from every attack and suspicion. Véronique Lossky who saw her in Moscow over a period of six weeks confirms that Ariadna was always biassed in her father's favour and defended his memory fiercely (*'défendait farouchement sa mémoire'*).[3]

> I wear his ring with a challenge!
> – Yes, his wife in eternity, not on paper!
> The extremely narrow face
> Resembles a sword.
>
> His mouth is silent, with its corners down,
> His brows are tormentingly magnificent.
> In his face two ancient bloods
> Have mingled tragically.
>
> He is fine, with the first fineness of branches
> His eyes are splendidly useless!
> Under the wings of his brows spread open
> Are two abysses.
>
> I am loyal to the chivalry in his face,
> – To all of you who have lived and died without fear
> – Those, who in fatal times
> Compose stanzas and mount the scaffold...[4]

This is how Tsvetayeva described her husband in 1914 and Slonim confirms that even in 1933 she saw him in exactly the same way.

Marina was, in fact, very much in love with her husband: 'If only you knew what a fiery, magnanimous, profound young man he is', she writes to Rozanov in a letter dated 7 March 1914.

> I constantly tremble over him. His temperature rises from the slightest excitement, he becomes possessed by a feverish thirst for everything... For three – or almost three years – of life together there has not been a single shadow of doubt between us. Our marriage does not resemble an ordinary one to such a degree that I do not feel myself to be married at all, and I have not changed in any way (I love everything I did at seventeen, and I live in the same way as I did at seventeen). We will never separate. Our meeting was a miracle.[5]

They were, however, completely different people. Seryozha needed an ideal which he could serve: at first this was Marina, then loyalty to Russia, and still later Communism. Marina, on the contrary, served only one ideal; the word and art. They probably began their life together too early and hastily: 'An early marriage (such as mine) is generally speaking a catastrophe, a blow which lasts for one's whole lifetime,' Marina writes on 26 May 1934 to Anna Tesková. And although Slonim maintains that she never really loved anyone but her husband, and despite the fact that she followed him only to face her own destruction, we do not know a single work of hers, from which we could conclude that she understood him with all his human qualities and weaknesses.

Immediately after Marina's wedding the publishing house Ole Lukoiye (a name invented by the young couple) brought out Seryozha's book *Childhood* and Marina's second volume of poetry, *The Magic Lantern*. This second collection appeared, like the first, in an edition of 500 copies. Only some of the poems were new; by their themes and the childish language one can conclude that the chapter 'Little Children' was written earlier than the collection *Evening Album*. The main part of the book, which appears under the title 'Not for Joy', contains poems written for Nilender, which Marina did not include in the first volume because they reveal too clearly her personal emotional experiences.

The Magic Lantern was not well received by the critics. They noticed with irritation that the young writer had failed to heed their benevolent advice, and had not achieved any new triumphs. Apparently, they did not notice that these poems were partly written before the others.

Gumilyov wrote:

> Marina Tsvetayeva's first book, *Evening Album*, forced one to believe in her, most of all, perhaps, because of her unfeigned childishness, which so naively does not recognise its difference from maturity. *The Magic Lantern* is already an imitation and has been published, moreover, by a stylised 'children's' publishing house, in whose catalogue are listed only three books. One finds the same themes, the same models, only they are paler and drier, as if they were not real experiences and memories, but only recollections of recollections. The same thing applies to form. The line does not flow freely and effortlessly as before; it stretches and snaps, and the poet tries to replace in it inspiration with a skill which is still not sufficient. There are no longer any long poems, as though she has run out of breath. The short ones are often constructed on the repetition or paraphrase of one and the same line. They say that with young poets the second volume is generally the most unsuccessful. Let us count on this.[6]

Bryusov found in *The Magic Lantern* the sarcastic poem which was addressed to him. He was offended and reacted to it without the slightest humour, and did not even notice that Marina had used, jokingly, the very words, with which he had criticised her first volume.

> True to herself Miss Tsvetayeva continues stubbornly to take her themes from the sphere of a narrowly intimate personal life, and is even proud of this: 'sharp feelings and requisite thoughts were not given to me from God'. In the end, we can reconcile ourselves with this as

everyone must write about what is near and familiar to them, but it is impossible to reconcile oneself with that carelessness of the line, which Miss Tsvetayeva is beginning more and more to display. Five or six truly beautiful poems drown in the waves of purely 'album' verses, which could only be interesting to her close friends.[7]

In May 1912 all the Tsvetayev children gathered around their father for the last time. The greatest event of this year for them was the opening of the Alexander III Museum of Fine Arts, which brought to Ivan Tsvetayev not only the conclusion of the work of a lifetime and long-awaited recognition, but also reconciliation with his daughters. The opening of the 'Colossal younger brother', as Anastasia Ivanovna called the museum, took place on 31 May 1912 and was preceded by a solemn 'Te Deum' service. The imperial family and leading members of the government and of society were present. This occasion was described by both sisters (by Marina in 'Father and His Museum'). Both sisters were expecting at the time and managed to get through the ceremony only with difficulty.

The birth of little Ariadna in September 1912 formed an important step in the emotional development of Marina Tsvetayeva. The godparents were Ivan Vladimirovich and 'Pra'. All of Marina's boundless love was concentrated on Alya, which from now on would be reflected in countless poems.

In March 1913 a collection of poetry with the title *From Two Books* (*Iz dvukh knig*) was published by the same press, Ole Lukoiye, in an edition of 1000 copies. Included in this volume were those poems from the first two which Tsvetayeva herself particularly liked. However, those which were too intimate were omitted. This volume found a large circle of readers and was positively received by the critics. V. Narbut wrote prophetically in the *Messenger of Europe* (*Vestnik Evropy*):

> One can almost believe that there has appeared at last a woman writer who will speak about herself, about woman, the whole truth, which will be as simple and understandable as what Pushkin said about the soul of man.[8]

Once again Marina could not resist writing some sarcastic poems. Here is one which can be found in the new collection:

TO V. YA. BRYUSOV

I had forgotten that your heart is only a night-lamp,
Not a star! I forgot about this!
That your poetry is from books
And your criticism from envy. Young old-man
For a moment you had again
Appeared to me to be a great poet!

This time, however, Bryusov preferred to remain silent: 'In the mountains (of his steep soul) the "response" lasted a lifetime'.[9]

Not long before his death Professor Tsvetayev saw another triumph: on the occasion of the fiftieth anniversary of the Rumyantsev Museum, where he was formerly the director, he was entrusted by the Academy of Arts and the Alexander III Museum with the delivery of their official congratulations. After this last effort, however, his strength was exhausted. He suffered a heart attack while on an estate not far from Klin. On 27 August he was taken, in a hopeless condition, to Moscow where he died on 30 August in the presence of Marina and Andrey.

Ivan Vladimirovich Tsvetayev was buried in the Vagankovsky cemetery next to the grave of his wife. His death deeply shook both sisters. They understood only now how much grief and anxiety they had caused their good, defenceless, aged father, in spite of the fact that their relations had improved at the end. Marina wrote to Rozanov:

> The very last year of his life he felt our love; earlier he had suffered a great deal on our account without any idea of what to do with us. When we married he was very worried about us. He did not come to know either Seryozha or Boris. Later he was able to love Seryozha, believing in his desire for further education, this was for him the most important thing. But as people he did not know Seryozha or Boris, he did not know at all those whom we loved. He was very fond of Alya and Andryusha, and was very happy about them, and, as we later learnt, told everyone about them. But he saw them only when they were very little, before they were a year old. This is a terrible shame![10]

One can see from the poems written between 1913 and 1915 that marriage, a child and an independent life strongly influenced Tsvetayeva, and that a new stage had begun in her emotional development; her personality was defining itself more precisely. Marina understood this very well herself and attached great significance to the poems of this period. Sometimes, when they resembled each other thematically, she joined them together in cycles, even if they were written at different times. All of this resulted in an organically integrated collection, which Tsvetayeva thought of publishing under the title *Poems of Youth* (*Yunosheskie stikhi*), as the third volume of her lyrical journal. But she did not hurry over it: Marina 'lived, the books lay'. It seems almost grotesque, but typically for Tsvetayeva, this volume was published in the form she wished only in 1976, more than sixty years after its creation and thirty-five years after her death. Several poems, however, such as those addressed to her daughter or the highly romantic ones about death and the grave, were known previously.[11]

When one becomes familiar with the contents of those parts which have come to light only relatively recently, then one understands why the poet herself hesitated to make this volume public. One reason is the poem 'The Enchanter', dedicated to Asya, where the story about Ellis is described. Another is the cycle of poems 'The Friend', about which we will speak later.

Poems of Youth, however, contains many happy, harmonious poems and there can be no doubt at all that the present was full of contentment for her. According to the dates of the poems, and scholarly research, one can ascertain that the Efron family spent the spring of 1913 in Koktebel.[12] As always, they were received there especially warmly. Voloshin painted a picture for Marina, and she and Seryozha gave 'Pra' copies of their books with dedications. They felt themselves to be surrounded by an atmosphere of friendship and understanding, which acted particularly productively on Tsvetayeva's work. A new feeling of certainty in herself and in her creative power is heard in the famous lines of 13 May 1913:

> For my poems, written down so soon in life, so early
> I did not know I was a poet yet,
> Forced loose from me like droplets from a fountain,
> A rocket's sparking jet,
>
> Poems storming from me, invading, like some tiny demons
> The sanctuary where sleep and incense twine,
> Their themes made up of youth and death, my poems,
> My always unread lines!
>
> Thrown here and there amid the dust of various bookshops,
> Untouched then, now, by any reader's thumb,
> For my poems, stored deep like wines of precious vintage,
> I know a time will come.[13]
>
> [translated by David McDuff]

Did she know in sunny carefree Koktebel in 1913 how true was what she had said? In the course of her whole life Tsvetayeva considered these lines to be some of her most important: 'This formula was in advance of my entire literary (and human) fate', she writes to Ivask on 4 April 1933, adding: 'I knew *everything* – from birth.'

Soon after the death of Professor Tsvetayev, Marina and Asya returned to the south. Moscow without their father seemed to both sisters to be unbearable. Moreover, each sister had a family problem; Asya's husband had abandoned his nineteen-year-old wife and one-year-old son Andryusha, and Marina's husband had

Marina and Asya, 1913

to recover from a fresh attack of tuberculosis and to try to pass his school-leaving examinations. For a short time the Efron family stayed in Yalta. On 18 October they moved to Feodosia, where they stayed in the *dacha* of Redlikh, on a small hill in the Karaimskaya Sloboda, from which there was a view of the coast and the entire city. Asya found a flat at a ten-minute walk's distance from her sister's *dacha*. Here they remained until the beginning of the war.

In the second edition of her memoirs, which were published in 1974, Anastasia Ivanovna describes this winter in Feodosia. The sisters often met and they took an active part in the cultural life of the city. As before, they recited Marina's poetry together, for example, on 24 November at the opening of the philanthropic 'Jewish Society for Aid to the Poor', in which Sergey Efron also participated; and on 15 December, together with Voloshin, at an 'Evening of Poetry and Music'. They also gave readings in private homes, for the most part in the company of Voloshin, who would come on foot from Koktebel. Marina, Asya and Seryozha greeted the new year of 1914 in Koktebel which they reached during a terrible snowstorn. On the same night, as Marina describes in 'A Living Word About a Living Man', Voloshin's 'Tower' almost burnt down.

From Feodosia Marina also wrote several letters to V. V. Rozanov (at present we know of three), which are especially interesting for their wealth of biographical details. Asya had initiated an epistolary acquaintance with the famous writer and friend of her father, having written to him after she had read his book *Solitude*, though without giving her surname.[14] Rozanov replied promptly, and this letter which was 'so genuine', pleased Marina to such an extent that she also decided to answer it. She told Rozanov about her background, and her marriage, admitting:

> I do not believe at all in the existence of God and the afterlife; from which comes despair, a horror of old age and death. There is a complete inability in my nature to pray and repent. I have a mad love of life, a convulsive and feverish greed to live. Everything which I have said is true. Perhaps you will reject me for this. But indeed I am not guilty. If God exists He indeed created me this way. If there is an afterlife I will, of course, be happy in it. Punishment – for what? I have never done anything on purpose.[15]

There were, however, more worldly concerns. Seryozha was still having difficulties at school. The director of the *gymnasium* was a great admirer of Rozanov. Marina therefore requested him to send the director one of his books with an inscription in his own hand

and hoped that this would influence the result of the forthcoming examination.

'If he fails, he can be enlisted as a soldier in the autumn, in spite of his affected lung and his narrow chest. He will then die.'

We do not know if Marina's request was fulfilled, but Sergey Yakovlevich did pass his exams.

On 1 June 1914 the Tsvetayev sisters and their relations left for Koktebel. During these last days of peace before the war the artists Yulia Obolenskaya and Kandaurov went to stay there as well. The latter was the stage-designer of the Maly Theatre and secretary of the journal *The World of Art.* 'A summer whirlwind of madness' is how Voloshin describes the summer of 1914 in his memoirs. He himself had left Koktebel just before the beginning of the war: he had wanted to see Rudolf Steiner and he returned to Russia only in the spring of 1916 with the greatest difficulty.

Aleksey Tolstoy recalls these last peaceful days in Koktebel:

> There was a levity and instability among the new arrivals which exceeded all bounds. It was as if some kind of gigantic solar flare which had been emitted on one fine July morning by the red-hot sun, destroyed the memory and good sense of hundreds of thousands of inhabitants of this city...

The Tsvetayev sisters were also, apparently, drawn into this whirlwind. On 9 July Yulia Obolenskaya wrote to a friend: 'Marina and Asya have argued with all the summer guests and after an almighty scandal left Koktebel the other day for good.'[16]

Both Seryozha and Marina returned to Moscow, while Asya remained for a short time in the south with her son and a nanny.

CHAPTER 9

Moscow – Outbreak of War
1914 – 1915

The reason for the hasty return of the Efrons to Moscow was not fear of the approaching war, but the unexpected arrival in Moscow of Sergey Yakovlevich's older brother, Pyotr, who until now had been an actor in Paris. He was terminally ill with tuberculosis and died within a few weeks. Marina was deeply shaken by this meeting. One can thus understand why, unlike those around her, she was not at this particular moment overly concerned with the war. In a cycle of poems dedicated to P.Ya. Efron, the following is included:

> War! war! – Pacing by the icons,
> And the rattle of spurs.
> But imperial accounts are not my affair
> Nor the quarrels of nations.
>
> On the seemingly snapped tight-rope
> I am a little dancer.
> I am the shadow of someone's shade
> The lunatic of two dark moons.[1]

This was written on 16 July, the day after Austria-Hungary issued its ultimatum to Serbia.

Hundreds of books have been written in the West about the beginning and course of the war, about the downfall of the imperial Russian régime and the revolutions of 1917. Accents have been placed differently, according to the positions and political convictions of the authors. One thing is clear, when people in Russia learnt about the ultimatum given by Austria, a wave of patriotism and hatred for Germany and Austria arose in the whole country. Soldiers and young officers hurried to join the army as volunteers, and everywhere committees were formed for military aid. Young women from the aristocracy enrolled in Red Cross courses in order to work as nurses in hospitals. Private individuals hastened to provide assistance where the government could not meet its goals. All the displays of patriotism, however, could not hide the fact that Russia was not ready for war; the main problem of the transportation of military units and materials had not been solved. This led, already in August 1914, to catastrophe in East Prussia.

These events had, of course, an influence on the future life of the Tsvetayevs. Andrey Ivanovich Tsvetayev turned the chocolate-coloured house on Trekhprudny Lane, which he had inherited, over to the authorities for use as a military hospital. Soon after this the Tsvetayev sisters' family home was half burnt down, and later, at the beginning of the Revolution, it was looted. Marina and Sergey decided not to return to their house on the Polyanka, as a psychiatric hospital had been transferred there. Once again they looked for a roof over their heads and in July 1914 they settled on Borisoglebsky Lane. Sergey entered university and Marina plunged into Moscow's intellectual life.

The young Nikolay Yelenev, whom we meet here for the first time, was caught at the beginning of the war in Austria. When he managed to return to Moscow, after many wanderings, he was struck by the difference between the moods of the charitable organisations which were trying to help and to entertain the wounded 'little soldiers', and the utter indifference of the intelligentsia to everything relating to the war.[2] While thousands of people were dying on the fronts the intelligentsia quite peacefully rotated in the same narrow circle of pre-war artistic and philosophical interests. Here too could be found Marina Tsvetayeva.

In February of 1915 Sergey Yakovlevich set out as a volunteer to work as an orderly in a hospital on the front. It is possible that one of the reasons for this was a serious crisis in the relations between husband and wife, which dated from the autumn of 1914 when Marina had met the poet Sofia Parnok. Parnok, who was considerably older than Tsvetayeva, 'belonged', as A. Saakyants expresses it, 'to the followers of Sappho'; that is she was 'openly and aggressively lesbian' to use the more precise words of S. Karlinsky. Marina immediately fell completely under her influence. Between October 1914 and February 1916 a stormy "romance" developed between them, the peripeteia of which are described in detail, but also with a certain amount of fantasy, in the cycle of poems 'The Friend' which is included in *Poems of Youth*. There is no doubt that this meeting had a strong effect on both of them; for Tsvetayeva it marked an important stage in her personal and poetic development. The friendship broke down for good in February 1916 in Koktebel. Traces of it are still to be found in 1916 in *Milestones (Vyorsty)*.[3]

During the years 1914-15 both women took a serious part in the literary life of Moscow. Yelenev relates that a year before the war A.Ya. Tairov, a former assistant to the famous director Mardzhanov, threw down a challenge to the even more famous Stanislavsky and opened on Strastny Boulevard a new, so-called 'Chamber Theatre', where the most recent Russian and European plays were staged, including Maeterlinck, Schnitzler, and Mayakovsky. All of Moscow spoke of these performances. Tairov, however, did not spend his time entirely on dramatic productions, he also organised soirées in the theatre, at which well-known literary figures and philosophers spoke before a select audience. Sometimes private evenings were held, and at one of these, which was in honour of the aged Marius Petipa, Yelenev saw Marina Tsvetayeva for the first time.[4]

> Tsvetayeva's face seemed younger, more relaxed, and more inspired. With her dark-brown cropped hair, fine clear-cut nose, thin lips, but with a rather wide oval Russian face, Marina was devoid of earthly inertia...If some people did not like Marina, and avoided her, then they had to admit, all the same, that Tsvetayeva was an exceptional person. Her poetic gift went beyond the limits of the artistic concepts and world-view of that era. This talent did not resemble either everyday feminine charm, or the hedonistic experience of the age-old call of beauty. The structure of Tsvetayeva's forms and ideas opened up untouched virgin territory...

Yelenev was struck by the spirituality of her face in which so much hidden emotional tension was reflected. Her face reminded him of that of the page in the Vatican fresco 'La Messa di Bolsena'.

> The shape of her nose, well-proportioned and slightly aquiline, went extremely well with her large, high, steep forehead. But her grey eyes were cold, transparent. These eyes had never known fear, and least of all supplication or submissiveness...

Marina was the centre of the evening. Accompanied by thunderous applause she turned to Petipa with an "impromptu" which shocked Yelenev:

> Never before, nor later, have I heard such open eroticism. What was amazing was the fact that the erotic theme was cold, chaste, and devoid of any kind of seductiveness. Tsvetayeva's sonnet was a remarkable example of poetic mastery and cold reason. A scarcely perceptible hint of irony, consciously, with calculation, destroyed its amorous meaning...

The year 1915 was the most successful and victorious for the

imperial Russian army: after a protracted siege in Galicia the
fortress of Przemysl and a large part of Galicia were taken. Already
in May, however, the Austrian and German forces had assumed the
offensive and the Russian army was forced to retreat. In August the
Tsar himself took supreme command of the army. He spent the
greater part of his time at headquarters in Mogilev. While
Rasputin's influence was growing in Petrograd, discontent spread
throughout the country. Grand Duke Nikolay Mikhailovich, an
uncle of the Emperor, and a very educated and intelligent man,
wrote to his friend in Paris, Frédéric Masson:

> While you have a threat which comes from the left, we have one from
> the incorrigible right, and especially from certain mystical tendencies,
> which have reduced social opinion to despair...

On 9 November he adds: 'As far as internal politics are
concerned, I fear very much what will happen after the war...'[5]

This terrible time, the horrors of war and the misfortunes of the
country, are not reflected in the collection *Poems of Youth*.

All the same, however, it is impossible to say that Tsvetayeva
took no interest in the events of the day. Two poems from this time
clearly show her feelings and moods, and are very indicative of her
character. In the first she addresses Germany, which was then
universally hated. It seemed to Marina that she had to take the side
of the weaker country, persecuted by everyone, which she loved like
a second motherland.

> You have been given over to the world for baiting
> And to your enemies there is no end.
> Yet, how could *I* desert you?
> Yet, how could *I* betray you?
>
> And how could I apply the commonplace:
> 'An eye for an eye, blood for blood', –
> Germany – my madness!
> Germany – my love!...[6]

Such lines, of course, could not be printed in Russia, which was
at war with Germany. But Tsvetayeva often read them at private
literary evenings. The other poem about the war, written on 15
October 1915, was published in the journal *Northern Annals*
(*Severnie Zapiski*) in August 1916. She expresses here her general
attitude towards war.

> I know the truth! All previous truths – away!
> People do not need to struggle with each other on earth!
> Look: it is evening, look: soon it will be night.
> *What* is it all about – poets, lovers, captains?

The wind has already settled, the earth is already covered in dew,
Soon the astral storm in the sky will be frozen,
And we shall all soon sleep under the earth,
We, who hindered each other from sleeping on earth.[7]

CHAPTER 10

Petersburg – Moscow – Aleksandrov – 'Milestones I'

1916

The Petrograd journal *Northern Annals*, which first appeared around 1910, was considered to be "left-wing". Its publishers Ya. L. Saker and S. I. Chatskina, continually sought young, new and talented contributors. Soon after the first issue of the journal they managed to enlist F. A. Stepun as a regular contributor. Sofia Parnok also published regularly with them and it was through her that Marina Tsvetayeva came into contact with the journal. From January 1915 until it was discontinued in 1917 *Northern Annals* published sixteen poems by Tsvetayeva and her translation of *La Nouvelle espérance* by the Comtesse de Noailles.[1]

The editorial office of *Northern Annals* was reputed to be the meeting place of all the radical intelligentsia of Petrograd. In the drawing-room of the publishers' home, where a fire was kept burning in the large fire-place day and night, and where poetry was also read day and night, the entire pleiad of Petersburg poets often put in their appearance. These included Vyacheslav Ivanov, Aleksey Remizov and the young, recently discovered Sergey Yesenin, who came here whenever he was in the capital. A special place was occupied in this circle by Anna Akhmatova:

> At our first and only meeting I did not take a liking to Anna Akhmatova, who was appreciated most of all by Sofia Isakovna and her circle. I did not see at first in the poetess that great, profound personality which Vyacheslav Ivanov had immediately divined in her. Perhaps it was because she was sitting with too great an effect by the fire-place on a polar bear skin, surrounded by a ring of various elegant over-powdered and scented morning-coats, after the Petersburg fashion...[2]

As they wished to introduce her to the literary circle of the capital, Ya. L. Saker and S. I. Chatskina invited Marina Tsvetayeva to Petrograd to celebrate the New Year of 1916. They had already met her previously in Moscow. Since Marina did not accept money for her work they brought her gifts: a three-volume edition of Russian folk tales by Afanasyev and two red fox stoles. In Moscow they took her to a restaurant with gypsy music. This was the first time that such a thing had happened in Marina's life and it made a great impression on her. In her memoir 'An Otherworldly Evening' she addresses her publishers: 'Sofia Isakovna Chatskina and Yakov Lvovich Saker – thank you for the holiday – I have so few of them!

She was right to be grateful to them: the impressions from this evening served as the source for the gypsy motifs which appear in Tsvetayeva's work after 1916. Tsvetayeva herself also stated that the Afanasyev collection of folk tales inspired much of her creativity. These new influences can already be detected in *Milestones I* of 1916.

Her stay in Petersburg also turned out to be most significant, as she could meet people who provided fresh impetus for her work. Tsvetayeva stayed with the family of the engineer Kannegiser and she became very friendly with his sons, Sergey, who was a great traveller, and the shy and less robust Lenya, who wrote poetry. Soon after this Leonid Kannegiser became a celebrity, but not as a poet. In August 1918, when a group of Social-Revolutionaries organised an attempt on Lenin's life, he killed one of the fiercest of the Chekists, Uritsky. With this venture a wave of repressions began, in which Leonid himself perished.

In the hospitable home of the Kannegisers Marina became acquainted with some of the poets of Petersburg, such as Yesenin and one of the young pupils of Gumilyov, Georgy Ivanov, who was later to play a great role in the literary circles of the Paris emigration. From the first minute they did not like each other. Georgy Ivanov describes in his memoirs how an argument '*à bâtons rompus*' arose at the tea-table. Marina maintained that the writers of Petersburg were not in a position to understand and appreciate the greatness of Rostand.[3]

The most important event of this visit was the evening of the first of January 1916, when Mikhail Kuzmin read his poetry. Tsvetayeva describes this episode in 'An Otherworldly Evening', which also includes a poem she sent to Kuzmin in 1921:

Two glowing orbs! – No, mirrors!
No two misfortunes!
Two seraphic mouths,

Two black circles
Charred remains on the mirror's ice,
On the pavement's stones,
Across the thousand-*vyorsted* hall
Smoke the polar fires...[4]

All literary Petrograd was present at this evening at the Kannegisers'. Everyone wished to meet Tsvetayeva and to hear her poetry. She recited 'Germany', 'I know the truth' and others for them, and she knew she was a success: 'But everything I have read is still not enough, and they all still want more. I clearly feel that I am reading in the name of Moscow, and that I will not allow this name to fall into the mud...'

Petersburg, however, was already in possession of a woman writer whom it adored:

> Akhmatova! The word is spoken. With my whole being I sense the intense, inevitable – at my every line – comparison between us...not only between Akhmatova and myself, but between the poetry of Petersburg and of Moscow, between Petersburg and Moscow. (But if certain of Akhmatova's followers listen to me, *against me* then I, however, do not read against Akhmatova, I read to Akhmatova,) I read as though Akhmatova were in the room, Akhmatova alone. I read for Akhmatova, who is absent. My success is necessary to me, as a direct line to Akhmatova. And if at the present moment I want to make an example of Moscow, then it is not in order to conquer Petersburg, but in order to give this Moscow to Petersburg, in order to give this Moscow, which is inside myself, inside my love, to Akhmatova, to lay it down at the feet of Akhmatova. (Indeed, the Poklonny Mountain itself has bowed down to her from the unbendable peaks of its heights.)[5]

The adored Akhmatova, however, was not able to receive this gift: she was not in the city. By a strange decree of fate the paths of the two greatest woman poets of twentieth-century Russia went their separate ways until it was too late for a real friendship. They met for the first time only in 1941 after Tsvetayeva had returned from France.

We know that Akhmatova did not show the same degree of enthusiasm for her great rival's work. Even in the sixties, when Akhmatova met Gleb Struve abroad she recalled Tsvetayeva 'with reserve'. But for Tsvetayeva, even that first "non-meeting" with Akhmatova in 1916 proved to be productive. Immediate results of her trip to Petersburg were the 'Poems to Akhmatova' and several of the 'Poems to Moscow'. These form important elements in the collection *Milestones*.

One meeting, which is more significant perhaps, from the personal point of view, did take place during that 'otherworldly

evening'. Marina was introduced to a person she had seen for the
first time the year before in Koktebel: this was the young poet Osip
Mandelstam. When he recited his poems he would throw back his
head, his eyes half-closed. Marina made such an impression on
him that already in March he went to Moscow in order to see her.
Mandelstam was in Moscow for the first time, so Marina took him
around the city to show him its sights. In the end she made a
present to him of the city she loved so much:

> From my hands – accept my strange, my splendid
> Brother, a city not made by human hands.
> With all its churches, forty times forty
> And the doves which soar above them.
> . . . .
>
> The incomparable circle of the five cathedrals
> Accept, my ancient, my inspired friend.
> . . . .
>
> And you will arise full of marvellous powers
> And you will not repent of your love for me.[6]

Mandelstam had no difficulty in replying:

> ...And the five-domed cathedrals of Moscow
> With their Italian and Russian soul
> Remind me of the appearance of Aurora
> But with a Russian name and in a coat of fur.[7]

In two letters to A. Bakhrakh she recalls these walks around
Moscow:

> I was then twenty years old. I said to your favourite poet: 'What is all this
> about?' 'Why Marina, when there is Moscow?! Marina, when there is
> the spring? Oh, you do not *truly* love me!' This always stifled me, this
> sort of narrowness. Love the *world* – in me, not *me* in the world. So that
> 'Marina' would mean: the world, and not the world – 'Marina'.
>
> (25 May 1923)

And later:

> Do you have a copy of Mandelstam's *Tristia?* It might be curious for you
> to know (as one of the reflections of me) that the poems 'In the
> discordant polyphony of a girls' choir', 'On the sledge covered with
> straw', 'But in this strange, wooden settlement of fools' and several
> others were written for me. This was in Moscow in the spring of 1916,
> and in place of myself I made him a gift of Moscow. Because of his wife
> (recent and jealous) he decided not to dedicate them openly to me. I
> have many poems to him...Because of his wife (recent and jealous) I
> decided not to dedicate these to him.
>
> (25 July 1923)[8]

About this matter Nadezhda Mandelstam says:

I knew very well that the poems were written for Tsvetayeva. The author of 'An Attempt at Jealousy' apparently despised all wives and lovers of her erstwhile friends, and suspected that it was I who would not allow Mandelstam to "dedicate" poems to her. Where had she ever seen dedications above love poems? Tsvetayeva knew perfectly well the difference between dedicating and addressing poems. Mandelstam's poems are addressed to her and speak of her, but a dedication is a neutral matter, something completely different, so that 'the recent and jealous wife', that is myself, had absolutely nothing to do with this affair. (Both Akhmatova and Tsvetayeva were highly jealous women, and were truly great and brilliant; I could be compared to them as to a star in the heavens.)[9]

In general Marina Tsvetayeva remained silent on the subject of the identity of the heroes of her romances, and of the addressees of the poems which flowed from her pen. When her feelings had cooled down, when everything was finished, the addressee of the poems no longer counted:

Once and for all: all such poems of mine, all such poems in general, are addressed to God. Not without reason have I never included dedications, and not because of posthumous feminine pride, but because of some kind of final purity of conscience. Over the tops of human heads – they are addressed to God. At least to – the angels. Even if each one of the mortal addressees received one poem, not one of them would accept it, would not appropriate it, would not attribute it to themselves, would not sign a receipt for it.[10]

For a long time Marina was silent about her friendship with Osip Mandelstam – the information in her letters to Bakhrakh was meant only for him. However, in 1931 when she read in an article by Georgy Ivanov that Mandelstam was living in 1916 in the Crimea with a brunette woman doctor, to whom he had dedicated poems from *Tristia*, she broke her silence, and in her essay 'The History of a Dedication' wrote down her memories of Mandelstam, knowing that in her lifetime they would not be published. (In this instance we will follow her account, even if, in the meantime Anna Saakyants has demonstrated, on the basis of a letter of Marina to her sister, that the real story was much less romantic and that Mandelstam, in fact, spent barely a day in Aleksandrov.)

In the meantime, we should add the "romance" with Parnok broke off for good in February. On 27 April, Marina Tsvetayeva addressed her husband in a very depressed mood:

I came to you at the dead of night
As the last resort.
I am a vagrant, who has forgotten her ancestry
A sinking ship...

At this time Anastasia Ivanovna was living with her second husband, Mavriky Aleksandrovich Mints, in the small town of Aleksandrov in the province of Vladimir. In May 1916, Marina came to stay in their house while Asya moved to Moscow where she gave birth to her second son, Alyosha, in June. The wooden house in which they lived was situated on the edge of the town, surrounded by a forest and gardens. M.A. Mints returned only in the evenings, and Marina looked after the children, Alya and Andryusha. The coachman Pavel and Andryusha's nanny, Nadya, a village girl who was deeply devoted to her mistress, also lived in the house.

> Aleksandrov. 1916. Summer.
> I am writing poems to Blok and am reading Akhmatova for the first time...

Suddenly Mandelstam appeared in Aleksandrov. He would go on walks with Marina and the children, but he was very displeased by the fact that Alya and Andryusha loved most of all to play in the old neglected churchyard, which was not far from the house.

> In the cemetery I was, according to his words, 'somewhat distracted' and forgot about him, Mandelstam, and was thinking about the dead, reading the inscriptions (instead of poems!) and calculating how old were those who were lying and how old were those who were still alive, in a word, I was looking either above or below, but invariably *away*. I was *ab*stracted!

Mandelstam was afraid of the dead, he himself did not know which he should fear more – their souls or their decomposing bodies. He wanted to return home, but from the house they would drag him out again to the churchyard. During one of these walks a young bull chased them; the children were thrilled, but the adults were panic-stricken.

> Now I know: all of my Red bull comes from that chase. It was dormant in me from May 1916 and was resurrected in 1929 in Paris in the final delirium of a volunteer soldier of the White Army. (I know that this bull was exactly the same as my – our – bull in Aleksandrov. And the laughter with which the man who was dying laughed, was the same laughter of Alya and Andryusha: the pure joy of flight, of the game and the bull.)

Mandelstam did not feel at home at all in Aleksandrov. He was also afraid of the nanny, who it seemed had 'wolf-like eyes'. When he saw the nun who came to help with the housework he was overcome by superstitious terror. After he had left for Koktebel at a break-neck speed ('He wanted – for the sake of his life – to leave...') and sent from there a profound love poem 'Not believing in the miracle of the resurrection', it became clear what the real

Marina and Asya with their husbands and children, Aleksandrov, 1916.

reason of his unrest was. Konstantin Mochulsky, who was at
Koktebel at this time recalls how Mandelstam wrote this poem:
'But these other misfortunes were nothing in comparison with the
real sorrow which he experienced at the end of this Crimean
summer of 1916. I remember the inspiration with which he wrote
one of his best poems...'[11]

Mandelstam's wife affirms as well the decisive role that the
meeting with Tsvetayeva played in his life:

> The friendship with Tsvetayeva, in my opinion, played a great role in
> the life and work of Mandelstam...This became the bridge by which he
> crossed from one period to another. The poems to Tsvetayeva open the
> 'Second Book' or *Tristia*. Kablukov, who was watching over Mandel-
> stam at that time, immediately felt a new voice and was distressed...
> Tsvetayeva, having granted him her friendship and the city of Moscow,
> had somehow freed Mandelstam from an enchantment. This was a
> fantastic gift, because with Petersburg alone, without Moscow, there
> was no freedom to breathe, no real feeling of Russia, no moral
> freedom...[12]

It was not only Mandelstam who began to speak with a different
voice after his meeting with Marina Tsvetayeva; the same thing can
be said about Tsvetayeva herself. In her lyrical journal of 1916,
Milestones, a new tone makes its appearance. S. Karlinsky calls this
volume the watershed of Tsvetayeva's creativity.[13]

One cannot, however, explain this development by the influence
of Mandelstam, but rather by that of the gypsies, whom Tsvetayeva
had heard in Moscow, and by the expressive language used by the
nanny Nadya and the coachman Pavel in Aleksandrov. Here, for
the first time, can be heard echoes of popular speech, folk poetry
and the Church Slavonic language, as well as the new rhythms and
nuances of sound, which will become so characteristic of the later
lyrical poetry of Tsvetayeva. Mandelstam, for all his genius,
remains entirely within the framework of the classical Petersburgian form, from which Tsvetayeva broke away when this form
could no longer contain her rhythms and harmonies. Perhaps this
explains why these two great twentieth century Russian poets did
not know how to appreciate each other's work.

But perhaps there was another reason for her misunderstanding
of Mandelstam. In Aleksandrov, Marina became more closely
acquainted with a friend of M.A. Mints, Nikodim A. Plutser-
Sarno. This knight of the old school, a member of the Polish
nobility, had been educated at the universities of Leipzig and
Heidelberg and loved to ride on trotters and present ladies with
flowers. He was perhaps the strongest romantic love of Marina. He

was also married. Plutser-Sarno is the friend 'from haughty Poland, with a princely coat of arms and a coronet', whom we meet on the pages of *Milestones I* and *II*, even at the height of the Revolution.[14]

Nikodim Plutser-Sarno was subsequently a victim of the repressions. He spent more than twenty years of his life in exile somewhere beyond the Urals, where he evidently died.

In *Milestones I* military events are hardly spoken of. Marina acted, in this regard, like many of the Russian intellectuals and writers, who even in 1916 were still discussing poetic rhythms, the spiritual crisis of old Europe, and other endless philosophical problems, without taking the slightest interest in the fate of their own country, which was slowly spilling its blood on the front, and which was facing internal disintegration. In 'An Otherworldly Evening' Tsvetayeva was later to say:

> Everyone paid. Seryozha and Lenya with their lives, Gumilyov – with his life, Yesenin with his life. Kuzmin, Akhmatova and I – with life imprisonment in ourselves, in this fortress which is more secure than the Peter and Paul Fortress.

But she did sense that something sinister was in the air. She felt that the earth was shaking beneath her feet. As though possessed by that prophetic spirit, which struck Nadezhda Mandelstam so much, she wrote on 2 July 1916 the following poem:

> Both hands were given to me to extend to everyone,
> Not to withold even one of them, my lips – to give names,
> And eyes, not to see, with eyebrows raised high above them,
> But to marvel gently at love, and more gently at hatred.
>
> But this bell, which is heavier than those of the Kremlin,
> Swings and swings unceasingly in my chest –
> This means – who knows? – I do not – that perhaps
> I have not long to remain a guest on Russian soil![15]

All the same, it seems strange that the last poem by Marina in *Milestones I*, the splendid, 'Here again is the window where again they do not sleep', written 23 December 1916, is completely untouched by everyday events. Indeed, only six days before this, on 17/30 December, three young people, Grand Duke Dmitry Pavlovich, Prince Feliks Yusupov (husband of the Grand Duchess Irina Aleksandrovna), and a right-wing member of the Duma, Purishkevich, murdered the universally hated Rasputin. The whole atmosphere trembled and the tension reached an unbearable state. On 30 December/12 January the French ambassador Paléologue and his attaché the Comte de Chambrun were invited to dinner by one of the Grand Duchesses at which they witnessed what appeared to be a conspiracy by members of the imperial family against Nicholas II with the purpose of elevating another Romanov to the throne. The French guests understood that a coup d'état had not been successful. The atmosphere was so tense that Paléologue said to Chambrun, as they left the palace, '*La révolution russe a commencé* !'[16]

Moscow – Koktebel – February Revolution – 'Milestones II' – 'Swans' Encampment' – 'October in a Railway Carriage' – Birth of Irina

1917

Voloshin once said to Tsvetayeva: 'Marina, you do harm to yourself by your abundance. There is enough material in you for ten poets, and all of them remarkable...' This saying applies very well to the year 1917, which saw the beginning of two volumes of poetry, which are so different in themes and styles that they could be attributed to different poets, and many prose pieces, 'all of which are remarkable'. The first collection includes poems from 1917-21 which according to Tsvetayeva's intention were to be published under the title *Milestones II*, but they never appeared in print in this form.[1] The central part of this collection is the cycle 'Don Juan', a set of poems expressing a new, triumphant love, overcoming all earthly difficulties. They are addressed to N. Plutser. These apolitical poems are, on account of their themes, not style, something of a return to the poet's romantic youth.

Parallel with this collection of 1917-20, a volume was compiled from Tsvetayeva's reflections on contemporary events such as the February and October Revolutions and the Civil War.[2] This volume, *Swans' Encampment* (*Lebediny stan*), serves as a lyrical diary and expresses the real feelings and hopes of the poet. If one adds to this that in 1917 Tsvetayeva began to write prose seriously and gave birth, as if incidentally, to her second daughter, then one cannot help acknowledging her versatility.

The year 1917 began with the publication of 'Poems to Moscow'

in the January edition of *Northern Annals*. Many years later
Tsvetayeva was to recall this:

> Yes, in 1916 I was the first to speak about Moscow like this. (And in the
> meantime, it would seem, the last). And I am happy and proud of this,
> for it was Moscow's final time and hour. *It was a farewell...* These poems
> were prophetic – (Re-read them and do not forget the date.)[3]

After that, however, people stopped taking an interest in
literature. This is not the place to describe in detail those events
which shook Russia and the West from February 1917, and about
which whole libraries have been established. The French attaché
de Chambrun described for his fiancée in Paris how even on 24
February he attended a noisy ball at an aristocratic palace ('...*un bal
sur un cratère...*'), and how the following day, after the founding of
the Provisional Government and the formation of the Council of
Workers' and Soldiers' Deputies, chaos began to reign in Petrograd. The streets turned black from the crowds of people, who
were wandering about, stealing and killing officers.

In Moscow events took a somewhat milder form. There the
commandant of the city managed to preserve order, but Marina
Tsvetayeva quickly understood that dreaming about revolution, as
she had done in 1905, and living through one, were two different
things. Already on 2 March she wrote:

> Above the churchtower there are clouds of blue
> The caw of crows...
> And there, of ashen, sandy hue,
> The revolutionary troops pass through.
> My lordly pain, my kingly anguish, you.
>
> They're without faces, without names.
> And without songs!
> You've lost your way, Kremlin chimes,
> Inside this windy wood of banners, deep.
> Pray, Moscow. Lie down to eternal sleep.[4]
>
> [translated by David McDuff]

The Russian intelligentsia reacted in various ways to the
February Revolution. Many welcomed it with joy. Fyodor Stepun,
who was an officer on the front at the time greeted it 'with delight'.[5]
He began to act as an agitator in his regiment, and was chosen as a
delegate to the Council of Workers' and Soldiers' Deputies. ('Like
the majority of the members of this formless and exaggerated
assembly, I, in fact, did nothing there, if one does not consider
making speeches and carrying on conversations as activities.') Later
he offered his services to the Provisional Government, and finally
assumed for a few months the high position of head of the Political

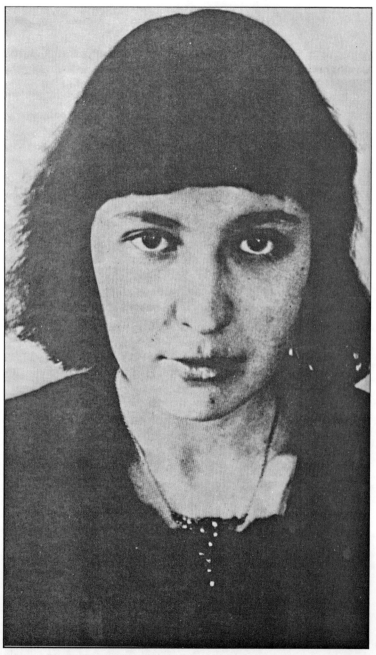

Marina Tsvetayeva, 1917

Division of the War Ministry. In his extremely interesting memoirs Fyodor Avgustovich describes how the revolutionary enthusiasm of responsible people gradually turned into the endless fierce arguments between the various small factions and parties, while the Bolsheviks knew exactly what it was necessary to do to obtain power, which they consciously prepared for from the first moment.

Andrey Bely was in raptures over the Revolution. He took part in all the demonstrations and street-fights, and wrote an article about 'Revolution and Culture', in which he pronounced revolution to be a constructive action of creative form. Still another intellectual, who until this time had lived in Paris as an émigré, Ilya Ehrenburg, returned in July to Petersburg. He understood nothing of what was happening and soon abandoned the stormy capital and journeyed south to the more peaceful Moscow, and then still further to the south...Apparently the discrepancy between the reality of revolution and that for which he had agitated while still a schoolboy, and for which he had left the country, was too great.

Among the intelligentsia, however, were also those who considered desertion to the new powers to be treason and who remained loyal to the Emperor and their oath of allegiance. Among these was Sergey Efron, in spite of the extremely anarchist past of his parents. At the beginning of the February Revolution, and in the summer of 1917, he attended the Alexander Officers' Academy in Moscow.

Marina Tsvetayeva whole-heartedly shared her husband's views, which is not surprising, considering her character. A deep-seated sense of loyalty and fidelity to one's word of honour, and hatred of every kind of desertion, defined her attitude to the Revolution:

> New crowds collecting – other flags waving!
> But we still stand by our word – unwavering,
> For they are devious captains – the winds.[6]
>
> [translated by Robin Kemball]

Without fearing the possible consequences, Tsvetayeva took the side of those whom the new government was persecuting, even if she had previously not sympathised with them. On 4 April 1917, within two days of Lenin's arrival in Petrograd, she passionately defended the Tsarevich Aleksey.

> Pray for the Son – the Dove – the Adolescent,
> For the young Tsarèvich, for the young Alexis –
> Russia, pray, who the true faith confessest!
> . . . . . .

Gentle mother, Russia, kind, caressing!
Is thy heart so hard as not to grace him
With thy loving-kindness, with thy blessing?

Visit not upon the son the father's trespass.
Russia of the country folk – be his protectress:
Spare the lamb of Tsàrskoye Selò, Alexis![7]
    [translated by Robin Kemball]

For the present moment, political events had to take second
place as, on 13 April, Marina's second daughter, Irina, was born.
Interest in the outside world, as well as her muse, soon awoke
however. Between 22 and 25 April Tsvetayeva composed a cycle of
three poems about her favourite folk hero, the robber Stenka
Razin. On 2 May she made a new acquaintance and on 13 May she
wrote:

What then! If the die is cast –
Let it be! Love!
In the stormy – insane – sky –
Ice and blood.

I await you tonight
After two.
At the hour when in me roar
Blood and spirit.[8]

On 19 May an adventure of a completely different character
occurred: walking with Alya, Marina passed by her former family
home on Trekhprudny Lane. By the fence a gypsy woman was
standing, who was reading the palms of people in the street. Over
two days Tsvetayeva wrote a cycle of poems 'Fortune-Telling', in
which she imitates the gypsy's speech. This language is masterfully
used in many of her poems of this period. Later in Prague,
Professor Kondakov, an internationally-known scholar, praised her
very much for these poems: 'He approved of the authenticity of the
gypsy speech. – Where did you manage to study the gypsies so well?
– Oh, they only told me my fortune...'[9]

If it had been possible in 1916 to ignore the war, in 1917 it was
not so easy to forget about what was happening from day to day in
the country. The Provisional Government was losing power and
confidence, while the Bolsheviks, under the leadership of Lenin
and Trotsky, were preparing to overthrow it. In the middle of May
the government was re-organised: P. Milyukov was replaced by the
Social-Revolutionary A. F. Kerensky, who became the Minister of
War and Navy. For several days Marina thought Kerensky would
become a Napoleon for Russia. On Pentecost Sunday, 21 May, she
wrote:

Bent over the map, unsleeping,
There stoops a man.
A Bonaparte breath goes sweeping
Across my land. [...][10]

[translated by Robin Kemball]

But this dream turned out to be an illusion. When Kerensky took the post of Prime Minister, after an unsuccessful Bolshevik uprising, it became apparent he was as completely incapable of dealing with the situation as his predecessor, Prince Lvov, had been.

Marina understood very well the growing danger, especially for her husband. On 7 August she wrote to Voloshin:

> Dear Maks, I have an enormous favour to ask of you: secure a place for Seryozha in the artillery in the south...Best of all in the siege artillery, if this is not possible, in the heavy...Only, Maks, I beg of you, do not delay!

On 25 August she wrote to Voloshin again and let him know that she was planning to go with her children to Feodosia, because in Moscow 'there was hunger, and soon there would be cold'. On the following day she sent a postcard:

> Dear Maks, convince Seryozha to take a leave and go to Koktebel. He dreams of this, but his will power is somehow weakened, and he can not make any decisions. He feels abominably, Moscow is damp, dank, hungry. They will, of course, grant him leave...Write to him Maksinka! Then I will go as well to Feodosia, with the children. Otherwise I am afraid of leaving him here in such a dubious state...[11]

In the south an entire colony of refugees from Moscow and Petrograd was already gathered: Maya Kudasheva, later the wife of R. Rolland, the actress Maria Kuznetsova, the second wife of Boris Trukhachov, and Asya with her son Andryusha. Somewhat later in the course of the Civil War, Boris Trukhachov, seriously ill, managed to reach Koktebel and died there from typhoid in the arms of both his wives. If one can say that the year 1917 was successful for Marina Tsvetayeva, if only from the point of view of her work, then for her sister it was a year of great catastrophes. On 21 May her second husband, Mavriky Aleksandrovich, died from purulent appendicitis; in July both her sons fell ill with dysentery, Andryusha recovered, but little Alyosha died on 18 July and was buried in Koktebel.[12] Anastasia Ivanovna remained alone with Andryusha in Koktebel, where the Civil War found her.

Marina made her way alone to Koktebel, to be with her unfortunate sister, and in order to find rooms for herself and her children. This is why the fatal night of the October Revolution (old

style: 24-25 October; new style: 6-7 November) caught her
unawares in the south of Russia without her family. She knew that
Seryozha, who had only just finished a course for officers, was
facing the greatest possible danger. She saw how in Feodosia
drunken soldiers had raided a wine cellar and realised what the
country could expect. She took a train on 31 October trying to go to
Moscow. The journey lasted three days. The closer she approached Moscow, the more terrible were the rumours. In order to
distract herself Marina began to write down her thoughts in a
notebook:

> Two and a half days without a bite or a drink. (My throat is parched.)
> The soldiers bring newspapers printed on pink paper. The Kremlin and
> all monuments have been blown up. The 56th regiment. The buildings
> of the cadets and officers, who refused to surrender have been blown
> up, 16,000 dead. At the next station – already 25,000. I am silent. I
> smoke. My travelling companions, one after the other, change to trains
> going back...

And then comes the heart-rending 'letter in a notebook':

> If you are alive, if I am destined to see you once again – listen: yesterday,
> approaching Kharkov, I read in *The Southern Region*: 9000 killed. I
> cannot describe this night to you, because it has *not ended*...(I am afraid
> of writing to you, as I would like, because I would begin to weep without
> ceasing. This is all a terrible dream. I try to sleep. I do not know how to
> write to you. When I write to you – there you are, once I write to you!
> But later – ah!) The 56th Reserve Regiment, the Kremlin...But the
> main, the main, the main thing, is you, you, you, with your instinct for
> self-destruction. Could you possibly stay at home? If everyone else
> remained, you alone would go out. Because you are blameless. Because
> you cannot witness people killing others. Because you are a lion,
> offering the lion's share: to give your life for everyone else, to the hares
> and foxes. Because you are selfless and balk at self-preservation,
> because the "I" is not important for you, because I knew all this from
> the first hour! If God performs this miracle – and leaves you among the
> living, I will follow you like a dog![13]

Early in the morning of 3 November, when Marina reached
Moscow, everything seemed quiet there. The fighting had ceased,
and the Kremlin was still standing: how many people had been
killed will never be completely ascertained. The cadets and officers
had defended themselves for five days, but the day before Marina's
arrival in Moscow, they had surrendered and were allowed to go.
Her fear for her husband proved to be groundless; she found him
in the flat of some friends, sleeping the deep sleep of the exhausted.
He had only one goal, to make his way to the south as soon as
possible, in order to continue fighting against the Bolsheviks.

On the evening of the day of her arrival Marina set out with
Seryozha and a friend of his on the long journey back to Feodosia.
Sergey's friend lay on the top berth and in order to distract himself
from gloomy thoughts, began to recite the poetry of one of his
friends whose name was Pavlik.

In the chaos of this urgent departure the Efrons forgot one thing:
to take their children with them. This turned out to be a fatal
mistake.

They arrived in Koktebel during a terrible snowstorm. Maks was
so glad to see Seryozha alive that his joy knew no bounds. But he
was more perspicacious than many of his contemporaries, and the
picture he drew of the Russia of the future was not optimistic:

> But now, Seryozha, there will be something to watch...And insinuat-
> ingly, almost enjoying it, like a good magician before children, he
> showed picture after picture, the whole Russian Revolution for five
> years to come: the terror, the Civil War, the executions, the Vendée, the
> bestiality, the loss of humanity, the unleashing of the spirit of the
> elements, blood, blood, blood...[14]

In the Crimea everything was quiet, the Tatars were living as
they had for centuries. It seemed that the gaudy posters on the
walls belonged to another world. It was decided that Marina would
go collect the children, and then spend the winter in Koktebel with
Maks and Pra. 'Only hurry, Marina,' Voloshin said to her,
'remember that from now on there will be two countries: the North
and the South.'

Seryozha left for the Don, and Marina boarded the train for the
third time in order to bring back Alya and Irina. But this was to be
her last trip. She reached Moscow, but it was already impossible to
return. The front between the 'Reds' and the 'Whites' had divided
the country into north and south, as Voloshin had predicted, for
three whole years. The Efron family was torn apart.

Marina, who had always lived in the clouds and who had no
conception of the practical side of life, suddenly faced the task of
struggling for her own life and that of her tiny children in
conditions which had nothing in common with what she had
previously known.

One immediate consequence of the events of October was,
however, at hand: the sketch 'October in a Railway Carriage'
marked the hour of Tsvetayeva's birth as a prose writer.

CHAPTER 12

October Revolution – Journal – Dramatic Works – Moscow

OCTOBER 1917 – 1918

Lenin knew exactly what to do in order to consolidate the power which fell so easily into his hands in Petrograd. In the country as a whole the Bolsheviks were in the minority; the general elections held on 25 November serve as proof of this, when they won only 25% of the votes, (all the Socialist parties together received 61% of the votes). Lenin did not waste time on dreams about the withering away of the state and other left-wing intellectual phrases. Blow by blow he issued orders which broke up the power of his opponents and completely undermined their influence. Provisional workers' and peasants' councils were organised; estates, factories, and banks were nationalised, the slogan 'steal the stolen' now became very popular. Already on 7/20 December Lenin sent a letter to Dzerzhinsky which served as the foundation of the 'Extraordinary Commission for the Struggle Against Counter-Revolution, Specu-lation and Sabotage', or 'Cheka'. This commission immediately began to exterminate all enemies of Communism.

F. A. Stepun, who had served in the War Ministry of the Provisional Government, managed to leave Petrograd and to reach Moscow while fighting there was still under way, that is, probably a day before Tsvetayeva's first arrival in Moscow after the Revolu-tion. He describes these months as he himself saw them:

> The terror grew from day to day, people were persecuted not only for their actions and thoughts, but also for their inactive silent existences. Death sentences were pronounced and carried out not as punishments for crimes, but in order to liquidate material which was foreign, and therefore, not suitable for the creation of socialism. Landowners, bourgeois, priests, kulaks, White officers were liquidated, just as on

rationally run farms one breed of cattle is liquidated for the sake of another.

Under the threat of this cold-blooded rational terror a process of internal and external repainting in the protective colouring of the Revolution began, which was unprecedented in its dimensions, throughout all of non-proletarian Russia. Thousands and thousands of people who had been forcibly driven from their estates, their city houses and even their modest "intelligentsia" flats by Revolutionary legislation and the arbitrary rule of the masses, discarded their entire cultural baggage and world-view, along with their accumulated property, if only to settle somehow under the saving shelter of Marxist ideology. Crowds of these impoverished, internally lost migrants ended up as employees and even directors of every kind of Soviet bureaucratic department, giving life an elusive, illusory and schizophrenic character. Surrounded on all sides by party spies, these newly appeared 'comrades' easily became entangled in the spy network, and in order to save themselves they sacrificed others.

There can be no doubt that the faceless and omnipresent system of espionage was the most terrible aspect of Bolshevik terrorism. The heart of every man did not beat in his own chest, but in the cold hand of an invisible 'Chekist'.[1]

Several wealthy people and foreigners managed to leave Russia already in the summer and autumn of 1917. The French attaché Comte de Chambrun was recalled in August. Bitter was the fate of those who could not follow his example. Landowners, industrialists, aristocrats, officers and high-ranking civil servants were hounded from the first moment. Members of the imperial family suffered particularly horribly. Grand Duke Nikolay Mikhailovich, who in other circumstances would certainly have served his country in the most responsible positions, was shot together with some of the other Grand Dukes on 20 January 1919 in the Peter and Paul Fortress. One can follow his tragedy by the letters he wrote from prison to Frédéric Masson. His testament from his last letter reads: *'Au nom du Ciel, préservez par tous les moyens votre pays de cette contagion du bolchévisme. C'est la plus dangeureuse forme de l'anarchie qui puisse seulement exister!'*[2]

The Bolsheviks had to cope with the extremely difficult tasks of governing the country, with its economic, political, and military problems. The after-effects of the Civil War and the centralisation of power were felt in the collapse of the economy. Years of calamity began for the general population. It is understandable then why the new rulers, in this difficult position, welcomed all collaborators and intellectuals, who were prepared to work with them, even if they were not party members. Several writers and poets attached themselves to the new government out of conviction and enthusi-

asm, such as Mayakovsky, for example; others, such as Blok and
Bely, believed at first in some kind of great idea of mystical
anarchism, but they were quickly disillusioned when they collided
with reality. A group of left-wing Christian philosophers close to
Berdyayev and Bulgakov attempted to assimilate the Revolution
spiritually in the summer of 1918. Their book, *Out of the Depths*,
however, was not even printed. Among the poets of the pre-war
time was one who joined the Communist party for purely
mercenary motives and who received an influential position: V. Ya.
Bryusov.

The overwhelming majority of the rest, however, rejected the
new ideas and did not want to associate any further with Bryusov or
Blok. Most likely they thought as Marina Tsvetayeva did, who soon
after her last arrival from Koktebel in December 1917 expressed
her opinion very clearly in poetry:

TO MOSCOW

When the red-haired impostor, fell Dimitri,
Laid hold of you, you did not bow the knee.
Where is your pride, my princess? – Where, my beauty,
The rosy cheeks? – the voice once wise and free?
　. . . . .

And Bonaparte's cold lips cannot forget still
The fiery draught you set before him then.
Once more now your cathedrals serve for stables.
The Kremlin's flanks will soldier to the end.[3]

　[translated by Robin Kemball]

Every day new decrees appeared on the walls. By one of these
Tsvetayeva was deprived of her 'unearned income' of 100,000
roubles in the state bank. She herself had always despised money
and wealth and in this she was in agreement with the teachings of
Communism, but this decree meant she now lost her only means of
existence. More painful for her, probably, was the requisition of her
house on Borisoglebsky Lane, which was now occupied by
proletarian families. Marina was fortunate though, she was left
three rooms, in which she lived with her two daughters and the
nanny Nadya, who had previously been with Asya. In December
1920 Marina wrote to her sister in Koktebel:

　I am living with Alya in the same place, in the dining-room. (The rest is
　occupied.) The house has been pillaged and is partially in ruins. It is a
　hovel. We are burning furniture as firewood...

This hovel on Borisoglebsky Lane consisted of the completely
empty dining-room, a second room where the children slept, and

where the stove stood, and where guests were received, and
Marina's refuge, a little room in the attic. These rooms were
described several times in contemporary Russian literature. In the
winter of 1917-18 Ilya Ehrenburg visited Tsvetayeva there for the
first time. He was horrified by the disorder which he found there:

> Entering the small room I was at a loss: it was difficult to imagine
> greater desolation. At that time everyone was living in anxiety, but the
> external way of life was preserved. Marina, however, destroyed her den
> as though on purpose. Everything was thrown about, covered in dust
> and tobacco ash...A very thin young girl came up to me and hugging me
> trustfully began to whisper: 'What pale dresses! What a strange
> silence...' I turned cold from horror: Tsvetayeva's daughter, Alya, was
> then only five years old, and she was reciting Blok's poetry. Everything
> was unnatural, contrived: the rooms, and Alya, and the conversation of
> Marina herself – she proved to be passionate about politics; she said she
> was agitating on behalf of the Cadets...[4]

But the thin pale girl who recited Blok's poetry denies the sharp
remarks of Ehrenburg:

> I do not recall Ehrenburg's first appearance in our rooms on
> Borisoglebsky Lane, I only know that at the age of five, I was naturally
> not familiar with Blok's love poetry, and that in the large, awkward, but
> comfortable rooms, that shipwrecked disorder, which struck everyone
> who entered them at the beginning of the 20s was not yet apparent.[5]

Ehrenburg was right about one thing, however, the little Alya was
an extraordinary child. 'The tiny shadow on the enormous horizon'
was educated by her mother in a very unorthodox and arbitrary
manner. Alya knew how to write at the age of four, and at six began
to keep a journal under her mother's supervision. She showed
herself, even at this early age, to be a consciously thinking and
perceptive individual. The note in her journal of December 1918
was probably written with her mother's help:

> My mother.
> My mother is very strange. My mother is completely unlike a mother.
> Mothers always admire their child, and children in general, but Marina
> does not like small children.
> She has light-brown hair which is waved on the sides. She has green
> eyes, a hooked nose and pink lips. She has a straight posture and hands
> which I like.
> Her favourite day is the Annunciation. She is sad and quick, and
> loves Poetry and Music. She writes poems. She is patient. She is patient
> in the extreme. She gets angry and she loves. She is always rushing
> somewhere. She has a large soul, a gentle voice and a quick step.
> Marina's hands are all covered in rings. Marina reads at night. Her eyes
> are almost always mocking. She does not like it when people come to
> her with some kind of stupid question, she then gets very angry.
> Sometimes she walks about like someone lost, but suddenly she wakes

up completely, begins to speak and then again it is as though she has left for somewhere else.[6]

It would be difficult to find a better characterisation.

The winter of 1917-18 was cold, chaotic and hopeless. But there still existed families which lived better than others, and which tried to help the starving intellectuals by inviting them to dinner. Among such people were the Tsetlins, who before the Revolution were rich owners of a tea firm; they had always supported poets and M. O. Tsetlin himself wrote poems under the pseudonym of 'Amari'.

'The times were difficult and everyone came – from Vyacheslav Ivanov to Mayakovsky,' writes Ehrenburg. Tsvetayeva arrested his attention because without any reserve she passionately defended the Tsarevna Sofia against her brother Peter the Great, whom she considered to be the root of all evil and the perpetrator of the rejection of law and custom.

At one of these dinners Marina sat next to Boris Pasternak. He said that he wanted to write a great novel with a romantic theme and a heroine, like Balzac. 'A poet' thought Marina and she invited him to come and see her. Pasternak did not go, however; like Marina he found it difficult to mix with people.

In the spring of 1918 the Tsetlins' house in Moscow was also requisitioned. They managed to make their way to Paris where they had a flat. The life of writers in Moscow became even more difficult.

Tsvetayeva wrote about life in revolutionary Moscow in her journal. In spite of the fact that she was adding all the time to *Milestones II* and *Swans' Encampment*, it seemed to her that prose was better suited for describing this time.

> These notes are not of a *personal*, nor of a *social*, character: they are thoughts, observations, conversations, scenes of revolutionary life – every sort of thing...Revolutionary Moscow, a certain spiritual chronicle.[7]

This journal, which covers the years 1917-20, was never published in full. In the 1920s short extracts appeared in Russian émigré newspapers. These notes illuminate Tsvetayeva's state of mind. Although she describes everyday concerns, hunger, heavy housework and the 'new people' around her, she tries, for the most part, to leave such realities to the side and to consider abstract themes: about love, friendship, gratitude; she dreams about Germany, which seems to her to be the promised land of wisdom, order, and freedom. In her brilliantly written aphorisms we are struck in particular by Tsvetayeva's talent for abstract thought.[8]

In the summer of 1918 Marina's love for Plutser became less
important:

> Simpler and simpler
> Are writing and breathing.
> Sharper and sharper
> Are sight and hearing.
>
> Less and less
> Are remembrance and love.
> Which means soon will come
> Sand and tatters.
>
> [18 August 1918]

However, even in the darkest times there were flashes of light:
Marina met new people and found friends, whom she would
probably not have met under normal circumstances. Straight after
her arrival from Koktebel she searched for the poet 'Pavlik' whose
poems had pleased her so much during her last trip to the south.

> The meeting was something of an earthquake, for the reason that I
> understood who he was, and he understood who I was. (I am not
> speaking about poetry, I did not even know then whether he knew my
> poems.) Having stood, for I do not know how long, in a magical daze, we
> both went out, by the small back entrance, inundated with poems and
> conversation. In a word, Pavlik departed and vanished. Vanished with
> me at Borisoglebsky Lane, for a long while.[9]

'Pavlik' was the well-known Soviet poet Pavel Antokolsky. In his
memoirs, written in 1966, which are 'somewhat lyrically coloured
and dictated by a feeling of profound gratitude and love to a poet
friend', Antokolsky speaks of Tsvetayeva, whom he recalls in the
following way:

> A stately, broad-shouldered woman with widely spaced grey-green eyes.
> Her reddish hair was closely cropped, her high forehead was hidden
> under a fringe. Her dark-blue dress was neither of a modern, nor of an
> old-fashioned design, but was of the simplest possible cut, recalling a
> cassock, and was tightly drawn in at the waist by a wide yellow belt. Over
> her shoulder was thrown a yellow leather bag resembling an officer's
> map case or a hunter's ammunition pouch, in this unfeminine sack two
> hundred cigarettes and a notebook with poems covered in oil-cloth
> found room. Wherever this woman went she seemed to be a wanderer, a
> pilgrim...Her speech was swift, exact, distinct. Any stray observation,
> any joke, any answer to my questions, were cast into easily found,
> happily sharpened words, and they could just as easily be turned into a
> poetic line. This meant that between her ordinary practical everyday self
> and her poetic self there was no difference: the distance between them
> was imperceptible and insignificant...She never lied, and never exag-
> gerated anything. Her vision and hearing were entirely her own, unlike
> anyone else's, she was on a wave-length of her own, to use a
> contemporary expression...Something weightless and winged emanated

from her whole appearance. She was full of Pushkin's 'inner freedom'.
In her continual striving, she was sleepless, daring. In fact, it was not
herself she loved, but her speech, her words, her work. But she could
love unselfishly the words of another person, and she was prepared to
blow the most gilded trumpets in honour of someone else's success.[10]

The young poets – Tsvetayeva was twenty-five and Antokolsky
twenty-two – sat through the night in the small room in the attic,
which seemed to Antokolsky to be the cabin of a ship sailing outside
time, and philosophised. They sat in the clouds and ruled the
world, as Tsvetayeva expressed it.

Antokolsky was studying under Vakhtangov in the third studio of
the Moscow Art Theatre. Later he worked there for many years as
a producer. He introduced Marina to this circle of bright
responsive people who were enthused by art. New artistic and
social perspectives opened up for Tsvetayeva.

Pavlik's best friend was the handsome actor Yury Zavadsky, who
had a brilliant career ahead of him. Marina fell very deeply in love
with him; it remained a one-sided platonic passion which lasted a
year. Under Zavadsky's influence Tsvetayeva began to write
theatrical pieces, and between 1918 and 1919 she wrote no fewer
than six. For the most part Zavadsky was the leading hero. She
tried to forget about the terrible present and took refuge in an
epoch she had always loved, the eighteenth century. These plays
are not masterpieces, and were not performed at the time. The
near-sighted Tsvetayeva drew her inspiration from sounds and
tones, rather than from the visible world; action on the stage and
the effects of a spectacle remained foreign to her. Karlinsky
remarks that these plays belong by their language, as well, to the
world of her early youth; they are certainly weaker than the lyric
poetry written by her at this period. These plays are still of interest
as they reflect, as if in a mirror, her emotional experiences at the
time, and the strong influence which the whole atmosphere at the
Vakhtangov theatre had on her.[11]

Aside from Zavadsky two other actors in the troups personified
certain ideals of Marina: the former officer of the Guards and
landowner A.A. Stakhovich and the actress Sofia Yevgenievna
Holliday who worked in the Second Studio. Stakhovich, who was
already in 1918 an old man, taught the art of deportment to the
actors. He appears as Casanova in the plays *The Adventure* and *The
End of Casanova*. Marina met him personally only once and this
proved to be a very typical Tsvetayevan meeting: he began to praise
some poems, which were not in fact by her, but by someone else,

while she decided that she should not see him again precisely because she was so taken with him. Later she could find no way of forgiving herself for this, as in February 1919 Stakhovich committed suicide. He paid his debts, gave his money to his valet and hanged himself. Life in proletarian Russia was beyond his endurance. For Marina he remained the prime example of an aristocrat of the old school, belonging to a vanished epoch and a vanished world.[12]

Marina saw Sonechka Holliday for the first time in December 1918 when she recited her play *The Snowstorm* on the stage of the Third Studio. Among the audience was Zavadsky, the main hero and inspiration of the play. But his presence was forgotten when Antokolsky introduced the young ecstatic actress Sonechka to Marina, whose admiration for her was reciprocated from the first moment. Judging from Tsvetayeva's description, Sonechka was in every regard a real *institutochka* (a well-bred schoolgirl) from an earlier Russian era, and the opposite of the reserved Tsvetayeva. For several months they were inseparable. Ariadna Efron recalls that among the many visitors to their house only Sonechka took an interest in her and the little Irina, bringing warmth and affection into their lives.

A third discovery was Volodya Alekseyev, another actor, who deeply respected Tsvetayeva. This idyll lasted until the summer of 1919 when Volodya joined the army of General Wrangel as a volunteer and from that time disappeared without a trace. Sonechka, shedding bitter tears, also bid farewell to Marina and left with the theatre for the provinces. After this Marina never saw her again.

These living human encounters, which took place against the background of the second post-Revolutionary winter, left deep traces in Tsvetayeva's work. Such people as the old aristocrat, the young man who embodied all the masculine and chivalrous virtues, and the delicate young actress who twittered like a bird and who was forever dissolving in tears, had no place in the new Russia: they were condemned to death, to extinction. Each one of them sought and found for themselves a way out of this situation. Under the influence of these events Marina wrote her 'Poems to Sonechka' and then several decades later, her *Tale about Sonechka*, which is perhaps her finest prose piece. It was published in full only in 1976.[13]

Friendship with these lively brilliant people from the theatre brought a certain relief; but grim reality, fear and anxiety could only

be forgotten for short moments. The news from the front of the
Civil War was not good. The 'Free Republic of the Don' created in
January 1918 was destroyed by the Red Army after the few weeks
of its existence. Tsvetayeva was to write:

> White Guard, your path is set noble and high:
> Black muzzles – your breast and temple defy.
>
> Godly and white is the cause you fight for:
> White is your body – in sands to lie.
>
> That is no flock of swans in the sky there:
> Saintly the White Guard host sails by there,
> White, as a vision, to fade and die there...
>
> One last glimpse of a world that's gone:
> Manliness – Daring – Vendée – Don.[14]

> [translated by Robin Kemball]

She had no idea of what had become of Seryozha. All
communication with him had been broken. Worries of a purely
mundane character were added to her daily anxieties and fears
about Seryozha: Tsvetayeva had no money, there was nothing to eat
and no hope for improvement. Marina describes a typical day in
1918:

> There is no flour, nor bread, under the writing-table is about twelve
> pounds of potatoes, the remains of the *pud* [36 lbs.] "borrowed" from
> our neighbours – this is our entire supply! The anarchist Charles took
> Seryozha's antique gold watch, I went to him a hundred times, at first he
> promised to return it, then he said that he found a buyer for the watch,
> but had lost the little key for it...In sum: neither watch, nor money. (At
> present such watches are worth 12,000, that is 1.5 *puds* of flour.) The
> same thing with the children's scales.
>
> I stay alive on gratuitous meals (for the children's sake). The wife of
> the shoemaker Gransky – ...a thin, dark-eyed woman with a beautiful
> suffering face – the mother of five children – sent me recently her eldest
> daughter with a ration card for dinner (one of her daughters has gone to
> a colony) and a "little bun" for Alya...

She also says about the wife of the lawyer Goldmann:

> It seems she helps me in secret from her husband, whom naturally as a
> Jew and a man of success, I – in whose house everything has frozen to
> death except the soul, and in which nothing has survived destruction,
> but books, – cannot fail to irritate.[15]

In another sketch, 'Free Passage', Tsvetayeva describes how at
that time people would go into the countryside for provisions.
One of the new occupants of the house was the influential
Communist Henryk Sachs, a close collaborator of Dzerzhinsky. He
tried to question Alya about her father, but for all this he turned out
to be a kind-hearted man and managed more than once to help

Marina. On one occasion, after Marina's half-brother, about whom she had heard and known nothing, turned up unexpectedly and asked for Marina's help in order to save his old grandfather, Professor Ilovaisky, from prison, Sachs was able to get him released from the Cheka. In the autumn of 1918 he also arranged for Marina to obtain some work, with a salary, at the People's Commissariat for Minority Populations, the so-called 'Narkomnats'.

Marina kept amusing and malicious notes entitled 'My Services' about her activities in 'Narkomnats' where she worked for almost six months, and about working conditions in general in Russian governmental departments in 1918. Her work consisted in cutting out of newspapers all despatches from the Civil War front, or transcribing them and pasting them on index cards. But the employees were occupied, for the most part, with other matters: during working hours they stood in queues for provisions, they improved and re-painted their offices, and dragged from the other offices everything they could (the commissariat was located in one of the sumptuous palaces of the nobility). They helped each other in solving personal problems and if they had no real work to do, they quickly invented, on their own, news from the front, which they pasted on their cards.

In 1925 Marina wrote to Anna Tesková:

> I remember almost with joy my work in Soviet Moscow – during this time three of my plays were written: *The Adventure*, *Fortuna*, and *The Phoenix*, as well as two thousand lines of verse...

On 25 April 1919 Marina gave notice at her office in 'Narkomnats'. She was not in a state to continue working and she did not understand a classification system which they required of her. This was probably for her good: to the end of her job she apparently did not know who the head of the department was, who was collecting information about enemy activity, not only on the front, but everywhere; this information he studied thoroughly and used in order, sooner or later, to destroy the enemy. His name was I. V. Stalin.

After this Marina worked still one more day, on 26 April, in a department which went under the name of 'Monplenbesh'. There she had to put a card-index into alphabetical order and to enter the cards into a catalogue; the norm was 200 cards a day. Everyone there was working with great zeal, scarcely raising their heads. Marina held out until lunch, she then leapt up and under some pretext ran away, never to return:

> It was not I who left behind the little cards: my legs carried me! The legs of the soul: without the hesitation of consciousness. This was indeed instinct at work![16]

Tsvetayeva wrote to her sister in 1920:

> I worked at one time for 5½ months (in 1918) and then left – I *could not* work any longer. It is better to hang oneself.

Marina was once again forced to cope with everyday tasks, without the support of a family or income. Seryozha had not given any sign of life. The children were hungry and neglected. Instead of speaking little Irina only sang to herself and nodded her head.

Silhouette by E.S. Kruglikova, 1920

CHAPTER 13

Moscow – Death of Irina – Epic Poems
1919–1920

> Do not be ashamed, country of Russia.
> Angels are always bare-footed...
> It is the devil who has made off with the boots.
> Whoever is not bare-footed now is terrible![1]

– wrote little Alya in 1919. This 'most plague-ridden, most black, most fatal of all the years of Moscow's history' was an indescribably dreadful experience for the Russian people and especially for Muscovites. The new rulers, who had destroyed the entire economic system of the country and who were carrying on a civil war, were in no position to deal with the problems of everyday life. The people vegetated in a state of complete chaos: they were famished, freezing, and deprived of every necessity. They also trembled in fear before the political terror. It is not recorded in any archive how many people perished during this winter.

Fortunately during difficult times people become kinder and help each other more. Such solidarity was shown to Marina Tsvetayeva as well, who was little suited to the exigencies of daily life. Without the assistance of her neighbours and writer friends it is likely that neither she, nor Alya, would have survived this winter.

Marina also helped others when she could and in those catastrophic times rose, in just purely human terms, to the occasion. Konstantin Balmont provides her with a good testimonial:

> I am walking down Borisoglebsky Lane, which leads to Povarskaya. I am on my way to see Marina Tsvetayeva. It is always a joyous occasion to be with her, when life oppresses one especially unmercifully. We joke, laugh, read poetry to each other. And although we are not at all in love with each other, few lovers can be as gentle and attentive to each other at their rendezvous.[2]

Balmont expressed himself even more clearly when he had left Russia and was living in the West:

> Remembering those, already distant, days in Moscow, and not knowing where Marina is now, and whether she is alive or not, I cannot help saying that those two poetic souls, mother and daughter, who were more like two sisters, gave an example of the most moving vision of complete estrangement from reality, and of a free life among reveries, under circumstances in which most people only moaned, grew sick and died. The spiritual love for love, and love for beauty, somehow liberated these two human birds from pain and anxiety. Hunger, cold, complete destitution...and yet eternal chatter, a firm step and a smiling face. They were two saints, and looking at them I more than once felt a strength in myself which seemed to have been extinguished completely.[3]

Marina later wrote to Bakhrakh:

> I had never been an admirer of Balmont; but I helped him drag his rations home. I despise literariness. All those flowers and letters and lyrical interludes are not worth a shirt which has been mended in time. 'Daily life'? Yes, this is a loathsome thing, and a sin to put it on one's shoulders, which are already, as it is, burdened with wings![4]

On one point all witnesses agree; although everyone who was in Moscow at that time lived very badly and had to struggle in order to survive, the position in which Marina found herself was particularly desperate.

Prince S. M. Volkonsky relates the anecdote, that even a thief, who broke into the rooms at Borisoglebsky Lane, offered Marina some money when he saw in what terrible poverty she was living. Stepun recalls one walk along the Tverskoy Boulevard, when the writer 'bare-footed, and wearing a torn dress, in which she probably also slept', came up to him and told him about her sad situation.

Precisely during this dreadful time, however, Marina's hovel on Borisoglebsky Lane, this house which was falling more and more into ruin, attracted the greatest variety of visitors: poets, writers, philosophers, and eccentrics of both sexes.

'No one faced any obstacle in being received in this chicken-coop,' wrote Mindlin. 'Tsvetayeva spoke patiently with everyone, smoking a cigarette and blowing away with her lips the spirals of cheap, bitter smoke.'[5]

In this way, the time which brought with it the most serious deprivation and material need, was also the time when Tsvetayeva was especially close to other people, closer than she had ever been, or would be.

After her unsuccessful efforts at working, Tsvetayeva remained without any kind of regular income. She tried to publish her poetry in order to earn some kind of money from it. In 1918 an anthology appeared in Petrograd entitled *Responses to the War and Revolution*. Among the thirteen contributors, Tsvetayeva's name is included with one poem. But this poem aroused Mayakovsky's contempt: 'Among other lines by Tsvetayeva we find: "For the life, the health of the servant of God Nikolay!" Respond, gentlemen, to something else!'[6]

Another enemy of Marina's, Valery Bryusov, had become head of 'Lito', a government department which functioned as censor. He did not allow the works of Tsvetayeva to be passed. In the summer of 1918 Marina sent for publication typewritten copies of *Poems of Youth* and *Milestones I*. A year later she somehow managed to get them back with Bryusov's memorandum: '...M. Tsvetayeva's poems, since they were not published at the time appropriate for them, and since they do not reflect contemporary life, are useless...'

Thus there remained only literary evenings as a means of earning a few roubles now and then. On 1 May 1919 Marina took part in a festive gathering at the Palace of Culture, the former residence of the Sollogubs, where she had worked for six months in the offices of 'Narkomnats'. On 7 July she again made an appearance there. Lunacharsky, the all-powerful commissar of education, was present in the hall. But on this occasion as well, as often happened with Marina, her temperament triumphed over reason; she chose from among her works the most compromising, Lauzun's mono-logue before execution from her play *Fortuna:*

> *I, Lauzun, with a hand whiter than snow, also*
> *Used to lift a goblet to drink the health of the mob!*
> *I, Lauzun, also prophesied that the nobleman*
> *And wood-cutter would enjoy equal rights under the sun!*

> I had never breathed so responsibly in my life. Responsibility! Responsibility! What a joy to be compared with you! And what kind of glory?! The monologue of a nobleman – in the face of a commissar – that is life! Only it is a pity, that it was to Lunacharsky's face, and not to...I wanted to write to Lenin, but Lenin would not have understood anything, nor the entire Lubyanka![7]

The audience applauded; Lunacharsky was a good listener, he even hushed the audience when they were making too much noise.

Another time Marina behaved even worse: in the large hall of the Polytechnic Museum Bryusov held an 'Evening of Women Poets'. The hall was packed. In his opening speech Bryusov maintained that women can write poems only about love and passion; they are not capable of anything else. Marina, who was wearing her dark monastic cassock, with her satchel over her shoulders, which already distinguished her from the other women writers, was the first to appear on the stage, where she read a few poems from *Swans' Encampment*:

> In committing such an obvious act of folly I was pursuing two, no three or four, aims: 1) To read seven poems by a woman without love, or the pronoun 'I', 2) To prove the pointlessness of reading poems for a large audience, 3) To reach at least one person who might understand me (even if only a student!), 4) And the main goal: to carry out here in Moscow in 1921 a *duty of honour*. And beyond purposes, to be without purpose – to be more than purposes! A simple and extreme feeling: – and well, what then?[8]

At first nothing happened. But it was probably this evening which angered Ilya Ehrenburg so much; in his article 'Portraits of Russian Poets' he wrote about her and her reading:

> The haughty gait, the high forehead, the short hair, cut with a fringe, is this an audacious boy, or perhaps, only a touch-me-not young lady? Reading her poems, she sings, and finishes the last two words of a line with a tongue-twister. The boy in her sings very well, he loves wild songs about the province of Kaluga, about Stenka Razin and the recklessness of the people. The lady in her prefers the Comtesse de Noailles and the banner of the Vendée...
>
> Somewhere she confesses that she loves to laugh, when one should not. To this I will add, she loves to do a great many things, which one should not do. These "should nots", prohibitions, laws, barriers, become the vital sources of the poetry of wilfulness...Coats of arms are now banned, so she glorifies them with the audacity which is worthy of all great heretics, dreamers, rebels...However, all this will one day be forgotten...The splendid verse of Marina Tsvetayeva will remain, as also will remain the thirst for life, the will for destruction, the struggle of one against all, and the love which is exalted by its proximity to death.[9]

Relations between Marina and Ehrenburg were good at this time, but not without complications. On one point, their characters were so radically different from each other, that a true lasting friendship was impossible: Marina remained loyal to her political convictions, once they had been adopted, but Ehrenburg knew very well how to look after himself, and how to ingratiate himself with the new state of affairs. In his memoirs, *People, Years, Life*, he himself hints at this:

> In the autumn of 1920, when I managed to make my way from Koktebel to Moscow, I found Marina in the same frenzied solitude. She had finished a volume of poetry, which glorified the Whites, *Swans' Encampment*. At the same time I had managed to see many things, including the 'Russian Vendée', and had thought about many things. I tried to tell her about the true nature of the White Guards – she did not

believe me; I tried to argue for a while, Marina became angry. She had a difficult character, and she herself suffered more than anyone from this.[10]

The problems of everyday existence were becoming too great. Following the advice of her friends, Tsvetayeva placed her daughters in a children's home in Kuntsevo. Soon after in February 1920 Alya fell ill with dysentery. Marina took her home, nursed her and learnt, only by accident, that at the same time, the little, weak Irina had died at Kuntsevo. Marina was horrified, she felt herself to be guilty: she had not worried enough about her, she had nursed her favourite elder daughter instead of looking after the younger. 'She died, without any illness, from weakness. And I did not even go to the funeral. Alya had a temperature that day of 40.7°. Shall I tell the truth? I simply *could not*.'[11]

She also wrote to her sister: 'Irina was almost three years old. She could hardly speak, she made a very sad impression. The whole time she would rock back and forth, singing. Her hearing and voice were amazing.'[12]

Marina remained alone with the seven-year-old Alya, with the rest of the house full of strange people. At twenty-seven she felt herself to be an old woman; her mood was very depressed. She wrote to V. K. Zvyagintseva:

> What I need now is for someone to believe in me, and say: 'All the same, you are good, do not cry. S. is alive. You will see him, you will have a son, all will be well.' I cling feverishly to Alya. She gets better, already I start to smile, but then – 39.3°, and again everything is taken from me, and again I am reconciled to death! Dear Vera, I have no future, nor will, I am afraid of everything. It seems to me it is better to die. If S. is not among the living I cannot live: think what a long life it would be, enormous, everything strange, strange cities, strange people, Alya and myself, so abandoned, she and I...[13]

Alya was a little, pale, starving Wunderkind, with large pale-blue eyes: in all the journals and memoirs of this time, at least some mention is made of Tsvetayeva's precociously developed daughter.

One can understand why she made this impression. In her depressed mood and isolation Marina forgot that Alya was still a small child; for her Alya was not only someone she could talk to, but also someone she could trust. She took her everywhere with her, even to literary evenings. She fell into the same mistake as her own mother, and wanted to make a poet out of Alya, although Alya was especially talented at painting. Ariadna Sergeyevna herself describes in her memoirs how her mother mercilessly destroyed her joy when she managed for the first time to draw a human figure.[14] Marina dedicated many poems to her daughter, but probably she, who was herself so young and so preoccupied with her own inner life, did not understand her talented daughter, who was already keeping a journal. Perhaps the future conflict between mother and daughter was rooted in these years?

Mindlin writes: 'It seemed that Alya was as lonely in her childhood as her twenty-nine-year-old mother, in spite of the wide circle of friends and the daily guests who spent hours by the stove.'

Soon after the death of Irina, Tsvetayeva's life improved: friends secured rations for her through official channels. Now Marina could write again without being dependent upon help from others. Her poems of the spring of 1920 show that her frozen soul was beginning to thaw out, and even rather rapidly. Already 27 April brought 'a breath of England – and the sea – and valour'. Anna Saakyants, who could make use of the notebooks of Tsvetayeva, reveals to us the name of 'N.N.V.', to whom are addressed twenty-seven poems – 'one whole poem of unrequited love'.[15] This was Nikolay Nikolayevich Vysheslavtsev, an artist, who had travelled a great deal before the war in France and Italy. To him is addressed the celebrated poem:

> One man is made of stone, another of clay –
> but I am of quicksilver, and I shimmer!
> My profession is betrayal, my name is Marina,
> I am the fragile foam of the sea...[16]

Among these poems is also one dated 18 May, which is movingly addressed to her husband:

> I used to write it out on schoolroom slates
> And on the folds of fans that had grown faded,
> On sea and river sand, on ice with skates,
> And with my ring on windows I'd engrave it, –
>
> On trunks of trees, a hundred winters old,
> Over again: I love you, love you, love you,
> And finally, so everyone was told,
> I'd register our marriage with a rainbow.
>
> How I wished that with me each would flower up
> For centuries! Beneath my fingertips!
> And how then, forehead bowing on table top,
> I'd cross his name out with a crucifix.
>
> But you, clutched by a scribe for sale, suffering
> That grip! Why do you wound my heart with sadness?
> Unsold by me! *Inside* the ring!
> You will come out unscathed upon these tablets.[17]

[translated by David McDuff]

Little by little, life began to become more normal. Old friends again appeared, whom Tsvetayeva had not seen for years. Marina met again such people as Vladimir Nilender and Sergey Mikhailovich Solovyov, who was living alone after his wife Tanya Turgeneva had left him. Solovyov was a priest, and in the spirit of his uncle considered himself to be both Catholic and Orthodox. Everywhere one could meet Andrey Bely, who was trying very hard to spread education among the people, and to enlighten them with anthroposophy. Marina often saw him from a distance, but no real meeting occurred.

Another meeting also failed to take place, that is, with her favourite poet, Aleksandr Blok. On 9 May 1920, already seriously ill, he gave a reading in the large hall of the Moscow Polytechnic Museum. Marina stood behind him, keeping in her pocket some verses dedicated to him. But she did not dare to give them to him; instead, she sent Alya with them to the dressing-room. Ariadna Sergeyevna writes that Blok was the only poet whom Tsvetayeva did not consider to be a colleague; rather she revered him as if he were a divine being.

The year 1920 marked a new stage in Tsvetayeva's artistic development: she turned for inspiration to the genre of the epic folk poem, the *bylina*. Between July and September she wrote a long epic poem in verse, *The Tsar-Maiden* (*Tsar'-Devitsa*), the first of the folk tales borrowed from Afanasyev. Between 31 December 1920 and 4 January 1921 she composed the unfinished verse-tale 'Yegorushka', followed by 'On the Red Horse' ('Na krasnom kone'), 'Byways' ('Pereulochki') in the spring of 1922, and *The Swain* (*Molodets*) later in 1924. What one notices, more than anything else in these "folk poems" is Marina's mastery of the Russian language, in all its popular forms and expressions. She drew from the deepest sources of speech and used melodies of sound and rhythm, which are impossible to convey in translations from Russian into other languages.[18] D. P. Svyatopolk-Mirsky says of these poems:

> Her work lives entirely according to the spirit and melody of folk songs...'The Tsar-Maiden' is simply an astounding creation. Apart from Blok in his 'The Twelve', no one, probably, has been able to create something like this; it is like an incomparable fugue on a folk theme.[19]

'My last great work, *The Tsar-Maiden*, belongs to Russia and to me', thus Tsvetayeva says herself about this work.

If one compares the content of the epic poems, written in 1920, with the romantic theatrical pieces of the previous years, one is struck by something new: the themes and language have changed, and the nostalgic escapism into the eighteenth century has disappeared. This turn to the folk tales of the Russian people is in agreement with the demands of the present; it can be understood as a "yes" to the Russian Revolution, if not in the political sense, then at least in recognition of it as an event unleashing elemental forces. Such an understanding could be expressed only with a new language. Marina Tsvetayeva, the most significant poet and "Singer" of the White movement, surpasses in the power and spontaneity of her speech all those who adhered to the new régime, or struggled against it. When she said that she had 'learnt this language from the Revolution', we must agree that she is right, although it would be more accurate to say she learnt this language from revolutionaries, such as Lann, Bessarabov and others.

Ehrenburg, who had managed with many adventures to cross the front of the Civil War, and to reach Moscow from Koktebel, was the first person to bring the news to Marina that Asya's first husband Boris Trukhachov had died in February 1922 in Koktebel from typhus. Her relations with him even after his second marriage to the actress M. N. Kuznetsova-Grinyova, remained good; Boris's death was a great sorrow for Marina.

In November 1920 the Russian Civil War ended with the complete victory of the Red Army at Perekop, and its subsequent occupation of the whole of the Crimea. The British and French, who had very weakly and unenthusiastically supported General Wrangel with money and arms, now felt themselves to be under some obligation, even if only to evacuate the remains of the defeated White Army to Constantinople. No one knew anything at that time about the fate of Sergey Efron.

At the end of November someone knocked one evening at the door. Behind it stood a tall young man who resembled Boris Trukhachov; he asked where he could find Marina Tsvetayeva.

'You do not know me, my name is Lann – I am acquainted with your sister, Asya, and I have come from Koktebel.'

Lann produced a letter from Maks Voloshin, the first letter after three years. 'This is the first – the old – joy, the first Easter from a man for three years', Marina wrote to her sister.

The young poet Yevgeny Petrovich Lozman-Lann was twenty-four; his stormy romance with Tsvetayeva lasted only two weeks, after which he left for Kharkov. From 6 December 1920 to September 1921 she wrote him several letters, which came to light in 1981, and sent him some poems dedicated to him.[20]

The news from Koktebel was terrible. Everything which Maks had predicted at the beginning had come to pass: the Crimea had shifted from one side to another, and the inhabitants of Koktebel had lived through all the terror and violence committed by both. Maks had defended Reds from Whites, and Whites from Reds; a heroic action in the name of love for one's fellow man. After the cessation of military activities terrible need and hunger reigned.

Marina somehow managed to send a letter to Koktebel. On 21 November/4 December she wrote to Voloshin, using only half-phrases and hints, so that the meaning would not be understood by the uninitiated. Did Maks perhaps know something about Seryozha?

> Dear Maks, I implore you, let me know – I can find no peaceful place for myself, every knock at the door throws me into icy horror – for God's sake!!! I do not write because I do not know, where and how it is possible...
>
> I am writing a great deal. The last thing is a long work – 'The Tsar-Maiden'. In Moscow we are leading a frenzied life, with every kind of passion. I stay as a guest everywhere, I am not attached to anyone or anything...Maks! I entreat you – at the first opportunity – let me know – I do not know what words to find.[21]

On 17 December 1920 Marina also wrote to Asya in Koktebel, for the first time in three years. In short words she conveyed to her sister what she had lived through during this time, and suggested that she should come to Moscow:

> Asya! Come to Moscow. You must be living badly, things will not improve there for a long time, with us things are improving, we have much bread; there are frequent payments for children, and since you are working anyway, I can arrange (with splendid contacts!) a fantastic position for you, with a large ration and firewood. I hate Moscow, but I cannot travel now, for this is the only place he can find me, if he is alive. I think about him day and night. I love only you and him. I am very lonely, although I know all of Moscow. They do not count as people. Believe me (or they have grown tired, which, for me, with my "gun-powder", is awkward, and for them, perplexing)...Asya! I am completely the same, and in the same way everyone deceives me, internally and externally. Only the desire for life has completely faded, I do not love anything anymore, except for the contents of my rib-cage. I am indifferent to books, and have sold off all my French ones; that which I need, I write myself...[22]

The year 1920 destroyed all hopes for a change in the political situation in Russia. Boris had died, Seryozha had disappeared without trace. Marina expressed her personal grief in the mouth of the Kievan Princess Yaroslavna, who mourns the death of Prince Igor.

PLAINT OF YAROSLAVNA

Hear Yaroslavna
Mourning her loved one
Ceaselessly –
From her bower, grievous she
Sobs – unabated –
Unmitigated:

– Igor mine! Prince
Igor mine! Prince
Igor!
. . . . . .

Woe then is *Rus*!
Igor mine! *Rus*!
Igor!
. . . . .

– Wind, wind! – Princess,
Behold thy fate!
Thy Prince lies lifeless –
For honour's sake!

[translated by Robin Kemball]

Swans' Encampment does not end, however, with these words of desperation. Perhaps Seryozha had managed somehow to survive?

Grief makes weary with its weight of sighs:
– My Son! – My Prince! – My Brother!
– Happy New Year, you – young *Rus* that lies
Beyond the wide blue waters![23]

[translated by Robin Kemball]

Yury Ivask remarks:

If the White Army had triumphed, which Marina Tsvetayeva had praised in the cycle *Swans' Encampment*, then she might have occupied in White Russia the position which Mayakovsky had in Red Russia, but it is possible that she would have also become disillusioned with the victorious Whites, as Mayakovsky, 'the heavy-footed archangel', as she called him, had with the victorious Reds.[24]

CHAPTER 14

Moscow – Departure

1921 – APRIL 1922

At the beginning of 1921 the sailors at Kronstadt revolted in protest against the Bolshevik regime. The mutiny was drowned in blood, but Lenin understood, all the same, that if he wanted to retain power, he would have to make certain concessions, even if only within the limits of the country's economic organisation. In one day he drastically altered his political course, and in February he announced his 'New Economic Policy', N.E.P. This abrogated the state's centralised management of the economy. Small businesses were once again permitted, the black market could again arrange its shady deals, and one could make a lot of money in a short time. In this way the situation in Moscow improved immediately, although by normal western standards it was still very grim. Louise Weiss, a young radical, intellectual French journalist, who was just beginning her career, was one of the first foreigners to succeed in glimpsing this newly created workers' paradise; she was horrified by what she saw:

> At the station I got into a jingling *droshky*, which was dragged by a horse swaying on its legs...The coachman crossed himself at every church, that is, at least twenty times. He was wearing some kind of caftan, of an indeterminate colour; it was the colour of catastrophe, the colour of the whole city, which was not so much grey as red: it seemed covered with blood, with red flags, red stars, red hammers, red sickles...Along both sides of the street stood the mutilated trees of an avenue. Their branches had long since disappeared into stoves. Under long banners with slogans wheezed processions of hobbling phantoms. Behind them they pulled little four-wheeled covered carts. There was nothing besides dislocated arms and legs, bent bodies, skulls without flesh, and without thoughts. In the hollows of their eyes burned only one desire – to survive...On the steps of the Ryazan station peasants were selling butter, flour, *pirozhki*. Whole families lie around the bonfires, which burn on the roadsides...Men are wearing evening trousers and leather jackets,

the women wear fur hats and bast shoes, others wear boots on their bare feet...Government office workers are selling separate sheets of paper from archives, which are used to roll cigarettes; young people adorned with red badges offered fox pelts and sheepskins and pieces of material; small girls tried to sell broken mirrors, and little embroidered bags; others traded in old bits of soap and used tooth brushes. And there are hundreds of people besides, who are paler than from any illness, more exhausted than death itself; professors, petty bourgeois, aristocrats, who in mute despair cling to each other, offering their last belongings, before they themselves descend into the grave.[1]

The after-effects of the introduction of N.E.P. were felt not only in material conditions. There arose, not only shops with foodstuffs, but also new artistic movements, literary circles and societies. It even became possible for the intelligentsia, who remained in Russia, to make contact with émigré literary figures in Berlin and Paris; a new movement was created which called itself 'Volte-Face' ('Smena vekh'). It tried to reconcile the émigrés with the Soviet regime, a tendency much supported by Moscow.

In 1921 it was still possible to re-found the old Union of Writers although there was not a single Communist in it. Boris Zaitsev was elected president. The union was given permission to open a bookshop, where members of the union could sell books which belonged to them. This gave many the chance to make some money. Whoever had no more books to sell made them himself: he would write in home-made notebooks and take them to the 'Writers' Book Shop'. Many years later Ilya Ehrenburg got hold of a list of these 'autographs":

> Recently a catalogue of manuscript books, which the 'Writers' Book Shop' carried, fell into my hands. Among the authors are Andrey Bely, V. Lidin, M. Gerasimov, Shershenevich, Marina Tsvetayeva, and many others. My book *Spanish Songs* is listed as well, at a price of 3000 roubles. The little book copied out by Shershenevich, is accompanied by the note 'at cost price 4 lumps of sugar is 2000 roubles, a jug of milk – 1800, 50 cigarettes – 6000'. Money had so little value, that few people thought about it; we lived on rations and hope.[2]

In this way 1921 can be considered as the year of the birth of 'Samizdat'. Marina Tsvetayeva mentions that Boris Zaitsev had already invented the expression 'Overcoming Gutenberg'.

Writers still had one more means of earning money: they could read their works at literary gatherings. As well as official readings held in large halls, there were also those organised by the so-called literary cafés. It was the custom that the writer who took part in the reading received a free meal. The most famous café in Moscow, which is mentioned in many memoirs, was the Domino, where one could meet not just starving writers, but snobs and speculators who had quickly become wealthy thanks to N.E.P. Tsvetayeva only rarely made an appearance at the Domino, but from time to time she did read her works in various cafés. At one such evening she saw her half-sister Valeria. Neither one suspected that this would be their last meeting.

The beginning of 1921 was a most successful period for Marina; within five days, from 13 to 17 January, she wrote her second epic poem, 'On a Red Horse'. In reflecting on her poetic inspiration she admits that she is not obliged to the Muses, but to a 'Sultan', a male genius on Pegasus, the winged red horse, who 'sets her house aflame'.[3] This Sultan was Yevgeny Lann, to whom she wrote on 19 January 1921 (Russian style):

> I had not written anything for two weeks, not a word, which is very rare for me – for Song is above everything! Rushing about with Asya it was as if I had driven you away – farther and farther, finally I had completely driven you away – no more Lann! Then I began to write poems, in a complete frenzy! From morning to night! Then 'On the Red Horse'. This was my final liberation: you were now in the clouds for good![4]

Tsvetayeva dedicated 'On the Red Horse' to Anna Akhmatova, and moreover, wrote a letter to her, asking her to read the proof-sheets, if the publishing house Alkonost agreed to print the text. We do not know if Akhmatova responded to this request.

At the end of January 1921 Marina made a new acquaintance: Boris Aleksandrovich Bessarabov, 'a young Red Army soldier, ruddy and blue-eyed, like a peasant', who had fallen in love with Romantic poetry.[5] His arrival in Tsvetayeva's life marked a new phase in her creative development. Bessarabov is 'The Bolshevik' (a poem of 1921) and the prototype of Yegorushka, who is portrayed in the long unfinished poem which Tsvetayeva began immediately after the completion of 'On the Red Horse'. Like the letters and poems to Lann, 'Yegorushka' was only published for the first time in 1971.

In the spring of 1921 a letter on official paper finally helped Asya and her son to return to Moscow from Feodosia. She was 'thin, ragged, but immediately alive and indomitable...' In her memoirs Anastasia Ivanovna draws a vivid picture of Moscow in 1921 and tells of her efforts to return to a normal life.[6]

Soon after Asya's return to Moscow, one of her acquaintances, a young poet by the name of Emil Mindlin, arrived from the south, and had nowhere to stay. Night after night he would sit in the Domino hoping that at least one of the literary figures present would invite him home to spend the night. Anastasia Ivanovna found him a room for a short while, and then sent him to Marina. In 1938 Tsvetayeva told Yury Ivask how this happened:

> Moscow in '21. The stove would not light, it smoked, but there was no heat. You could not cook the *kasha*, (the same old millet *kasha*): A knock at the door. A young man enters, wearing some kind of bast sack. But his eyes – are the eyes of David. It turns out he is a poet who has come from the south. I say to him: light the stove! He lit it and we began to talk, while the *kasha* burnt. His poems did not amount to much, but all the same – he is David! Milya Mindlin. A principled idler...[7]

Mindlin lived there for a short time; he stoked the stove, and sat in the evenings with Marina and Alya on the floor, watching the flames of the fire while Marina read her poems. He accompanied her everywhere. Tsvetayeva wrote for her companion of 1921 a cycle of poems 'The Youth' ('Otrok'), which later, already after her departure from Russia, she dedicated to her Berlin publisher, A. G. Vishnyak.

In his book Mindlin extolls Marina with hymns of praise. He found everything about her wonderful: how she could blow spirals of cigarette smoke with her lips, how she managed with the detested, distracting housework, 'as though she ruled a kingdom', how she took him around Moscow and showed him the city. He emphasises how selflessly Marina, who had nothing of her own, helped others near to her who were destitute.[8]

In the second half of 1921 her heart belonged entirely to the old Prince Sergey Volkonsky, a sixty-five year old former landowner, whom she loved 'more than all and above all others'.

> I myself loved the 60 year old Prince Volkonsky, who could not bear women, very much. I loved with complete submissiveness, with complete selflessness, and finally I captured him as an eternal possession! I conquered with the stubbornness of love. He did not learn to love women, he learnt to love *love*![9]

In 1934 Marina wrote to Ivask:

> I became friends with him in Moscow in 1921 and then, out of sheer enthusiasm and gratitude, I copied out for him the manuscripts of three of his long books in this very hand-writing. I did not write a line of my own, there was no time, and suddenly I exploded with 'The Pupil', and with *The Craft*.[10]

Unfortunately, however, on this occasion as well, the recipient of the poems was not worthy of them. Prince Volkonsky, though himself a writer of memoirs, understood nothing about poetry, and did not even suspect the existence of these lines, which, out of modesty, Tsvetayeva did not dare to show him. But to make up for this, the wise old prince, who was not embittered by all his losses, did appreciate the love of his young friend. He dedicated to her his book *Daily Life and Being* (*Byt i bytie*) and wrote in the foreword:

> Dear Marina,
>
> Why am I dedicating this book to you? You yourself know why...You remember how we lived? In what filth, in what disorder, in what homelessness? Yes, and what else! You remember the impertinence which burst into the room wearing a fur cap? Do you remember the insolent demands, the mocking questions? Do you remember the terrible knocks at the door, the loathsome searches, the abusiveness of "comradely" behaviour? Do you remember what the sound of an automobile meant by the windows: would it stop, or not stop? Oh, those nights!...They cannot, cannot understand, those who did *not* live there – they cannot. (It is strange, that people do not know how to place themselves in those circumstances, in which they have not been themselves – human imagination does not suffice...But another thing still amazes me: how people are not capable of applying to themselves what others have lived through. To pass from the reality of another's suffering to the possibility of one's own suffering – how few people are able to make this step!)...Do you remember all this? Such was *Soviet daily life*.
>
> And do you remember our evenings, our vile, but dear "coffee", made on a kerosene stove, our readings, our writings, our conversations? You read to me poems from your future volumes. You copied out my books *Wanderings* and *Monasteries*. How much strength there was in our tenacity, how much reward in our inflexibility! Such was *our* state of *being*.[11]

Tsvetayeva's new collection of poems *The Craft* (*Remeslo*) begins with the cycle 'The Youth' which is dated: 'Second of April (Russian style) 1921'. In this volume are collected all of Tsvetayeva's poems from before April 1922, that is, her last lyrical works written in Russia. The volume was published in Berlin in 1923.[12]

The Craft contains two cycles dedicated to Seryozha: 'Separation' ('Razluka') and 'Georgy'. Marina still did not know whether her husband was alive, or had perished.

SEPARATION

A peal from a tower
Somewhere in the Kremlin.
Where on the earth
Where is

My strength
My gentleness
My valour
My holiness

A peal from a tower
A peal cast out

Where on the earth is
My
House,

My – dream
My – laughter
My – light
The track of narrow soles.

As though cast
By a hand into the night. –
A peal.
　　　　　　– My abandoned one![13]

In the spring of 1921 Ilya Ehrenburg became one of the first
Soviet citizens to receive an official passport and permission to
travel abroad. He promised to enquire about the fate of Sergey
Yakovlevich. One evening in July Boris Pasternak appeared at the
door of the hovel on Borisoglebsky Lane although Marina hardly
knew him. He gave her a letter from Ehrenburg:

> Overcoming my initial greed, I deafened my joy with a rush of words
> (the letter lay unopened before me) – and questions: how are you? Are
> you writing anything? What is new in Moscow? And your response – so
> indistinct! 'The river – by steam – is the shore moving to me, or I to the
> shore...And perhaps there are no shores – perhaps...'[14]

Ehrenburg wrote that Sergey Yakovlevich was alive, healthy and
living as an émigré in Prague. In a new cycle of poems 'The Good
News' ('Blagaya vest') – a reference to the feast of the
Annunciation – Marina tried to express her joy:

> The lark announced
> To me from the heights –
> That you are beyond the seas,
> Not beyond the clouds![15]

In 1921 it was still possible to leave Soviet Russia legally with a
passport, although not all requests for permission to leave were
granted, and all the necessary formalities could take several
months. Now that Tsvetayeva knew that her husband was alive she
applied for a passport for herself and Alya, as she wished to follow
her husband. She began the process just in time: about a month
after she had written the poems of 'The Good News', an event took
place which promised nothing good for writers. On 2 August 1921
Nikolay Gumilyov was arrested in Petrograd and on 24 August he
was executed as a monarchist. The Cheka now began to take an
interest in Russian writers. Rumours were current in Moscow that
Akhmatova too had perished. On 31 August Marina Tsvetayeva
wrote to her:

Dear Anna Andreyevna! All these days terrible rumours have been spread about you, every hour more stubborn, more irrefutable...I can tell you – from my knowledge – that your only friend (a friend=action!) among the poets is Mayakovsky, who with the look of a down-trodden bull wanders around the cardboard box of the 'Poets' Café'. (*Down-trodden* with grief, I tell you, such was his appearance). Through his friends he even sent a telegram to make enquiries about you, and I am indebted *to him* for my joy at hearing news of you...Dear A.A., in order to understand my evening yesterday...it would be necessary to know what my three previous days were like...which are *indescribable.*[16]

Marina wanted to give a lecture about Akhmatova, but this never took place. Out of gratitude she did dedicate some poems to Mayakovsky.

Within several days of Gumilyov's arrest, Russian literature suffered a second heavy blow. On 7 August Aleksandr Blok died at the age of forty-one. His application for permission to go abroad for his health had been turned down by the authorities. His death served Andrey Bely as a pretext for writing a letter of ardent protest to the government: he accused them of the death of his friend and drew their attention to the inhuman conditions in which intellectuals were vegetating. It is possible that this appeal helped him and others to receive permission to leave Russia.

Marina's grief at losing her favourite poet was expressed in several poems written immediately after Blok's death. Later she joined them with the poems written in Aleksandrov in 1916, and published them the next year in Berlin with the title *Poems to Blok* (*Stikhi k Bloku*).

More bad news began to arrive. In the autumn of 1921 Voloshin managed to inform the Tsvetayev sisters of the desperate situation in which, a year after the Civil War, writers found themselves in Koktebel. He told them that the Gertsyk sisters were on the verge of death from hunger. Marina and Asya now rushed to their assistance: among their Moscow acquaintances they organised a society to save those who were destitute. Marina even managed to reach Lunacharsky.[17] The hostility which Marina felt for the rest of her life towards Nikolay Berdyayev, began at the moment when he apparently said in response to her appeal for help: 'You yourself have nothing: it is *foolish* to give to others!'[18]

Tsvetayeva's creative energy did not fail her in the beginning of 1922 either. In February she wrote the cycle 'Snowdrifts' ('Sugroby'), which she dedicated to Ilya Ehrenburg. In April she completed the long poem 'Byways', which concludes *The Craft*.

'Byways' is a poem based on folk motifs, and is dedicated to an actor friend, Podgayetsky-Chabrov, 'in memory of our last Moscow'.[19] Very few people understood this work at the time. The explanations which Marina Tsvetayeva herself tried to give to Yury Ivask in the thirties did not help.[20] Contemporary critics preferred to remain silent about it. Karlinsky speaks of it as 'one of the most colourful explosions of verbal fireworks in the whole of Russian poetry', despite its incomprehensibility.

Thanks, perhaps, to the influence of the all-powerful P. S. Kogan, a good friend of Tsvetayeva's, several volumes of her works were finally published in 1922; *Milestones*, in this case a selection from *Milestones II* (poems from 1918-22), was brought out by the Moscow publishing house Kostry. The printing of 1000 copies was immediately sold out, so that a second edition had to be published. The collection *Milestones I* (i.e. the poems from 1916), and the play *The End of Casanova* (*Konets Kazanovy*), which Bryusov had rejected in 1918, also appeared in print, along with, finally, 'The Tsar-Maiden'. Each of these works was printed in an edition of 2000 copies.

Not long before her departure from Moscow, Marina Tsvetayeva met yet another old friend, but the occasion was not a success. Osip Mandelstam turned up at Borisoglebsky Lane with his young wife Nadya and wanted to present her to Marina. Nadezhda Mandelstam describes this meeting with a rather sharp pen. One can see that from the first moment she was inclined against Tsvetayeva. She was disgusted by the dirt and disorder in the entrance-hall:

> We knocked at the door – bells had been abolished by the Revolution. Marina opened the door. She gasped on seeing Mandelstam, but scarcely offered me her hand, looking, all the while, not at me, but at him. With her entire behaviour she made it demonstratively clear that she had nothing at all to do with wives of any kind. 'Let's go see Alya,' she said, 'you must remember Alya,' and then, without looking at me, she added: 'But you wait here – Alya can't bear strangers.'[21]

Mandelstam turned green from annoyance, but all the same he went to see Alya for a few minutes. He immediately returned and refusing to sit down, he began, with his wife, coldly to say goodbye. 'She evidently felt that she had gone too far, and tried to start up a conversation...'

But it was impossible to make up for the insult. In her memoirs Nadezhda Mandelstam regrets that she was too young and inexperienced then to be able to make conversation with Tsvetayeva. In her books she speaks very positively of her: 'Marina Tsvetayeva made on me an impression of absolute naturalness and astounding wilfulness...'

And suddenly the unexpected happened: Marina and Asya received a passport and permission to leave the Soviet Union. On 11 May 1922 they left, passing the former estate of the Meyn family 'Yasenky' on the way. After a journey of four days they reached Berlin travelling via Riga. Within a few months a large group of Russian philosophers, scholars and thinkers, among them, N. Berdyayev, S. Bulgakov, S. Frank, and F. Stepun, followed Tsvetayeva. All of them had not left according to their own wishes, however; the authorities had exiled them because what they were thinking and writing could no longer exist in the new state.

In Marina Tsvetayeva's life, as in the life of the Russian nation, a new epoch had begun.

PART THREE

Emigration

My refuge from savage hordes,
My shield and armour, my last fortress
From the evil of the good, and the evil of the evil,
You, my verse, thrust into my very ribs! [1]

Contemporary Annals, vol. 7, 1921

CHAPTER 15

Berlin – 'The Craft'

MAY – JUNE 1922

When Marina Tsvetayeva arrived in Berlin she would not have felt the loss of her native milieu. Aside from waiters and tram conductors she probably did not meet any Berliners, as she mixed exclusively with Russians.

Berlin's appearance in 1922 must have been rather strange. R.C. Williams, who has written an extensive study on the life of the Russian emigration in Germany, maintains that in 1922 approximately 250,000 Russians were living in Germany, of whom 100,000 were in Berlin.[1] This population consisted of former prisoners of war, who had not returned to Russia, the remnants of various corps of White Army soldiers, who only recently had been fighting the Bolsheviks, émigrés who had fled or had been exiled, and also, finally, temporary visitors from Russia with Soviet passports, who had not yet decided whether they would return or not. All of these people were divided into different groups and parties, which carried on their political activities exactly as if they were still in Russia, and as though the hurricane had not passed over their heads.

Berlin was especially attractive, at that time, for the Russians: on the one hand, life was not expensive, on account of inflation, and on the other, the German capital had a large number of printing presses of high quality, which were not being used to their full capacity. Thus, it was now possible for the Russians to publish all those numerous memoirs, political tracts and literary works, which had sprung up like mushrooms after a rainstorm. Certain enterprising literary figures tried their luck at the publishing business; as German currency was losing its value from hour to hour, one had to spend it as quickly as possible. Whoever had a manuscript could count on it being published. In 1924 one hundred and forty-two Russian publishing houses existed outside the borders of Soviet Russia, of which eighty-six were in Berlin. Two excellent Russian newspapers were also published here, *The Rudder* (*Rul'*), the paper of the Constitutional Democrats and *Days* (*Dni*), which was close to the Social Revolutionaries. Many literary journals were frequently founded by writers who had come to Berlin only for a short while. Very often such journals lasted only for a few months, then either there was no more money for the journal to be continued, or the publisher left for the other émigré centres, Prague or Paris, or else returned to Russia.[2]

This Russian Fata morgana ended as suddenly as it had begun: the German currency reform in the summer of 1923 dealt a fatal blow to it. Many Russians remained in Germany, but the brilliant literary era was over.

In 1922 'Russian Berlin' extended, for the most part, from Prager Platz to Nollendorferplatz, and possessed its own Russian shops, hairdressers, bookshops, and even a theatre, in which Marina's friend, Chabrov, gave a triumphant performance in the summer of 1922 in Schnitzler's play *Schleier der Pierette* (he took the rôle of Harlequin). Intellectual life went on here in a number of local cafés: the Union of Writers met in one, in another, the House of Arts. The café Prager Diele on the Prager Platz acquired a certain notoriety and it entered into Russian literature, thanks to Tsvetayeva and Andrey Bely, as a neologism: *pragerdil'stvovat'* (i.e. 'to frequent the Prager Diele').

Not only did former Muscovite and Petersburgian literary people meet each other in the cafés (sometimes for the first time in their lives), but Soviet citizens could also meet there with émigrés. In their passionate literary discussions, which were so reminiscent of Russia, politics, surprisingly enough, found little place. Between the 'true believers' and the 'renegades' the iron curtain had not yet fallen; everything was still in motion, and final decisions about remaining in the West or returning to Russia had still not been made.

Aleksandr Bakhrakh recalls: 'Berlin in the twenties was a paradoxical and unrepeatable phenomenon. In some ways it was an even more fantastical city than the one which E.T.A. Hoffmann had described a century before.'[3]

Tsvetayeva and Alya arrived in Berlin on 15 May 1922, and stayed at the hotel Trautenau-Haus, at no.9, Trautenaustrasse, in Berlin-Wilmersdorf. Ehrenburg and his wife, who had found them this room, were staying in the same hotel.

Tsvetayeva's stay in Berlin was only a temporary sojourn. In spite of this, however, these ten weeks were a very important period in her life: during this time the transformation of one mythical hero, Andrey Bely, into a man of flesh and blood, occurred, as well as the transformation of a man of flesh and blood, Pasternak, into a myth. This was accompanied by the cooling off of old friendships, the birth of new love and meetings with new people, and finally the reunion with her husband after a separation of four years. But deep involvement in the actual life of the refugees and serious preparation for the coming heavy years in exile, did not take place in Berlin.

The first impression which Marina Tsvetayeva received in Berlin must have been flattering; she was greeted as celebrated poet. It is to Ehrenburg's credit that two of her collections of poetry had already been published at the time of her arrival in the West. These were: *Separation*, that is, the poems of 1921 addressed to her husband, supplemented by the long poem 'On the Red Horse'; and the volume *Poems to Blok*, covering the period 1916 to 1921. In 1921 Konstantin Balmont had already published a selection of Tsvetayeva's poetry in the Paris journal *Contemporary Annals*, placing her, in his foreword, together with Akhmatova, in the first place among Russian women poets. *Separation*, published by Helikon, which belonged to Ehrenburg's friend A.G. Vishnyak, enjoyed, in particular, great success. Somewhat later, a second edition of 'The Tsar-Maiden' was published by Epokha, which also attracted considerable attention. In Berlin Tsvetayeva also compiled the volumes *Psyche* (*Psikheya*) and *The Craft*.[4]

Yevgenia Kannak, who worked as a typist at Helikon recalls that she often saw Marina Tsvetayeva there. She would come in leading her heavy nine-year-old daughter by the hand and would read pages from her journal with special pride.[5] Tsvetayeva could hardly have read aloud, though, the following lines by Alya, who was perspicacious beyond her age, which relate to A.G. Vishnyak:

> Helikon (i.e. Vishnyak) is always torn in two – between the mundane and the spiritual. The mundane is that weight, which keeps him on the earth and without which, so it seems to him, he would immediately fly off... In fact he might just not be able to be torn away – he has little soul, since he needs peace, rest, sleep, comfort, and this is exactly what the soul does not give. When Marina visits his office, she is like that Soul which disturbs and removes peace, and raises a man to itself, without lowering itself to him... Marina speaks to Helikon like a Titan, and she is as incomprehensible to him as the North Pole is to an inhabitant of the East, and just as magnetic... I see that he is drawn to

Marina as to the sun, with his entire sickly stalk. Meanwhile, the sun is far away, because Marina's whole being lies in restraint and clenched teeth, while he himself is frail and soft, like a shoot of sweet-pea.[6]

As can be seen from the poems dedicated to Helikon in *The Craft*, a close bond had arisen at this time between Tsvetayeva and Vishnyak. These poems had, at first, been written for Mindlin, but later Marina "seized" them from him. We are indebted to Serena Vitale for giving us further details; Tsvetayeva had fallen in love with the young publisher. At the beginning of their acquaintance Vishnyak had given Marina a copy of Heine's *Florentine Nights*, which according to Ariadna Efron is the name Tsvetayeva later gave to a story in epistolary form which she "wrote" in Berlin. In fact, this "story" is simply a re-working of nine letters she sent to Vishnyak between 17 June and 9 July 1922. His reply of 29 October is also included in the "story".[7]

This infatuation was very romantic and brief. When they met five years later Marina no longer even recognised Avram Vishnyak. During the war he died tragically in a German concentration camp.

A shadow had also fallen on Tsvetayeva's relations with Ehrenburg. The close friendship which had begun in Moscow, where Tsvetayeva had dedicated 'Snowdrifts' to him, was now threatened by their differences. In his book, *People, Years, Life*, Ehrenburg quotes one of the letters which Marina sent him at this time:

> Then in 1918, you swept aside my Don Juans (the 'cloak', which neither conceals, nor reveals) and now in 1922, my 'Tsar-Maidens' and 'Yegorushkas' (that is, the old Russia in me, i.e. what is secondary). Both then and now you wanted one thing from me – myself, that is, a skeleton, without cloaks and caftans, best of all, in rags. The plot, the cast, the means of expression, are all for you mere stage props. You have wanted to remove from me the main thing, without which – I am not myself. Not once have I misled you (I do that to myself continually, and shall do): you have turned out to be more perceptive than myself . . . [8]

The real reason, however, was probably something else, even if Ehrenburg could not speak about this openly; they argued, as they had previously, about political questions, and about the poems of *Swans' Encampment*. He was to write later: 'In Berlin I once talked with her right through the night, and at the end of our conversation she said that she would not publish her book.'

In a letter Tsvetayeva provides another version of the rift between her and Ehrenburg:

> I parted from Ehrenburg because of the immensity of the feelings involved: his principled emotions collided with my elemental ones. I

> demanded monstrous trust and understanding (in spite of the visible, I despatched him into the invisible!) ... I always had the feeling with him, that everything valuable in him he considered to be a weakness, which in fact he loves, but has to forgive himself for. In his views my "virtues" play this rôle of "weaknesses", all my pluses (that is, everything which I have loved and fiercely defended) were for him only minuses to be forgiven ... I did not want to be a dear child, or a romantic monarchist, or a monarchist romantic, I wanted to *be*. But he had *to forgive* my being![9]

Tsvetayeva expressed herself even more clearly and maliciously in 1933 in a letter to Ivask: ' ... never, not even for a second did I ever feel that he was a poet. Ehrenburg has fallen under the influence of everyone, he is *spinelessness* itself. Besides that, a cynic cannot be a poet.'[10]

At the Prager Diele, the meeting-place of all the new arrivals, Ehrenburg had a table, at which he worked and held forth. At this table meetings were celebrated, friendships made and broken; and publishers, manuscripts and life companions were all exchanged at once. Not everyone who had come from Russia had left for political motives, certain people simply were escaping from family circumstances: 'Many people silently carried on, before one's eyes, transitory love affairs (not one of them for real!) Everything at the Prager Diele was something of a joke ... '[11]

Literary figures with well-known names also gathered here. Nina Berberova, who had come to Berlin, with V.F. Khodasevich on 30 June 1922, met Tsvetayeva on 5 July. She quotes an extract from Khodasevich's journal, in which he describes a literary gathering at the Prager Diele on 24 July. Among the numerous names are Ehrenburg, Tsvetayeva, Pasternak, V. Shklovsky and Andrey Bely. (There is an obvious mistake here: Pasternak came to Berlin only in August.) One should add that all these writers spent their time not only socialising, but also working very seriously.

At the beginning of June, however, within two weeks of Tsvetayeva's arrival, a literary scandal took place in Berlin, which changed the atmosphere and signified the beginning of the end of the apolitical situation there and the peaceful co-existence between writers of the two political camps. Aleksey Tolstoy, who had already lived in the West for a few years, decided to make a volte face and return to Russia. In order to prepare for this he published in a literary supplement of the Volte Face movement's newspaper *On the Eve* (*Nakanune*), a letter by his friend Korney Chukovsky, who lived in Moscow, which was obviously not meant for publication. In it Chukovsky mentions the names of several writers belonging to the House of Arts, who, as he put it: 'receive rations, hold meetings, write nothing and curse the Soviet authorities'.[12]

The publication of this letter in Berlin aroused deep consternation among the writers, particularly in Tsvetayeva, who, knowing the situation understood how dangerous such a denunciation was for people in Soviet Russia. On 7 June her open letter to Aleksey Tolstoy was published in *The Voice of Russia* (*Golos Rossii*).

> Aleksey Nikolayevich!
> Before me lies ... Chukovsky's letter to you. If you were not an editor of this newspaper, I would see what has happened as a disservice carried out by one of your friends. But you are the editor ... If you divulge these lines of a letter out of friendship to Chukovsky, then Chukovsky's action might be clear. More obscure is your intention, in turning inside out such a cesspit. To render such a service is to betray ... Either you are, in fact, a three-year-old child, who does not suspect either the existence of the G.P.U., or the closure of the *Chronicle of the House of Writers*, or much, much else ...
> Aleksey Nikolayevich, there is above personal friendship, private letters and literary vanity, a collective solidarity belonging to the profession, a collective solidarity of humanity.
> Five minutes before my departure from Russia, a man came up to me, a Communist, a nodding acquaintance, who knew me only from my poems, he said: 'A Chekist will be travelling with you in the train. Do not say anything unnecessary.'
> I shake his hand, but I will not shake yours.
> MARINA TSVETAYEVA.[13]

This became Marina Tsvetayeva's visiting card in the West.

Among the other visitors to Berlin was Andrey Bely. He had not come in order to find a new wife, but to recover his first, Asya Turgeneva, whom he had not seen since 1916. His real acquaintance with Tsvetayeva, which had not taken place in Moscow, occurred at the Prager Diele.

> Ehrenburg's table was surrounded by people he knew and did not know. The animation of publishers, the euphoria of writers. The exchange of payments and manuscripts. (The fear that one and the other will soon drop in value.) ... And suddenly, two extended hands, curls of hair, a radiance: 'Is it you, you?' (He did not even know my name). 'Here? How happy I am! Have you been here for long? Have you come for good? ... Why did we see so little of each other in Moscow, and so briefly? ... We had a friend in common, Ellis ...'[14]

Bely then reminded her of some of the other things they had in common: that they were both professors' children and both had connections with Tarusa. The new friendship grew by the minute: everyone else present at this occasion withdrew discreetly and left them to themselves. On the same evening Bely read Marina's *Separation* for the first time – his enthusiasm knew no bounds. For a short time they were inseparable. Bely found a room in Zossen, near Berlin, from where he would come to visit Marina and Alya. They would often go to the zoo together, or else Marina and Alya would visit him in gloomy Zossen. Bely was in a pathetic state, he poured his heart out to Marina, and talked to her about Asya Turgeneva and Lyuba Blok. He spent every free minute writing his memoirs of Blok. And just as suddenly he disappeared from Berlin.

Russian literature benefited from this encounter in Berlin. Andrey Bely began to write lyric poetry again and gave the volume which resulted the name, *After the Separation* (*Posle Razluki*). The last poem is dedicated to Tsvetayeva. In return, Tsvetayeva portrayed Bely many years later in a literary sketch, 'A Captive Spirit' ('Plenny dukh'), which is a masterpiece of her prose writing.

On another occasion, the poet Sasha Chyorny introduced Marina to a young man in a café on the Kurfürstendamm, whose name was not yet well-known among the Russian intelligentsia. He was a critic and literary editor for the Prague journal *Freedom of Russia* (*Volya Rossii*), and was called Mark Lvovich Slonim. In his review in *Freedom of Russia* he had declared that *Separation* was a major literary triumph, and he now wanted to speak with its author about literary matters. Tsvetayeva, however, was only interested in what was going on in Prague, to where she was planning to move. They arranged to meet again, in order to continue their discussion, at the journal's offices in Prague, which were situated in the house where Mozart had composed *Don Giovanni*.

> I warned her about the political orientation of the journal, as we were affiliated with the Social Revolutionaries. She responded with a quick retort: 'I am not interested in politics, I do not understand it, and, of course, Mozart has already decided the matter for me.' To this day I am convinced that Mozart indeed influenced her decision.[15]

Slonim was struck by the same things in Tsvetayeva's appearance which other people also noted: the large grey-green eyes, which looked to the side; the large head on its long neck, which she would throw back, with a gesture which sent her light golden hair flying; the silver bracelets she wore on the wrists of her strong arms; the somewhat large fingers covered with silver rings, which clenched a wooden cigarette-holder, and finally, the strong masculine handshake. 'There was something neat about her fine svelte body, and all her habits made the impression of strength and lightness, of impetuousness and restraint.'

Soon after her arrival in the West, Marina received a long letter from Moscow, which she deciphered with difficulty. It appeared someone else was also in raptures about *Separation*. Only when the letter mentioned the funeral of Tatyana Skryabina did she understand who had written it: Boris Pasternak. On 29 June Marina replied politely and formally; she addressed him as 'Respected Boris Leonidovich . . .' She then recalled how they had met in Moscow, and said that she hoped to see him in Berlin soon. She also reminded him that she did not know his poems well, and that she had only heard them once when he read at the Polytechnic Museum in Moscow. She sent this letter, with two of her books, to his father, the artist Leonid Pasternak, who was living in Germany, with the request that he forward it.[16]

In reply, Pasternak sent her his volume *My Sister, Life* (*Sestra moya zhizn'*). Marina was thunderstruck by these poems. In one breath she wrote her essay 'A Cloudburst of Light', which Andrey Bely published in his publishing-house, Epopeya. She wrote:

> I am reading Pasternak's poetry for the first time. I had heard about them from Ehrenburg, but on account of my innate rebelliousness (no, the gods forgot to bestow the gift of collective love on me in my cradle!!), my immemorial jealousy, and my complete inability of loving something together with someone else, I was quietly resistant to what I heard: Perhaps it has genius, but it is not necessary to me![17]

Her interpretation of Pasternak's verse is not based on his rhythms and metres ('That is the business of specialists of poetry. My specialty is life!'), but rather on her poetic intuition. She could only compare his work to a 'cloudburst of light'.

Sometime in July, Ariadna Efron does not recall the precise date, Sergey Yakovlevich finally received permission to go to Germany in order to meet his wife and daughter again after a separation of four years. Very soon after this, on 31 July, they left for Czechoslovakia. In Berlin Tsvetayeva had not visited a single museum, or attended a single play or concert.

On the day following their departure Pasternak arrived in Berlin.

> In her departure from Berlin on the eve of Pasternak's arrival, there was something reminiscent of the nymph's flight from Apollo, something mythical and not of this world . . . And perhaps there was something no less mythological about her flight itself, with a treasure entrusted to her hands, which she had recognised, appropriated and abducted; that is, her desire not to share Pasternak with everyone else in the airless space around the little tables of the Prager Diele. This was accompanied by her fear of the eyes of strangers, of the 'evil eye', which was so natural to Marina, with her longing for and devotion to the mystery of the possession of a treasure: be it a book, a piece of nature, a letter or a

human soul. For Marina was a great proprietor in the world of
immaterial valuables, in which she did not tolerate joint-owners and
spies ... [18]

'Russian Berlin' of 1922 has literally vanished from the face of
the earth. Not only has fate scattered its inhabitants in all
directions, but their houses and their entire part of the city were
destroyed during the Second World War. The present-day Prager
Platz resembles the original only in name. That which survived the
bombings gave way to the bulldozers of modern West Berlin. Even
the Russian church on Nachodstrasse, where Father Sergey
Bulgakov and later, Father John Shakhovskoy (who became still
later the Archbishop of San Francisco), served as priests, no longer
exists. The only witnesses who can tell of the short starlit hour of
Berlin's Russian cultural life, would be the old poplars on the
Prager Platz which miraculously survived the air raids.

And one more thing will remain forever; Tsvetayeva's declaration of love for Berlin:

> The rain lulls the pain,
> Under the storm of lowered shutters
> I sleep: The hooves along
> The shuddering asphalt are like applause.
>
> The rain made its greetings and poured.
> In gilded abandonment
> You have taken pity, barracks,
> On the most fabled of orphanhoods![19]

CHAPTER 16

Czechoslovakia – Pasternak

JULY 1922 – AUGUST 1923

A detailed description of the life of the Russian emigration in pre-War Czechoslovakia during its short existence as a democratic state has not been, and probably never will be, written. In May 1945, when the Red Army occupied Prague, one of the first tasks of its various "organs" was the seizure of all documents and sources relating to the history of the Russian emigration and their transportation to the Soviet Union. That which they did not take at the time was given to them by the Communist government of Czechoslovakia in 1948. The majority of the people who witnessed this epoch are either very old or now live in other countries. Today one can judge the size and importance of the Russian colony in Prague by visiting the cemetery at Olšany. One thing, however, is beyond dispute, the Czechoslovak Republic, then headed by President Masaryk, through its aid and hospitality rendered an enormous and indispensable service to Russian scholarship and culture abroad. Without this help and support Marina Tsvetayeva's work could not have been realised either.

Already in the nineteenth century many Czechs had come to love their great Slavonic brother nation. At the end of the First World War Austrian prisoners of war of Czech and Slovak descent organised in Russia the so-called 'Czech Legion', which took an active part in the Civil War. In fact, the Czech Legion played a decisive rôle in its outcome. At first it fought on the side of Admiral Kolchak, but later it unexpectedly abandoned him, ceased its military activities and returned to the newly created Republic of Czechoslovakia. After this, as the remains of the defeated Volunteer Army were being evacuated across Gallipoli to Turkey, Masaryk organised extensive assistance for the émigrés. In this way many participants in the Civil War found refuge and a new homeland in Czechoslovakia. Officers who had had no special training received stipends in order to finish their education and free accommodation in student hostels. Famous Russian scholars were invited to teach at Czech universities, such as the art historian and Byzantinist N.P. Kondakov at the University of Prague,[1] the linguist N.N. Durnovo at the University of Brno, and the philosopher N.O. Lossky at the University of Bratislava. We must also mention Roman Jakobson in Prague, and Prince N.S. Trubetzkoy in Vienna, who were the chief founders of the celebrated Prague School of Linguistics. The rising generation of youth were given the barracks at Moravská Třebova, which had been used formerly for prisoners of war. A Russian *gymnasium* and boarding-school were now established there. The Czech government was particularly generous to Russian intellectuals. Many writers received financial support over the years, which allowed them to continue their work. Marina Tsvetayeva and her family could live on the stipend which she, and, at first her husband as well, received. Even when the Efrons settled in France, the Czech stipend remained their main source of income.

Parallel with this aid from the state there were also private organisations, such as the Czech-Russian Society ('*Česko-ruská Jednota*'), which was founded as early as 1919. The aim of this charitable society was the creation of ties between local Czech intellectuals and the Russian émigrés. At the head of the Jednota was the Czech writer Anna Tesková, who was born in St Petersburg. At the centre of the Church oriented émigrés were the Russian Orthodox Bishop of Prague, Sergey (Korolev) and Princess Natalia Yashvil, a founding member of the Kondakov Institute. The left-wing circles gathered at the editorial offices of *Freedom of Russia*, the influential journal of the Social Revolutionaries.

In the winter of 1922 a large group of leading thinkers and literary figures exiled by the Bolshevik régime met in Prague. Among them were several of the authors of the famous volume *Landmarks* (*Vekhi*), and others, who after long deliberation had returned to religion and the Orthodox Church. In Prague they came into contact with a mass of young Russian students, former soldiers and White Army officers, many of whom, after all the upheavals and catastrophes, began to reflect on the reasons for the collapse of Russia. Many of them, in turn, found an answer in Christianity. At first in Belgrade, where the young Zernovs then

Marina Tsvetayeva: Prague, 1924

lived, and later everywhere in the Russian diaspora, Orthodox student brotherhoods were formed and a remarkable Christian revival began, which subsequently had a strong influence on the spiritual life of the West as well. In this regard a great deal of credit belongs to Bishop Sergey of Prague, one of the strongest personalities among the Russian Orthodox hierarchy in the West. The first two conferences of Russian students from Czechoslovakia and the rest of Europe was organised in Přerov in 1923 and 1924, with the participation of Berdyayev, Father Sergey Bulgakov, A. Kartashev, V. Zenkovsky, and others. The result of this was the birth of the 'Russian Student Christian Movement', its journal the *Messenger* (*Vestnik R.S.Kh.D.*), which is still in existence, and a plan for the establishment of a theological institute in Paris.[2]

These professors lived in the so-called 'Professors' House', by the church in the centre of Prague, while the students were accommodated in the former barracks on the outskirts of the city, which was named 'Svobodárna'. This is where Sergey Efron lived until Marina's arrival. Nikolay Yelenev describes it vividly:

> Along both sides of its narrow tunnel-like corridors the building contained several hundred 'cabins', which stretched from one end to the other. Thin partitions separated them, which reached neither to the cement floor nor to the ceiling...[3]

There the Russian émigré students lived and studied, so diligently, in fact, that they came first in almost every subject, even in sport. All of them were convinced that they would be returning very soon to their native land and that they would then be able to serve their country with their knowledge.

When Marina and Alya arrived in Czechoslovakia on 1 August 1922 Sergey Yakovlevich had to find them a place to live. Since life in Prague itself was too expensive, the family settled in the small village of Mokropsy, not far from the city, where many Russian refugees were already living. Sergey Yakovlevich continued to study at the University of Prague and kept his place at the Svobodárna, but he often went into Prague only for the day.

For Marina the year spent in Mokropsy (which to a Russian ear means literally 'Wet dogs') was a year of sobering up, when she could rethink and reassess many things. It was also a time of productive work in the quiet solitude of the country, which was so different from the ant-heap of Berlin. Tsvetayeva describes her surroundings thus:

> A tiny mountain village: we live in its last house, in a spacious hut. The dramatis personae of our life: a well with a chapel, where I run for water

> (down the hill), mostly at night or early morning; a chained dog; a
> squeaking gate. Directly behind all this lies the forest. To the right, a
> high crest of rock. The entire village is criss-crossed with streams.[4]

And further:

> A third of the day goes towards stoking the enormous tiled stove. Life is
> not very different from that in Moscow, its material side is perhaps even
> worse, but to poetry has been added family and nature. I do not see
> anyone for *months on end.* I write all morning and then go walking.
> There are wonderful mountains here.[5]

Anxiety about her family was certainly present; without a doubt
life was different here from the Bohemian existence led in Moscow.
As with the majority of Russian émigrés, the Efrons almost always
did not have enough money for life in Prague. They migrated in the
countryside around the outskirts of the city, often pursued by ill-
disposed landlords. They had to heat, clean and paint their rooms;
the family had to be fed, and they often did not have even the most
primitive household articles. Sergey Yakovlevich continued to
study in Prague. He would take the train early in the morning, at
dawn, and would return late at night completely shattered. Marina,
and for the most part, Alya as well, had to cope with the exigencies
of daily life without help of any kind. These new conditions
completely changed the relations between mother and daughter. In
revolutionary Moscow they had lived like sisters, and had divided
between them all their duties – Alya was not only the double, but
also the property of her mother. The ten-year-old Alya now began,
however, to play with dolls, and turned into a child, that is, into
what she was naturally. Marina was worried: Alya was beginning to
slip away from her. 'She is completely indifferent to me,' she wrote
to Bakhrakh.

The greatest problem for Marina, however, was probably her
husband, with whom she had to live again. He no longer appeared
to be that St George she had imagined him to be while living alone
in Moscow. In fact, he was now a broken man. At the same time
that Marina was still believing in all the ideals of the White Army,
and did not want to hear anything about Communism, with which
she had become intimately acquainted, Seryozha began to have
doubts. It now seemed to him that he had been fighting on the
wrong side during the Civil War. Ariadna Efron recalls her father's
words on the subject:

> ... Imagine a railway station in war-time, a large junction station,
> crowded with soldiers, black marketeers, women, children, all that
> anxiety, confusion, crush, everyone trying to get into carriages, pushing
> and pulling each other. You are pulled in too, the third bell rings, the

train starts, a minute of relief – glory to you, oh Lord! – but suddenly you realise with mortal terror that in the fatal confusion you have ended up, along with many, many others, in the wrong train, that your regiment has left from the other platform, that there is no way back, that the rails have been dismantled. One can go back, Marinochka, only on foot, along the sleepers, for one's whole life ... [6]

Inspired by Seryozha's morning trips to Prague, Marina wrote one of her well-known poems, 'Dawn on the Rails':

While day has not yet risen
With its conflicting passions,
I resurrect Russia
Out of dampness and sleepers ... [7]

Ariadna Sergeyevna recalls with pleasure her childhood in Czechoslovakia, in spite of the different conditions:

We spent the winter in an honest and friendly fashion, even if with difficulty. These difficulties became evident to me only afterwards; as a girl I simply did not understand them, perhaps because I had never known an easy life. I considered it not only natural, but also pleasant, that part of the housework should fall to my lot; the fact that I had two dresses in all did not force me to dream about a third ... that gifts and presents were rare only elevated their magic value in my eyes. The main thing was the courageous poverty of Marina and Seryozha, their dignity, endurance and the frequent humour with which they struggled with all their daily hardships, supporting and encouraging each other; all this inspired in me such a warm feeling of love for them and solidarity with them, that this in itself was already happiness. Happy were the evenings which we sometimes spent together, at the table, which had been cleared of food and dishes, and wiped with a damp cloth and comfortingly and magnificently headed by a kerosene lamp, with a brilliant glass cover ... Seryozha would read aloud the books he had brought from Prague; and Marina and I would listen while we darned, mended and patched ... [8]

In the 'Russian' villages around Prague, Mokropsy, Všenory, Jiloviště, Radošovice, and others, lived many 'comrades in misfortune'. Soon the Efrons began to make friends with their neighbours. Marina had already become acquainted with Lyudmila Chirikova, the daughter of a well-known writer, in Berlin; she now met the rest of her family.[9] There were also strong ties with the Yelenev family. Marina was particularly friendly with Yekaterina Isaakovna Yeleneva, 'a friend and comrade-in-arms from Mokropsy'.[10] With Nikolay Yelenev, however, misunderstandings soon arose. Tsvetayeva had lived for five years under the Communist régime which Yelenev had been fighting against. Some of the several habits of those years had left their trace on Marina. Yelenev recalls:

Marina brought with her across the border, if not fear, then the spectre of hunger. Coming in she would hold out to me a large saucepan, somehow covered in newspaper: 'I have brought you some *kasha*. We cooked too much of it. I thought we should not throw it away...' Although my means of existence at that time were very limited, I did not need such a gift. It seemed strange to me, awkwardly inappropriate. But Marina's motive became clear to me somewhat later. Soviet reality had not entered, or had almost not entered, into my daily life. But on Marina it had left its mark, even on her, who with her whole being was a born rebel... [11]

A certain distrust of the 'Soviet' in Tsvetayeva was to remain among some of her compatriots in the West.

Her relations with politically left-wing circles were, from the very beginning, apparently better than with others. Already in September, she visited the editorial offices of *Freedom of Russia*, as Slonim had arranged, where she was amicably received by the entire editorial staff.[12] Her conversation with M.L. Slonim began in his office, but was soon transferred to the café Slavia, on the banks of the Vltava.

The first conversation lasted several hours. They spoke about literature and Slonim was quite amazed that Tsvetayeva knew so much about Casanova and had even written several plays in verse about him. It was agreed that *The Adventure* and the re-worked *The End of Casanova* (re-named *The Phoenix*) would be printed in *Freedom of Russia*. Already, however, at this first meeting, a heated argument arose between them in regard to the translation of the epigraph for *The Adventure*.

I was struck by the passion with which M.I. insisted on her own version and put forward the most unexpected arguments. 'But this is a mere trifle,' I said, trying to stop her. 'A trifle?' she asked with some kind of ominous hiss, exactly as if I were guilty of blasphemy: 'The choice of words is the most important thing.' How many times after this did I not notice how M.I.'s calm and patience would vanish as soon as it was a question of the precision of individual words, of the legitimacy of little used expressions, or rhythmic stresses. At moments like this she would become an Amazon, ready to annihilate her opponent: for her the first line of the Gospel of St John was sacred: In the beginning was the Word, and the Word was with God and the Word was God.

From this day Marina had a loyal friend in Prague. They often saw each other and walked around the city, delighting in its beauties; they usually ended their wanderings in one of the city's many cafés.

Over a period of three years, from 1922 to the end of 1925 we would often meet. We would talk for hours on our walks, and we quickly became intimate. Literary interests soon turned into a personal

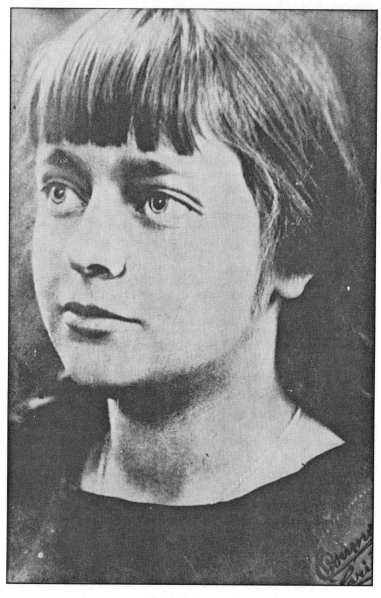

Alya (Ariadna), 1925

friendship. It lasted for seventeen years, but was uneven and complicated, with disagreements and reconciliations, highs and lows. In one thing I remained unchanged: I considered her to be a great poet, on a par with Pasternak, Mayakovsky, Mandelstam, and Akhmatova, and even in 1925 I wrote that her only equal in the emigration was Khodasevich.

Slonim praised Marina's extraordinary and penetrating mind, in which were united common sense, clarity of thought and a talent for abstract thought. All of these qualities could flare up together in moments of true feminine intuition.

> Marina was extremely intelligent: she possessed a sharp, strong and cutting mind, which combined a certain sobriety and clarity with a gift for abstraction and universal ideas, logical consistency and unexpected flashes of intuition. These qualities appeared with particular brilliance when she was in conversation with those she considered to be worthy of her attention. She was an exceptional, and at the same time, very difficult, – many said exhausting –, interlocutor. She sought and valued people who understood her on the basis of half-words; a certain intellectual impatience lived in her, as though she had no desire to comment on thoughts or images thrown at random. One had to catch them in flight; conversation thus turned into a verbal tennis-match; one had to be on one's guard the whole time and to parry metaphors, quotations and aphorisms, to guess at the essence of the conversation through hints and fragments. The most important thing for her was lightning quick retort, her own or another's. Otherwise all the heat of the game, all the excitement from the speed and moments of illumination would falter. At times I felt exhausted after two or three hours of such intensity, and was ashamed of this because of my age; I saw it as a sign of inferiority, and concealed it.

Mark Lvovich did a great deal for Marina Tsvetayeva, then and later; probably more, in fact, than she ever knew. Thanks to his good relations with important Czech circles, he could secure for her a stipend. He also persuaded *Freedom of Russia* to publish her works periodically, although the editors and readers of the journal were not at all enthusiastic about this poet of the White Movement.

In September 1922 Marina met some new people. One of the first poems she wrote in Czechoslovakia, 'Trees', is dedicated: 'To my Czech friend Anna Tesková'. The president of the Czech-Russian Society soon became very interested in Tsvetayeva, and wanted her to read her poems at the meetings of the society. In a short note of 2/15 November 1922 addressed to Anna Tesková, the first in their extensive correspondence, Marina thanked her for the invitation, which she accepted.[13] On more than one occasion she was later to take part in the evenings organised by this society in the Prague hotel 'Beranek'. At one of them she met the Czech writer and translator František Kubka. He speaks of this event in his book *Voices from the East (Hlasy od východu)*.[14]

In spite of the fact that Marina often went into Prague, where she had friends who looked after her, (aside from Slonim, Yelenev also speaks of strolls around Prague, and visits to the 'Knight of Prague' under the Charles Bridge), this year at Mokropsy was a quiet one of productive work, against the background of the splendid unspoiled landscape.

On 27 September, far from her native land, Marina celebrated her thirtieth birthday. She wrote on this day a poem, which, as she later told Pasternak, was one of her favourite works:

GREY HAIRS

These are ashes of treasures:
Of hurt and loss.
These are ashes in face of which
Granite is dross.

Dove, naked and brilliant,
It has no mate.
Solomon's ashes
Over vanity that's great.

Time's menacing chalkmark,
Not to be overthrown.
Means God knocks at the door
– Once the house has burned down!

Not choked yet by refuse,
Days' and dreams' conqueror.
Like a thunderbolt Spirit
Of early grey hair.

It's not you who've betrayed me
On the home front, years.
This grey is the triumph
Of immortal powers.[15]

[translated by David McDuff]

After this Tsvetayeva ceases for some time to write short poems. She was working on a large piece which she had begun in Russia. Over the course of several months this turned into an epic poem which was something of a continuation of 'Byways' and the uncompleted 'Yegorushka'. This served as proof that mentally and spiritually she was still in Russia: 'I am finishing a long composition in verse which I love passionately, and without which I will be orphaned.'[16]

The 'long composition' is the epic poem *The Swain*

(*Molodets*). In 1924 it was published by the Prague publishing house Plamya. The theme of this work is based on an ancient Russian legend about a village girl Marusya, who falls in love with a vampire. *The Swain* was greeted both positively and negatively. Olga Chernova later asked Marina why she had chosen this theme in particular. Marina answered with the following:

> ... I must name my subjects, that is realise those, who have summoned me. It is as if my compositions chose me on their own, and often I write them against my will. Russia wishes to express herself through certain things and choses me to do this. And by what means was I convinced and captivated? By my own personal strength: you alone! Yes, me alone. And having surrendered myself to this summons, sometimes seeing, other times blindly, I have obeyed, seeking out with my ear some kind of aural lesson. And it is not I who have chosen out of a hundred words the hundred and first, it (the thing itself) resisting the first hundred words will say: that is not my name.[17]

In her solitude Marina developed still another form of self-expression: she began to write letters. She made contact with her friends who had stayed in Berlin, and was soon carrying on a correspondence with several people. In her letter writing she also remained the professional author; before sending a letter she would polish every word, and every phrase, and first copy her letters into a notebook. In this way a large part of Tsvetayeva's archive of personal correspondence has been preserved at the Central State Archive of Literature and Art (TSGALI) in Moscow, even if certain originals of these letters have perished or have simply not yet been published. This is very important as these letters, along with her poetry and prose, form an independent part of Tsvetayeva's literary legacy.

The contents of the letters vary, naturally, in accordance with the addressees. For example, in the correspondence with Roman Gul we find questions mostly about concrete matters, such as the printing of her works, negotiations with the publishers, whom Gul was supposed to find, and so forth. We learn also a great deal from these letters about Tsvetayeva's life and opinions. On one occasion she reveals her annoyance with a review of her 'Tsar-Maiden' by Yuly Aikhenvald, in which the well-known critic had written:

> I should like to mention the beautiful edition by Epokha of the still more beautiful semi-folk poem by Marina Tsvetayeva 'The Tsar-Maiden'. The talented poetess has created an artistic plaything in the Russian folk style ... It is full of surprises and caprices, one does not always immediately follow its development, but you surrender yourself gladly to the humour and fantasy of the author, with a smile of attention and pleasure ... The whole piece fascinates you with its charms, its national

> spirit, you whirl away on waves, along the river of Russian speech. One can truly say that it 'has the spirit of Russia', and 'savours of Russia'.[18]

This is Marina's reaction:

> I have been moved, but in the wrong way! So, it is Baroque – Russian speech, a plaything written with talent, and not a word about its inner substance: the fates, characters, heroes, as if nothing remained except for the *ringing in one's ears*. It is annoying. I have not written for the sake of the Russian language![19]

Tsvetayeva also wrote, however, another kind of letter. She would turn to people she did not know, or barely knew. She judged these people only by their replies to her letters and, therefore, often judged them incorrectly. But these were the contacts she liked the most: that friendship between souls which prosaic reality could not disturb. She wrote to Pasternak on 19 November 1922:

> My favourite forms of communication are otherworldly, the first is by dream; and the second is correspondence. A letter is a form of otherworldly communication, less perfect than a dream, but the laws are the same. Neither one, nor the other, come by command: one neither dreams nor writes when one wishes, but when they want to: the letter to be written, the dream to be dreamt. My letters *always* want to be written!

And in the same letter:

> I do not like meetings in life: the collision of two foreheads. Two walls, that one does not break through. A meeting must be an arch: then the meeting is *above*, with heads thrown back![20]

The dangerous consequence of this attitude soon made itself felt: Marina fell deeply in love, more than once, with the heroes of her dreams, and each time she was deeply disillusioned and saddened. She would reveal the secrets of her soul to the correspondent in question, then her hero would suddenly fall silent and retreat from her, or would turn out to be completely different from what she had imagined. All of her correspondence is essentially a monologue, which relates not so much to the people to whom she is writing, but ' . . . above their heads, to God, or at least, to the angels . . . '

The first of these heroes, whom Marina met in a dream, was Boris Pasternak (and this was despite the fact that she had scarcely even noticed him while in Moscow). His volume of poetry, however, *Themes and Variations* (*Temy i variatsii*), which he sent her from Berlin in February 1923, was a 'burn': 'Your book is a burn . . . I caught fire from it and am burning – there is no sleep, nor day . . . '

She wrote to him as though uttering prophetic words: 'Do you know, Pasternak, you need to write a large work. This will become your second life, or rather, your first, unique to you, nothing and no one will be necessary to you.'

On 9 March 1923, however, terrible, bitter news arrived: Pasternak had made his decision, he had turned his back on the West and was returning to Moscow. He wanted to say goodbye to Marina, and suggested that she come to Berlin. Marina could not: she had no money, and she could not obtain in such a short time the documents necessary for this trip. Besides, she could not leave her family. The heavy tasks of daily domestic life were beyond their strength. She wrote to Pasternak:

> I will not come, because it is too late, because I am helpless, because Mark Slonim (for example) will obtain permission for travel in an hour, because my fate is loss ... A great insomnia lies ahead, of Spring and Summer. I know that every tree, which I choose with my eyes, will be you. How can one live with this? (It is not a question of the fact that you are there, and I am here, but that you will be *there*, that I will never know whether you are alive or not. Longing *for* you and fear *for* you, a primitive fear, I know myself.) ... A meeting with you would be for me a certain liberation from you, a legitimate one. Is this clear to you? A way out! I would (away from you) breathe in you. But only do not become angry! These are not extreme words, these are immense *feelings*: feelings which already exclude the concept of measure![21]

Marina sent Pasternak a proof-copy of her, as yet unpublished, volume *The Craft*, and instructed Gul to find in Berlin a copy of Eckermann's *Conversations with Goethe* and to present it to Pasternak in her name at the station.

Marina saved herself from despair at losing a poet, who had become for a moment a brother, in her art. Between 17 March and 11 April she wrote the cycle *Cables* (*Provoda*), which consists of ten poems, and between 8 and 23 April the cycle *The Poets*; both of these are dedicated to Pasternak.[22] Once again she expressed in verse something that she had already written to him in a letter.

It is difficult to imagine a more accurate and apt description of Tsvetayeva:

THE POET [3]

What is left for me, sightless and fatherless,
In this world where all have sight, a paternal home,
Where the passions must brave anathemas
Like trenches! Where weeping is
Called a head cold!

What is left for me, who by my nature, my knowledge,
Live to sing – like cables! tan! Siberian wastes!
Over my infatuations as over a bridge!

With their weightlessness
In a world of weights.

What am I to do, singer and first-born,
In a world where grey is the blackest that's found!
Where inspiration is kept as in thermos flasks!
With this boundlessness
In a world of bounds?!²³

[translated by David McDuff]

The spring of 1923 brought Marina not only grief, but also vexing mundane problems; the owner of the house in which the Efrons lived lodged a complaint about them in court, because they had not properly washed the floors of the house. Moreover, Tsvetayeva was very angry that her review of Prince Volkonsky's book, which had appeared under the title 'The Cedar: An Apologia', in the literary journal Notes of an Observer (Zapiski nablyudatelya), was attacked. The critics came down on both Tsvetayeva's review and Volkonsky's book itself. Yuly Aikhenvald wrote in the newspaper The Rudder, that Tsvetayeva was clearly mistaken if she thought she had written a review, or an apologia; what she had produced was a panegyric.

After this Marina experienced something even worse; she could find no one to publish her journals of the Revolution. She wrote to Gul:

> Helikon has replied; the conditions are magnificent, – but there is one stipulation, they must be *apolitical.* I answered in my turn. Moscow 1917-1919 – what was I doing, rocking in a cradle? I was between the ages of 24 and 26, I had eyes, ears, hands, feet: and with these eyes I saw, with these ears I heard, with these hands I chopped wood (and wrote!), with these feet I walked through the markets and the barricades, wherever they took me! There are no *politics* in the book: there is passionate truth: the most passionate truth of cold, hunger, anger, of a *year's* worth! My youngest daughter died of starvation in an orphanage – this is also 'politics' (a Bolshevik orphanage).²⁴

Apparently, however, the Berlin publishers, who still hoped to sell their editions in Soviet Russia, preferred to stay aloof from such 'omens of the earth'. On Marina's part there was also a further condition, she wanted Alya's journal to be published as a postface to her own.²⁵

In the spring Helikon did publish The Craft. It enjoyed a great success and the critical reception was splendid. Vera Lourié, for example, wrote:

> With The Craft Tsvetayeva has shown that she has found a solution to her spiritual explosiveness. She belongs to those great poets who do not know the middle way, either they fall headlong overboard or they

triumph. Tsvetayeva has triumphed over herself and over others ... Behind all the daring, coarse masculine manners and strength, an infinitely great deal of the feminine is concealed in Tsvetayeva; all her aspirations to sacrifice and heroism are purely feminine ... How petty and pale seem the femininity and gentleness of Akhmatova in comparison with the romantic impulse of Tsvetayeva. The mature genuine craft of Tsvetayeva has only just begun, she is rich with infinite possibilities. With one's whole soul, with sincere love and affection one wants to say, together with her, 'Preserve, oh Lord, her muse!'[26]

Another laudatory review of *Separation* and *The Craft* appeared in the newspaper *Days*, under the heading 'Poetry of Rhythm'. It was signed by a critic about whom Marina knew nothing: Aleksandr Bakhrakh. It immediately seemed to her that he, of all the critics, did not stamp her with the label *'style russe'* but, on the contrary, understood the spirit of her poetry. Tsvetayeva was impressed by his intuition. On 20 April she jotted down in her notebook 'A Letter to a Critic':

> I do not know whether it is acceptable to answer criticism, other than with caustic remarks – and in print. But poets do not only observe rites, they also create them! Allow me now, in this letter to establish the rite of gratitude to a critic: from a poet.

Only on 9 June did she decide to send this letter, to which she added one more phrase: 'The occasion is sufficiently rare for one not to count too much on others!'[27]

Thus began the 'romance in letters' between Tsvetayeva and a young man who at the time had just turned twenty. This was a very important episode in Tsvetayeva's life.

Aleksandr Vasilievich Bakhrakh, a man of letters and a critic, who subsequently wrote a great deal about Russian émigré writers, apparently displayed in his letters to Tsvetayeva (which have not yet been published), those qualities, which as Slonim has described, she valued in her interlocutors.

His reply to her letter, in which he said that her new book had nothing in common with 'craft', hit the mark directly. Tsvetayeva's interest in this perceptive young man continued to grow. On 30 June she wrote:

> An unknown man contains all possibilities, he is the one from whom you expect everything. He does *not* exist yet; he will exist only tomorrow (tomorrow, when I will no longer exist!) I grant to another human being everything which I should have ...

On 14-15 July she wrote:

> You are a stranger, but I have taken you into my life. I walk with you on

the dusty village road, and along the streets of Prague ... I want you to grow up great and magnificent, and having forgotten *me*, never to separate yourself from the other world, *my* world! ...

I want from you a miracle. A miracle of trust, a miracle of understanding, a miracle of detachment. I want you to be, at your age of twenty, a seventy-year-old man, and a seven-year-old boy, at the same time. I do not want age, calculations, struggles, barriers. I do not know who you are, I do not know anything about your life, I can be perfectly free with you, I am speaking with a spirit ... Everything is of the hour ...

To this letter was attached the first poem of the cycle *Hour of the Soul.*

On 25 July she again wrote:

I want you to be irreproachable, that is proud and free to the extent that you go under reproach like a soldier under fire: 'You will not kill my soul!' Irreproachableness is not blamelessness, but responsibility for one's defects, to realise them, even to the point of defending them ... Little friend, the destruction of form consists in excessiveness. I practise this tirelessly in my poetry, if I were younger I would do nothing else in life! I will understand everything ...

On the same day, apparently, Marina received a letter from Bakhrakh, in which he somehow supported her notion of him. She read this reply in the forest lying on a grassy slope above her house, and wrote him an 'excessive' letter, in which she proposed a plan; she would go to Berlin and meet Bakhrakh there. Not surprisingly, the young man took fright and did not answer.

Before the reader's eyes the tangle of the 'romance in letters' turns into an emotional drama. Marina's soul had fallen deeply in love with the soul of the magical being she had invented; she was far from thinking that she herself was probably guilty of his silence. She waited with despair for a letter from Bakhrakh. On 17 August she wrote briefly:

I have written to you twice and have not received a reply ... If my letters have reached you, every explanation of your silence is superfluous, just as every of your future worries about my earthly affairs will be declined with gratitude.

A letter which has remained unanswered is a hand which has not met another. It is not my business to enquire about reasons, and not yours about my feelings ...

On 27 August she tried again:

I have exhausted myself this month with suffering ... not one of my last letters received a reply ... Put yourself in my place for a second, understand what this means, neither a line, nor a word, for a whole month, day after day, hour after hour ... Oh many have been my thoughts and cries and feelings. And such pain of loss, such an insult to my living soul, such bitterness that if it were not for poetry, I would throw myself at the first person I met: to forget myself, to extinguish myself, to drown. Friend, I am not a little girl (although in some ways I will never grow up) I have burned, been burnt, caught fire, suffered; all this I know, but I have never been SO broken up, as I have been broken up about you, with the whole force of one's trust – thrown against a wall! – never. I have fallen from you, as from a mountain.

On that day she must have finally received some kind of word from Bakhrakh, because on 28 August, beside herself with joy, she wrote to him and included extracts from her journal written between 26 July and 25 August, which she called a 'Bulletin of Illness', and some poems written for him. The following conveys her mood especially well:

THE LETTER

Thus one does not wait for letters,
Thus one waits for *the* letter.
A ragged shred,
Around it a ribbon
Of paste. Inside – a word
And happiness. And that is all.

Thus one does not wait for happiness,
Thus one waits for the end:
A soldier's salute
And in the chest – three
Slugs of lead. Red in the eyes.
And nothing more. That is all.

I am too old for happiness!
The wind has blown away the colour of
The square of the court-yard
And of the black muzzles.

(A square of a letter:
Ink and charm!)
For mortal sleep
No one is too old.

The square of a letter![28]

In this letter, however, she also writes something else:

Difficult days lie ahead of me. I will be separating from Alya and am sending her to a *gymnasium* (in Moravia) S. is already there. We had decided that Alya would travel with some other children (it is now the end of the holidays and the children are all going back) and that I would go to Prague, where we had already rented a room, and that I would live there. These were to be the 2-3 free weeks which I had written to you about. Today I have received a letter: my presence is required, it is necessary to take Alya myself to introduce her to life at the *gymnasium* ... I am now at an internal (yes, and at an external!) parting of the ways, a year of my life – in the forest, with poetry, with trees, and without people, has come to an end. I am on the eve of a great new city (perhaps, of a great new grief?!) and a great new life in it, the eve of a new self...[29]

CHAPTER 17

Prague – Všenory – 'Poem of the Mountain' – 'Poem of the End'

1923 – 1924

'On the first (of September) I am moving to Prague ... I have a house on a mountain, and the whole city at my feet ... '

This is how Marina Tsvetayeva describes her room at no.1373 Švedska Street on Smichov hill, from where there is a magnificent view of a part of the city.

After moving to Prague Tsvetayeva took her daughter to the boarding-school ('to the camp', as she called it) of the *gymnasium* in Moravská Třebova, and remained there with her for a few days, from 8 to 16 September. Alya at once felt at home in the school, and was probably happy to be a child, at last, among other children. No one forced her here to behave as a celebrated "Wunderkind". Marina was disillusioned; she wrote to Bakhrakh:

> Alya is already accepted, she has immediately got used to life here, she is happy; her eyes are unanimously declared to be stars, and she immediately answers the questions of the children (500 of them!) about who she is, and where she is from, by saying: I am a star from the sky! She is very beautiful and very free, she is not confused for a second, ingenuousness itself. They will love her here, because she is in need of no one. My whole life through I have done the loving *myself*, and have still more done the hating, and from the time I was born I wished to die; I had a difficult childhood and a gloomy adolescence. I recognise nothing in Alya, but I know one thing: she will be happy. I never wanted this (for myself). And here is ten years of my life, as if taken away by a hand. (This is almost a catastrophe, but this separation will make me younger.) A ten year experience removed, I now begin to live *my own* life.

Moravská Třebova (Mährisch Trübau) was at that time a purely German town and reminded Marina of her years as a child in

Germany. Here, at a distance from her daily worries, she recalled
her summer love, but in terms full of foreboding:

> The air which I breathe is the air of tragedy; there are no unexpected
> events in my life, because I have anticipated all of them. But aside from
> inner, underwater currents, there are also confluences, even if mere
> circumstances, simple events in life, at which you cannot guess in
> advance. I have a definite feeling of being on the eve of something, or at
> the end. (Perhaps they are the same thing!)... Wait for a moment
> before answering, there is no need for answers here, the answer will
> come later, when I, having blown up all bridges, will ask of you the
> strength to blow up the last... You were the first, *it seemed*, to call
> directly to me (in space). Oh, but now I hear it as a call to the other
> life... And I responded, and gave in to the voice, which I felt like a
> hand... Indeed I am not made for life. Everything I have is a
> conflagration! I can carry on ten different relationships (a good way of
> putting it, 'relationships'!) at once, and can convince each one from the
> profoundest depths that he is the only one. But I cannot tolerate the
> slightest turn of the head away from me. I am in *pain*, do you
> understand? I am a person skinned alive, and you are covered in armour.
> All of you have: art, society, friendships, amusements, family, respons-
> ibility, while I, at heart, have NOTHING. Everything falls away, like
> skin, and under the skin is living flesh or fire: I am Psyche. I do not fit
> into any form, not even into the simplest forms of my poems! I cannot
> live. Nothing is as with other people. I can live only in dreams...

Ten days after this letter, on 20 September, Bakhrakh received
the following news from Prague, which was like a clap of thunder:

> My friend, gather all your courage with your two hands and listen to me:
> *something* has ended. Now the most difficult thing is done, listen further.
> I love another man, one cannot say this more simply, crudely and
> honestly. Have I ceased to love you? No, you have not changed, and I
> have not changed. Only one thing has changed, my painful concentra-
> tion on you. You have not ceased to exist for me, I have ceased to exist in
> you. My *hour* with you is finished, only my eternity with you remains.
> Oh, linger on this point! Aside from passions there are still spaces. My
> meeting with you is now in these spaces. How did this happen? Oh
> friend, *how* does this happen? I rushed, another responded, I heard
> great words, there are none which are simpler, and which I heard,
> perhaps, for the first time in my life... What will come of this, I do not
> know. I know there is great pain. I am going to suffer.[1]

The hero of this new romance of Tsvetayeva, was not invented
this time. He was Konstantin Rodzevich, who belonged to the
Prague Russian colony. A former White officer, he was now a
fellow student and friend of Sergey Efron. Yelenev speaks of him
very maliciously. He seemed to Slonim to be: 'clever, crafty, not
without humour, but also someone of a slightly tarnished and
mediocre calibre'. Ariadna Efron, however, defends him fiercely:

Marina Tsvetayeva, Yekaterina Yeleneva, Konstantin Rodzevich (sitting). Sergey Efron, Nikolay Yelenev (standing). Czechoslovakia, 1923.

The hero of the poems was invested with a certain rare gift of a charm, which combined courage with spiritual gracefulness, affectionateness with irony, responsiveness with carelessness, enthusiasm, (passionateness) with selflessness, gentleness with irascibility . . . [2]

The stormy liaison between Tsvetayeva and Rodzevich, which brought Marina a great deal of doubts, despair and self-reproach, is described by Irma Kudrova.[3] It only lasted a few weeks. As early as 27 September, her birthday, Marina wrote one of her most famous poems, which was inspired by the 'Knight of Prague', a statue under the Charles Bridge. She was especially fond of this knight and found that she resembled him:

THE KNIGHT OF PRAGUE

Pale faced
Guard over the lapping of centuries
Knight, knight,
Watching over the river.

(Oh, will I find in it
Peace from lips and hands?!)
Sen-try
At the post of partings

Vows, rings . . .
But, like stones into the river
How many there are of us,
Over four centuries! . . . [4]

Between this moment and the bitter confession of 12 December 1923 only a few weeks were left. On this day Marina, 'in order to understand', 'plunged into verse, in order to see it from there' that which she probably did not want to admit to herself earlier:

> You, who loved me with the deceptions
> Of truth – and the truth of lies,
> You, who loved me – beyond all distance!
> – Beyond boundaries!
>
> You, who loved me longer
> Than time – your right hand soars! –
> You don't love me any more:
> That's the truth in six words.[5]
>
> [translated by David McDuff]

For such a woman as Marina Tsvetayeva, there was only one possible way out of this position: she broke with the man she passionately loved, 'in the full heat of love', as she told Bakhrakh: 'I would have been *happy* with him (I had never thought of this!). I had wanted a son from him ... Only one thing remains – poetry ...'

In *Poem of the Mountain* (*Poema gory*) and *Poem of the End* (*Poema kontsa*) Tsvetayeva describes in detail what led to this break.[6] The first was written between 1 January and 1 February 1924, the second was begun on the same day, 1 February but was not completed until 8 June.[7] She wrote to Pasternak:

> The 'mountain' is earlier and has a man's face to it; from the first moment of excitement I kept it on a high tone, but the 'Poem of the End' is already about the grief of a woman, who has burst into tears; I when I lie down, not when I get up! The 'Poem of the Mountain' is the mountain seen from the other side. The 'Poem of the End' is the mountain on top of me, I under it.[8]

These long poems belong to the best work of Tsvetayeva; in them the rhythms seem to gallop and chase after each other. The content is the same, always contemporary, always repeated theme of a woman's disillusioned love. Here one can say, a woman has truly expressed everything a woman can experience. Today we can accept and appreciate the mastery of these works. At the time they were written, however, this unadorned, authentic emotional outburst aroused the indignation of the greater part of the Russian writers living in the West; beginning with Gorky and ending with Bunin, everyone reproached Tsvetayeva for her stylistic and rhythmic innovation and for the 'tactlessness' of her expression. To all this was added the scandal, which in the closed circle of the Prague émigrés could not remain unnoticed and served as the theme of endless conversations and gossip.

In spite of all these events Marina's life went on. Writers and
people involved in Russian literature often gathered in Prague.
Between 4 November and 6 December 1922 Vladislav Khodasevich and Nina Berberova stayed there on their way to visit Maksim
Gorky. Marina often saw them, but a close friendship did not
develop between them.[9] Vladimir Nabokov also recalls a 'Strange
poetic walk in 1923 along some hills of Prague in a strong spring
wind', which he took with Tsvetayeva.[10]

It seems that Andrey Bely also thought of settling in Czechoslovakia for good. Even on the day of his final departure for the Soviet
Union he turned to Marina in desperation, asking her for
assistance in obtaining permission for him to enter Czechoslovakia.

A frequent guest in Prague was F.A. Stepun; he was living in
Germany but came to Prague to give lectures. He suggested to
Marina that she work as a literary critic. 'He wants to make a critic
of me, but I resisted, for I am not a critic, but an apologist,' she
explained to Gul, in a letter of 10 April 1924.

Life in 'the house on the hill' brought Marina some joyful
peaceful days as well. In the neighbouring flat lived Olga
Kolbasina-Chernova, who had only just separated from Viktor
Chernov, the last president of the Social Revolutionary Party, along
with her fifteen year old daughter, Ariadna. She and her three
daughters had spent several weeks in the Lubyanka, when Ariadna
was only ten years old.[11] Adya Chernova and Alya Efron, like their
mothers, also became friends immediately. In her memoirs Olga
Chernova describes how on the day after her arrival in the new flat,
a young woman came to see her, who held out her dry wiry hand
and said: 'I am your neighbour, Marina Tsvetayeva-Efron. I have
come to ask if you can lend me some knives and forks. Some guests
are coming this evening, and we do not have enough of them.'

Olga Chernova also had next to nothing, and could only offer a
Corsican dagger, which sent her neighbour into raptures. Their
friendship was strengthened by a shared enthusiasm for Pasternak:
they would recite from memory poems from *My Sister, Life* for
hours. Olga Chernova relates several interesting details about
Tsvetayeva:

> I soon learnt of her habit of writing from very early in the morning. No
> power on earth, no circumstance could force her to give up her work.
> When her ten-year-old daughter, Alya, would come home from
> boarding-school, Marina would make her clean the room in the
> mornings, and prepare dinner. Two years later she would also have to
> look after her new-born brother, which is why Alya could not go to

Ariadna Efron, Sergey Efron and Ariadna Chernova, Czechoslovakia, 1925

school or study systematically. This did not prevent her, however, from learning to write correctly in two languages, and from acquiring a great deal of knowledge; and all of this was entirely through her own efforts and talents. Marina said: 'Either me, and my life, that is my art, or she, who has still not proven herself, who is still in the future. But I already *am*, and I cannot sacrifice my poetry'.[12]

Marina Tsvetayeva understood very well that Alya's life was not of the easiest. She told Olga Chernova:

Adya, at the age of fifteen must sit entire nights through, working on dolls for other girls, and, Alya, at eleven, spends all day running between the broom and dustbin, while hundreds of thousands of *nonentities* of the same age, dislocate their jaws, yawning at the prospect of a golden, free, endless, rich day. He is a fool who does not feel the injustice of this, and a scoundrel who does not stand up for them![13]

The fact remains, however, that Alya's formal education only lasted a year. She herself writes that weak spots were discovered in her lungs.

After the completion of the long lyrical poems in the summer of 1924, Tsvetayeva again returned to a work begun in the previous year, during the Bakhrakh episode: the dramatisation of the Theseus legend. She wanted to present Theseus as a hero, who has had good fortune in all his undertakings, but has not known the happiness of love. She thought of making Theseus the central

character of a trilogy of plays. The first part, *Ariadna*, was to depict
the hero's youth; the second, *Phaedra*, his adulthood, and the third,
Helena, his old age. Already in the spring of 1923 she wrote several
poems which show that she was earnestly studying Greek
mythology. Her themes and motifs were borrowed, for the most
part, from Gustav Schwab's adaptations of Greek myths for
children. After the events of 1923, however, Marina created a
completely new conception of this work: Theseus abandons the
sleeping Ariadna on the island of Naxos, because only through his
sacrifice can her destiny, preordained by the gods, be fulfilled. The
third part of the trilogy was never written.[14].

In the autumn of 1924 the Efron family moved to another village
near Prague, Všenory, a much less picturesque suburb. The
Chernov mother and daughter moved to Paris, where Olga
Yeliseyevna's twin daughters from her first marriage were already
living. Thanks to this, we are very well informed about the
following months (until 26 October 1925) in Tsvetayeva's life. She
and Olga often wrote copious letters to each other. This
correspondence speaks less about lofty questions of poetry and
ethics, than about the small, sometimes minor, daily concerns of
the refugees in joyless Všenory.

Although the Efrons lived here under the same roof, they saw
little of each other. Seryozha was still studying in the city, and
moreover, was preoccupied with other very interesting, but in no
way renumerative, activities: he took part in the publishing of a left-
wing student newspaper, *In One's Own Way* (*Svoimi putyami*), and
also, together with Marina and V.F. Bulgakov, he edited the
anthology *The Ark* (*Kovcheg*), in which the 'Poem of the End' was
published for the first time. In addition, Sergey was a member of
the administration of the Union of Writers in Prague, and also
devoted himself enthusiastically to his favourite occupation, the
theatre. At the time when he was leaving for Prague early in the
morning, and returning late at night, Marina, like many other
émigré wives, would sit in her small shabby flat and would try to
earn some money by writing. The payment which *Freedom of Russia*
gave her for her contributions was the main source of their income,
and it covered the family's everyday needs. The second source was
the stipend granted by the Czech government. In Všenory Marina
could not take the long walks, which were so necessary for her
mental equilibrium, as she used to in the forests and hills around
Mokropsy. It is easy to imagine how depressed her mood was. She
wrote to Olga Chernova on 25 January 1925:

Do you remember Katerina Ivanovna from Dostoyevsky? That is me –
exhausted, embittered, indignant, in some kind of frenzy of self-
abasement and its opposite. There is the same hatred, which falls on
innocent heads. The whole world for me is the landlady Amalia
Lyudvigovna, *everyone* is guilty. But the fury of the feelings does not
obscure the accuracy of my judgements, and that is the hardest thing.

Marina knew that she had to stay in Všenory for at least another
year.

I am living in a box without air. I do not make a secret of the fact that
this is not life, for life (without people) – nature is necessary, *new* nature,
with voices replacing those of people; and freedom is necessary. I do not
have one or the other, or a tenth of what I need; I have my notebook.
And this it will be for another year! (I am speaking about my soul, about
my essential, demanding indignant self!)

Guests rarely came from Prague:

Visits from people give me little. The first minute is a joy (from the
change! A break in the routine...) and then immediately after, the
primus stove, the oven, dishes, washing, cooking; you cannot do
anything right, everything is filthy, everything gets burnt, later you
finally manage to read some poems, and it is already dark, and already
people are asking about trains. Aside from this, I am not good with
people, I do not need people, but one person, a support, even if for one
evening.

The reason for Marina's difficulties and her bad humour was not
only emotional; she was expecting her third child, a son, who, as
she wrote, she had promised her husband. She was thoroughly
convinced that it would be a son. She stayed at home clumsily
knitting scarves, and writing little. When the literary · world
suddenly turned its attention to her, when Anna Tesková invited
her to give a lecture at her society, her first reaction was to refuse.
But she did ask Tesková to visit her in Všenory.

I am expecting the visit today of a Czech lady, middle-aged and
enthusiastic, who had invited me to give a lecture, about anything I liked
at the Charles University, on 7 May 1925 at seven o'clock in the
evening, whereupon I informed her of my own seven month condition
and the uncertainly predicted hours and dates which certainly however,
will fall in February 1925. It is a pity she is not a midwife! It is always
pleasant to converse with a business-like (knowledgeable, as Dostoyevsky would say) person. But alas, she is an old maid![15]

It is not known for certain if Anna Tesková visited Tsvetayeva in
Všenory in January or February. But this letter about Marina's
lecture at the Charles University marked the beginning of her
regular correspondence with the 'middle-aged enthusiastic Czech
lady', which ended only on the day of Tsvetayeva's departure for

the Soviet Union.[16] From this day onwards the wise Czech woman, who was many years older than Tsvetayeva, carefully and benevolently entered the writer's life. She knew how to encourage and help her tactfully and unobtrusively. Perhaps Tesková's letters, which are suffused with sympathy, maternal concern and affection, contributed more than anything to helping Tsvetayeva repeatedly to find the strength to overcome all her difficulties and catastrophes. Perhaps, also, Tsvetayeva's life would not have come to such a terrible end in Yelabuga if Anna Tesková had somehow been at hand. And Marina loved her Czech friend to the end of her life.

In her letters to Anna Tesková, Marina often mentions a certain M.L. It is not difficult to guess that this is the same man who is referred to in her letters to Chernova as 'the dear one' and that Marina was not indifferent to this 'dear one.' This was Mark Lvovich Slonim, who in 1970 wrote a warm article about his friendship with Tsvetayeva.[17] He states that after her break with Rodzevich, Marina Ivanovna needed especially a 'friendly shoulder, on which to bury her head, cry and forget herself...' There occurred at this point, however, 'a collision of individualities, temperaments and aspirations'.

Further on Slonim says:

> First of all, M.I. had, as usual, created around me a certain illusion; she imagined me to be the incarnation of spirituality, and every kind of virtue, knowing absolutely nothing about my personal life, nor about my inclinations, passions and vices. Having lifted herself up into heights beyond the clouds, she soared for a short time up there, and her coming down to earth, as always, caused her injury and suffering.

There was another reason for the cleft in their relations:

> First of all, she demanded from those close to her an undivided reciprocal devotion, a complete separation from everything else, to the point of total self-sacrifice, which she wanted brought to her, not by a weak man, but by a strong one; she would have despised a weak man.

Slonim was not an invented mythical hero, but a man of flesh and blood, whith whom at every meeting there had to be new explanations. Here the pose of Marina's ideal, Tatyana, from *Yevgeny Onegin*, was inapplicable.

She wrote to Olga Chernova 10 May 1925:

> Of many people, for many years, he is the closest to me: on account of his face, which is neither masculine, nor feminine, but one belonging to a third realm, which is sometimes darkened, by the eyes of a stranger... And what pain there has come to me from him (and probably will come!) Lord! Who and what has not been painful to me in my life?... And if it were not for the triteness and awesomeness of the word (not the feeling!) I would say simply that I love him.

Against the background of this confession, we can understand Marina's malicious and even perfidious reaction, when she noticed that between them was not that 'ideal harmony, both literary and personal, about which she dreamt' (as Slonim expresses it).

On 19 November Marina wrote her famous poem 'An Attempt at Jealousy'. The immediate impetus for this is described in detail in a letter to Chernova of 17 November. On 3 December she again wrote to Chernova about it:

> I am sending my poem to him for the New Year, which I sent to you ('How is life with another woman ... '). I hope it tears his heart or lashes his pride (on that evening, at least, his 'plaster dust' will be poisoned).

> How is life with another woman –
> Is it not simpler? Like the stroke of an oar! –
> Has the memory of me,
> A floating island

> (Not on the waves, but in the sky!)
> Quickly receded, like a coastline.
> Souls, souls! – Sister should one be
> Not mistress – to you!

>   . . .

> At the price of your head: are you happy?
> No? In a bottomless pit
> How is life my dear? Is it harder
> Than life for me with another?[18]

In the Soviet Union there was, until recently, much argument about the identity of the addressee of this poem, as Tsvetayeva sent this explosion of wrath on more than one occasion to various men, when they were in disgrace.

And how did Slonim himself respond to this poem? He wrote carefully:

> The rift in our relations occurred at the end of 1924 and at the beginning of 1925, when it became clear that between us did not exist that ideal harmony, literary and personal, about which she dreamt. Yes, our basic views on poetry and on literary creativity coincided in general, but a series of my opinions and evaluations diverged from Marina's, and in spite of all her 'attempts at tolerance', as I sarcastically called them, she felt dissatisfied and disillusioned with me ... [19]

Despite all this, Slonim remained loyal to Tsvetayeva to the end of her life, and, afterwards, he did a great deal to resurrect her memory. Shortly before his death he admitted that 'An Attempt at Jealousy' was not addressed to him.

CHAPTER 18

Všenory – Birth of Georgy –
'The Pied Piper'
FEBRUARY – OCTOBER 1925

The birth of her son Georgy on 1 February 1925 created a "caesura" in Tsvetayeva's life, which was greater than, for example, her moving to Paris. If she was burdened before with work and worries about house-keeping, then these difficulties became insignificant in comparison with those the birth of a child brought. Moreover, Marina's lack of knowledge about coping with the practicalities of life complicated the situation. The baby demanded all of her time; he became the centre of her existence. Marina now transferred to him all the accumulated surplus of love in her, that love and affection which neither her husband, nor the heroes of her "romances" knew what to do with. In her life the little Georgy now began to play first violin, and Marina obeyed unquestioningly.

The baby was born two weeks before the predicted date, on a Sunday during a terrible snowstorm. He was not able to breathe at birth, and was unconscious. His life was saved only by the speedy assistance of the Russian doctor Altshuler. In the beginning neighbouring women friends helped (Tsvetayeva mentions several times Anna Ilinichna Andreyeva, the second wife of Leonid Andreyev, and Maria Sergeyevna Bulgakova), but without doubt the greatest burden of the new family fell on the weak shoulders of Alya. Marina describes for Anna Tesková, who was the first to be informed about the birth of her son, the new difficulties of her life at that time:

> It is impossible to find a servant, the local women (dailies) are very expensive, 12-15 korunas, per day. They will not come here to live ... S.Ya. has three exams in the near future (Niderle, Kondakov and another) and spends all day in the library. The whole house rests on

> Alya, for even if I got up, I would still be an invalid for two more weeks, that is I must be one. I am not complaining, but simply relating (and all this will pass, of course).[1]

And further:

> I have a great request to make, not perhaps a modest one: can there be found somewhere in your circle a simple washable dress? All winter I have been wearing a woollen one, which is coming apart at the seams. I do not need a good one, as I never go anywhere – something simple. To buy or sew one now is hopeless; yesterday 100 kr. went to the mid-wife for three visits, in a few days 120-150 kr. to the charwoman for ten days, also there is the deposit for the children's scales (100 kr.), and then medicines and the sanatorium! – It is impossible to think about a dress! But I would like very much something clean for the baby's sake. A snake must sometimes change its skin.

Gifts for the baby poured in from all sides. The editors of *Freedom of Russia* gave a pram, for which, if we believe Slonim, Marina did not really thank them.

Marina badly wanted to call her son Boris, 'In honour of my beloved contemporary, Boris Pasternak'. Only after long hours of coaxing on the part of her husband did they agree on the name of Georgy. Marina confessed to Olga Chernova why she consented to this name:

> Thus the boy is Georgy, and not Boris; Boris has thus remained within me, in a nowhere, like all my dreams and passions. It is a pity... Calling him Georgy, I keep, by the same token, the right to *his* Boris, a Boris from him; is this madness? No, dreams for the future... I could never live together with B.P. I know. For the same reason, for both of the same reasons, (S. and I) why Boris is not Boris, but Georgy; my tragic impossibility of leaving S. is the first, and the second, no less tragic, stems from my inability to construct *life* out of *love*, carve days out of eternity. I could not live with B.P., but I want a son from him, *so that in him, through me, he might live.* If this does not come true, my life, and its design, will not come true...[2]

Boris Pasternak was for her the personification of a bright shining world. Dreams about this world appear in the poem 'My bow to Russian rye', which Marina wrote during these days for Pasternak.[3] It ends the volume *After Russia* (*Posle Rossii*):

> ... Give me your hand for the whole other world!
> Here both my hands are engaged.

On 8 June 1925, on Whit Sunday, Father Sergey Bulgakov christened the baby Georgy in Všenory. The godmother was Olga Chernova and the godfather was Aleksey Remizov. Soon after this the diminutive name 'Mur' took root, which remained with him.

It was now impossible to think even about taking walks, which

Marina loved so much. The dirty country road in Všenory seemed to be an almost insurmountable obstacle for the pram. When it became warmer in the summer Marina spent long hours in 'a summer-house, right in the middle of a dung heap'. While Mur slept in his pram, Marina wrote there a large part of her lyrical satire *The Pied Piper* (*Krysolov*), which is one of her best works. We can tell she worked very hard on it as her notebook of 300 pages contains up to ten different versions in some places.

The Pied Piper soon began to appear in *Freedom of Russia* in instalments, which guaranteed the newspaper with material for almost an entire year.[4] The idea for this satire first occurred to Tsvetayeva already in the autumn of 1923 while she was staying in Moravská Třebova. The little town served as the model for her 'city of Hameln', that epitome of sated German bourgeois life. The poem is a re-working of the familiar legend of the Pied Piper, who takes vengeance on the prosperous inhabitants of the town, who have treated him badly, by entrancing all the children of the town with his flute playing, and leading them to their death. The feelings of disdain and hostility towards the self-satisfied bourgeois which appear in *The Pied Piper* undoubtedly derive from Marina's distant childhood, and her mother's influence, who regarded with contempt all the forms of conceit and arrogance which accompany wealth. We can also see in this the helpless malice of little Marina against the philistinism of the German boarding school run by the Brink sisters in Freiburg, as well as Tsvetayeva's irritation with certain types she met among the émigrés. The rats, however, who overrun the city, use the Bolshevik jargon of the early twenties.

At Easter of 1925 Sergey Yakovlevich performed with great success in a play by Ostrovsky, produced in the students' theatre. On this occasion Marina went into Prague for the first time since the birth of her son. In other matters, however, failure pursued her husband; the day before the examination set by Professor Kondakov, the famous scholar died.[5] Sergey's student stipend was not continued, and to add to these difficulties, symptoms of his old lung ailment again appeared and he had to go and stay at the sanatorium run by the Russian organisation Zemgor. From the letters of this period it is clear that Tsvetayeva was beginning to think more and more about how she could create a more settled way of life for her family. More and more often the thought of moving to Paris is mentioned, at first as something of whim. In Czechoslovakia Tsvetayeva was suffering from her poverty, but she apparently was not aware of the fact that the life of the refugees in

Paris was also difficult. She could not understand why the intelligent, talented Chernova was working in a factory, and was amazed that she did not see anyone, and had still not even met Bakhrakh.

In the summer Tsvetayeva interrupted her work on *The Pied Piper*. Learning that her old enemy, Bryusov, had died in Moscow, she began to write her recollections of him. A deeply thoughtful portrait of the writer emerged from the short sketch which she had planned.[6]

> It turned out, as always, that it was five times longer than as I had planned it; instead of anecdotal notes about Bryusov the man, it became an evaluation of his entire poetic and human personality, with a multitude of accompanying observations. (I will be curious to know how you like it.) The task was a difficult one; despite the repulsion he inspired in me (and not only in me) I wanted to give an idea of his peculiar greatness. To judge without condemning, although it seemed the verdict was prepared.[7]

This article about Bryusov, 'A Hero of Labour', contains several openly anti-Communist passages; its author makes no effort to conceal her political convictions. As her works were still in print in Soviet Russia, what she wrote was, to say the least, undiplomatic. This is probably why Gorky repudiated 'A Hero of Labour' so fiercely. In a letter of 20 December 1925 to Khodasevich, Gorky has absolutely nothing positive to say about this article.[8] Since Gorky's every word carried such enormous weight in Soviet Russia, Tsvetayeva acquired there a new and powerful adversary. When another memoir 'My Services' (her satirical description of Moscow during the Revolution and her work at Narkomnats), appeared at approximately the same time in *Contemporary Annals* (in Paris), all those 'holding power' in the Moscow literary world branded her once and for all. Her works were no longer printed, and if they were mentioned at all, then only in a negative way.[9]

Matters did not end with this, however. Tsvetayeva's characteristic openness and frequent tactlessness incited many émigrés against her. Shortly before her departure from Czechoslovakia, an article by the journalist N.A. Tsurikov appeared on 5 October 1925 in the Paris newspaper *The Renaissance* (*Vozrozhdenie*). Entitled 'Emigré Business' ('Emigrantshchina') it severely criticised Sergey Efron's newspaper *In One's Own Way* for its pro-Soviet attitude. As a reply, Marina wrote a fierce attack on *The Renaissance*, called 'Renaissance Business' ('Vozrozhdenshchina'), which was published as an open letter in the Paris newspaper *Days* on 16 October.[10]

Another short article was certainly not appreciated either by émigré circles. It is Tsvetayeva's response to a questionnaire sent by *In One's Own Way*. Replying to the question put to several émigré writers: 'What do you think about Soviet Russia and the possibility of returning there?' she says:

> One's native land is not dependent on the accidents of territory, but on the immutability of one's memory and blood. Only he who has conceived of Russia outside himself can be afraid of not being in Russia, or forgetting Russia. Whoever possesses Russia inside himself will lose her only with his life ... Lyric poets, epic poets, and storytellers, who are far-sighted by the very nature of their art, can see Russia better from a distance, the whole of it, from Prince Igor to Lenin, than when boiling in the dubious and blinding cauldron of the present. Aside from that, it is better for a writer to be in a place where he is least prevented from writing (breathing). 'But they do write in Russia!' Yes, with the cuts of the censorship, under the threat of literary denunciation, and one can only be amazed at the heroic vitality of so-called Soviet writers, who write like grass growing between prison flagstones in spite of everything. As for me, I will return to Russia, not as a tolerated 'vestige of the past', but as a welcome and expected guest.[11]

These words were addressed to everyone who was in favour of returning to Russia unconditionally, that is, to her own husband, among others.

What Tsvetayeva had said about nationalism did not coincide at all with the general opinion of émigré circles. In her letters she speaks still more clearly about this:

> I feel a general aversion to any form of nationalism, outside of wartime. A literary pose. It sticks in one's ear. I *cannot* stand the words 'God-bearing', I want to scream. I drown the 'Russian God' in the Dnepr like any other idol. Gul, ethnicity, are also a kind of dress, perhaps a skin, perhaps the seventh layer (the last), but they are *not* the soul.[12]

Tsvetayeva did not even want to be a 'Russian writer': two years later she wrote to Rilke in German:

> To write poetry, already means one is translating, from one's native language, into another language, whether into French or German it amounts to the same thing. No language is one's mother tongue. To compose is to transpose. Therefore I do not understand it when people speak of French or Russian etc. poets ... I am not a Russian poet and I am astonished when people take me for one, and treat me as such. That is why one becomes a poet (if it is at all possible to *become* a poet, if one were not one before everything else!) – in order not to be French, or Russian etc. but to be everything ... Nationality is exclusiveness and self-isolation. Orpheus breaks down nationality, or else extends it so widely and broadly that everything (past and present) is included.[13]

One can easily imagine that as a result of such statements

Tsvetayeva's popularity was not increased among her compatriots in Prague. The longer their return to Russia was delayed (those who were more perspicacious had already clearly realised that their stay abroad would not be ending soon), the greater their nostalgia for the lost motherland, and their love for Russia. Many people also did not like the political views of Sergey Yakovlevich. 'I remember Marina Tsvetayeva in Prague,' one elderly émigré has written in a letter to the author, 'she was still young, but, poor thing, everyone avoided her. They regarded her with apprehension entirely on account of her husband. He, in fact, was a very unpleasant gentleman, even at first sight.'

In the summer of 1925 Marina's fear at spending a second winter in Všenory was expressed more and more often:

> *I do not want to think about the winter here:* it would be fatal for all of us. Alya's mind grows dull (housework, geese); I grow bitter (in the same way), S. is living on his last strength, and poor Mur, I hardly dare think about him living in all this soot, dirt, damp, and vileness. To raise a child in a basement is to raise a Bolshevik, or in the best instance, a bomb-thrower. And he would be right.[14]

Olga Chernova was a true and loyal friend. She invited Marina to come to Paris and to share her flat with her. At first it was only a question of a literary evening, from whose proceeds Marina hoped to improve her financial position. In a letter to Tesková she writes:

> I have a question and a favour to ask: could you possibly keep at your house for a certain time our basket with our things in it? I say, for a certain time, because: either I will return in three months, or, I will settle in Paris (about which I am *very* doubtful). S.Ya. can send it 'par petite vitesse' ... A foreign passport will be ready in a few days, M.L. has promised to get a visa, but there is still no money for the time being. I am going with Alya and Mur ... I do not know exactly how I will travel: I am terribly unprepared ... I do not know, for example, how to organise Georgy's feeding. He needs food four times a day, and everything has to be heated. How is this done? One can hardly use a spirit stove ... Do not tell anyone about my departure, that is, about the *possibility* of my not returning, and if I return, help me to settle in Prague, somewhere on the outskirts. It would be good to be not far from you. We could take walks and wander together. Life outside the city is oppressive beyond measure, even to me (there is so much work, and everything is so expensive, aside from housing).

Concerning Paris, Tsvetayeva says:

> I am not going to Paris for the sake of Paris (I do not like places I have loved too much, like people I have loved too much: it is always suspect!) I am just going away in general, it has become essential to go somewhere! And to Paris only because they have promised to arrange a reading (paid) and because I have friends there. I have few of them.[15]

Slonim writes:

> I had little certainty that M.I. would find in France the realisation of all
> her plans, but I did not want to argue with her, all the more so, as her
> departure was attended by a multitude of practical and financial
> difficulties, and she had asked for my help . . . I was well acquainted with
> the French consul and obtained for the Efrons the necessary visa. It was
> then essential to secure for M.I. her Czech stipend and an advance from
> *Freedom of Russia.* Against these future blessings Tesková managed to
> obtain a loan from a lady she knew for her, and on 31 October 1925
> M.I. set out, trembling and anxious, with Mur and Alya, temporarily
> leaving her husband behind in Prague. In the same train was also
> travelling Anna Ilinichna Andreyeva, who took on herself all the
> troubles which so frightened M.I., even to the point of looking after the
> feeding of her ten-month-old baby.[16]

With this departure a four year period of Marina's life came to an
end. She probably only half suspected that it was one of the richest
and most productive periods in her life. This departure, about
which she had dreamt so much, also made her sad:

> Prague, basically, is also a city where only the soul matters. I love Prague
> first after Moscow, and not because of any 'Slavonic affinity', but
> because of my own affinity with it, because of its mixture of elements
> and characters. From Paris, I think I will write about Prague, not in
> gratitude, but because of the hold it has on me. From afar I will see
> everything better.

She recalled once again the 'Knight of Prague', whom she
imagined as the symbol and personification of her life in that city.
'For me, he is a symbol of fidelity (to oneself! *not to others*).'[17]

During these three years in Czechoslovakia Marina Tsvetayeva's
creativity attained the high point of its perfection. What she said
later about her volume of poetry, *After Russia*, applies as well to the
other works written at this time: 'Of 153 pages of text, 133 pages
belong to Prague. Let the Czechs be convinced that they did not
support me all those years in vain.'[18]

CHAPTER 19

Paris

1925 – 1926

There is at our disposal considerably more material for the history of the Russian emigration in France than for the emigration in Czechoslovakia. Aside from memoirs and letters there are several books about its literature, the most important of which is Gleb Struve's fundamental, *Russian Literature in Exile* (*Russkaya literatura v izgnanii*),[1] but in spite of all this, the Russian emigration in France (as elsewhere) still awaits its historian. The task is a difficult one, for during the numerous catastrophes of the last half-century, many primary sources have disappeared. An account of the fate of the Russian émigrés in the West cannot be the goal of this book, although one can understand Marina Tsvetayeva's life abroad only if one sees it against this background. Otherwise it is easy to come to conclusions which are far too grim.

There were several reasons why the Russian refugees preferred to settle in the French capital: to begin with, there was the tradition of the nineteenth century, and the more recent, though largely inaccurate, idea of France created at the turn of the century by the francophile writers of Moscow and St Petersburg, as well as by the wealthy Russians who travelled abroad and who owned flats in Paris; such people, however, could only partially know and interpret French reality. By the time that large numbers of refugees were arriving in France, around 1920-22, Paris had already become the political centre for the Russian emigration; from 1919 the so-called 'Russian Political Conference', which collected the majority of the pre-Revolutionary political activists, had been in existence, and from the first moment a literary life had begun. The intelligentsia, in particular, tried to consolidate itself in Paris, although the French government in no way facilitated this.

Permission for permanent residence was restricted by a great many unpleasant bureaucratic procedures, and worst of all, permission for working in France, for holders of the Nansen refugee passports, was given only for the most unskilled labour, such as at the Renault automobile factory at Billancourt, or cleaning cloakrooms and the carriages of the French railways. Apart from this, only freelance professions remained open to the émigrés: they could become taxi-drivers, waiters, singers and musicians, who performed in Russian restaurants, tennis trainers, or language teachers. Women who had often formerly commanded a multitude of servants, now had to become maids, milliners or dress-makers. Many of the former officers and young men without a formal education joined the Foreign Legion, where several of them made successful careers for themselves, as, for example, the French generals Pechkov and Andolenko.

In spite of all this, by 1925 more than 150,000 Russian émigrés were living permanently in France, the majority in Paris. They consisted of former landowners, industrialists, officers, ordinary soldiers and intellectuals of various political shades, who included among themselves many literary figures. One can imagine that it was especially difficult for such people to become accustomed to their new surroundings. It is also necessary to emphasise, however, that very often they did manage this, and that many of them, through their own self-sacrifice not only survived the worst times, but also put their children on their feet. They continued to write and to think and with all this made a most valuable contribution to Russian culture. One should also add that a great deal of credit belongs to those patient, heroic Russian women, who along with everything else, bore uncomplainingly the burden of their families and the demands of daily life. A typical example of such women was Marina Tsvetayeva.

Paris had also become the capital of the Russian emigration because of the presence of many cultural institutions. The majority of the approximately three hundred émigré cultural, political, social and philanthropic organisations were concentrated here. In 1925 next to the church of St Sergey, on the rue de Crimée, was founded a theological institute, whose great rôle in acquainting Western Christianity with the Eastern Church, and encouraging a *rapprochement* between them, is impossible to overestimate. Several of the Russian newspapers and journals had their editorial offices in Paris. They had a strong influence on Russian émigré cultural life, if only by the fact that they provided their employees with poorly paid, but continual work, and printed the works of writers and poets (even if offering only very limited honoraria). For many such money was their main source of income.

The following newspapers had their offices in Paris during this period: *The Latest News* (*Poslednie novosti*) which lasted from 1920 to 1940 under the editorship of P.N. Milyukov, and which from its foundation accepted contributions from all the famous, and less famous writers; and *The Renaissance* (*Vozrozhdenie*) (1925-36), the newspaper of the right-wing circles, to which Bunin, Zaitsev, Shmelyov and others contributed. Besides this the "thick journal" *Contemporary Annals* (*Sovremennye zapiski*) (1921-40) was also established in Paris. It was left-wing in orientation, and was edited by M.V. Vishnyak. Works by Berdyayev, Shestov, Father Sergey Bulgakov, Merezhkovsky and Zinaida Hippius were all published in it. During its first year some poems by Marina Tsvetayeva, which Balmont had brought from Russia in 1920, appeared on its pages, accompanied by Balmont's foreword, which we have already mentioned.[2] There were also other literary journals, such as *Russian Thought* (*Russkaya mysl*), (1921-27) edited by P.B. Struve, and *The Link* (*Zveno*) (1923-28), whose principle literary editor was Georgy Adamovich.

Literary activity seethed not only in the editorial offices, but, as formerly in Moscow and Petersburg, in various cafés. The centre of Russian literary life in Paris was Montparnasse, where the intellectual groups and groupings would meet regularly, usually at night after working hours, in the cafés Napoli, Select or La Bolle.

The Petersburgian Georgy Adamovich played a leading rôle in Montparnasse. A pupil of Gumilyov, he continued to write according to all the canons of Acmeism, which its founders, Akhmatova, Gumilyov and Mandelstam, had soon abandoned. Adamovich, as a severe critic, demanded that the poets of Paris observe this tradition, and was the inventor of the so-called 'Paris Note'. It is not surprising that such a climate was uncongenial to Tsvetayeva.

Much has already been written about the literature of Montparnasse. When Ehrenburg came from Moscow he constantly frequented La Bolle. The young Zinaida Shakhovskaya, who came to Paris for the first time in 1924, looked on the 'nightly Russian sessions in Montparnasse' somewhat from the side. She writes that '... everyone at that time was homeless, and took shelter in places where it was impossible for anyone to visit. The café was a club, and saved people from loneliness'. And further: 'One must not forget also the beneficial presence of several financially well off young Jewish women, the loyal guardians of émigré literature. They organised balls and evenings, distributed and bought tickets, collected money for the publication costs of volumes of poetry, consoled and fed, and were sometimes the sources of inspiration as well ... '[3]

In a better position than the other refugees were the Merezhkovskys, who, although they were not well off materially, at least had kept possession of their pre-Revolutionary flat in Paris. As they had previously done in Petersburg, they held "open house" on Sunday afternoons, where tea was served and philosophical, religious and literary conversations were held. They also organised the meetings of the Green Lamp society, which Yury Terapiano has described in detail.[4] Zinaida Hippius (Merezhkovsky's wife), a witty and often malicious woman, wrote venomous reviews under the pseudonym 'Anton Krainy', and was very much feared. From the first moment she and Tsvetayeva hated each other.

All of this activity did not reach Tsvetayeva, for even if she had wanted to throw herself into the literary life of Montparnasse after her arrival in Paris, she would not have been able to do so, as all her energy was spent on settling her family in their new circumstances. Olga Yeliseyevna lived with her three daughters – Adya, and the twin sisters from her first marriage, Olga and Natalia – in a three-room flat on rue Rouvet, in the proletarian 19th *arrondissement*. With her usual hospitality she offered one of her rooms to the Efrons, in which there was even a writing-table. At this table Marina finished her *Pied Piper*. In a letter to Tesková she complains that because of all the demands on her she had still not seen anything of Paris:

> I have been in Paris for a month and a week now and have still not seen Notre Dame. Until the fourth of December (it is now the seventh) I was writing and re-writing my long poem. Everything else is as in Všenory: cooking Mur's *kasha*, dressing and undressing him, taking him for walks, bathing him; other people are, on the whole, unnecessary. *Fruitless* efforts at arranging an evening: to rent a hall costs 600 francs plus a third of what you make. There are halls which are free, private ones, but no one has offered one. There have already been three refusals, on this score. The quarter in which we live is terrible, straight from a cheap novel, *The Slums of London*. A rotting canal, a sky which cannot be seen because of the chimneys, continuous soot and continuous noise (lorries). There is nowhere to take a walk. There is not a shrub in sight. There is a park, but it takes 40 minutes to walk there, and in the cold this is impossible. Thus we walk along the rotting canal.[5]

The most difficult thing of all was having to endure the closeness

of the flat and the continual presence of other people. In January
1926 Slonim visited Marina and found her in a bad state. He
reproached her for her ingratitude towards her hostess, but he
forgot how impossible it was for a sensitive writer to work in such
conditions. Tsvetayeva herself described this situation very vividly:

Quieter, praise!
Don't slam the door!
Fame!
    The corner
of a table – and an elbow.

. . . .

If only a kennel –
Only without other people!
The taps leak,
The chairs scrape,

Mouths open,
Filled with *kasha*
And thank me
'For beauty'.

. . . .

God of the horde!
The steppe – a casemate –
Paradise – is where
No one speaks!

. . . .

A god will be the one
Who can give me

(Tarry not!
The days are numbered!)
Four walls –
And silence.[6]

But even such unfavourable conditions did not distract
Tsvetayeva from her work, as can be seen from her correspondence
with the young Prince Dmitry Alekseyevich Shakhovskoy, who was
studying at the University of Louvain in Belgium, and was
preparing the publication of a new literary journal, *The Well-
Intentioned* (*Blagonamerenny*). Shortly before Tsvetayeva's departure
from Czechoslovakia he turned to her twice with the request that
she contribute to it.[7] From Brussels Shakhovskoy also tried, albeit
unsuccessfully, to find a hall for Tsvetayeva's literary evening.

We know from Ksenia Kuprina's book about her father how
difficult it was for Russian writers to organise such evenings, which
brought their authors only enough revenue to pay for their most
pressing debts. She quotes a letter by Tsvetayeva in which she

thanks Kuprina's mother for her help in selling tickets for Marina's first reading:

> I know that no one has any time for poetry or poets: they are not even luxuries, but a demanding diversion, which makes any participation and sympathy all the more appreciated.[8]

In the Chernovs' flat Marina finally met the hero of her 1923 romance in letters. Not surprisingly, this meeting was not a success. Aleksandr Bakhrakh recalls:

> ... This meeting took place in front of numerous witnesses, and was surrounded by an atmosphere of overt "gentility", with biscuits and tea. Something in the setting sounded like a false note. Tsvetayeva herself was aware of this, and a few years later wrote to me: 'I am guilty before you, I know. Do you know why? Because of the inappropriate cheerfulness of our meeting. Do you want another one, a first one, in earnest?'
>
> But something had disappeared after all these years. If one wants to be superstitious, then one has to admit that Fate ... was against us, and that some kind of "little demons" had got into our friendship, which could not be put right ... And it turned out that for all of her years in Paris, one could count the number of times I visited her ...[9]

Already at the beginning of Tsvetayeva's stay in Paris, an unpleasant incident occurred with Mur's godfather, Remizov. He allowed himself one of his famous jokes at her expense: he placed in *The Latest News* a notice that Tsvetayeva had come from Prague in order to start a new literary journal called 'Pincers' ('Shchiptsy'). Tsvetayeva was very angry about this, and wrote to Shakhovskoy:

> At the request of *The Latest News* I had to refrain from my sharp reply to Remizov, but they did print my refutation. I hate such jokes, and in general I never understand jokes at my expense. In childhood I used to throw things, now alas, I must limit myself to a verbal riposte, but these are always harmful and instantaneous. To make jokes at my expense shows a lack of feeling, and bad taste. It is a pity that Remizov has done this, who is *all* feeling ...[10]

The editors of the journal *The Link* organised at Christmas 1925 a competition for lyric poetry. The jury consisted of Adamovich, Zinaida Hippius and Konstantin Mochulsky. Of the two hundred poems received, the twenty best were to be selected for publication. One cannot reproach the members of the jury for the fact that they made their selection according to their own tastes. Adamovich writes:

> I recall that we all three unanimously rejected as wholly unsuitable Marina Tsvetayeva's poem, which was sent anonymously according to the terms of the competition ... Tsvetayeva, however, could not recover for a long time from her indignation, and even wrote a letter to the

editors of *The Link* demanding the incident be made public. It was
infamy, she said, a scandal, poems by various Petrovs, Sychevs, and
Chizhovs, were approved of, but Tsvetayeva – Tsvetayeva! was
rejected ... Moreover, the poem submitted by Tsvetayeva was, in fact,
weak and made little sense, despite all her customary forced energy,
with exclamation marks in almost every line.[11]

This poem 'Ancient Piety' ('Starinnoye blagogovenie') was
published in the first issue of *The Well-Intentioned*, with a
dedication to D.A. Shakhovskoy.

From the very beginning Marina did not have that success
among the Russian literary critics already established in Paris,
which she herself expected. Many years later Adamovich explained
why:

> ... In addition there was Marina Tsvetayeva, with whom there was a
> lack of affinity from the beginning. It is difficult to say with whom the
> fault lay. Tsvetayeva was a Muscovite, with a challenge to the
> Petersburg style in her every gesture and every word; it would have been
> impossible for us to tune our "note" to suit her, without distorting it.
> And who ever denied that there were some incomparable lines in
> Tsvetayeva's poetry? 'Like a certain cherubim ... ', without any
> exaggeration. But there was nothing to be learned from her. Tsvetayeva
> was without doubt very intelligent, however, she was too demonstra-
> tively intelligent, too intelligent after her own fashion, (which is almost a
> sign of weakness), and with continual "flights". There was in her the
> eternal *institutka* [public school girl]; Princess Dzhavakhva, with her
> 'head proudly thrown back', which, naturally, was 'light brown' or,
> better, 'golden', with her imagined crowd of young admirers around
> her; no this was not to our liking! There was apparently something else
> in her as well, something very sad; unfortunately this remained
> unknown to us.[12]

Bakhrakh, however, understood that the roots of all these
misunderstandings lay much deeper:

> We are all partially guilty for the fact that she, who was so helpless in
> life, was not given that minimal attention, which she merited more than
> others, and that the material precariousness of Tsvetayeva's family went
> at times to such extremes. And to this must be added still the dispiriting
> lack of understanding of her art, not only on the part of the large mass of
> readers, but also, more often than not, on that of the so-called "cultural
> élite" ... All the same, no matter what one says, a certain portion of the
> blame for the situation which arose falls on Tsvetayeva herself. She did
> not want to get on with, not only her readers, but also, which was worse
> for her, her editors and employers, stubbornly offering them material
> which was not according to their "standard", that is, not on the same
> level as their publications. She was opposed to any kind of compromise,
> and everything she did was carried out as some kind of challenge. To
> whom? In the first place, to herself, to her own destiny ... [13]

All of these attacks and misunderstandings, which were more or
less barbed, irritated Tsvetayeva a great deal. All her vexation is
reflected in one of her most intelligent and brilliant, but also
extremely malicious essays, 'A Poet About Criticism', written in
Paris at the beginning of 1926. She added to the concept of 'poet'
several remarkable definitions;

> ... A poet is first of all someone who has gone beyond the boundaries of
> the soul. A poet is *beyond* the soul, but not in the soul (the soul itself is –
> *beyond*!). Secondly, someone who has gone beyond the boundaries of the
> soul in the word. Thirdly, the 'soul of a poet', what kind of poet is he?
> Homer or Ronsard? Derzhavin or Pasternak...? The equality of gifts
> of soul and speech, this is a poet. Therefore there are no non-writing
> poets, nor non-feeling poets. You feel, but do not write – you are not a
> poet (where is the soul?). Where is the essence? Where is the form?
> They are identical. The inseparability of essence and form – that is a
> poet.

She also reflects on her own art:

> I obey something which I hear within me, continuously, but not evenly,
> at times giving directions, at times commanding. When giving direc-
> tions, I argue, when commanding, I obey.
> The commanding voice is a primary, immutable, and irreplaceable
> line, the *imminent essence of the poem*. (Most often it is the last two lines,
> towards which the rest later grow.) The voice giving directions is the
> aural path to the line: I hear a melody, I do not hear words. I have to
> seek for the words.

In her article Tsvetayeva wished to show that only poets, and not
literary critics, have the right to express their opinion about other
poets and their work. She saw this as an opportunity to settle
accounts with several well-known people she did not like, such as
Bunin, Zinaida Hippius (in whom she felt not simply the lack of
good will, but the presence of bad will), and even the old
benevolent Aikhenvald, who had regarded her so favourably ('rose
coloured water, dripping all over his articles...') She attacked
Adamovich most of all, appending to her essay a 'Flower-Bed'
composed of extracts from literary "chats" by Adamovich, which
showed how he would change his attitudes to various writers
depending simply on his moods. (Years later Gleb Struve
confirmed that Tsvetayeva was right about this.)[14]

But before 'A Poet About Criticism' was published in the second
issue of *The Well-Intentioned*, Tsvetayeva's first literary evening was
finally held on 6 February 1926. Gleb Struve managed to find a hall
at 79, rue Denfer. All the Russian newspapers announced the
forthcoming evening. It ended as a triumphant success. Marina
wore a black dress which Anna Tesková had sent from Prague; the

Chernov sisters altered it, and ornamented it with a butterfly, to symbolise Psyche. Before the packed auditorium Marina read some of her old poems, including *Swans' Encampment*. The audience and critics, which comprised *'le tout Paris littéraire russe'*, greeted her favourably. We can assume that not only Prince Svyatopolk-Mirsky, who had come from London, was present, but also Prince Shakhovskoy, from Brussels. From her letters to him, we can assume that Tsvetayeva had become acquainted with him in person at the beginning of February 1926.

The success of this literary evening was doubtless one of the reasons which influenced the Efron family to settle in France permanently. The second reason was Sergey Yakovlevich's enthusiasm for Paris, and the Paris based group the 'Eurasians', a political movement which arose in the 1920s and which sought the salvation of Russia in the rejection of the 'rotting' West in favour of the primitive traditions of the Asiatic tribes still untouched by Western influence. The 'Eurasians' by no means welcomed the Revolution, but were prepared to accept it out of patriotic and historical considerations. Efron threw himself with great zeal into the new movement; he and Svyatopolk-Mirsky began to work on the first issue of the new 'Eurasian' journal, in which they planned to print articles by Soviet authors along with those by émigrés. Here in Paris, as well, Sergey Yakovlevich apparently did not think it necessary to find some paid employment to relieve the financial situation of his family. But perhaps his poor health prevented him from doing this.

In May 1926 Mirsky invited Marina to London for two weeks, where he was teaching Russian at the School of Slavonic Studies at the University of London, and writing a history of Russian literature. Dmitry Petrovich loved good food very much and took Marina to the best restaurants in London, but without success; Marina was not interested in fine cuisine, and lived quite happily on the simplest food. The two weeks she spent in London were the first holiday she had had in eight years. Here she finally had time to put the finishing touches to her essay 'A Poet About Criticism', and to correspond with Shakhovskoy about its being printed in *The Well-Intentioned*.

Returning to Paris, Marina left rue Rouvet. On 24 April she moved with her children (along with Olga Chernova and her daughters) to Saint-Gilles-sur-Vie in the Vendée, for the whole summer. She could afford to do this with the proceeds from the literary evening. The choice of this place of residence also had sentimental reasons, as she explained to Tesková: 'All the same, I am glad that I am in the Vendée, which once produced such a magnificent explosion of *the will*.'

Aside from Olga Chernova and her daughters, Anna Andreyeva and her children also spent the summer in Saint-Gilles. The friends of the Andreyevs' sons often came from Paris; they included the young journalists and contributors to *Freedom of Russia*, Vladimir Sosinsky, and Daniil Reznikov. Subsequently, Vadim Andreyev married Olga; Daniil Reznikov, Natasha; and Vladimir Sosinsky, Adya Chernova. However, Marina Tsvetayeva's presence created a tension in this circle. In spite of the fact that Marina was a confidante of the young Valentin Andreyev, not so much with regard to romantic, as spiritual matters (as he later told Akhmatova in 1960)[15] and that the tie with V.B. Sosinsky was not broken until Marina's departure for Russia, the name of Olga Chernova disappears from her letters, or at least, from those letters which we know of at the present time.

As soon as Marina had settled in Saint-Gilles, a literary scandal broke out in Paris. Almost simultaneously, 'A Poet About Criticism' appeared in the second (and last) issue of *The Well-Intentioned* along with the first issue of the new 'Eurasian' journal *Milestones (Vyorsty)*, whose title page reads: 'under the editorship of Svyatopolk-Mirsky, S.Ya. Efron and P.P. Suvchinsky, in close consultation with A. Remizov, M. Tsvetayeva, and L. Shestov'. The name of the journal was clearly taken from Tsvetayeva's collection of poetry.

'A Poet About Criticism' exploded like a bombshell, and the new journal stirred up a storm of indignation. Its first issue contained Tsvetayeva's *Poem of the Mountain*, and new works by Remizov, Shestov, Nikolay Sergeyevich Trubetzkoy, Pasternak (his 'Potyomkin') and Artem Vesyoly. The publication was collaborating with Bolsheviks! The disturbance was universal and lasted a long time. P.B. Struve, who had never previously written on literary matters, called *Milestones* 'a disgusting superfluity'. Mikhail Osorgin, a writer and influential critic, decided to break completely with Tsvetayeva. Yuly Aikhenvald wrote to his nephew Slonim that he was deeply offended and did not understand why a writer he had esteemed so highly had attacked him so harshly.[16] Zinaida Hippius set in motion the complete register of her powers of intrigue in order to annihilate the 'gang of Shakhovskoy, and Svyatopolk-Mirsky, including Marinka'. From her letters to Vladislav Khodasevich it appears that Hippius was trying to organise a concentrated persecution of the editors of *The Well-Intentioned* and *Milestones*. Moreover, she did not even stop at putting into circulation insulting innuendoes touching on the honour of these people.[17]

During this time only one person remained silent; Georgy Adamovich. But he never forgave Tsvetayeva 'The Flower-Bed'. Later on he only spoke negatively of her, whenever he could. Apparently Adamovich suffered from his own kind of "Tsvetayeva complex".

All these stormy reactions, which she apparently did not expect, told very heavily on Marina. She described these attacks to Anna Tesková, and added: ' "Laissez-dire" is what is written above the door of one of the fisherman's houses here. This is what I shall say as well'.

But on 8 June she writes:

> Your letter was a great joy and support for me. The greatest rarity is a pure approach to a piece of writing – it and you, this is how you approached my 'A Poet About Criticism'. The article is *simply* written (this does not mean that I did not work on it – simplicity is not achieved immediately, complexity, (heaping up!) is easier) but is read with a bias . . . *There was not one voice of defence.* I am completely satisfied. But all this already belongs to the past. The present of a piece of writing is when you are writing it. That which has been written to the end – is past. The independent existence of a piece of writing beyond me – this is the goal and the result.[18]

All of this, indeed, was soon behind her. Even the fact that Dmitry Shakhovskoy abandoned (for a time) his literary career and departed for Mt Athos, where he became a monk, inspired in Tsvetayeva more sympathy than surprise. She wrote to Tesková: 'A pure heart is better than an editorship.'[19]

Her own heart at this time was far away: it was rushing between Moscow and Muzot in Switzerland. She had found a new friend, with whom she was corresponding. This time the person in question was of equal stature to her, he was Rainer Maria Rilke.

CHAPTER 20

Saint-Gilles-sur-Vie – Rilke

SUMMER 1926

At the beginning of April 1926 Boris Pasternak received two letters in Moscow, probably on the same day. The first was from Tsvetayeva and contained a copy of the *Poem of the End* in her own hand, and the second was from his father, Leonid Osipovich Pasternak, who was living in Munich. He was a friend of Rilke's and wrote to his son that Rilke had praised Boris ('... *Der junge Ruhm Ihres Sohnes Boris hat mich von mehr als einer Seite her angerührt...* ')

Hitherto Pasternak had known and loved Rilke as a poet only from a distance. The idea of entering into correspondence with him never would have occurred to him. Now, however, on 12 April 1926 he sat down and wrote a long letter to Rilke in German, of which he had perfect mastery.

> Great and beloved Poet!
> I do not know where this letter might end and how it could be distinguished from life itself, were I to give full expression to my feelings of love, admiration and gratitude, which I have experienced for the past twenty years. I am indebted to you for the fundamental traits of my character, for the direction of my spiritual being. They are your creation ... The magical accident which brought me to your attention has profoundly shaken me ...

He continues:

> On the same day that I had news of you, I also received by the roundabout means in use here, a poem written so sincerely and truly, as none of us here in the USSR would be able to write today. This was the second shock of the day. The poetess is Marina Tsvetayeva, a born poet, a great talent of the calibre of Desbordes-Valmore. She lives as an émigrée in Paris. I would like, oh please forgive this audacity and apparent presumptuousness, I would wish, I would dare to wish, that she might, on her part, experience something of the joy which I felt,

> thanks to you. I can imagine what one of your books, such as perhaps the *Duino Elegies* (whose name I know only by hearsay) would mean to her, with an inscription from you...

He also asked Rilke to send him, as well, a copy of the *Duino Elegies*, to Tsvetayeva's address: '...one never knows about things posted from Switzerland'.[1]

Rilke immediately responded to this letter. He sent Marina copies of the *Duino Elegies* and the *Sonnets to Orpheus*, and included a short note:

> ...I am so overwhelmed by the depth and force of his words that I cannot say anymore today: however, please send the enclosed note to our friend in Moscow. As a greeting.[2]

This 'enclosed note' consisted of a few words of thanks and the assurance that he had fulfilled Pasternak's request:

> ...The *Elegies* and the *Sonnets to Orpheus* are already in the hands of the poetess. You should receive copies of the same books in the near future...

Marina received Rilke's parcel and letter on 7 May in Saint-Gilles. For her this was a 'strike at the heart'. She forwarded the lines written by Rilke to Pasternak, and added as a postscript only the phrase which Rilke had used in his letter to her: 'I am so overwhelmed by the depth and force of his words...'

Marina now sat at her table and also wrote to Rilke a long letter in German, in which she confessed her love for his poetry. She calculated approximately when he might receive this letter and post-dated it 9 May. To her great joy she received a reply dated 10 May:

> Marina Tsvetayeva, were you not just here? Or: *where* was *I*? It is still the tenth of May...[Marina Zwetajewa, sind Sie nicht noch eben hier gewesen? Oder: *wo* war *ich*? Es ist mir immer noch zehnter May...]

Marina probably received this letter on 12 May, and on the same day replied to it and mailed it by the next post. Rilke answered just as promptly, on the seventeenth. In this letter he tells her about his life, and his solitude, and remarks that he was not able to understand Tsvetayeva's poetry as his knowledge of Russian was not sufficient. From Rilke's letters one can conclude that he generally understood Tsvetayeva as a person, and a poet, but perhaps he over-estimated her sensitivity and her ability to understand the reality of his situation. Behind Rilke's suggestion that she could always write to him when she wished, regardless of his delays in replying, Marina apparently failed to perceive the exhaustion of a mortally ill man.

At the same time Pasternak, who had promoted this acquaintance, was waiting for Rilke's reply in Moscow and was reading over
and over again the *Poem of the End.* He was delighted at finding a
'kindred soul' in Tsvetayeva. What was now happening to him was
what had often happened to Tsvetayeva; he was falling in love with
a phantom, who seemed to be very far removed from the tedium of
his domestic life in Moscow, from the over-crowded flat and his
sick child.

He wrote to her in a rather confused state on 20 April 1926:

> I began to write five letters to you today . . . Do not destroy me, I want to
> live with you, for a long, long time . . . I will put a question to you today,
> without any explanations on *my* part, because I believe in *your* reasons,
> which you must have . . . You must answer it, as you have never
> answered anyone, – as to you yourself. *Shall I come to you now or a year
> from now?* This indecision on my part is not *foolish*, I have very good
> reasons to be uncertain about the timing . . .³

Suddenly, instead of a reply to this question, the brief message
from Rilke arrived. As Pasternak had failed to reckon properly with
the delay caused by the 'roundabout means', which meant Marina
could not have even received his last letter yet, he only noticed that
the postscript written by the beloved hand did not contain a single
word addressed to him. It is not surprising that Pasternak was
offended and felt that Rilke and Tsvetayeva were neglecting him.

> Before this there were three which were not sent. This is like an illness.
> This must be suppressed. Yesterday I received your copy of his words:
> your absence, the palpable *silence* of your hand. I never knew that such a
> beloved hand could conduct such funeral music. I do not remember in
> my life ever feeling such anguish as I did yesterday . . .⁴

And again on 23 May:

> I am not writing to Rilke at the moment. I do not love him any less than
> you, and it makes me sad that you do not see this. Why did it not occur
> to you to write about how he inscribed his books to you, and in general
> how it all happened, and perhaps something from his letters. (Indeed,
> you stood at the centre of the explosion, and suddenly, you are on the
> side.)⁵

During this time Pasternak was concentrating on his 'Lieutenant
Schmidt'. In his letter to Tsvetayeva he included his poem 'A
Dedication', whose initial letters of each line form the acrostic '(to)
Marina Tsvetayeva'.

Tsvetayeva knew nothing about the feelings which her letters to
Pasternak had inspired. On 23 May she wrote to him from Saint-
Gilles and enclosed copies of her first two letters from Rilke. Not
suspecting anything, she told him about her stay by the sea, and

then adds:

> I am not writing to Rilke. It is too great a torment. And fruitless. The rising 'Nibelungenhort' confuses me and unsettles my poetry; do you think it is easy to manage this?! He does not need this. And it hurts me. I am not less than he (in the future), but I am younger than he. Many lifetimes younger. The depth of the bow is a measure of the height. He has bowed very deeply to me, perhaps deeper, *than* ... (it is not important) – and what have I felt? His *stature*, I knew it even before, but now I know it towering *over me*. I wrote to him: 'I will not diminish myself, that will not make you greater (or me smaller!), it would only make you *more lonely*, for on the island *where we were born*, we are all alike.

She added in German:

> *Durch alle Welten, durch alle Gedenken, an allen Weg-Enden,*
> *Das ewige Paar der Sich-nie-Begegnenden.*[6]

On 25 May Tsvetayeva received Pasternak's letter of 19 May. She hastened to clarify matters with him:

> Boris, you did not understand me. I love your name so much, that for me not to write it an extra time, in sending Rilke's letter, was a real deprivation, a renunciation. The same as not calling out of a window a last time when someone has gone away (when everything for the next ten minutes has departed with that person, and there is only the room from which it seems even you have departed, where only longing remains). Boris, I did this deliberately, in order not to diminish the blow of joy from Rilke. Not to break it in two. Not to mix two liquids. Not to turn *your event* into an occasion for myself. Not to do something beneath me. To have the wisdom to do this.

She digresses from this theme and philosophises about Orpheus and Eurydice and remarks on her hatred of the sea. She then continues:

> About Rilke. I have already written to you about him, (I am not writing to him). I am experiencing the peace of the total loss of the divine countenance, of *renunciation*. It came of itself. I suddenly realised it. And now to put an end to the matter of my absence in the letter (I wanted so much to be *obviously*, truly absent.) Boris, it was the simple politeness of not entirely, or entirely, simple things. That is all.[7]

Marina did not, however, hold out for long: on 3 June she wrote to Rilke again. She explained to him why she had kept silent:

> There is a phrase in your letter ' ... In case I should suddenly fall silent, this should not prevent you from writing to me as often as ... '
>   The way I read it; this phrase implores for rest. And rest has come. (Are you a little rested now?)
>   My love for you was divided up into days and letters, hours and lines. Hence the unrest. (Hence your request for rest!) A letter today, a letter tomorrow. You are alive, I wish to see you. A transplantation from the

always to the now. Hence the pain, the counting of days ... To *be* in the other person, or to *have* the other person (or to want to have, or to *want* in general, are all one!) When I realised this I fell silent ... [8]

And further on 14 June:

Listen Rainer, from the beginning so that you will know. I am wicked. Boris is good. And I was silent because of my wickedness ...

I am a multitude of people, do you understand? Countless, perhaps! (An insatiable legion!) No one should know of the others, that would upset everything ... When I am with you – there should be exclusiveness and isolation. Not only around me, but even within me, I do not want to have any witness. Which is why, in life, I am given to lying (that is to say, given to silence, and, if I am forced to speak, to lying), although in another life, I pass for being truthful, and so I am. I cannot share ... My whole life thus passes in a false situation. 'For where I am bent, there I am made false.' Made *false*, Rainer, not given to falsehoods! [9]

Rilke answered the first letter immediately. On 8 June he wrote from Muzot about the poor state of his health. And then:

I wrote today a long poem for you, sitting on a warm (though unfortunately, still not thoroughly warmed through) wall between the hills of the vineyards mesmerising the lizards with its prelude ... [10]

This poem is the famous 'Elegie für Marina Zwetajewa-Efron', which was known to publishers of Rilke's complete works only through fragments.

Oh, those losses to space, Marina, the plummeting stars!
We do not eke it out, wherever we rush to accrue
To which star! In the sum, all has been ever forereckoned.
Nor does he who falls diminish the sanctified number.

[*ll.*1-4]

Did Rilke sense with his fine poetic intuition Marina's recurring desire and aspiration 'to pass without leaving a trace'?

(Oh, how I grasp you, she-blossom grown on the same
Unwithering stock ...)

[*ll.*43-44]

answers Rilke, but he also provides a warning:

.... You know it, how often
A blind decree would bear us across that glacial forecourt
Of a rebirth ....

[*ll.*29-31]

Those who love, Marina, they ought not, they must not
Know so much of perdition. Must be as new.
Old is at most their grave, only their grave remembers ... [11]

[*ll.*35-37]

Here, finally, these two people met, who could understand each other and speak the same language: the mortally ill, lonely, homeless Austrian, and the equally homeless Russian, who had been thrown mercilessly into the torrent of life.

> Yes, that 'Dichterin' about whom Rilke writes to Pasternak, is me. I was his last *Russian* joy, his last Russia and friendship.[12]

On 2 July Marina received a new gift from Rilke, his volume of poems written in French, *Vergers*, with the inscription; 'À Marina Zwetajewa-Efron':

> Marina: voici galets et coquillages
> ramassés récemment à la française plage
> de mon étrange coeur... (J'aimerais que tu connusses
> toutes les étendues de son divers paysage
> depuis sa côte bleue jusqu'à ses plaines russes.)
>
> Fin de Juin, 1926, Muzot

On 2 August Marina acknowledged a further letter from Rilke:

> Rainer, I received your letter on my name-day 17/30 July, for I also have a patron saint, although I feel that I am the first person to bear my name...
>
> Rainer, if I want to go to you, it is also because of my new self, which can only arise with you, in you. And then, Rainer, ... do not be angry, it is only *me*, I want to sleep with you, fall asleep with you, fall asleep and sleep. The splendid folk expression, how deep, how true, how unambiguous, how precisely what it says. Simply, to sleep. And nothing further...[13]

As there was no reply to this letter, she wrote another on 14 August.

> Dear friend,
> Did you receive my last letter? I am asking you, because I threw it into a departing (mail) train...
>
> Rainer, this winter we must meet, somewhere in the French Savoy, close to Switzerland, somewhere you have never been...Or in the autumn, Rainer, or in the spring. Say yes, so that I will have a great joy from today onwards...[14]

This letter was followed by Rilke's cry: 'In spring? I am afraid! sooner! sooner!' (*'Im Frühling? Mir ist bang! Eher! Eher!'*)[15]

After this, however, Rilke fell completely silent, and did not even acknowledge a note written in Bellevue on 7 November, which consisted of one line: 'Dear Rainer! This is where I am living, do you still love me?' (*'Lieber Rainer! Hier leb ich. Ob Du mich noch liebst?'*)[16]

In the meantime, in Moscow, Pasternak was waiting for a reply. Marina's silence relating to her friendship with Rilke, and her refusal of his offer to go and see her must have acted like a cold shower. Tsvetayeva wrote on 10 July:

> I could not live with you, not because of a lack of understanding, but because of too much understanding. To suffer on account of another person's righteousness, which is at the same time one's own, to suffer for righteousness at all is a degradation I will not endure.
>
> To this day I have suffered because of unrighteousness, I alone was right, and even if I came across similar words (rarely) and gestures (more often), then the motive was always different... Meeting you, I would meet myself, with all the points turning against me...

She concluded that life together would be possible only in the other world.

> Boris, Boris, how happy we would be together, in Moscow, and in Weimar, and in Prague, both in this world and especially in the next, which is already *entirely within us*. Your eternal departures (as I see it) and your eyes which would gaze up from the floor. Your *life* in correspondence with all the streets of the world and the return to me at home... We would get along fine.[17]

A few years later, Marina mentioned this episode to Anna Tesková.

> In the summer of '26, having read somewhere my 'Poem of the End' B. wanted to rush to me, to come here. I *replied* that I did not want an *all round* catastrophe...[18]

But neither Rilke, nor Pasternak, nor the bright young people at Saint-Gilles could distract Marina from her work; even her son, who was just beginning to walk, could not do this. She wrote for Pasternak a poem with the title 'From the Sea', which describes a meeting in a dream.

Immediately following upon this she wrote another long poem *Attempt at a Room* (*Popytka komnaty*). Again it concerns a meeting in a dream. This time the attempt is to create a 'dream-room' in which the concepts of time and space do not exist. She wanted to meet Pasternak there, but this poem unexpectedly took on a life of its own, and turned from Pasternak to Rilke:

> A very important piece of information Boris, about which I wanted to speak. The poem about you and me (the beginning of it...) turned out to be a poem about him and me, *each line*. A curious substitution took place, the poem was written during the days of my most extreme concentration on him, but was directed consciously and deliberately towards you. It has turned out to be now (after 29 December) [Rilke's death], not about him as such! – but an anticipation, i.e. a premonition about him. I simply told him, the living man, whom I *was not intending to see!* why we had never met, and how we had met *in another way*. Hence the strange lack of love, which saddened me at the time, the alienation, the *renunciation* of every line. The poem is called 'Attempt at a Room', and every line, yes, every line I renounced...[19]

In Saint-Gilles Tsvetayeva also finished the poem 'The Stair-case' ('Poema lestnitsy') in which she describes a house in a poor district of Paris and the Russian émigrés living there. It is a protest against poverty and injustice, which is somewhat contrary to the general mood of this summer. She worked further on this theme, however, in order to stifle her omnipresent attachment to Rilke.[20]

This poem, however, did not give her as much trouble as the continuation of the trilogy she had begun about Theseus. After a lengthy and voluminous exchange of letters with Sosinsky and Tesková, Marina finally obtained her copy of the classical legends compiled by Gustav Schwab. Marina worked on the second part of *Phaedra* during the summer and up till the end of the year, when she received the news of Rilke's death. At this time two scenes were completed.

Financial difficulties, however, continued to pursue her in the Vendée as well. An unpleasant letter had arrived from Prague, which caused a great deal to trouble: Marina was requested to return without delay to Czechoslovakia, or renounce her stipend from the Czech government. Since Sergey Yakovlevich would not consider leaving Paris and his work for *Milestones*, they had to think of other possibilities. The house in Saint-Gilles was rented until 1 October, but Marina proposed to return to Prague on 15 September, and asked Tesková to find her a flat. Meanwhile, with the help of friends, among them probably Tesková, she managed to have the stipend continued for another year.

The trip to Prague remained only a fine dream. On 24 September Marina informed Tesková that a flat with a garden had been leased to her in Meudon, but their move was being delayed.

For the time being the Efron family settled in Bellevue (near Paris) at 31, boulevard Verdun, in a flat which, again, they had to share with another family. The difficulties of this year differed little from those of the previous. Sergey Yakovlevich was hardly to be seen; Alya started to take lessons from an old French lady, who died a few weeks later, and Marina was strained to breaking-point with housework, looking after Mur, writing *Phaedra* and continuous anxiety about Rilke, who had now fallen completely silent. In addition she had a further quarrel with the leading émigré journal:

> I have completely broken with *Contemporary Annals*; they would like poems by the *former* Marina Tsvetayeva, that is, of 1916. I recently had a letter from one of the editors: 'You, a poet by the grace of God, are either consciously disfiguring yourself, or are fooling the public.' I shall

keep this letter. It is the height of impertinence. Its author is *Rudnev*, the former mayor of Moscow.[21]

On the last day of 1926, a guest appeared at Bellevue who had not been seen for a long time; it was Slonim on his way back from America. He broke the news of Rilke's death to Marina 'very carefully', as he himself says, because he knew 'how much she idolised him'.

> M.I. was very upset and said: 'I never saw him, and now I never will'. Before I left, I asked whether M.I. and Sergey Yakovlevich wanted to celebrate the New Year with some of our friends in common, together with some colleagues from *Freedom of Russia*. I had at that time a great personal sorrow of my own and I could not think of any kind of festivities or restaurants, it was a question of a quiet evening among friends. Sergey Yakovlevich, as always, waited for M.I. to decide; she declined the invitation, but agreed to write, at my request, about Rilke for *Freedom of Russia*. Within a short time she sent me in Prague her essay 'Your Death'. This prose piece was published in our journal in March 1927.[22]

On this New Year's Eve, Marina stayed at home. She wrote a short letter to Pasternak telling him of Rilke's death:

> Boris, Rainer Maria Rilke has died. I do not know the date, perhaps three days ago. People came to invite us to a New Year's party and at the same time they told me.
> His last letter to me (6 September) ends with the cry: 'Im Frühling? Mir ist bang! Eher! Eher!' (We had spoken of a meeting.) He did not answer my reply, then, I sent him a letter of one line from Bellevue:
> 'Rainer, was ist's? Rainer, liebst Du mich noch? . . .
> Will we ever see each other? Greetings with *his* new era, Boris![23]

Following this she wrote Pasternak a second letter, and enclosed a copy of a letter of New Year's greetings to Rilke, written in German. This was later re-worked in Russian in poetic form and is known as the *New Year Letter* (*Novogodneye*), or the 'Letter to Rilke'. In it she describes how she learnt of his death:

> Shall I tell you how I learned of yours?
> There was no earthquake, no abyss's yawn.
> Someone walked in – not loved, just anyone.
> 'It's an event that's causing great distress.
> In *News* and *Days*. I hope you'll do a piece?'
> 'Where?' 'In the mountains.' (Window, fronds of firs,
> A bedsheet.) 'Don't you read the newspapers?
> You'll do one, then?' 'No.' 'But . . .' I make excuses.
> Aloud: 'Too hard.' Inside: 'I'm not a Judas!'
> 'In a sanatorium.' (A rented paradise).
> 'When?' 'One, two days ago. My memory's not precise.'

'Will you talk in Alcazar?' 'No, I think not.'
Aloud: 'His family.' Inside: 'All, but Iscariot.'[24]

[*ll.*12-25, translated by David McDuff]

'In the full heat of her letter to him' Tsvetayeva received a letter
from Rilke's last secretary, a young Russian woman, Yevgenia
Chernosvitova, about his death. In reply Marina wrote:

> ...I am *living for* this 'Letter' of 31 December, for which I have
> abandoned *Phaedra*...Its openness still inhibits me. An open letter
> from me to him...A letter, which will be read by *everyone*, but
> him...Do you want to know one truth about poetry? Each line means
> collaboration with 'higher forces', and a poet is already a great deal, if a
> secretary! (Have you thought, by the way, about what a splendid word
> this is: secretary – secret?) Rilke's rôle has changed only in so far as,
> while he was alive he collaborated with the 'higher forces', and now, he
> is one himself.[25]

Her piece of 'lyrical prose', 'Your Death' ('Tvoya smert'')
followed the *New Year Letter*. Into this work Marina weaves the
deaths of Rilke, Alya's teacher, and that of a young Russian boy she
knew. In 1929 Tsvetayeva returned to Rilke, with the publication in
Freedom of Russia of 'A Few Letters of Rainer Maria Rilke'. Since
the time he died she felt that he was her possession, that there were
now no language barriers between them, and that eternity belonged
to them both.

The Efrons were becoming increasingly impoverished; they
could only afford the cheapest horse meat for dinner, and many
émigrés of the Russian colony were avoiding them. Marina had
found in Rilke, however, something of a defender and protector.
Rilke dead, she could never see him, and could thus never be
disillusioned with him. He now belonged to her and became her
private property, her 'Nibelungenhort', a fortress in which she
could take refuge when reality became too grim.

CHAPTER 21

Meudon – Pontaillac – 'After Russia'
1927 – 1928

One of the legends which surrounds Marina Tsvetayeva, and which she herself often helped to create, states that no one among the émigrés was capable of understanding and appreciating the great writer, and that loved by no one she vegetated in isolation, alone with her notebook, which was her only means of communication with the outside world. Even Ariadna Efron, however, subjected this legend to careful criticism. In 1969 she wrote:

> Contrary to the legend which has been created, identifying Tsvetayeva's *creative* solitude, which was caused by the lack of acceptance of her non-canonical art on the part of her émigré contemporaries, with her *human* solitude, which is treated as some kind of inborn condition, Marina Tsvetayeva was an open, sociable person, who responded to any voice which called to her, and who did not merely reach out to people, but rushed to them . . . [1]

It goes without saying that many of the literary figures and writers in Paris did not understand Tsvetayeva, and attacked her; but there were also others who appreciated and helped her, and who were friendly with her in a completely natural way. Tsvetayeva's letters of 1926 and 1927 to Lev Shestov, for instance, clearly reveal that not everyone was against her.[2]

Even more convincing proof of this is the fact that several Russian émigrés leased a flat for the Efrons, paid the rent and furnished it. We know that Prince D.P. Svyatopolk-Mirsky, Salomea Halpern-Andronikova, Ye.A. Izvolskaya, and others, belonged to this circle. The flat was in Meudon, at no.2, avenue Jeanne d'Arc, several minutes' walk from the forest. It consisted of three rooms with gas heating, a kitchen and bathroom, and was located in the heart of the 'Russian quarter' of Meudon. The hero

of the *Poem of the End* lived very close by with his wife, Muna
Bulgakova, Marina's friend from her days in Czechoslovakia.

> We see each other constantly, between us there is a friendly good
> humour and equability, we go to the cinema together and buy gifts, I for
> my family, she for him. I threw the key to his heart off one of the bridges
> in Prague, and it rests with the 'treasures of Libusha' on the bottom of
> the Vltava – or perhaps – of Lethe.[3]

Yelena Aleksandrovna Izvolskaya, the daughter of the former
Russian minister of foreign affairs, who earned her living by
translating, met Tsvetayeva at an evening of the 'Eurasians'. They
immediately took a liking to each other. Before this evening
Izvolskaya had known Marina only from photographs.

> For me, Marina did not resemble her portrait in *Milestones*, because in
> the photograph she is too "pretty", with a round face, elegant clothes
> and her hair done. The person I saw that evening was neither elegant,
> nor pretty; she was thin, pale, almost wasted. The oval of her face was
> narrow, severe; her short hair was still light, but already strands of grey
> were showing. Her eyes were lowered. Altogether, she was not pretty,
> but *icon-like*. However, despite a certain reserve, she quickly entered
> into the spirit of our evening party, and took part in the conversation. I
> would like to emphasise here that Marina was not at all as "uncivilised",
> "isolated" and "unsociable" as she is now often depicted, and as she too
> liked to portray herself. At least *on the surface* she did not avoid people,
> but was even very eager to meet them, and was interested in them. She
> had a great sensitivity to people, and sincerely wanted to associate with
> them, but did not know how, or could not, perhaps, bring herself to do
> this . . . [4]

Yelena Izvolskaya lived with her mother not far from the Efrons
in a house occupied almost entirely by émigrés (it is described in
the essay 'History of a Dedication'). Marina often visited here and
would read 'Swans' Encampment' or 'The Swain' to its occupants,
depending on their political convictions. She was loved by everyone
there, and her visits were returned. Yelena Izvolskaya writes:

> We often visited Marina. She was always glad to see us and carried on
> endless conversations with us, about poetry, art, music, nature. I have
> never met a more brilliant conversationalist. We would drop in on her
> and she would give us tea or wine. And on feast days she would spoil us,
> with *bliny* before Lent, and with *paskha* and *kulich* after the Easter
> matins service. We would go with her to the small church at Meudon of
> St John the Warrior, which was very modest but beautifully painted.
> Marina rarely spoke about religion, but observed the rites of the Church
> simply and sincerely. The matins service in Meudon was somehow a
> continuation of the Easter Night in Moscow . . . [5]

The basic dilemma, however, continued to exist: Marina had no
time to write. The hours before dinner had to be devoted to

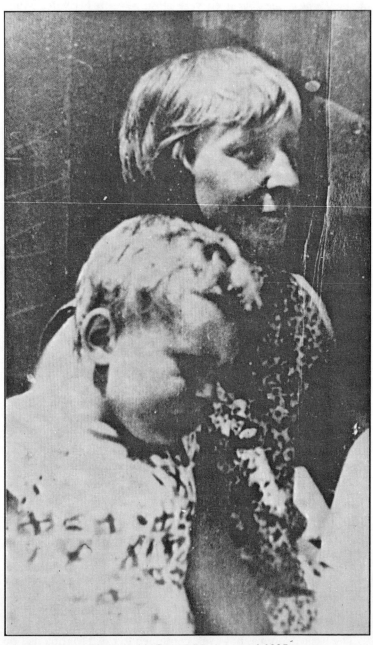

Marina with Georgy (Mur), around 1927

housework, and to looking after Mur. Friends would often drop in, so that by the evening her mind was empty. She found it impossible to catch up with her lost thoughts and feelings. Marina wrote to Tesková:

> It is not my mind, but my soul, which has grown dull after all these years and years (1917-1927). A surprising observation: it is for feelings that one needs time, and not for thoughts. Thought is a flash of lightning, feeling is a ray of light from a distant star. Feeling requires leisure, it does not live under fear. A simple example: rolling 1½ kilos of small fish in flour, I can think, but feel – no: the smell of the fish prevents this! The smell prevents this, my sticky hands prevent this, the spattering oil prevents this, the *fish* prevents this: each individually, and the whole 1½ kilos together. Feeling, evidently, is more demanding than thought. Everything, or nothing. I cannot give my feelings anything: neither time, nor quiet, nor solitude: I am *always* with people (from 7 in the morning until 10 at night, and around 10 o'clock I am so tired that – well, what is there to feel!) Feeling demands *strength*![6]

The persecution of *Milestones* continued as well:

> With rare exceptions, they hate me in Paris. They write every sort of rubbish, and imply every sort of thing etc. Hatred towards my absent presence, for I am *never* to be seen at social gatherings, and do not respond *in any way to anything.* The press (newspapers) make up their own stories. Participation in *Milestones*, a Eurasian husband, and finally, in the end, they say I write 'Komsomol' poems and that I am being kept by the Bolsheviks. Schwamm (und Schlamm!) drüber![7]

And further:

> Have you read the badgering of the Eurasians in *The Renaissance, Russia, Days*? 'Precise information' that the Eurasians have received *enormous sums* from the Bolsheviks. Naturally, there is no proof of this (for there cannot be any!), those who write know the emigration. Any day now the denials should begin, how ever vile it is to have anything to do with known liars, it is necessary. I am removed from all this, but my political passivity is also shaken. It is the same as accusing *me* of receiving Bolshevik sums! It is just as sensible and plausible. S.Ya., naturally, is upset and has lost his last vestige of strength over this affair. His earnings: for working as an extra at the film studio from 5.30 a.m. to 7-8 p.m. he receives 40 francs a day, of which 5 fr. go for transport and 7 fr. go for lunch; leaving 28 fr. a day. And such days amount to a great deal if there are two in a week. These then are the Bolshevik sums![8]

No, at that time there was certainly no Bolshevik money in the Efron household. Yelena Izvolskaya describes their situation thus:

> Before our eyes Marina Tsvetayeva wrote, and before our eyes, alas! she worked beyond her strength, grew poorer and often went hungry. Russian Paris realised the full tragedy of her position, after all, can one possibly earn a "living wage" on poetry and belles-lettres? But she had no other "profession", and she could not have any other. A 'Society to

help Marina Tsvetayeva' was created, which somehow paid for the flat and the family's rations. The heart is not a stone, but how is the heart any better than a stone? I had rarely seen *such* poverty in the Russian emigration. We, her neighbours in Meudon, shared her troubles, all the more so, as we were constantly with her. We helped her out as we could, but she, on her part, gave *so much*, that there was nothing, absolutely nothing, we could repay her with.[9]

Until recently it was not known who was the Maecenas who published at his own expense Marina's last volume of poetry, *After Russia*. The preparatory work for this edition lasted the whole of the summer of 1927.

I am publishing this as my last volume of lyric poetry, I know it is the last. Without sorrow. That which you can, you must not do. And that is it. In that sphere I can do everything. Lyric poetry (I must laugh here, as though *epic poems* were not lyric verse! But let us agree that lyric refers to short poems) has served as my faith and truth, saving me, rescuing me and guiding each hour, according to its own, and my own, intentions. I am tired of being torn up and divided into pieces like Osiris. Every volume of poetry is a book of leave-takings and sunderings, with the finger of Thomas in the wound between one line and another. Who of us could draw the last line, however, without a sinking feeling in the heart: and what next?[10]

Tsvetayeva's main work for 1927 was the *Poem of the Air* (*Poema vozdukha*), which was inspired by Lindberg's trans-Atlantic flight of 20-21 May. The theme of this fairly long poem is essentially the same as those of the previous year: she again speaks of an encounter in a dream, which this time takes place in the air. Again her interlocutor is apparently Rilke. Marina says in a letter to Pasternak: 'This is the driest thing I have ever written, or ever will write ... '

In 1927 Tsvetayeva not only published her new volume of poetry, but also set to work on her next composition. As Gleb Struve maintains, this year saw the beginning of the flowering of Russian émigré literature. Bunin, Zaitsev, Shmelyov, Remizov, Berdyayev, Merezhkovsky, Aldanov, Kuprin, Khodasevich and Osorgin, all wrote, or published, at this time their best work. To this group of older literary figures were added the members of the younger generation who were beginning to write, such as Vladimir Nabokov, Boris Poplavsky, Nina Berberova, Vladimir Varshavsky and a whole circle of young poets. In the evenings, after a day of exhausting work, they would meet in the cafés of Montparnasse, and, despite their hunger, would philosophise. Members of both generations visited the Merezhkovskys at their flat on Sunday afternoons, and attended the meetings of their society 'The Green Lamp'.

In his interesting book V.S. Varshavsky turns his attention to the inner spiritual state of this younger 'unnoticed generation',[11] made up of twenty-five to thirty-year-old 'veterans' of the Civil War, and the sons of émigrés. Their position was still more difficult than that of the older men of letters, who had managed to create names for themselves while in Russia, and whose works were still published by various presses, even if rather sporadically. But no one took an interest in the young writers. They went hungry far more often than the older generation, and suffered a great deal from loneliness and a passionate love for the Russia which was no more. In the 1930s their work began to appear, for the most part, in the journal *Numbers* (*Chisla*), where Adamovich was their protector and patron.

At the end of the twenties, during this flowering of Russian émigré literature, a bitter argument arose between Adamovich, Khodasevich and Slonim about the meaning, necessity and even the very possibility of this literature beyond the borders of Russia. They were all more or less of the same pessimistic opinion: it was unnecessary and impossible. As Russia, as such, had ceased to exist these authors had no more readers, and it was assumed that a Russian author would not be able to work outside Russia. One can find echoes of this argument in Tsvetayeva's work as well. The idea that the time might come when readers in Russia itself would take an interest in the literature of the émigrés did not even occur to them: the feeling that they had "brought" Russia away with them, and that nothing remained behind, was too strong.

In September 1927 Marina Tsvetayeva had an unexpected guest: her sister Asya arrived from Italy. At this time she was working in Moscow at the Museum of Fine Arts (which had been created by her father), and was planning to write a book about Maksim Gorky, who was then living in Sorrento. At the beginning of 1927 she wrote to him and Gorky invited her to Italy for a month. He also invited Marina, suggesting that the sisters could meet, if they wished, at his home. Anastasia Ivanovna, however, preferred to make the trip to Paris, instead.

Anastasia has described in detail her stay in Paris. She was delighted by Alya and Mur, and the flat made a great impression on her. But it seemed to her that Marina was exhausted and had aged. She noted that she treated her son more gently than she had Alya, and that she was less energetic and vivacious than she had been living in the chaos and ruins of her old flat in Moscow.

In the evening Marina reclined on her small divan, where she also slept (in her room I remember only her divan, her writing-table and books), and said, with tears in her eyes, blowing away cigarette smoke, 'You understand: how can I write when I must go to the market in the morning, buy food, choose it, making sure I have enough money, we of course buy the cheapest provisions, and thus, having found everything, I drag myself home with my bag, knowing that the morning is lost. After this I will have to clean and cook (during this time Alya has been walking with Mur), and when everyone is fed, everything clean, I lie down, just like this, completely empty, not a line written! But in the morning I am dying to be at my writing-table, and this happens day after day ... [12]

Asya tracked down in Paris her former school-friend from Moscow, Galya Dali (at that time still married to Paul Éluard), and met Ilya Ehrenburg, who was working in Paris as a correspondent for a Soviet newspaper. Nothing on earth could persuade Marina to accompany her sister on this visit, and she got out of it on the pretext that she was frightened by the terrible traffic on the streets of Paris. There is no record of whether Asya saw any of her other old friends from Moscow; and it also remains uncertain whether Sergey Efron met one of his former Moscow school-friends, Marcel Orbec, when he was in Paris.

It turned out that Asya's presence was particularly welcome; soon after her arrival Mur fell ill with scarlet fever, and after him Marina and Alya. For a few days Marina's life was in danger, but her strong constitution held out. She got up for the first time on the day of Asya's departure. Seryozha took her to the station where Rodzevich found them just as her train started to leave. He handed Asya a farewell letter from Marina. Did the two sisters feel then that this was in fact their last parting?

We saw each other for the last time when she was thirty-five and I was thirty-three. We corresponded for almost another ten years. Later on life was to separate us for ever. [13]

Asya's trip to Gorky in Italy had its consequences in Moscow. Pasternak was apparently so horrified by her stories about Marina's life as an émigré that he decided to do everything he could to facilitate her return to Russia. When Gorky thanked him for the copy of his book *The Childhood of Luvers*, Pasternak brought Marina Tsvetayeva's plight to the attention of the famous writer, who was now living in the USSR.

Amidst that complex web of faces and facts, which you touched on with such magnanimity this summer, particularly important and close to me is the tremendous talent of Marina Tsvetayeva and her unfortunate tangled fate ... If you asked what I am planning to *write* or do, I would answer: everything that is required that can help her, and that will support and return to Russia this great person, who perhaps, does not know how to align her talent with her destiny, or, rather, the reverse.

Gorky answered completely ungraciously:

> It is difficult for me to agree with your high estimation of Marina Tsvetayeva's gift ... Her talent seems to me clamorous, even hysterical; she has a poor mastery of the word, but, instead is mastered, like A. Bely, by the word. She has a poor knowledge of the Russian language, and handles it in an inhuman fashion, distorting it in every possible way. Phoenetics is not yet music, but she thinks: it is music already. M. Tsvetayeva should, of course, return to Russia, but this is hardly possible.[14]

After this letter relations between Gorky and Pasternak ceased for a long time.

Following the recovery of her health and Asya's departure, Marina's longing to see Anna Tesková and Prague again grew immensely. In her memory the years spent in Czechoslovakia, of which the 'Knight of Prague' was the symbol, became more and more splendid. Marina wrote to Tesková:

> (*How I would like to go to Prague!* – Will it happen? Even if *not*, say: yes!) I have never wanted in my life to return to any city, *I do not at all want to go to Moscow* (anywhere in Russia, *but* there!) but I want to go to Prague, evidently transfixed and bewitched. I want to return to *that* self of mine, the unhappy-happy self of the Poem of the End and of the Mountain, that self, that soul without a body, of all those bridges and places ...[15]

The wise Tesková, however, understood that Marina was not seeking the reality of her Prague life, but her dream of it. Slonim, who now often lived in Paris, recalled:

> Every time I was in Czechoslovakia I spoke with M.I.'s loyal friend, Anna Tesková, to whom she wrote repeatedly about this, but we both clearly understood all the difficulty, or rather, the impossibility, of such an undertaking. I had the impression that the intelligent and sensible Tesková, knowing M.I.'s talent for creating myths and believing in them, was afraid that a trip to Prague would bring M.I. not joy, but disillusionment.[16]

Tsvetayeva had to write many letters and to ask many people in order to find subscribers for her new volume of poetry, *After Russia*. Leonid Pasternak found three subscribers in Berlin, but in general it seems no one was particularly interested in the book. When it finally appeared, it did not inspire anything resembling that enthusiasm which the first volumes of Tsvetayeva's poetry had produced. The critics were either silent, or rejected *After Russia*. Only Slonim found encouraging words to say about it. At the end of the fifties one could still find copies of it lying around in bookshops in Paris. One would now have to pay a great deal for one of them.

In June 1928 Tsvetayeva again organised a literary evening. It came off successfully, although the choice of the day was not fortunate. A play by the Moscow Vakhtangov Theatre, which was on tour, was being staged on the same evening. This was the theatre previously called the 'Third Studio', and its director in Paris was none other than Marina's old friend, Pavel Antokolsky. She managed to meet him twice. In 1966 Antokolsky described in *Novy Mir* a visit to Marina in Meudon, and their second hurried meeting in a café on Boulevard St Michel. Apparently, they did not know what to say to each other, and found few themes for conversation.

> We did not recall the past at all, and she avoided expatiating about Moscow or Russia; this was obviously painful for her. We bid farewell hastily, at a foreign busy intersection, without a thought of a future meeting, without hope for such a meeting.[17]

Another encounter with the past struck Marina deeper than the one with Antokolsky. With the preparations for her literary evening and with the sale of tickets Marina was helped and supported by Vera Nikolayevna Bunina, the wife of Ivan Bunin (who hated Tsvetayeva as much as she hated him). Only after her third letter did Marina realise that Vera Bunina, *née* Muromtseva, was in fact a friend of her sister Valeria's, and a close relation of Professor D.I. Ilovaisky. Suddenly the world of Marina's childhood rose before her: the house on Trekhprudny Lane, Nervi, her beloved Nadya Ilovaiskaya.

On 10 April Anna Tesková received from Marina an unusually good-humoured letter:

> We have had at home some unexpected good fortune in the guise of a foreign relation, who is staying with us for a while. For the house this means order, for me, some leisure, the first in ten years. The first feeling is not 'Now I can write', but 'I can walk'! The second day of her stay I walked to Versailles, 15 kilometres, bliss. My companion was an 18 year old puppy who taught me everything he has learnt at his *gymnasium* (which is a great deal!) and I taught him everything which goes into one's notebook. (Writing is learning, one does not learn it in life!) We exchanged schools. (Only I am self-taught. And we are both excellent walkers.)

Thus began the friendship between Marina and the young Nikolay Gronsky. He was the son of a former city councillor of Moscow, who now edited the newspaper *The Latest News*. The young man loved hiking and was an Alpinist. Moreover, he wrote poetry. The novice in poetry and the great poet quickly took a liking to each other and undertook long walks during which they would become deeply absorbed in conversation on themes of common interest. Marina was impressed by Gronsky's poetic talent, and she saw in him the first real poet among the émigrés and considered him to be her spiritual disciple.

In the summer of 1928 the whole Efron family settled in Pontaillac on the Atlantic Ocean. She agreed with Gronsky that he would come for a few days in September. In anticipation of this meeting a great many letters flew between Meudon and the Atlantic coast; twenty-seven from him, and as many from her.[18] Only fragments of this correspondence are known to this day. In the end Gronsky had to cancel this trip; once again Marina had rejoiced prematurely. She wrote sadly to Tesková:

> He did not come to the ocean, just as I will not be going to Prague. – That is the order of things. – I was not at all surprised, and grieved only for a day, but internally, I am devastated, neither joy, nor grief, but dullness. I am losing in him not only him, in fact I will not be losing him in the least! – but *myself – with him, him with me*, a specific constellation, in a specific month of eternity, on a specific point of the earthly sphere.[19]

Marina later recalled:

> It lasted a year. Then the inevitable divergence of our *lives*, considering my non-freedom, began, (and in the spring of 1931 we separated completely, hermetically).

In the meantime Gronsky had fallen in love with a young woman of his own age and re-dedicated to her all the poems he had written for Tsvetayeva, with the exception of one poem where Marina's name appears. Marina did continue to appreciate him later as a poet, and had particular praise for his epic poem *Belladonna*.[20]

Among all the works of this summer, at least one lyric poem is addressed to Nikolay Gronsky, 'Conversation with a Genius'. In it 'Higher Forces' dictate to the young poet how he must write.[21] Another work of this summer was 'The Red Bull', a short poem with Bolshevik allusions. It is about a White Army volunteer soldier who dies at the age of twenty-eight in Paris of tuberculosis. In his delirium death appears as a young red bull happily prancing about, at which point Marina understands that this is the same red bull which had frightened her and Mandelstam so much in Aleksandrov in 1916.

Did the death of the young White Guardsman remind Marina of the heroic struggle of the White Army during the Civil War? Or was it the 'lively conversation' she had in the summer of 1928?

(' "In ten years they will forget!" "In two hundred years they will remember!" The second speaker – is me.')[22] In any case Marina began a new work in Pontaillac. She wrote to Tesková:

> I am writing a large work: Perekop (the end of the White Army). I write with great love and enthusiasm, with incomparably greater love than, for ex. *Phaedra*.[23]

For this epic poem she began to make use of her husband's journal. At this point, however, one of those purely 'Tsvetayevan' disasters befell her. Just as Marina was joyfully and devotedly creating a monument to the White Army, and *The Latest News* was printing in instalments *Swans' Encampment* and was persistently enquiring about poems from the period of *Poems of Youth*, Mayakovsky arrived in France and was the cause of an event which profoundly compromised Tsvetayeva in the eyes of the Paris émigrés. Mayakovsky read his poems at a literary evening; Marina had always admired him. She now printed in the first issue of *Eurasia*, the newspaper published by her husband, the following 'greeting' to Mayakovsky:

> On 28 April 1922 on the eve of my departure from Russia, I met Mayakovsky in the early hours of the morning on the perfectly deserted Kuznetsky Bridge.
>   Well, Mayakovsky, what should I convey from you to Europe?
>   That the truth is here.
>   On 7 November 1928, late at night, while leaving the Café Voltaire, I answered the question: 'What do you have to say about Russia after Mayakovsky's reading?' by saying, without further thought, that:
>   Strength is over there.[24]

This fatal declaration, made moreover in the new 'Eurasian' newspaper which had already been accused of collaboration with the Bolsheviks, incited a storm of universal indignation. *The Latest News* ceased printing *Swan's Encampment* (a complete edition appeared only in 1957 in Munich), and from this time Tsvetayeva was considered among the émigrés to be a Bolshevik collaborator. Later on *The Latest News* did begin to publish some of her works again, but many of the intolerant leaders of political opinion broke with her for ever.

And how did Mayakovsky react? Was he even grateful to Marina for her daring speech? He "forgot" his copy of *After Russia* with its inscription to him at Elsa Triolet's. Later, on 26 September 1929 he declared at the second plenum of the directors of RAPP (the Russian Proletarian Writers' Association):

> They say, regarding the poetess Tsvetayeva, she has good poems, but they miss the mark. It therefore follows: one must give Tsvetayeva ... so

that she does not miss the mark. She is a Polish dreg, who 'goes her own way', who agitated for the re-publication of Gumilyov's poetry, which 'are good on their own'. And I consider that anything directed against the Soviet Union is directed against us, and has no right to exist, and our task is to render it maximally worthless, and not to learn anything on the basis of it![25]

CHAPTER 22

Meudon – Belgium – French Prose
1929

After the political scandal of Tsvetayeva's 'greeting' to Mayakovsky, a second one soon followed. On 22 January 1929 Marina wrote to Tesková:

> A schism has occurred among the Eurasians...Professor Alekseyev (and others) allege that S.Ya. is a Chekist and a Communist. If I met him I am afraid of what I might do...Professor Alekseyev...is a scoundrel, believe me, I do not say this in vain. I am personally pleased he is leaving, but I suffer on S.'s account, with his purity and fervent heart. He, aside from two or three others, is the only *moral force* of Eurasianism. Believe me! They even call him the 'conscience of Eurasianism', and Prof. Karsavin says of him: 'He is the golden boy of Eurasianism'.

The Eurasian schism was aggravated by the departure of Prince N.S. Trubetzkoy, and others, from the society, which was even then under Communist influence.[1] What rôle did Sergey Efron actually play in it? Was he then living only according to his dreams and ideals, or was he in fact already collaborating in 1929 with Communists? It is now no longer possible to ascertain this precisely.

Slonim, and his circle of young writers, who called themselves the 'Ark', did not take part in the political persecution of the Efrons. Among them Marina was still a welcome guest. At the beginning of 1929 Slonim introduced her to Natalia Goncharova, the famous artist, who was also a great-niece of Pushkin's wife, and who bore the same name. They met at the end of January in the well-known Petit Saint Benoit on the Left Bank, which was the favourite restaurant of Larionov and Goncharova. Over their coffee at the nearby Café de Flore Marina said that she would like to write

something about the two Natalia Goncharovas. It was decided that
Marina would come visit her *atelier* in order to become better
acquainted with her model.

> My approach to her was from within the person, the same principle, I
> think, as the one she uses when approching her pictures. Nothing of the
> external. I have never met such an enormous 'I' among artists
> (painters).[2]

Goncharova, for her part, made illustrations to *The Swain*, and
gave some drawing lessons to Alya. Marina appreciated Goncharova very much, but she found the other woman to be too quiet and
too passive for a real friendship to develop between them. In this
regard she herself admitted:

> I am always ashamed to give more, than another person needs (that is,
> can take!), previously I would give, the way people take by direct assault!
> Later I resigned myself. People need something other than what I can
> give. M.L. once said to me: 'Nothing but a naked soul. How
> frightening!'[3]

The long 'non-article' entitled 'Natalia Goncharova' was published in 1929 in three issues of *Freedom of Russia*. It comprises a
brilliant study of the similarities and interdependencies between
various forms of art; a sketch, executed with a great deal of
imagination and intuition, about the frivolous and superficial wife
of Pushkin, as well as a whole treasury of autobiographical
information about Tsvetayeva herself, but it is not a biography of
the artist Goncharova. Tsvetayeva's intuition abandoned her when
she had to deal with a living person, and she did not understand
Goncharova's paintings in the least. Once again this confirms that
Tsvetayeva approached art only through her aural sense.[4]

In the spring of 1930 Marina again returned to Rilke. She
translated for *Freedom of Russia* some of Rilke's 'Letters to a Young
Poet' (and others), and wrote a foreword to them, in which she says:

> I am still convinced that when I shall die, he will come for me. He will
> *translate* me into the other world, just as I am now *translating* him (by
> hand) into the Russian language. This is the only way I understand
> translation.[5]

At the same time work on *Perekop* was progressing. But on 15
May she had to discontinue it: the material for her description of
this event, Seryozha's journal, had suddenly disappeared.

> I did not write the end of Perekop, because the diary was no longer
> available, and the Perekop campaigner himself had already cooled
> towards Perekop, and the rest of those who were there, and who have
> *not* cooled towards it, do not know how to tell me things, or else *I* do not
> understand (i.e. the military jargon). Thus the last part of Perekop has

remained without me, and I without the last of Perekop. It is a pity.[6]

Marina wrote this in the autumn of 1939, when she was copying her work into a notebook; with her departure for the Soviet Union this notebook remained in the West. However, on 7 January 1939 she added the following afterword on the last pages of the notebook: 'N.B. But perhaps it is just as well that my 'Perekop' ends with a victory: it means that this victory will *not* come to an end.'[7]

Already from her time in Prague the Lebedevs (husband and wife) proved to be good friends to Tsvetayeva; they were also contributors to *Freedom of Russia*. In the summer of 1929 they invited Alya to go with them to Brittany. As there was not enough money for them to go as well, Marina and Mur had to stay in Meudon. But Marina's longing and nostalgia for the green hills of Všenory only grew stronger. As a reward for her summer, unbroken by any holiday, Marina dreamt of going to Prague in the autumn to see Anna Tesková, and to 'look after her soul'.

Plans were again made for a literary evening in Prague; it even seems as though, on this occasion, everything was arranged successfully. Their letters already speak specifically of ticket selling and the rental of a hall. Marina was to give a reading in Belgium, and from there she wanted to go to Czechoslovakia. But this time apparently, it was Tesková herself who cancelled the event at the last minute.

At the same time, another crisis occurred. Just before her departure for Brussels, Marina wrote to Tesková:

> *Eurasia* has come to a halt, and S.Ya. is in anguish, this man cannot live without a burden which is beyond his strength to bear. He lives on the hope of its revival and on his love for Russia...

A postcard arrived from Brussels:

> S.Ya. has earned nothing since the interruption of 'Eurasia'; you know what my income is. If the 500 hundred Czech korunas come to an end, I do not know what we will do...[8]

After this Tesková received an undated letter:

> Dear Anna Antonovna! For a long time I have had no news from you... And we have sad news: on account of his *extreme* exhaustion S.Ya.'s old lung condition has returned, for the time being it is not active, but is is threatening because of his exhaustion... Medical help is provided for, but the important thing is a sanatorium (getting away, relaxation, good air, rest) which means a great deal of money. Eurasia is finished, and with it the modest fee for the editor; we are living in debt, how then can we afford a sanatorium! For God's sake, if only the Czech subsidy would not end in 1930. Then we would all be ruined. I spent

half a year writing Perekop (the long poem about the Civil War), no one will accept it, the right, because it is too 'left' in form; the left, because it is 'right' in content. Even *Freedom of Russia* refused it (gently, of course, not offensively, it was rather *deflected*, than rejected. In a word, half a year's work in vain; this time they are not only not paying anything, they are not publishing it, that is, they will not even *read* it).

On this occasion, as well, friends came to their assistance. They managed to send Seryozha to the Château d'Arcine, near St Pierre-de-Rumilly, in the Haute Savoie, where a Russian sanatorium had been established, close to the Swiss border near Geneva.

The spring of 1930 proved to be a hard trial for Tsvetayeva. She was alone with everything. Since that year Alya was studying at the art school of the Louvre, Marina had to make decisions about everything herself, and to deal with the treatment of her sick husband and the chronic lack of funds '. . . alone with my hands . . .' as she wrote to Vera Bunina. She described for her the situation in detail:

> My husband is very ill (tuberculosis of the lungs, in three places, plus a liver disease, which complicates the treatment, because of the diet). The Red Cross has paid, for the second month, 30 fr. a day, but the sanatorium costs 50 fr. a day. I need 600 fr. a month to pay the extra, aside from all this, the stipend could end from one day to the next. There is no guarantee, but the illness comes with a guarantee, it will not come to an end.[9]

The following letter begins: 'Christ is risen, dear Vera Nikolay-evna! And at the same time let me answer, Indeed . . . ' [He is risen!] This is accompanied by words of gratitude. Apparently Vera Nikolayevna came to her aid immediately.

In spite of all these misfortunes, Marina continued to write. She translated *The Swain* into French, and in this way hoped to become known among French readers. In April she was busy with organising a literary evening, and placed all her last hopes on a possible financial profit. This evening was held on 26 April in the hall of the Geographical Society. The theme of the evening was romantic verse. Among the celebrities who helped make this evening a success through their participation were not only S.M. Volkonsky, but also even Georgy Adamovich, Georgy Ivanov, Nikolay Otsup, Boris Poplavsky, and N.A. Teffi, who all read from their works.[10] The financial returns afforded Marina not only relief from her everyday worries, but also the chance of renting an old chalet near the Château d'Arcine where her husband was being treated, and of staying there until October 1930, when Seryozha was discharged from the sanatorium. The house was tiny and primitive, but the surrounding landscape was magnificent. Yelena Izvolskaya spent a part of the summer with Marina and describes herself what a splendid time she had there, with endless walks and endless conversations which lasted into the morning. The tedium of housework was kept to a minimum.

The results in terms of literary work from this time of solitude and peace was the completion of the translation of The Swain (in French Le Gars) and a cycle of poems on the death of Mayakovsky.[11]

In October 1930 the Efrons returned to Meudon. Sergey Yakovlevich was no longer able to work, any kind of strain being beyond his strength. He enrolled in a course on film-making and hoped at the end of the course to be able to work as a cameraman. With great difficulty Marina managed to return to the demands of keeping house, but she also set to work on more literary enterprises. She wrote to Tesková: 'I am now continuing a long piece begun last winter. I have no time to write, but I write all the same ...'[12]

All of Marina's hopes now centred on the publication of Le Gars, with illustrations by Goncharova. This poem was to have been published in a French literary journal, and Marina carried on a correspondence about it (in French) with Charles Vildrac. From this correspondence only one letter has survived in a Russian translation. It contains Tsvetayeva's reply to the question why she wrote this work in verse. Her answer can be summarised by one phrase: 'For a work to last, it has to turn into a song ...'[13]

Tsvetayeva received an invitation to read Le Gars in a well-known Paris literary salon. Yelena Izvolskaya accompanied her:

> Marina read her translation of The Swain. It was listened to in sepulchral silence. Alas! The Russian lad did not suit the snobbish atmosphere which reigned in this house. I think that in other Parisian circles it would have been appreciated, but after the unsuccessful reading, Marina retreated into her solitude.[14]

In the course of all these years Yelena Izvolskaya was a most loyal and loving friend to Tsvetayeva. The news that this beloved person was planning at the beginning of 1931 to get married and go to live in Japan was a heavy blow for her. Izvolskaya recalls:

> Marina turned my departure into a real drama. This does not mean that she grieved particularly over me. No, in her eyes the 'ordinary' days of my life had come to an end, and a time of anxiety, uncertainty and a descent into the unknown had begun. Marina began to visit me, frequently, dropping in several times a day, she spoiled me, gave me

books, entertained me with poems and stories, and helped me pack, or rather, hindered me from doing so with her fussing. My imminent journey turned into a myth. The parting became a real tragedy. I remember Marina at the station, when I got into the carriage. She stood on the platform, pale, silent, motionless, like a statue. This send-off was more like a funeral ...

Alas, neither she, nor I, thought that soon there would be a separation of another kind. Or, perhaps, then, seeing me off on the station platform, she had already bid farewell to me for ever, not only in the earthly scheme of things. There was something prophetic about this motionless figure. Yes, it was a premonition of catastrophe, *her* catastrophe. Marina departed into the night, and nothing remained with me, but my sorrow about her, which was to last for ever.[15]

Tsvetayeva's memoir, the 'History of a Dedication', begins with this scene of packing at Yelena Izvolskaya's, before her departure, and their attempt at sorting and destroying unnecessary papers. The 'History' itself bears the dedication: 'To my dear friend Ye.A.I. – a belated wedding present'. In fact, the destruction of some of Izvolskaya's personal papers was the direct cause of this delightful work, as it inspired Marina to do the same at home. In the process of going through her own things she found a newspaper clipping which contained a fanciful tale by Georgy Ivanov which claimed to be his memoirs of Osip Mandelstam. Aside from various anecdotes and stories, Georgy Ivanov tells how in the Crimea in 1916 Mandelstam met and fell in love with a brunette woman doctor (who was living with a wealthy Armenian); and how Mandelstam dedicated to her the opening poems of his volume *Tristia.* Full of indignation Marina tells of her acquaintance with Mandelstam and how the poem 'Not believing in the miracle of resurrection' arose. She also describes the summer of 1916 and the time they spent together at Aleksandrov. This essay provides the reader with a chance to become more familiar with Marina's personal life, her memories of her parents' house in Moscow and her life in Meudon.

The 'History of a Dedication' also failed, however, to win for Marina the desired success; like *Perekop* and *Le Gars* the 'History' remained in a desk drawer. Perhaps this was intentional, as the mendacious storyteller, in whose memoirs fantasy prevails over truth, was too well-known.

After Izvolskaya's departure Marina became immersed again in solitude and silence. The friendship with the much admired Goncharova also came to an end of its own accord: the biography was finished and Alya was no longer taking lessons from the famous artist. The monotonous routine of daily life and housekeeping,

and the necessity of looking after every *sou* prevented Marina, as
often happened, from getting to know people better. Once again all
she had left was her notebook, and – and this was something new –
a book she had fallen in love with, Sigrid Undset's *Kristin
Lavransdatter*. Marina felt as though the heroine of this novel was
somehow herself. She wrote to Tesková:

> Sometimes I think that such a life, with my ceaseless work, is
> undeserved. I have been ruined by my patience, my seven-fold pride, as
> though omnipotent: able to pick up, drop, bear and *endure* everything. If
> I were like all the women of my circle (N.B. and do I have a circle!?), or
> like all writers (of my circle, which is unknown to me!) everyone would
> do everything for me, and I would look on. The woman would look on,
> and the writer would write. If I live another time, I will know ... [16]

CHAPTER 23

Meudon – Clamart – Prose Writings
1930 – 1932

As a result of the Great Crash on the New York stock exchange on 'Black Friday', 23 October 1929, and the subsequent ruin of many banks and speculators, everything suddenly changed in the West. In the course of several hours countless Americans, and then Europeans, lost their property, work, optimism, and any sense of security in life. Unemployment, poverty and fear about the future began to reign. In the recently defeated countries of Europe a process of political radicalisation took hold: in Germany, at the elections for the Reichstag held on 14 September 1930, a somewhat obscure party under the name N.S.D.A.P. ('National Socialist German Workers' Party') headed by the failed Austrian artist Adolf Hitler, who promised work for everyone and the restoration of Germany's honour, received so many votes that it now had at its disposal 107 mandates, instead of the previous 12.

In France life became more and more difficult, not only for the Efrons, but also for the other émigrés. The world economic crisis affected everyone, including the general population of the country, but at least French citizens had more opportunities and rights to defend themselves from destitution. One by one publishing-houses and printing-presses began to close, the bookshops became as impoverished as their customers, journals were ruined and hardly anyone published volumes of lyric poetry. People worried only about themselves, and nothing remained among writers of the fraternal assistance of the twenties. The fate of indigent Russian writers ceased to interest anyone; and no one wanted to buy tickets for the same old literary evenings.

In addition to all this, there occurred among the Russians a similar political radicalisation. If before 1930 French society was indifferent to its "uninvited guests", then now, in the present circumstances, French intellectuals began to take a great interest in Soviet Russia, especially after several French writers had gone there in order to become better acquainted with the Communist experiment of creating a "new man". They returned in raptures, and when Bunin and Balmont published a number of documents about the oppression of artistic creativity in the USSR, Romain Rolland fiercely attacked them in the press.

The difficult economic situation sharpened further the political polarisation of the Russian émigrés. Many were enthusiastic about Italian Fascism, or even looked sympathetically at Hitler's attacks on Jews and Bolsheviks. During the thirties several revolutionary movements arose among the "superfluous" younger generation, which imitated Fascism or sympathised with it; they included, for example, the 'Union of Young Russians', the 'National Labour Union of the New Generation' (both of a nationalistic anti-democratic character), and the 'National Maximalists' who had anti-Semitic, and national-Bolshevik tendencies, and preached the need to return to Soviet Russia. A 'Union for Repatriation to the Motherland' also appeared on the scene. Vladimir Varshavsky, who has described all these movements in detail, maintains that all the members of his generation had to pass through the temptation of these extremist ideas.[1]

It is impossible to establish exactly when Sergey Efron fell completely under Soviet influence. Zinaida Shakhovskaya is of the opinion that he helped to 'Sovietize' the newspaper *Eurasia*.[2] According to the stories of those who knew him, Efron always needed an idea which he could serve. Most likely, the desperate situation of his family, his illness and the hostile attitude of émigré circles all played a certain rôle in his *rapprochement* with the Soviet government. He now had only one goal in mind: to return to Russia. He certainly understood that a high price would be demanded from a former officer of the White Army for this.

Sergey's children soon fell under his influence in this respect: Alya, who saw no future for herself in France, and the adolescent Mur. The fact that Marina did not share the political aspirations of her husband can be seen even in the severely censored letters to Tesková; her attitude to the Bolshevik régime had not changed. She also wrote to Ivask on this subject:

> You wish to say, perhaps, that my hatred for the Bolsheviks is too weak for them [i.e. the émigrés, Yury Ivask's note]? To this I answer: it is *another kind* of hatred, of a different nature. The émigrés hate them,

because they took their estates from them, I hate them because they will not allow Boris Pasternak (as it happened) to go to his beloved Marburg, and me to my native Moscow. As far as executioners are concerned, my dear, all executioners are brothers: I swear that the recent execution of a Russian, following a *proper* trial, and with a lawyer in tears, and the Cheka's shot in the back, are one and the same, whatever they are called, an abomination, to which I will not submit *anywhere*, as in general I will not submit to any kind of organised violence, in the name of whatever it is, and with whatever name it is called ... [3]

In spite of this, Tsvetayeva's interest in events in her homeland and a longing for Russia gradually developed during the thirties, under the influence of her family and external circumstances. Although she would later repudiate this development, we can see it in certain poems of this period, such as the following:

THE TORCH

To the Eiffel Tower
Is but a step! Take the step and climb,
But each of us has seen already,
And sees, as much. But today, I say

That your Paris seems to us
Boring and ugly.
'Russia mine, Russia,
Why do you burn so brightly?'

This attitude is expressed even more definitely in the 'Verses to My Son':

Our conscience is not your conscience!
Enough! At ease! Having forgotten everything,
Children, write yourselves the tale
Of your own days and your own passions.

The saline family of Lot
That is your family album!
Children! Settle your own accounts
With the city which poses as Sodom.

Not having fought with your brother –
Your plate is clean, curly head!
Yours is the land, *yours* the epoch, *yours* the day, *yours* the hour,
Ours is the sin, *ours* the cross, *ours* the quarrel, *ours*

The wrath. You who were wrapped
From birth in an orphan's travelling cape –
Cease holding memorial services
For the Eden in which you

Never were! For the fruits which you
Did not even see! Understand: blind
Is the one who leads you to the requiem
For the people who are eating bread

And who will give it to you, as soon as
You leave Meudon for the Kuban.
Our quarrel – is not your quarrel!
Children! In your own time
Wage your own wars.[4]

The strangest irony of this poem is that Marina failed to realise, as did, evidently, the rest of her family, that part of the Russian people at this time were not 'eating bread', but were dying of starvation because of the "de-Kulakisation" of the country.

Tsvetayeva began to write fewer and fewer poems (the journals were no longer accepting them), but to compensate for this, the period of her 'lyrical prose' began. It can also be seen from some of this work that she was particularly close to those writers who remained in Russia. At Slonim's request she wrote in February 1931 an article called 'About the New Russian Children's Book',[5] where she explains to the reader that children's books in Soviet Russia are far superior to those of the past. She was very offended when the newspaper, for which the article was written, refused to publish it.

> I wrote about the new type of children's book which exists in Russia, about its richness, its fairy-tale realism (or, if you prefer its earthy imagination), about its incomparable advantages over the pre-school literature of my childhood and of the emigration. (Everything is based on quotations.) Here 'da liegt der Hund begraben', a letter arrives; they cannot accept my article, because there are bad children's books in Russia also. I have written in vain. (N.B. In the article, by the way, the word 'sovetskaya' is not used once, only 'Russian' appears; there is not a trace of politics in my article, which has nothing to do with my theme (the pre-school child). Obviously the money which is behind the newspaper is émigré ... Thus I am becoming estranged, arrogantly and silently. Everyone is forcing me towards Russia, where I *cannot go*. Here I am *not needed*. There I am *not possible*.[6]

A particularly unusual work of this summer is the poem 'Siberia', which intermingles a description of the city of Tobolsk with Eurasian themes and pride in the famous conqueror of Siberia, Yermak. The poem ends rather unexpectedly with the lines:

> Tobolsk, Tobolsk, wooden monastery!
> Tobolsk, Tobolsk, wooden grave!

It is quite clear, as Marina hinted many times, that this poem is related to her long poem about the demise of the Imperial Family, (a work which remains lost to this day), and that 'Siberia' is the only fragment of it ever to be published.[7]

Tsvetayeva's article about children's books in Russia was printed in *Freedom of Russia*, but with editorial reservations. If anything, it further damaged her political reputation. No one tried to understand her any more:

> My trouble with my milieu is that I *do not get through to anyone.* The fate of my books: everyone wants them to be 1.) simpler, 2.) more cheerful, 3.) more charming. I have never been so lonely as during these five years. At home I am some kind of gendarme ... the most thankless rôle. All day I have to patrol everything, direct everything, and all this effort goes on trifles. I sometimes think with bitterness: everyone at home and everyone else around me are "poets" more than I am. Of "poetry" I have only my hapless notebook.[8]

A piece of news which had arrived from Moscow also left a heavy impression on Tsvetayeva: her adored Pasternak had abandoned his family, because he had fallen in love with another woman. Marina wrote to Tesková:

> For years I have lived on the dream that we would see each other. Now it is futile. I have no one in Russia to go to. The wife and son – I have respected. But a *new* love means I must withdraw. Understand me correctly, dear Anna Antonovna: this is *not jealousy.* But once someone manages to do without me! I used to have the feeling about B. that: if I was dying, I could summon him. Because I felt that he was, despite his family, completely alone, and mine. Now, my place has been usurped ...[9]

The Efrons' financial situation grew still more hopeless. Seryozha was unemployed and was not capable of working; three of Marina's compositions, which should have improved their domestic budget, lay in the drawer:

> All of this is for later, when I am no more, when they will discover me (not when they will unearth me!) ...

More and more of her friends disappeared from the scene. Izvolskaya was far away (although she later returned to Paris, their former intimacy was not renewed); Svyatopolk-Mirsky, who had helped Marina for all these years, sent her the last cheque. This unfortunate, rebellious, doomed man would become, as Izvolskaya remarks, gentle, childishly trustful and almost happy, only when he could sit in the Efrons' kitchen and grind coffee for hours in a little Turkish coffee-mill. He had joined the Communist Party in England and in 1932 he returned to Russia. Around 1937 he disappeared and died in a camp.

In this way, the members of the 'Committee to Help Tsvetayeva' had either dispersed, or were themselves in need of assistance.[10] *Freedom of Russia,* Tsvetayeva's saving anchor of many years, began to be published with more and more irregularity, an ominous warning that even the editors in Prague were threatened with a crisis. On top of all these misfortunes, the Czech stipend was arriving with greater delays. The government of Czechoslovakia had informed almost all the recipients of its stipends that they could no longer count on its support. Some guardian angel in Prague arranged it so that Tsvetayeva and Remizov, the poorest of the Russian writers, would not be deprived of this assistance. In the autumn of 1931 when 'the catastrophe of our term' was approaching (i.e. the quarterly payment of the rent), once again their friends, among them Tesková, collected enough money to pay the Efrons' rent till the end of the year. Marina wrote to Tesková:

> I am living on the last of my (emotional) strength, without any kind of external or internal impressions, without even the slightest grounds for the latter. In brief: I am living like a poorly functioning automaton, poorly, because of the remnants of a soul which interferes with the machinery. I am like an unfortunate, unsuccessful automaton, a mockery of an automaton ... The demands of daily life have destroyed my brains. I lead the life of any housewife in Meudon or Všenory, without any distinction; I *must* do everything she must do and I do not dare to do anything she does not dare to do, and there is much which I do not have, which she has, and there is much I do not even know how to do. In these same circumstances (but are the circumstances ever the same??) another woman (i.e. not myself, which means that already everything would be otherwise) would be happy, i.e. because then the circumstances to begin with would be different ... But the things which are mine which I have not done (poems which I have abandoned, the letter I have not answered) gnaw away at me and poison everything. Sometimes I do not write for weeks (N.B. I always want to, but I simply do not get down to it.)[11]

At exactly this most unsuitable time a friend from Prague appeared: Nikolay Yelenev. He recorded what he saw:

> In 1931, at the end of the summer, I visited the family of the producer T. in Meudon, near Paris. During supper the bell rang at the entrance. Efron unexpectedly entered the dining-room ... Our relations had broken off long before this. We had not corresponded. He asked about life in Czechoslovakia, about our friends in common, and then he insisted by every means of persuasion that at the end of the meal, despite the lateness of the hour, I visit them. 'Marina will be so glad to remember old times. After all it has been so many years since we last saw each other!' ... Before this my friends, who were living in Paris, had warned me that something incomprehensible was happening with Tsvetayeva: people had stopped trusting her politically. But it was impossible to decline this invitation ... The room in which Marina lived contained two beds by the wall, head to head. On the colourless walls there was neither a single painting, nor photograph. There was an untidy wooden table, unwashed dishes, and a cloud of tobacco smoke, in which an electric light glimmered. Efron's expectations were mistaken; not only did Marina not rejoice at my arrival, but she met me rather

indifferently, even drily. She looked stubbornly to the side and smoked constantly. Her complexion had turned a dull yellowish colour (Marina did not use rouge). Autumn had arrived not only in the courtyard ... One could no longer feel Marina's radiant halo, it had been extinguished. Something alien and unfriendly now came from it ... Efron sensed my embarrassment. He tried to draw Marina out of her gloomy state, but to no avail. It only remained for me to take my leave. No one had ever heard Marina's confession, probably not even a priest, still less then could I expect one. Neither Marina's past, nor France with its tradition of social manners had taught her how to dissemble. On leaving them I did not feel disappointment, I only knew that we would never see one another again. Marina's silence was the silence of a person, who no longer has a way out ... [12]

Slonim partially confirms the observation of Yelenev. Marina Tsvetayeva's mood in 1931 also struck him as particularly despondent and depressed. He attributed this, for the most part, to the political disagreements within the family. He also recalls, however, one amusing event: he and the Prokofievs undertook a visit to Marina. Although Prokofiev was a terrible driver, he insisted on driving the car himself. On the way home he was still so much under the charm of Tsvetayeva's personality that he drove into a telegraph-pole and almost killed all his passengers.

Despite the difficult circumstances of her life, Marina still had the strength and energy to carry out her creative ideas. In the course of the summer she wrote the cycle *Poems to Pushkin*,[13] and the 'Ode to Walking',[14] which appeared in print only after Marina's death. She also began a lyrical 'self-portrait' called 'The House'.

Perhaps because of her immersion in Pushkin, Marina returned to one of her favourite themes, which was always particularly close to her. In spite of her usual domestic obligations Marina continued during the winter and most of 1932 to work out with great zeal her attitude to the relation between art and the artist or writer. Taking Pushkin and other great writers as examples, Marina defines what the essence of art is for her; it is the moral obligation of a poet to the time he lives in and to his own conscience. The result of these reflections was her 'magnum opus' and artistic 'Credo': *Art in the Light of Conscience.*

It is more important simply to be a human being, because this is what is needed more. The doctor and the priest are more necessary than the poet, because they are present at the deathbed, and not us. The doctor and the priest are humanly more important, the rest are socially more important. Whether society itself is important is another question, which I would only have the right to answer from an island. With the exception of parasites, in all their varieties, everyone is more important than us.

And knowing this, in full possession of my mind and realising it with my sound memory, I assert, with no less fulness of mind, and no less sound memory, that I would not exchange my own profession for any other. Knowing the greater, I do the lesser, which is why I will not receive forgiveness. Only those like me will have to answer for themselves before the Last Judgement of conscience. But if there is a Last Judgement of the word, I will be innocent there.

Art in the Light of Conscience never appeared in its entirety as a book. Although it is possible that Tsvetayeva never finished it as such, some of the blame for its incompletion falls on *Contemporary Annals*; in spite of the frequently repeated protests of the author, the editor, Rudnev, cut this work by half.[15] Thus only two chapters were published. One carries the title given by the author ('Art in the Light of Conscience') and the second is called 'The Poet and Time'.[16] Before this, Marina read these two chapters on 21 January and 25 May 1932 in front of a large and interested audience. On the first evening during the discussion which followed the reading, a young Russian poet from Prague, Aleksey Eisner, attracted her attention. Later on he would be of great help to Tsvetayeva. He advised her to invite G.P. Fedotov to the second evening and discussion. Marina's first letter of 16 May to Fedotov mentions briefly her theme.

Georgy Petrovich Fedotov, whom Gleb Struve considered to be one of the most brillant writers and publishers of the emigration, was an enthusiastic admirer of Tsvetayeva after reading *Poem of the Mountain* and *The Pied Piper*. He had been one of those pre-Revolutionary Marxist intellectuals who subsequently became profound Christian believers, and belonged in Paris to the leading figures of the 'Russian Student Christian Movement'. At the beginning of the 1930s this group sought a solution to the contemporary situation in a combination of Christianity with social democratic thought. In 1931 Fedotov, Stepun and I.I. Fonda-minsky-Bunakov founded the journal *The New City* (*Novy grad*), which accepted contributions from Berdyayev, and S. Bulgakov, as well as Mother Maria (Skobtsova), who was more involved in active social work.

G.P. Fedotov invited Tsvetayeva to write something for *The New City*, which brought her into contact with this very energetic circle. Her letters to Fedotov relate, for the most part, to the article she wrote for them, 'The Epic and Lyric in Contemporary Russia: Mayakovsky and Pasternak'.[17] In this essay she returns to another of her favourite themes: she places alongside the 'statuesque' born fighter Mayakovsky, the 'dynamic' born poet Pasternak. According to Tsvetayeva, these two poets are related to each other 'only by the singular presence of their strength' which is accompanied by a 'common want: the lack of song which unites them...'

'My lecture 'The Poet and Time' was given on the 21st,' Tsvetayeva informed Tesková on 27 January 1932. 'There was not a single free place in the hall; the audience was very well-disposed, although I spoke some harsh truths...'

In the spring of 1932 the Efrons were forced to leave Meudon. Without the help of wealthier friends they were simply unable to pay the rent any more. They moved to another suburb of Paris, Clamart, where many Russians were already living. At first they settled in a small flat at no.101, rue Condorcet. The following year they moved to no.10, rue Lazare Carnot, next to Nikolay Berdyayev.

At the house on rue Condorcet Marina finished *Art in the Light of Conscience*, and during the entire summer, 'without letting up', she wrote one of her most charming literary portraits, her memoir of Maksimilian Voloshin, 'A Living Word about a Living Man', which was inspired by the news of the death of her friend and protector from Koktebel.[18] These memoirs are written so vividly that the living man, as well as his mythical image as a hero, rises before our eyes. Khodasevich could not resist from remarking drily in *The Renaissance*: 'Tsvetayeva's memoirs about Voloshin are much more significant than Voloshin himself. In this consists her incomparable literary art and the obvious error of her memoirs.'

Between 16 October 1932 and 7 March 1933 there is a break in the correspondence between Tsvetayeva and Tesková. This occurs at the same time as Marina was writing a short composition in French, whose theme, the love between two women, it was difficult at that time to associate with the concept of "propriety". Subsequently called 'Mon frère féminin' with the subtitle, 'Lettre à l'Amazone', it was a belated reply to the book by the French author Natalie Clifford-Barney, *Pensées d'une amazone*. According to Tsvetayeva two women who love each other form the ideal union, but this is flawed by the absence of the child:

> L'impossible, ce n'est pas de résister à la tentation de l'homme, mais au besoin de l'enfant. Seul point faible qui ruine toute la cause. Seul point attaquable qui laisse entrer tout le corps ennemi. Car même si nous pourrons un jour avoir un enfant *sans lui*, nous ne pourrons jamais avoir un enfant d'*elle*, une petite toi à aimer...[19]

In 1933 *Freedom of Russia* ceased publication. This was a heavy blow for Marina Tsvetayeva, and not only from the financial point of view. The Prague newspaper had granted her not only complete

Mur, Clamart, 1933

artistic freedom, but had also published everything she wrote
without the slightest alteration. There now remained only *Contemporary Annals*, where Rudnev, who found Tsvetayeva's style
incomprehensible, was in charge of the literary section. Marina's
letters were now full of complaints about him, his interferences
with her text, his deletions, and in general, his refusal to publish
her work under the pretext that the journal's readers did not like
her poetry. Mark Vishnyak, who was for many years editor of the
journal, refutes the greater part of these complaints.[20]

The Efrons' dire need did not come to an end at rue Condorcet.
Marina wrote to Fedotov:

> Dear Georgy Petrovich, I *implore* you to write once more to Fondaminsky about the honorarium, we have been put under distraint; for the
> first time in our lives.

On 24 May she apologised for not being able to pay a visit:

> Dear Georgy Petrovich and Yelena Nikolayevna, I did not forget, but at
> the last minute, yesterday, one of my rubber soles refused to work, and
> departed this life, that is, it simply fell off, and since these were my only
> shoes ...[21]

At the same time Marina was working on a new composition, about
which she hints in her letters to Tesková and Bunina:

> I wrote few poems this winter, but instead a long work about M.
> Voloshin and a translation of one of my own things into French: nine
> (my own genuine) letters and one, a reply from a man, with an
> afterword, Postface ou Face posthume des choses, followed by a
> description of a final meeting with my addressee, five years later, on
> New Year's Eve. It has proved to be a work *of one piece*, written by life
> itself. But with my usual luck, although there is praise (from the French)
> on all sides, the manuscript lies untouched. And evidently will remain
> thus, like my French Swain illustrated by Goncharova ...[22]

In this regard Tsvetayeva had predicted correctly. The 'translation of one of her own things' into French, are the letters of 1922 to
A.G. Vishnyak. The text of this book, *Les Nuits florentines*, as
prepared by Tsvetayeva in 1933, was published for the first time
only in 1983 in French with an Italian translation accompanying it.
The Russian version appeared only in 1985.[23]

Within her family Marina felt increasingly isolated. She confided
to Tesková:

> S.Ya. has gone completely over to Sov. Russia, he sees nothing else, and
> in Russia he sees only what he wants.[24]

Thanks to František Kubka we know that in 1932 Sergey Efron
joined the 'Union for Repatriation to the USSR' and that Alya, who
had now turned twenty, shared the political views of her father. She

also began working for a French Communist newspaper.[25]

Marina Tsvetayeva was profoundly depressed by the estrangement between herself and the daughter she had previously adored so much. According to the words of V.V. Morkovin, the publisher of the letters to Tesková, the greater part of the deletions in the edition of this correspondence relate to this theme. Alya supported the family as much as she could; it often happened that the few francs she earned was the only money in the house. Her character was, however, completely different from that of Marina, she had not inherited the romantic impulses and stormy nature of her mother and grandmother.

> She is very "harmonious", that is, she prefers nothing, accepts everything: both the morning paper and my desperate leap into dreams, everything is somehow equivalent for her – she does not get this from me, it is not mine.[26]

A similar problem occurred with the adored Mur, who was eternally attached to her and terribly spoiled: he too had no spiritual affinity with his mother. He lived on hopes for the future, and often repeated: 'Poor mama, you are so strange: it's as though you were *very* old!' This is, however, essentially the spirit which Tsvetayeva had herself imparted to Mur in her 'Poems to My Son'. But even if the people closest to her were gradually moving away from her, one thing remained faithful to her, her writing table, to which Tsvetayeva turned whenever she needed consoling:

> The thirtieth anniversary
> Of our union, more faithful than love.
> I know your every wrinkle
> As you know mine and of
>
> Which you, are you not the author?
> Having eaten quire after quire,
> Teaching there's no tomorrow,
> That today is all there is here.
>
> Table, hurling money and letters
> The mailman brings, into the fray.
> Insisting that the deadline
> For every line is today.
>
> Threatening that counting of cutlery
> Doesn't give the Creator his due,
> That tomorrow they will stretch me,
> Poor idiot woman, on you.[27]

> [translated by David McDuff]

CHAPTER 24

Clamart – Autobiographical Prose – Vanves

1933 – 1934

In the spring of 1933, soon after Hitler had come to power in Germany, Marina learnt from her sister in Moscow that on 8 April their half-brother Andrey had died from the family disease, tuberculosis of the lungs. This sudden encounter with the past evoked in her the forgotten world of her childhood, the world of Trekhprudny Lane. She wanted to raise a monument to this past and to her brother. But she was soon convinced that she did not know enough about this world, and that which she did know she saw only through the eyes of a child. There was in France, however, someone who did know the Ilovaisky family and its milieu. This was Vera Nikolayevna Bunina. On 6 August Tsvetayeva sent her a letter with a long list of questions, and soon after she received a detailed response. Vera Bunina did even more, she sent Marina her own notes about D.I. Ilovaisky and his children,[1] and in this way rendered her a great service, for which Marina was very grateful to her. Both women, who shared common childhood memories, and similar literary aspirations, entered into an intense correspondence. For a certain time Bunina became Marina's best friend and confidante; even her correspondence with Tesková took second place. Marina's memoir 'The House at Old Pimen', bears the dedication: 'To Vera Muromtseva, of the same roots as myself'.[2]

'The House at Old Pimen', on which Tsvetayeva worked from August to October 1933 and 'The Tower in Ivy', her memoirs about her stay as a girl in the Freiburg pension, mark the beginning of a new stage in her prose. Quickly, one after the other, she wrote several autobiographical essays, which in varying degrees relate to her childhood and youth. Taken together they form a brilliantly written collection of memoirs, a mixture of truth and fantasy.[3] Certain events are illuminated differently than in the memoirs of Anastasia Tsvetayeva, which shows the distinction between the perception of the past by a poet of genius, and by a painstaking biographer.

These autobiographical sketches of 1933-1937 have a dual significance, they earned Tsvetayeva some money, as *The Latest News* and *Contemporary Annals* published her prose enthusiastically (although they still refused to print her poetry); and they also gave her the chance to escape into the past, the only place where she felt she was safe from danger.

> I have no place in the present day, in the future. I do not have a single square inch of the surface of the earth on which to stand, not even this minimal amount, for me there is not even an inch in the whole wide world. I am now standing on my last inch of space, which has not been seized only because I am *standing* on it, like a monument, with all my weight, like a stylite on a column. There is (for me, and for everyone like me: for there are such) only a crevice, which leads out of time into the depths, into the stalactic caves of pre-history; into the underground realm of Persephone and Minos, where Orpheus bid farewell, into H-a-d-e-s. Or into the blessed realm of Frau Holle ... For I *also* do not want to go into *your* atmosphere, mechanical and aeronautical, which, in the meantime is merely fit for excursions, and which tomorrow will become, you know yourself what. But who are you to say 'me', 'to me', 'I'? No one. I am a lonely spirit. Who has no air to breathe. (And Pasternak has none. And Bely has none. *We* exist, but we are the last.) The epoch is not only against me ... not so much against me, as *I* against it, I really hate it, the whole realm of the future ... The epoch is against me, not personally, but passively; I am against it actively. I hate it. It does not see me.[4]

In her relations with Vera Bunina, Tsvetayeva was the one asking questions, Suddenly, however, a voice resounded completely unexpectedly, a voice from afar, which turned to her with questions; someone was interested in her. The young Russian writer Yury Ivask, who was then living in Revel (Tallin) wanted to write an article about Tsvetayeva. He sent her a draft of this, and enclosed a whole list of questions: about her works and her opinions regarding various events. On 4 April 1933 Marina replied with a long and detailed letter. The future American professor George Ivask performed a great service in continuing his correspondence with Tsvetayeva even after the publication of his article in the Revel newspaper *Innovations* (*Nov'*, no.6, 1934). He knew how to ask the right questions, so that these twelve letters which

Tsvetayeva wrote to him have become one of the most important sources for her biography.[5] Tsvetayeva condescended to provide Ivask with some explanations for her more difficult works, such as *The Swain* and 'Byways'. She replied to questions of a personal nature as well.

One can guess that already in his first letter Ivask was interested in Marina's political convictions and must have asked if she sympathised with one of the new Russian nationalist groups. Her answer was unequivocal:

> In those places where they say: Jew and mean: Yid, there is *no place* for me, a colleague of Heinrich Heine. I will say more: that place where I will not stand, will itself not accommodate me; that place senses me, like a gunpowder store-room *senses* a match.

And further:

> As far as the 'Young Russians' are concerned, here is a little scene from real life. A lecture was given by the former editor and contributor of *Freedom of Russia* M. Slonim (a Jew): 'Hitler and Stalin'. *After* the lecture the 'Young Russians' appeared in full force. They stood 'with their arms crossed on their chests'. At the end of the discussion I move towards the exit (I live in the suburbs and am dependent on trains) so that I am standing in the very thick of it. A respectful whisper 'Tsvetayeva'. They hand me some kind of leaflet, which I do not unfold. On the stage Slonim is saying: 'With regard to H. and the Jews . . . ' At this, one of the 'Young Russians' (who if not a "pillar" is a *post*) shouts to the whole hall: 'We understand! He is a Yid himself!' I, distinctly and clearly say: 'Lout!' (A whisper: they do not understand). I repeat 'Lout!' and tearing the leaflet in half, make my way to the exit. Several threatening gestures. I say: 'You did not understand me? Those who say Yid instead of Jew and interrupt a speaker are louts.' I pause and repeat contemplatively: 'Louts.' After this I leave. I speak to everyone in their own language![6]

Although the Russians in Paris became more and more immersed in their political differences under the influence of world events, their literary life continued unabated in the various cafés. In spite of Hitler, Stalin and Mussolini, Russian Montparnasse followed with interest the arguments between Adamovich and Khodasevich, about whether poetry should reflect the inner world and be 'truthful', as Adamovich demanded, or be simply 'good' verse as Khodasevich wanted. In the summer of 1933 an important event occurred in Russian émigré literature, which probably, however, passed unnoticed; this was the reconciliation between Tsvetayeva and Khodasevich.[7]

The paths of these two poets had crossed already earlier, when they had both been published in the Musaget anthology of 1911. In Berlin and Prague they had become better acquainted, but they did

not like one another. Tsvetayeva's art continued to grow and
develop in exile; Khodasevich, however, soon fell silent. Right up
until his death he worked for *The Renaissance* as a strict literary
critic, whom everyone feared. On more than one occasion he wrote
negative reviews of Tsvetayeva's works, especially her dramas. But
for all this, he was still one of the few critics who took account of
the volume *After Russia*, and even praised it. In Tsvetayeva's
memoir about Voloshin, Khodasevich appears in a short scene.
When Marina sent 'A Living Word about a Living Man' to
Contemporary Annals, Rudnev was not pleased with this passage; he
was afraid of the dangerous critic and wanted to cross out the whole
scene. Marina then, on 11 May, wrote to Khodasevich herself,
asking whether he had anything against her mentioning his name.
Apparently Khodasevich gave his consent immediately, because
already on 19 July Marina sent a second letter:

> Dear Vladislav Felitsianovich! It is still easier to be reconciled with me
> than to quarrel. I simply do not remember our disagreement, I even feel
> that it was not *ours*; someone quarreled and even, one might say,
> something, near us, and it seemed as though we were arguing, or were
> even argued about. This is all nonsense. For one genuine poet, or even
> for half a poet (or as the Czechs say, for an eighth) if one can separate a
> whole one! – I would give a hundred genuine non-poets.[8]

This was the beginning of a warm friendship, based on mutual
understanding. They shared not only identical views on artistic
taste, but they also felt themselves to be alone in a strange and
hostile milieu. To this union of lonely people Tsvetayeva added
Zamyatin, who had recently arrived as an émigré. Khodasevich now
understood and appreciated better Tsvetayeva's creative spirit and
responded more favourably to her latest work. Their friendship was
not even broken during Marina's fatal year of 1937, and it ended
only with Khodasevich's death.

Tsvetayeva's letters to Khodasevich have been published in *The
New Review* (*Novy zhurnal*) in New York; but another important
letter was printed in 1969 in *Novy Mir*. It contains the following
passage:

> No, one *must* write poetry. One must not grant this triumph either to
> life, or to the emigration, or to the Vishnyaks, or "bridge players", or to
> all and sundry: to force a poet to go without poetry is to make of a poet a
> prosaist, and of a prosaist, a corpse. Into your hands (ours!) has been
> given something, which we do not have the right to drop, or to place in
> the hands of others (who are not there)...Of course, there can be a
> feeling of satiety. But there is also atrophy from lack of practice. Do not
> renounce, do not abdicate, remember Akhmatova:

> And if I die, who then
> Will write my poems to you?

Not even to *you*, and not to everyone, but simply, *who*, and, *my poems* ... No one. Never. This is irretrievable ... And precisely because there are few of us, we do not have the right ... [9]

In the autumn of 1933 Mur finally began to go to school. Until now his mother had kept him with her, fearing that French schools were 'too exhausting'. 'This means that I too am going to school,' she wrote on 5 October to Bunina. To all the difficulties at home was added the task of taking Mur to school twice a day, and of walking with him for an hour before lunch and two hours after, as it was necessary for him to have some exercise. 'Everyone thinks this is madness,' Marina complained to Tesková. Her friends were probably more annoyed by the fact that Mur was enrolled in an expensive private school; the explanation which Marina gave on this account did not, of course, increase the sympathy of the people around her:

> Why is he not in a state school? Because my father sent university students abroad at his own expense, and paid for so many *gymnasium* students as well, and dying left 20,000 roubles for a school in his native village of Talitsy in the district of Shuya; also I have the *right* to educate Mur in a *good* ... school. That is, the right to pay for him out of my own pocket, and when it is empty – to beg. (Only do not say all this, dear Vera, to the "ladies", simply remind them so that they will not forget me when they divide up their money, and *inspire* them to give as much as possible.)[10]

In the autumn of 1933 Ivan Bunin received the Nobel Prize for literature, as the leading Russian writer of his day. This was a great event for the Russian colony of Paris. Tsvetayeva wrote about this in a letter to Tesková on 24 November 1933:

> On the 26th I will have to sit on a platform and congratulate Bunin. To avoid this would be a sign of protest. I am not protesting, I am only in disagreement, for incomparably greater than Bunin, is Gorky, who is greater, and more human, and more original and more necessary. Gorky is an epoch, but Bunin is the end of an epoch ... I still have not seen Bunin. I do *not like* him: the cold, cruel presumptuous *seigneur*. I do not like *him*, but I love his wife very much ... [11]

Marina did not know at the time, and the rest of the world would only learn decades later, that the financial support Tsvetayeva received from Vera Bunina was a part of Bunin's Nobel Prize. Remizov also received help in the same discreet manner.

On 8 January 1934 Mur brought home some sad news: he had read in a newspaper a notice about the death of Andrey Bely in Russia. Father Sergey Bulgakov held a memorial service at the

church of St Sergey, at which Marina was present. After the
service, she met the writer and journalist Vladimir Weidlé, who
makes no secret in his memoirs of the fact that the famous poetess
made a deep impression on him. Later Marina often received him
at home in Clamart.

Weidlé maintained good relations with French intellectual
circles, and managed to have published several of Tsvetayeva's
translations of Pushkin in the Dominican paper *La Vie intellectuelle.*
These lines in French had to wait more than half a century before
they became available to readers again. One can see from them that
Marina Tsvetayeva was also a remarkable translator:

ADIEUX À LA MER

Adieu, Espace des Espaces!
Pour la dernière fois mon oeil
Voit s'étirer ta vive grâce
Et s'étaler ton bel orgueil.

Telle une fête qui s'achève,
Supplique d'une chère voix –
Ta grave voix, ta voix de rêve
J'entends pour la dernière fois

. . . .

Adieu, ô Gouffre! l'heure presse,
Mais en tout temps et en tout lieu
Me poursuivra sans fin ni cesse
Ta voix à l'heure des adieux.[12]

At about this time Alya and Mur fell ill with measles. For some
time the trips to school and the midday walks had to be curtailed,
and this gave Marina the chance to write her memoirs about Bely
('Ça me hante!'). This article 'A Captive Spirit' was dedicated to
Khodasevich in gratitude for his remarkable lecture about Bely. On
15 March 1934 Tsvetayeva read her work in the Salle de
Géographie in Paris. Soon after this it was published in *Contemporary Annals* with fewer cuts than usual.[13]

V.I. Lebedev arranged for some of Marina's still unpublished
works to be published in Belgrade for the 'Russian Archive', which
was created for the purpose of helping émigré writers and which
paid well. These works, which appeared in Serbian and Croatian
translations, included an article about a new volume of poetry by
Pasternak, and the work of Akhmatova, Blok and Mandelstam,
called 'Poets with History and Poets without History' (in Serbo-
Croatian: 'Pesnici sa storijom i pesnici bez istorije'), and later 'A
Speech about Balmont' ('Reć o Baljmontu') and an article about

Gronsky, 'The Alpinist Poet' ('Pesnik Alpinist'). For these works Slonim was able to obtain for Marina a triple honorarium.[14]

In spite of the fact that Tsvetayeva railed against the émigré journals in Paris at every opportunity, during the years 1933-37 her prose work often appeared on their pages. At this time she was writing almost only prose as her poetry was still in disfavour. Along with her brilliant purely 'Tsvetayevan' pieces one can also find some uninteresting occasional articles which were hastily jotted down. Among the better pieces are: 'Two Forest Kings', a comparison between the 'Erlkönig' poems of Goethe and Zhukovsky, which was published in *Numbers*; the childhood memoirs, 'Women of the Flagellant Sect' ('Khlystovki') and 'The Opening of the Museum', which appeared in the short-lived journal *Encounters* (*Vstrechi*); the story 'The Devil'; the splendid lyrical-psychological study 'My Mother and Music' (in *Contemporary Annals*); and finally, the stories 'The Chinaman' and 'Mother's Tale' (in *The Latest News*).[15]

All the same, there was still not enough money, either for life or for death. The writer's mood was deeply depressed. Slonim recalls how once in 1934 she said to him when they met in a café in Paris: 'My faith has been destroyed, my hopes have vanished, and my strength has dried up.' In the edition of the letters to Tesková one notices an especially large number of cuts in the letters of this period.

At the end of 1934 the Efrons were forced to move from their flat in Clamart. Marina and Mur settled for a few weeks in the village of Elancourt (Seine-et-Oise) two stops after Versailles. For a short time Anna Andreyeva, whom Marina considered to be one of her best friends, stayed with them. Alya spent the summer in Normandy, with the family of a banker from Germany. She was supposed to give all the members of the family French lessons. In her letters Tsvetayeva complains that Alya was earning very little money. She simply did not understand that this once fantastically wealthy German Jewish banker had suddenly become the same kind of political refugee as herself. This whole time Efron was carrying on his own secret life.

Beginning in October, a new address appeared on Marina's letters: 33, rue Jean Baptiste Potin, Vanves.

Towards the end of the year a new disaster befell Marina '...pure and sharp, like a diamond...' On 21 November 1934 her former "pupil" and hiking companion of 1928, Nikolay Gronsky, fell under the wheels of a train in the Paris métro and was crushed to death. They had not seen each other since the spring of 1931, but this unexpected death profoundly shook Marina. She suddenly found that she could write poetry again. Over several days the cycle of poems *To the Memory of N.P. Gronsky* arose:[16]

> There are happy men and women
> Who *can't* sing. Well, they must
> Shed tears! How sweet it is for them
> To pour their grief out in a cloudburst!
>
> So that under the stone there stirs something.
> But my calling is like a whip's sting –
> Amidst all the funeral's sobbing
> Duty commands – to sing.
>
> Though grief-cloven when his friend fell,
> With his song for him David continued.
> If Orpheus had not gone to hell,
> But his voice, instead, had descended
>
> Alone there in the dark wood,
> While he himself stood on the threshold,
> Superfluous – Eurydice would
> Have come out on it as on a tightrope.
>
> As on a tightrope and as to light's joys,
> Beyond going back, and unshaken.
> For, poet, once you're given a voice,
> From you all else is taken.
>
> [translated by David McDuff]

These poems were printed in volume 58 of *Contemporary Annals*, but her obituary about Gronsky 'A Posthumous Gift' was not accepted by *The Latest News*, where Gronsky's father worked in the editorial office. They preferred instead a colourless and dull obituary by Adamovich. In April 1935 Marina read her 'A Posthumous Gift' before her usual audience and sent it to the 'Russian Archive' in Belgrade.[17]

Marina was working with great ardour and effort. Like an ostrich she was trying to bury her head in the sand in order not to know what was happening around her, just as she had during her childhood on Trekhprudny Lane, when she saved herself in the world of her dreams. She wrote to Bunina:

> Events, wars, Hitlers, Herriots, Balbos, Rossis, and whatever they are called ... The NEWSPAPER is what impresses people as being truly alive, and which knocks me dead with boredom.[18]

She hid her head so deeply in the sand that she did not even notice what was going on under her own roof. Or did she, all the

same, suspect that not everything was in order with her husband?
As Slonim says:

> From 1935 Sergey Yakovlevich had become a paid employee of the
> 'Union for Repatriation to the Motherland', but M.I., of course, did not
> suspect that the money he was bringing home came from the special
> fund of the Soviet secret service.[19]

Slonim correctly assessed the situation, only he was mistaken
about the date. In an article which appeared in *Literaturnaya gazeta*
at the end of 1990, which summarised what was known for certain
about the Efron affair up until then, it was stated that already in
1933 Efron was recruited by the NKVD as a secret agent, along
with his friend N.A. Klepinin.[20] One can assume from then on he
was also paid by them.

CHAPTER 25

Clamart – La Favière – Vanves – Savoy
1935 – 1936

'Events, wars, Hitlers', however, very actively continued to make their presence felt. In Germany opponents of 'The Party' had already begun to be arrested, and the persecution of the Jewish population was underway, as well as the burning of books by authors who had not submitted themselves to the official ideology. Among the people rumours were spreading about some kind of terrible prison camp in Dachau near Munich. Intelligent and sober minds could already guess where Germany was headed, and with it, the rest of the world.

In June 1935 the French left-wing parties, with the participation of the Communists, organised in Paris an international congress of writers, in order to call attention to the dangers of Fascism. A delegation was also sent from the USSR, and by order of Stalin himself, Boris Pasternak was among its number. Thus it happened that Marina met Boris, something which she could not even have dreamt of, in the corridors of the building in which the congress was held. This meeting turned out to be a complete fiasco.

She wrote to Tesková on 12 July:

> I will write about my meeting with Pasternak (and what a *non-meeting it was!*) when you reply. Now it is too painful (and uncertain, as perhaps you have already left for your *dacha*, and this letter will not reach you) ...

Here is Pasternak's own account:

> In the summer of 1935, half out of my senses and on the verge of mental illness after almost a year of insomnia, I arrived in Paris for an anti-Fascist congress. There I met the son, daughter and husband of Tsvetayeva, that charming, fine, and upright man, whom I loved like a brother. The members of Tsvetayeva's family insisted on her return to Russia. They expressed in part their nostalgia for their native land, and

their sympathy for Communism and the Soviet Union, and in part their belief that Tsvetayeva had no place in Paris, and that she was disappearing into a void without response from her readers.

Tsvetayeva asked me what I thought in this regard; I had to say I had no definite opinion. I did not know what to advise her, and was very much afraid that she and her remarkable family would find it difficult and awkward to live among us. The total tragedy which befell this family immeasurably surpassed my apprehensions.[1]

Slonim says:

> When I asked her about this meeting, she said with a bitterness which I will never forget: 'It was a non-meeting', and then she suddenly repeated without finishing it, the last stanza of her poem to Blok:
>
> > But my river – with your river
> > But my hand – with your hand,
> > Will not meet...[2]

Only much later did Marina confess in a letter to her Czech friend, how she had become disillusioned with Pasternak:

> When I read the word "Furchtlosigkeit" I feel a shiver down my spine: *fearlessness*. That is the word which I have been repeating during this whole time inside myself, and sometimes aloud, as my last stronghold: the first and last word of my whole existence. (Which links me with almost all people!) Boris Pasternak, to whom I turned for years on end, across hundreds of *versts*, as to a second self, said to me in a whisper at the writers' conference: I did not dare not to come, the secretary of S-n [Stalin] came to me. I was frightened...

She then added maliciously, apparently without thinking of the conditions in which Pasternak lived in the Soviet Union: 'He did not at all want to go without his beautiful wife, but they sat him in the aeroplane and brought him here.'[3]

Thanks to Olga Ivinskaya, we now know why he was on the verge of a mental breakdown after nearly a year of insomnia. The year before, Pasternak had been forced to take part in a trip organised by the Union of Writers through some regions which had been "de-Kulakified", so he witnessed at first hand the terrible deprivations which the remaining population suffered. And then, at the insistence of the organisers of the Paris congress, Barbusse, Aragon and Malraux, he was taken directly from a sanatorium and put on a flight to Paris.

Could Pasternak have saved Marina Tsvetayeva from the terrible fate which threatened her and her family, if he had told the truth in 1935 about what was happening in Russia? And would Marina have believed him?

Olga Ivinskaya writes:

> Pasternak suffered greatly from the disaster which befell Tsvetayeva

and her family, all the more so, as he himself had asked M. Ts. to return to her native land.[4]

In the summer of 1935 Marina was given the opportunity of going with Mur to Provence. Two Russian families had organised a Russian colony there at the foot of the Esterel Massif, not far from the resort of Le Lavandou, in the quiet bay of La Favière. One of these organisers was Baroness O.M. Wrangel, the daughter of the writer Yelpatievsky, a cousin of Ivan Vladimirovich Tsvetayev, in whose *dacha* Marina had lived in Yalta in 1905. She now leased a room in the attic of Baroness Wrangel's summer home.

For the first time in her life Marina saw the Côte d'Azur, but the celebrated beauty of this place did not impress her. She wrote to Tesková:

> We are here for the second week. I am languishing. I will now explain why, and I hope you will understand me. I do not at all need *such* beauty, nor *so much* beauty; the sea, the hills, the myrtle, the flowering mimosa etc. For me, one tree in a window is enough . . . Such beauty imposes on me the responsibility of uninterrupted rapture . . . This continuous beauty oppresses me. I have *nothing* to give in return. I have always loved modest things; simple and deserted places, which no one likes, which trust *me* to convey them, and myself, I feel this, *to others*. But to love the Côte d'Azur, is the same thing as loving a twenty-year-old heir to a throne: it would never occur to me.[5]

At first Marina did not feel at ease at La Favière. Here, as well, she could not be separated from Mur for a second. He had recently undergone an operation for appendicitis, and therefore could not overstrain himself. According to a precise schedule she walked with him on the beach. She did not know how to swim and she could not bear to be idle in the sun. At home she had to cook Mur's food on a primus stove; after lunch, when he took a nap, and after nine in the evening when he went to bed, Marina had nowhere to sit but in the stuffy kitchen. She could not even write as the table which she needed was in the other room where Mur slept. Moreover, she had no one to talk to as none of the Russians paid her any attention. She wrote to Tesková:

> I am "aus dem Spiel", completely "aus jedem". I look at the twenty-year-olds present, and see myself (and at the same time – *not myself*!) of 20 years ago, but they do not look at me, for them I am boring (and perhaps "strange"), though still young, I am already greying, which means: not young, a lady with a little boy. But perhaps they simply do not see me, I am just an object. It is a bitter sensation to leave suddenly the ranks of the living.

She also speaks to Vera Bunina about another worry:

> Over the last few years I have written little poetry. Because they did not

accept poems from me, they thereby forced me to write prose. (While *Freedom of Russia* was alive I could calmly write a long epic knowing that they would take it. (They accepted *everything*, and I will be grateful for this as long as I live, and, if it exists, in the hereafter.) But when F.R. ended there only remained Rudnev, and he immediately said: We do not print long poems. We need 15 poets for 12 pages.

But where could I go with my large works? Thus my Perekop was lost, seven months of work and 12 years of love. Thus the poem about the Imperial Family was never (and will hardly ever be) finished. Thus my French Swain – Le Gars, had gone to waste; and all for the same reason, *long poems are not needed*. But I needed to earn money; and *outwardly* to justify my existence. And thus the prose began, which I love *very* much, I do not complain. But all the same, it is somewhat forced: I am doomed to prosaic words.

Of course, lines of verse do come to me, but as if in a dream. Sometimes, and this more frequently, they also leave me in the same way. Indeed poems do not write themselves. But all of my little free time ... goes on prose, for prose demands *physically* more time ... Fragments do land in the notebook, sometimes 8 lines, sometimes 4, sometimes only 2. Other times poems burst forth, or else I fall into a torrent of them. Then there were whole cycles, but again nothing was finished: there were solid blanks, either there was a line missing, or a whole quatrain; that is, in the end, there was only a rough draft.

Finally I became frightened. And what if I die? What then will be left from these years? (For what did I live then??) And then another fear: what if I lose my art? That is, if I were no longer capable of writing a *completed* work; of *finishing writing*. And what if I am doomed to fragments to the end of my days?

And yet this summer I have begun to finish something. It was simple: I took a notebook and wrote from the first page. I accomplished something. That is, a series of poems which exist. But during these past years I have noticed that my demands have also risen: in terms of both sound and meaning. Vera! I can spend a *whole day* seeking an epithet; i.e. one word, and sometimes I do *not* find it, and I become frightened, ... that I will end like Schumann, who suddenly began to hear (day and night) *in his head*, beneath his skull, trumpets in B flat ... [6]

At the end of this summer, Marina's mood improved. She met some more sympathetic people, among them the Slavists Boris Unbegaun and Yelizaveta Mahler, a Swiss woman born in Russia, who taught the Russian language at the University of Basle. Marina even went swimming, and was, in the end, very satisfied with this summer on the Mediterranean.

Speaking of her stay at La Favière, Tsvetayeva told Tesková on 30 September: 'As a result there are several poems: not a great deal, and half a long poem (about a *singer*: myself).' Not only did this work remain unfinished, but it became known only in 1981 when Ye. Korkina published it in Moscow in 1981 in the Moscow literary collection *Poezia*. The manuscript is kept at TSGALI. The

beginning of the poem was known earlier, it is a self-portrait with
the title 'The House' (' . . . out of which souls watch with all their
eyes . . . ') In this part Tsvetayeva describes her house in Vanves,
the refugee milieu, and a young man (' . . . with a face, pure as the
moon . . . '), who after hearing the voice of the singer coming from
the top storey, goes up and follows her into a dark corridor:
' . . . and thus he went, farther, farther, farther . . . ' The poem
broke off 'suddenly and for ever' on 10 September 1935.[7]

The winter of 1935-36 was monotonous and lonely for
Tsvetayeva. She lived alone with Mur in Vanves; Alya and Sergey
Yakovlevich hardly ever appeared at home. Disagreements in the
family were constantly growing. Marina wrote to Tesková:

> Do you know, dear Anna Antonovna, a good fortune-teller in Prague?
> For I do not think I can manage without one. Everything comes to the
> same thing: to go or not to go. (If to go, then this is for ever.) In short:
> S.Ya. and Alya and Mur are dying to leave. Around us is the threat of
> war and revolution, in general, catastrophic events. I have nothing to live
> for here, on my own. The emigration does *not like* me. *The Latest News*
> has got rid of me; they will no longer publish me. The lady-patronesses
> of Paris cannot bear me for my independent character. Finally, Mur has
> no kind of prospects here. I can see, after all, what has happened to
> these twenty-year-old young people. The are in a *dead end.*
>
> In Moscow I have my sister Asya, who loves me, perhaps, more than
> her own son. In Moscow I have, at least, a circle of real writers, not
> wrecks. (The writers here do not like me, they do not consider me to be
> one of them.) Finally, there is nature and space over there.
>
> Thus the *pro*. The *contra*: Moscow is turning into New York; into an
> ideological New York, neither deserts, nor hills: lakes of asphalt with
> megaphones, loud-speakers, and colossal posters. No, I did not begin
> with the main thing: with *Mur*, whom this Moscow will immediately and
> entirely seize from me. And the second main problem: me with my
> Furchtlosigkeit. I who do *not know* how not to answer, I who cannot sign
> a welcoming speech to the great Stalin, for it is not *I* who have called
> him great, and even if he is great, this is not my kind of greatness, and
> perhaps, most importantly of all, I hate every kind of triumphant
> bureaucratic church.

And on 29 March:

> Dear Anna Antonovna, I am living under a cloud of departure. As yet
> there is still nothing real, but for me, for feelings, reality is not
> necessary. I feel that my life is breaking in two, and that this is its final
> end.
>
> Whether it will be tomorrow, or in a year's time – I already no longer
> live here ("this short while is not worth the trouble") nor live at all for
> that matter. I fear for my manuscripts, what will happen to them? *Half* of
> them cannot be taken! and what kind of worry (love) and mad pity I feel
> for my last friends; and for my books; again, half of them cannot be
> taken! And which to leave?? and which to take?? Already . . . breathing

heavily I live (not-living). Getting up in the morning I am either full of
joy (having overslept!) and throw myself immediately at my manuscripts;
suddenly I remember everything and think à quoi bon? It does not
matter if I do not finish writing anything, for if I do finish something, I
will abandon it all the same: in the best instance I will bury it alive in
some archive. I will then never be able to re-read it! (not to speak of
reading it to anyone, or publishing it)...

I cannot keep S.Ya. here any longer, nor will I keep him, but he will
not go without me, he is waiting for something ('the recovery of my
sight') not understanding that *I will die the way I am*. In his place I would
feel: either – or. In the summer I am going. Are you going? And I would
say, of course, yes, in order not to be separated. Besides this, I would be
lost alone with Mur. But he will not take this on himself, he is waiting
for me to burn my bridges *of my own free will* (or as he sees it: for me to
unfurl all my sails!)...More than anything I want to go to you in
Czechoslovakia – for ever![8]

Marina's apprehensions that she could no longer finish a work
she had begun, proved to be unfounded: when she learnt of the
death of Kuzmin she wrote in a short time, 'An Otherworldly
Evening', her recollections of Kuzmin and the New Year's Eve of
1916 in Petersburg. The essay was published in volume 61 of
Contemporary Annals.

Mark Slonim is the only person who can tell us about another
work of Tsvetayeva, to which she herself referred only in hints.
This is the epic poem about the life and death of the Imperial
Family, which included descriptions of Tobolsk and Yekaterinburg. Marina was writing this at the same time as her family was
becoming whole-heartedly devoted to Communism. The poem was
completed in 1936. It was not possible, of course, to publish it; she
therefore decided to read it to the Lebedev family circle, Marina
also insisted that Slonim be present:

...M.I. explained that the idea for the poem was conceived a long time
ago, as an answer to Mayakovsky's poem 'The Emperor'...She
insisted on what she had declared repeatedly: the poet must be on the
side of the victims, and not of the executioners, and if history is cruel
and unjust, then the poet is obliged to be against it. The poem was quite
long, with a description of Yekaterinburg and Tobolsk, which recalled
various parts of Tsvetayeva's 'Siberia'...They almost all seemed to me
to be very vivid and daring. The reading lasted more than an hour, and
after it everyone immediately began to speak up. Lebedev considered
that, deliberately or indeliberately, it turned out to be a glorification of
the Tsar. M.I. reproached him for confusing two levels of meaning, the
political and the human. I said that several cantos moved me, they
sounded tragic, and were successful verbally. M.I. quickly turned to me
and asked: 'And would you decide to publish the poem if you now had
your journal?' I answered that I would, but with an editorial proviso,
because the poem would be received as a political declaration,

independently of the idea and intentions of the author. M.I. shrugged her shoulders: 'But everyone knows perfectly well that I am not a monarchist, in fact Sergey Yakovlevich and I are accused of Bolshevism.' At this point everyone tried to convince her: it was not a question of what one thinks, but of the kind of impression one's words make. As always, the serene Margarita Nikolayevna Lebedeva restrained our ardour: after all, the disagreement remained purely theoretical, as the poem would not be published anywhere. M.I. pondered this and then remarked with a bitter smile that, perhaps, it would some day be written on the title page: 'From the posthumous legacy of Marina Tsvetayeva'. But this prediction was not to be fulfilled. Before M.I.'s departure for Russia in 1939, the poem about the murder of the imperial family, and a significant number of poems and prose works, which M.I. had rightly declared 'unsuitable for import into the USSR' were sent, with the help of our foreign friends, to the International Socialist Archive in Amsterdam for safe-keeping. During the occupation of Holland it was bombed by Hitler's planes and all this material went up in flames.[9]

In May 1936 Marina was invited to Belgium to read some of her works. Zinaida Shakhovskaya, who was living in Brussels, organised two appearances for her in the small Russian colony. At the first evening Tsvetayeva read an essay in French 'Mon père et son musée', which has come down to us only in Russian.[10] The programme for the second evening consisted of the 'Speech about Balmont' and 'An Otherworldly Evening'. From the point of view of earnings, the trip was a success, not only could Marina buy new clothes for Mur, but she could even put some money aside for herself. But her dream of a friendship with her hostess, Olga Wolters, a Russian married to a Belgian, was not realised. Tsvetayeva complained to Tesková:

> I dreamt of a *friendship* with her, for this and with this I went, but the friendship did *not happen*...there was no room in her soul *for me*. Therefore, in spite of all the success of the trip, I returned with a feeling of failure: with my soul empty-handed. I still need people to love me: to allow me to love them, to need me – *like bread*. And this demand is both modest – and mad.[11]

Soon after this trip Zinaida Shakhovskaya visited Marina in Vanves. She recalls how Marina spoke of Rilke while she was boiling some eggs in a small saucepan:

> ...Captivated, I can still hear the unique rhythm and unique weight of her speech, but I do not remember anything about Rilke. I only recall Marina Tsvetayeva's face and those heights on to which she led me with such irrepressible energy, not realising that I could not follow her. And the demands of everyday life, of course, immediately took their revenge on such disdain: the water had boiled away, the eggs were not cooked, but had curdled and exploded, and the aluminium was burnt...[12]

Between her return from Brussels and the summer holidays, that is, from the end of May to 16 June 1936, Marina was busy with the re-working of a poem, begun in 1934, with the title 'The Bus'. This is an amusing, carefree description of a ride on a bus, during which her travelling companion can think of nothing better to say than to compare a tree in blossom with 'a cauliflower covered in white sauce'. The cheerful tone of this poem in no way reflects Marina's real mood at the time.[13]

In July Marina moved with Mur to a small town with a medieval appearance, Moret-sur-Loing. According to the letters which she wrote to Tesková and Shakhovskaya, one might conclude that she intended to spend the entire summer here in order to do some serious work: she wanted to translate all of her favourite poems by Pushkin into French. She did not explain to her friends why she then spent August and the first part of September at the Russian convalescent home of Château d'Arcine in the Haute Savoie.

During this summer a miracle suddenly occurred again in Marina Tsvetayeva's life. A letter reached her in Moret-sur-Loing, which again awakened all the hidden sources and strengths of her soul. The person writing to her was a young Russian of Swiss descent who belonged to Adamovich's circle and was a poet of modest talent. He was called Baron Anatoly Steiger. In his letter, which he sent from a sanatorium in Switzerland, he informed her that he was very ill with tuberculosis and was about to undergo an operation in a few days. He also sent her a copy of a recently published volume of his poetry.

Marina's letter in reply (which remains unknown) apparently made such an impression on him that he sent her a sixteen page 'confession' of his life and asked for her frendship and help 'for his whole life'. The sick young man, who was afraid of possibly dying, sought the assistance and spiritual support of the mature woman poet, whom he had long admired from a distance. He made, however, a terrible mistake; as his friend Kirill Vilchkovsky explains, he had touched a volcano.[14] Marina interpreted this letter after her own fashion: she understood only that there was someone who needed her, and who was waiting for her. The realisation of this struck her like an earthquake. She wrote to him every day, and offered him her 'maternal love'. She was prepared to give herself entirely to her new mission, but she also wanted to have complete control over Steiger's fate. She did not stop to consider that the seriously ill man needed her solicitous sympathy more than her tyrannical love. On 29 July she wrote to Steiger:

If I said *mother*, then it is because this word is the *most* inclusive and all-embracing, the most extensive and the most exact, which excludes *nothing*. The word, before which *all, all* other words are boundaries. And whether you like it or not, I have taken you to that place inside me, where I keep everything which I love without taking the time to examine it, *seeing* it already *from the inside*. You are my booty and catch, like the ruins of the Roman viaduct I saw today, through which the dawn shone, and which is absorbed in me more truly and eternally than in the Loing river, into which it has been gazing for centuries ...

During these days, before and after his operation, Marina wrote to Steiger every day in order, as she promised the sick man, to give him pleasure. She wrote also, probably, because the image of the ill and abandoned young man had become for her the embodiment of the principal causes and goals of her life. She wrote to him: 'Do not be surprised at my gigantic step towards you, I have *no* other ...' and 'Sometimes I think that you are me ...'

She waited for his letters, as she had waited at one time for Bakhrakh's and especially for the first news after his operation.

Marina spent this time wandering through the ancient halls and enormous empty attics of the château; her fear and anxiety about the young poet made her happy, probably for the last time. As proof of this is her cycle *Poems to an Orphan*, which like a living stream, suddenly poured forth as before.

> Finally I met
> The one I need
> Someone who had a mortal
> Need of me.
>
> What the rainbow is to the eye
> And black earth to grass
> Is the need of a human being
> For a human being.
>
> More necessary to me than rain and rainbow
> Or a hand – is the need
> Of someone's hands
> For my hand.
>
> And because this palm
> Reached me with a *sore*
> I would put my own hand directly
> Into the fire for you![15]

It is not surprising that Steiger did not understand these letters very well. He withdrew and was even more frightened, when from his point of view, the older poet invited him to Savoy. Steiger carefully declined, but she did not understand and began to take steps towards obtaining a Swiss visa in order to visit him in Berne. He then, after 11 September, decided to break off this correspondence.

Tsvetayeva's letters to Steiger after 1 September, and his replies, are not known to us; only one of these letters, her last, dated the end of September, has been published in *Novy mir*. According to Vilchkovsky, this correspondence ends with a refrain from a German folksong which Marina was fond of:

> Behüt Dich Gott, es wär so schön gewesen,
> Behüt Dich Gott, es hat nicht sollen sein!

The awakening after this bright summer dream was bitter and painful. Returning home Tsvetayeva related to Tesková what she had been through:

> The doctor wanted him to spend the winter in Berne with his parents, and of course, his parents wanted this too; but he himself decided to go to Paris, because in Paris there is Adamovich, literature and Mont-parnasse and sessions until 3 in the morning with the tenth cup of black coffee; because he is after all (after that love) – dead ... This is what I have wasted and even squandered 'le plus clair de mon été' on. To this I responded with the truth of my whole being; that we do not share the same *road*: that my road, and the road to me, is a solitary one. And to this I then added everything about Montparnasse; and everything about *spiritual* weakness, with which I have nothing to do; and gratitude for a whole summer of anxiety and dreams; and gratitude for the truth ... [16]

In her last letter to Steiger she wrote:

> For friendship with me, or service, which amounts to the same thing, a healthy root is needed. Friendship with condescension means *only* pity and abasement. I am not God, who can condescend. I myself need someone who is higher, or at least, equal to me. About what kind of equality do I speak? There is only one, the *equality of effort*. I am completely indifferent to how much you can lift, what is important to me is how much you can exert yourself. Effort is desire. And if this desire is not in you, then I have nothing to do with you. [17]

It is possible that Marina did not send this letter, but only entered it into her notebook.

All the same, Steiger considered it his duty to visit Tsvetayeva after he arrived in Paris. They had nothing to talk about. 'Everything which is human in him has gone into his short poems, there is nothing left for the rest; immediately the bottom shines through,' Tsvetayeva wrote to Ivask. [18] She did not, however, refuse her 'adopted son' a last favour: she recommended him to Ivask with the request that he help Steiger in his literary career. After this they never met again. For Marina, Anatoly Steiger had ceased to exist. In 1944 he died in Switzerland of tuberculosis.

For one last time, however, Tsvetayeva succeeded in transform-ing a personal grief and injury into a radiant work of art. We are indebted to the era of the encounter with Steiger for the inspiration behind one of her best prose pieces, the essay 'My Pushkin', which was written in the autumn of 1936. One can find in it countless traces of the summer's experience:

> But there is still one more, or rather, not one, but many things which *Yevgeny Onegin* predestined in me. If later, throughout my whole life, up to the present day, I have always been the first to write, the first to extend my hand, both hands, not fearing judgement, it was because, lying at the dawn of my days, Tatyana, in this book, did this before my eyes, by the light of a candle, with a tousled plait of hair across her breast. And if later, when everyone went away (they always went away), I not only did not hold out my hand after them, but did not even turn my head, it is only because, at that time in the garden, Tatyana froze like a statue.

What was Sergey Yakovlevich doing at this time? Why did his wife and son urgently have to leave their village and move to the distant Château d'Arcine on the Swiss border? One explanation might be that here Efron could keep in contact with N.A. Klepinin, who was staying nearby.[19] Efron's name unexpectedly turns up in a small booklet *L'Assassinat politique et l'URSS*, which did not attract much attention when it was published in 1939.[20] One of its authors relates several strange incidents.

In 1936 the GPU became interested in Lev Sedov, the son of Trotsky. A group of five people in the service of the GPU rented a flat near him, and when Sedov and his wife went in August to Cap d'Antibes, the "shadows" followed him. They were: the young Swiss woman Renata Steiner, an admirer of the Soviet Union, who was told that when the occasion arose, she could receive a Soviet visa through the 'Union for Repatriation to the Motherland'; her "chief" Marcel Rollin, alias Dmitry Smirensky; her lover Pierre Schwarzenberg, who subsequently disappeared during the Spanish Civil War; the Frenchman Pierre-Louis Ducomet, and – Sergey Yakovlevich Efron.

Once again during this period, we come across Sergey Efron. When Kirill Khenkin, a young Russian of the second generation of émigrés and a student at the University of Paris, decided to fight in the Spanish Civil War on the side of the Republicans, it was Efron, a long-standing friend of the family, who smoothed the way for him to get to Valencia, and instructed him to get in touch with the NKVD agent there, a certain Orlov, who would assign him 'some interesting work'. Later, Orlov was one of the very few who succeeded in escaping Stalin's agents, and who fled to safety in America.[21]

CHAPTER 26

Vanves – Departure of Alya – Reiss Affair
1937

The terrible year of 1937, over which hung the black storm-cloud of the Stalin purges and the systematic preparation for war in National Socialist Germany, the year, which finally destroyed the Efron family, began rather well for Marina. This was the year of the centenary of Pushkin's death, and Tsvetayeva worked, therefore, especially intensively on two essays about her favourite poet, 'Pushkin and Pugachov'[1] and 'My Pushkin'.

'This is about my early childhood: Pushkin in the nursery, with the amendment, *in my* nursery,' she explained to her Czech friend defending herself against the accusations of megalomania which had been made about the title.[2] On the occasion of the 'Pushkin Year' *Contemporary Annals* published her cycle of *Poems to Pushkin*, although at first Marina had doubts that this would ever happen, as she considered them to be 'too revolutionary'.[3] She read these poems and 'My Pushkin' on 3 March 1937. As it later turned out, this was her last public appearance in the West.

During this time we also come across the name of Sergey Yakovlevich, not as a member of the audience attending his wife's literary evening, but in connection with other events: he was the head of the group of Renata Steiner, Smirensky, and Ducomet, which we have mentioned. In January 1937 they followed Lev Sedov to Strasbourg, in order to learn what he was discussing with his Swiss lawyer. But a telegram sent by Efron immediately summoned them back to Paris. Here they were entrusted with a far more interesting task; they had to shadow an agent of the GPU who was residing in Paris, and who, under the influence of the Stalin purges had begun to entertain doubts about the ruling élite in Moscow. He came from Podwoloczyska and was called Ignaz Poretsky, but was known in party circles as 'Ludwig'; he also used the alias of Ignaz Reiss.[4]

The president of the 'Union for Repatriation to the USSR', managed to perform yet another duty, this time official: his own daughter Ariadna returned to the Soviet Union of her own free will on 15 March. She made this trip full of excitement and enthusiasm. The few remaining friends of the Efron family showered her with gifts, and Alya, trembling from happiness and hopes for the 'radiant future', left to meet her fate. Marina wrote to Tesková:

> The departure was a happy occasion, people only leave like this for their honeymoons, and not even all of them. She was dressed entirely in new clothes, and looked very elegant [1 line deleted]. She ran from one person to another, chatting and joking. [7 lines deleted]. Then for a long time she did not write. [2 lines deleted]. Then the letters began and continued [5 lines deleted] . . . She is living with S.Ya.'s sister, who is ill and an invalid, in a tiny, but separate room. She is studying English with my sister (the best expert of English in all of Moscow). I do not know how and with whom she spends her time. The first pay which she received as soon as she arrived was 300 roubles, and she has all sorts of prospects for work as an illustrator. One thing is clear: she is *very* happy [22 lines deleted].[5]

The consequences of Alya's departure were instantly felt. Marina's Russian friends and correspondents no longer wanted to have anything to do with her. Or, perhaps she herself broke off all her correspondence? Her last letter to Vera Bunina (of 19 or 26 February) mentions only the Pushkin evening; in a letter to Ivask of 27 February she keeps to her theme about the problem of mediocrity in literature; and in her last letter to Khodasevich she writes, among other things:

> Do not be surprised by my silence, Alya is leaving on Monday, that is, the day after tomorrow. The whole house and the whole day have gone mad, there are heaps of things everywhere, the last purchases and errands: all this is indescribable. As soon as she leaves I am yours . . . I embrace you and will soon call you.[6]

After 15 March we know of only a few insignificant notes to Vladimir Sosinsky. Finally, there remain the letters to Tesková, who did not fail Tsvetayeva as a source of support.

In her first letter from Moscow Alya told her mother that the actress Sonya Holliday had recently died. This news profoundly shook Marina, and it evoked a whole epoch of her youth. Marina dedicated to the memory of Sonya her last large work in prose, *The Tale about Sonechka*, which is among Tsvetayeva's best. As much as her portrait of Goncharova appeared flat and colourless, the one of Sonya is vivid and convincing. Before our eyes arises the petite eccentric actress, who behaved like an *"institutochka"* and was constantly in tears, but who in decisive and difficult moments proved brave and kind. It seemed to Marina that she had never loved another woman so strongly as Sonechka. She summed up her joyless life and wrote:

> And now, farewell Sonechka! You shall be blessed for the minute of beatitude and happiness you gave to another lonely and grateful heart! My God! A whole minute of happiness! Is this really that little, even if over a lifetime?

Marina was so immersed in her memories of Sonechka and her life in Moscow in 1919 that she did not appear to notice what was happening around her. She finished this work in the summer of 1937. She was then on holiday on the Atlantic coast, in Lacanau (Département Gironde). On 16 July she sent greetings from here to Anna Tesková, which are in the cheerful spirit of summer holidays. She writes about her work and about the books she was reading by Sigrid Undset and Selma Lagerlöf, and recalls how ten years ago she had lived in the same place, and mentions, as if in passing, that her husband was planning to come in August to spend a few days with her and Mur on the coast. We do not know whether this took place; we also do not know, unfortunately, if Marina met Sergey Yakovlevich when she returned to Vanves on 20 September. One can conclude from a letter of little interest which she sent to Tesková on 27 September, that at the time she still did not suspect anything untoward, and that her world was still in order.

In fact, however, everything had changed: on 17 July 'Ludwig' Poretsky took a decisive step, which became the turning point for Marina Tsvetayeva as well. In a letter written in the style of a manifesto, he renounced Stalin and his own political position, which had been one of loyalty to the régime. Such a gesture demanded great courage on his part.[7] He managed to escape unnoticed from Paris with his wife and small son, in spite of the fact that this letter, addressed to Stalin, was already in the 'hands of the appropriate people' in the Soviet embassy in Paris, that is, the members of the group who were following him, Lidia Grosovskaya and the commissar for special affairs, Spiegelglass, 'Accidentally' one of the letters which 'Ludwig' received through the embassy was from a former acquaintance in Germany, Getrud Schildbach, who wrote that she too was planning to break with Moscow, and asked 'Ludwig' to set a date for a meeting. In this way still another person was added to the group of people assigned to follow 'Ludwig'. Poretsky then made his terrible mistake. Before going into hiding in the mountains of the Haute-Savoie, not far from the Swiss frontier,

Sergey Efron: Paris, 1937

he wrote to his former friend and arranged to meet her in Lausanne.

This meeting between Schildbach and Poretsky took place on 4 September. Later his wife and son waited in vain for his return. On the following day on a road in the outskirts of Lausanne the body of a man who had been shot several times was found.

In a free country with a free press every reader has the right to free information. Thus the *Neue Zürcher Zeitung* did not conceal what it had been able to discover about the murdered man. The morning edition of 6 September 1937 contained the following:

> 'A Political Murder?' Pully. On Saturday night the police found ... on the road near Chamblandes the bullet-ridden corpse of a man. He had apparently been shot by a light machine-gun. Since no one in the vicinity had heard shots, one can conclude that the crime was committed in another place. The wallet of the man, which contained bank-notes, was untouched. The person in question was a Czech citizen by the name of Eberhardt.

By the evening edition of the same day the Pully police had already learnt some more about the murder:

> Enquiries have shown that on Saturday evening Eberhardt had taken a room alone in a hotel. From that time no one had seen him. That night his body was taken in an automobile from Lausanne to the place where they found him; the car stopped for a short time and quickly returned by the same road. On Sunday evening the Geneva police found a grey car with a Berne registration number near the railway station of Cornavin. In the car were found traces of blood, and on the floor, ten empty cartridges of the same calibre as the revolver, which was discovered near the body. Thus there is no doubt that the car belonged to one or another of the murderers, who, apparently, fled to France on the train.

On the following day the *Neue Zürcher Zeitung* added further information:

> Since the circumstances in which the body of the Czechoslovak businessman Eberhardt was found completely exclude the possibility of suicide, there are more and more grounds for believing that this was a political crime.

On 8 September 1937 the midday edition stated:

> The police of the canton of Vaud have united their efforts with the security police of Valais after it had been established that a suspicious Soviet citizen had left Lausanne on Saturday for Martigny. There he received a telephone call from someone, and he again left in the direction of Chamonix. Enquiries made in Prague have shown that the passport found on the body of the murdered man is a forgery.

On 9 September the police had already established that a suspicious couple were driven by a chauffeur from Geneva to

Annemasse. On 13 September the *Neue Zürcher Zeitung* published a communiqué from Budapest, in which several members of the Socialist Workers Movement there identified Eberhardt as the deputy of the commander of the Red Army during the time of the Communist dictatorship of Béla Kun in Hungary.

Only ten days later the newspaper revealed more sensational news:

> *Neue Zürcher Zeitung*, 23 September 1937 (evening edition): 'Another Kutepov Affair?' Paris. The Paris police have announced that General Miller, the president of the Union of Russian Combined Forces yesterday afternoon *disappeared without a trace.* They are afraid that General Miller has suffered the same fate as General Kutepov, who was kidnapped in 1930, and whom no one has seen since. General Kutepov was the predecessor of General Miller as president of the Union of Russian Combined Forces...

> *Neue Zürcher Zeitung*, 25 September (page 3): The Kidnapping of General Miller... On Thursday night the police found a new clue which led them to Le Havre. The chief of police in Le Havre has reported that around 4 o'clock on Wednesday evening, that is, within several hours of General Miller's disappearance, a car arrived at the harbour with three foreigners, and after 3½ hours it returned in the direction of Paris with only two people. It was noticed that the car stopped very close by the Soviet ship *Maria Ulyanova.* This ship left Le Havre one and a half hours later, suddenly and without notifying the port authority. As it became known, the ship sailed directly to Leningrad. In police circles the question is being raised: could General Miller have been taken on board this ship? At the present time the police are trying to learn where the suspicious car came from and who was in it...

> *Neue Zürcher Zeitung*, 25 September (page 1): Paris. The Soviet embassy in Paris has announced that the mysterious car found near Le Havre belongs to the embassy. The car, which has a diplomatic number plate, took not three, but four, people to Le Havre; namely, the Vice-Consul of the USSR, a Soviet trade official, an employee of the embassy and a chauffeur. The first two people named boarded the merchant ship *Maria Ulyanova*...

By 30 September the police of Vaud had made considerable progress in their investigation of the murder in Chamblandes: the president of the Revolutionary Socialist party of Holland, H. Sneevliet, identified the dead man as his friend Ignaz Reiss. The police had also succeeded in discovering that Gertrud Schilbach had visited the deserter Reiss, who was in Montreux with his wife and child, under the pretext that she too had been troubled by Stalin's executions and no longer wanted to return to Moscow, and had arranged another meeting with him. In view of this it was still not clear who had killed Reiss. On 8 October the newspaper published a dispatch from Berne:

> Berne, 7 October: 'The Cheka Murder in Pully'. Just over a month has
> passed since the murder in Pully. During this time the investigation has
> been able to illuminate some aspects of this crime. The principal
> culprits are still at large, and it is not known where they are, but it is
> probable that they have fled to the USSR.
> ... The supervision of Reiss was entrusted (along with others) to the
> Swiss citizen Renata Steiner from St Gallen. Her "chief" was a certain
> Rossi (probably a false name) a Frenchman from the south of France.
> On 1 September she travelled with him to Berne, where they hired a
> car. Soon after this Reiss arrived in Switzerland. Rossi, a certain Getrud
> Schildbach (born in 1894 in Strasbourg) and another unknown person
> met him in Lausanne. These four people travelled together in the
> direction of Berne. Rossi drove and in Chamblandes Reiss was killed by
> a machine-gun. In the hotel in Lausanne the police found traces of the
> murder; among them, a bottle with a strychnine solution and poisoned
> chocolate bonbons. These traces led to a certain Kudratiev, a former
> officer of the White Army, who now works for the GPU, and lives in
> Paris, where he watches the movements of officers of the former
> Russian army... Not long ago Kudratiev left Paris and went to stay in
> the Haute-Savoie, not far from the Swiss frontier...

In December the French police discovered that Lidia Grosovskaya, who worked in the Soviet embassy in the department of the
GPU, was one of the most important figures in the Reiss murder;
for it was into her hands that Poretsky's letter fell. The Swiss
government demanded that she be extradited to Switzerland, and
on 17 December she was arrested. Through the intervention of the
Soviet embassy, however, she was released after three days on bail,
and then immediately vanished.

On 22 February 1938 the *Neue Zürcher Zeitung* included in an
editorial everything which was known at the time about the 'Reiss
Affair'. This murder was soon ousted, however, from the minds of
most people in Switzerland by the entry of the German army into
Austria:

> 'The Cheka in Europe' ... It was so obvious that the hand of Moscow
> was involved in Grosovskaya's escape, that the Soviet government and
> its representatives in Paris have preferred to remain silent about it. Lidia
> Grosovskaya, her husband, and "Doctor" Beletsky, all three of whom
> worked in the trade delegation, together with the head of the so-called
> 'Society for Repatriation to the USSR', Efron, have been identified as
> the figures responsible for the murder of the agent Reiss. Grosovsky,
> Belitsky and Efron escaped in time, but L. Grosovskaya was arrested
> and regained her liberty after the Soviet government paid a bail of
> 50,000 Frs. Although the police watched her closely, she managed to go
> into hiding at the Soviet embassy on rue de Grenelle, where she was
> taken in a car by the head of the press division of the Soviet trade
> delegation. Since then she has vanished without a trace ...

The murder in Chamblandes was perfectly conceived but poorly carried out. Although the old Communist Schildbach led her former friend and comrade to his death, she, all the same, did not give the poisoned sweets to his wife and child, as she was instructed. Apparently her nerves gave way. Thus Elisabeth Poretsky survived and could soon give the police the necessary information. Thirty years later she wrote a book in English about the 'Reiss Affair' called *Our Own People*. The first person, however, who tried to explain this affair was Victor Serge. A few days after the killing, he met Reiss's widow in Paris, who had completely lost her wits in despair. His book *L'Assassinat politique et l'URSS* came out in 1939, but because of the outbreak of war it went unnoticed.

In the end, all the figures involved in the 'Reiss Affair' disappeared without a trace, and in 1938 the criminal case about the murder of the 'Chekist Ignaz Reiss' was dropped, 'in view of insufficient evidence', as the *Basler National Zeitung* announced on 17 November 1938.

According to Elisabeth Poretsky, Renata Steiner hired the car in Berne, in which Poretsky was killed on 4 September, and then went first to Martigny in order to find the Poretsky family, who were in hiding. With her were Getrud Schildbach, the former White Russian officer Kondratiev (not Kudratiev, as the Swiss newspapers spelled it), and two Russians, whom Steiner knew in Paris: Efron and Smirensky. Kondratiev returned to Paris from Martigny, and three weeks later was one of the kidnappers of General Miller. The driver of the car, Rossi, also vanished.

In 1937 the French government of the 'Front Populaire' regarded the Soviet Union sympathetically. At first the French police did not want to become involved with the murder of an agent of the GPU carried out on foreign territory. When the Swiss government lodged a complaint against Efron and Smirensky, they were summoned for questioning, but they were immediately released. Elisabeth Poretsky believes that they escaped through Spain.

After the kidnapping of General Miller however, the mood in France changed; the police set out for Vanves in order to arrest Sergey Efron, but when it turned out that he had fled the country, they arrested his wife.

We do not know from Marina Tsvetayeva herself, who suspected nothing, how she reacted to the accusations made by the investigation agencies of the French police against her husband. Her letter to Anna Tesková written on 17 November (consisting of

64 lines) is not included in the Prague edition of her correspondence. But the stories of her friends about this terrible night confirm
one another. Yelena Izvolskaya writes:

> ...Knowing nothing about Seryozha's activities, which he carefully
> hid, Marina could not answer the questions of the French police. One
> can imagine her terror and fear. At the same time, her loyalty, and
> absolute trust in Seryozha were not shaken. She suddenly began to
> speak very quietly in French. The police listened to her in bewilder-
> ment. From her lips flowed poem after poem after poem. Strangely
> enough, this recital made a great impression on them. They listened to
> her with great respect and finally they let her go. From that time no one
> troubled her any more.[8]

Aside from Corneille and Racine, Marina declaimed her own
work in French *Le Gars*, which thus succeeded in saving its
creator. Zinaida Shakhovskaya says that when they presented
Marina with proof of her husband's guilt during their questioning,
she replied: 'Sa bonne foi a pu être surprise, la mienne en lui reste
intacte.'[9]

Decades after these events, Véronique Lossky, for the purposes
of her research, obtained access to the protocol of this interrogation
carried out by the French security police. It turned out that it had
disappeared, along with other parts of the Miller file. The name of
Efron, for example, does not appear anywhere in the archives of the
French police. Evidently this material had, at some stage, been
removed.[10]

In October Slonim met Marina at the Lebedevs'. He had the
impression that she had aged and somehow withered:

> When I met her in October at the Lebedevs' I did not recognise her
> face, I was struck by how quickly she had aged and how she had
> somehow withered. I embraced her and suddenly she began to cry,
> softly and silently; it was the first time I had ever seen her crying. Then,
> having mastered herself, she began to relate, almost in a humorous tone,
> what she called her 'misfortune'. Mur was not present at this
> conversation. I was moved both by her tears and her lack of complaint
> against fate, and by her hopeless certainty that there was no point in
> struggling and that it was necessary to accept the inevitable. I remember
> how simple and ordinary her words sounded: 'I would like to die, but I
> have to live for Mur's sake, Alya and Sergey Yakovlevich no longer need
> me.'[11]

It seemed to him that during these days something had definitely
snapped inside Marina Tsvetayeva.

It is important to emphasise that even at this terrible time, several
friends still remained loyal to Marina, who tried in every way to
help her. Aside from Slonim and the Lebedevs, such a friend was

Berdyayev, who worried about her as though she were an invalid, and I.I. Fondaminsky, that 'tireless defender of all who toil and are burdened', as Ye. Fedotova called him. Finally, there were Izvolskaya, Sosinsky and Khodasevich, who was then already seriously ill.

In general, however, a universal boycott of Tsvetayeva began. One can easily imagine what disturbance the 'Efron Affair' created among the Paris Russians. Nina Berberova describes Marina's last appearance in Russian circles:

> I saw M.I. Tsvetayeva for the last time at the funeral (or was it a memorial service?) of Prince S.M. Volkonsky on 31 October 1937. After the service at the church on rue François Gérard (Volkonsky was a Catholic of the Eastern Rite) I went out to the street. Tsvetayeva was standing alone on the pavement, and looked at us with eyes full of tears. She had aged and the hair on her uncovered head was almost grey. She stood with her arms crossed on her chest. This was soon after the murder of Ignaz Reiss, in which her husband S.Ya. Efron was involved. She stood as though plague-ridden, no one went up to her. And I, like the rest, walked past her.[12]

Marina spent her last winter in Vanves alone with Mur. Lonely, without much money or earnings she occupied herself with laundering clothes and stoking the fire. They celebrated Christmas alone, but the small Christmas tree was decorated with gilded pine cones from Všenory. She sent brief New Year's greetings to Tesková on a postcard dated 7 February:

> [15 lines deleted]...I have written nothing for the whole winter. Of course it is a difficult life, but when was it easy? But there is simply no spiritual peace (the essential and only kind). Rather, there is the reverse. (Forgive the boring postcards; such stately buildings are always boring, but now there is nothing else at hand, and I am not capable of a letter.)[13]

Marina Tsvetayeva's most important occupation this winter was the sorting, copying and examination of her manuscripts. And there was also another business, which she detested: visiting offices. She was trying to obtain Soviet citizenship for herself and her son, in order to follow Seryozha and Alya to Russia.

CHAPTER 27

Paris – 'Poems to Czechia' Departure for the USSR
1938 – JUNE 1939

At the beginning of March 1938 the European crisis had reached alarming proportions. As if hypnotised the whole world was watching Vienna, and almost no attention was paid to the Bukharin, Rykov and Krestinsky trials which were being held at the same time in Moscow. Within a day after Hitler's 'report to history on the occupation of Austria' was delivered on Vienna's Heldenplatz, Bukharin and the other men were sentenced to death. Marina Tsvetayeva did not react to these events, she had no ties with Austria, aside from the Duc de Reichstadt, and she probably knew next to nothing about what was happening in Moscow. None of this, however, could possibly have been conducive to her peace of mind.

Hitler's satisfaction with his easily won gains did not last for long. On 1 May 1938, less than two months after the occupation of Austria, 'various excesses' and 'bloody skirmishes' began in Czechoslovakia, which forced the Czech government on 21 May to mobilise the army and to close the country's borders. Marina now realised the danger. She wrote to Tesková on 23 May:

> Dear Anna Antonovna, I think of you constantly, and I am in anguish, pain and indignation, and in *hope* with you. *I feel Czechoslovakia to be a free spirit, over which bodies have no power.* And in a personal sense I feel that she is my country, my *native* land, for all of whose actions I will answer, and to which I will put my signature ahead of time. This is a *terrible* time![1]

In the spring several articles against the now absent Sergey Efron appeared in Russian émigré newspapers. Although Tsvetayeva's name is nowhere mentioned, it became impossible for her to remain in Vanves. It was also impossible for any of her new work to appear in print. Although *Russian Annals* (*Russkie zapiski*) had published the first part of 'The Tale about Sonechka' in its third issue, they refused to take the second part (which remained, unpublished, in the library of the University of Basle until 1975). Marina left Vanves and settled with Mur in the small hotel Innova in Paris, at 13, boulevard Pasteur in the 15th *arrondissement*. She retreated here and waited, alone and unhappy, for the answer to her request to return to the USSR. She also watched with despair the thickening clouds of war, and continued to sort and copy her works; it was far from possible to take all of them with her to the USSR.

It seemed that Marina had reached the lowest point of her life in the emigration, it could not be worse. But at the end of August, events were happening which were such a heavy blow to her, that she forgot, for a time, her own troubles: Hitler was trying to invade Czechoslovakia.

In her little, shabby and uncomfortable room at the hotel Innova, Marina followed the days and weeks of the National-Socialist blackmail of the small country; the threat of war, the capitulation in Munich, and the final betrayal by the Western powers of her favourite country. Czechoslovakia had become for her the magical land of her reveries, her aspirations and dreams, personified for her by the 'Knight of Prague'.

On 24 September she wrote to Tesková:

> There are *no* words for this, but they must exist. Day and night, day and night, I think of Czechoslovakia, I live in her, with her and by her; I feel her from within: her forests and hearts. All of Czechoslovakia is now one enormous human heart, beating with one rhythm: the same as my own... To the last minute and at the very last I believe and will believe in Russia: in the loyalty of *her hand*. Russia will *not let* Czechoslovakia be devoured: remember my words...

Marina asked her friend to send her as mementoes of Czechoslovakia a necklace made of glass beads, a book of Czech fairy-tales, and a photograph of the 'Knight of Prague'. On 3 October she wrote:

> I love Czechoslovakia infinitely and am infinitely grateful to her, but I am not going to *weep* over her (one does not weep over the healthy, for she alone among nations is healthy, the sick ones are the others!), thus I do not want to mourn her, but to sing her...

And so Marina Tsvetayeva began to 'sing' Czechoslovakia. Suddenly her silence was sundered and she could again write poetry. She found the words to express her pain and her love for this unfortunate country.

Thus was born the first part of the *Poems to Czechia*, which is called September:

> Reserved for aurochs, mountainsides.
> Black, the forests lie.
> Valleys look into the rivers,
> Mountains look into the sky.
>
> Most free of any region,
> More generous, there's none.
> These mountains: native country
> Of my child, my son.
> . . . .
>
> God's own land. Bohemia.
> Don't lie still as a moraine.
> God gave to you with both His hands
> And He will give again.
>
> In solemn oath they've raised their hands,
> All your sons, your children –
> They swear to die for the native land
> Of those who've none to live in![2]

> [translated by David McDuff]

During the entire winter of 1938-39, up to the final liquidation of Czechoslovakia, Marina Tsvetayeva and Anna Tesková carried on an intense correspondence. Several letters bore the stamp of the Czech censors. Marina wanted to console her friend, but it is clear that she herself was seeking consolation; Anna Tesková was obviously her last support.

> I am terribly lonely. In all of Paris there are only two houses where I go. Everything else has fallen away. If these friends of mine went away, no one would be left. In the whole city of three million . . . If I were now in Prague, it would be better for you and for me. Here my existence is perfectly meaningless. But there I could begin to love everything with a new fervour. And perhaps I could begin to write again. Here I feel – what is the point? All last year I was finishing things off, sorting and selecting (later you will understand why). Now everything is finished, and I do not have courage to begin something new. Especially, if in any case, it will not survive. I am like the cuckoo, I have left my offspring in different nests. But to raise something new for the slaughter . . . [3]

Sometimes pleasant things did happen, even if rarely. Irina Odoyevtseva tells how in the summer (of 1938?) the reconciliation took place between Tsvetayeva and Georgy Ivanov. Odoyevtseva and Ivanov had gone to visit some friends, where they found Tsvetayeva, as well. After several seconds of hesitation and silence, Ivanov and Odoyevtseva went up to the slandered writer and began to assure her with great warmth how glad they were to see her. Later they composed a letter together asking for help for a young unknown woman writer. According to Odoyevtseva, when Tsvetayeva was walking home with them that night through the streets of Paris, she turned to Odoyevtseva, who, on the verge of tears, was looking at her pale, tired and despairing face, and said:

> 'But you are completely different from what you seemed to me. It is a great pity! It means one more meeting which has not come off. How many of them have I had in my life, these non-meetings! And here is another one.' She offered me her hand. 'Farewell. Farewell for ever. Be happy. But do not wish me happiness or a happy journey. There is no point to that with me...'[4]

In spite of her withdrawal to her den, several of her friends managed to find her: 'Yesterday, after a very long interval, I saw M.L....and we saw eye to eye on everything. But such conversations occur once in a year...'[5]

Entirely by accident, Ye.N. Fedotova, the wife of G.P. Fedotov, found Tsvetayeva in her hotel. While looking for another acquaintance, she was told that Tsvetayeva was also staying there and that she was very unhappy. Fedotova recalls:

> I decided to knock at the door. Marina Ivanovna, it would appear, rejoiced at the sight of a visitor, and she began to explain that she had to go to Russia, that she had had to flee from her neighbours in Clamart, that it was impossible to keep her son at school (a French one??) because of his class-mates, that, finally, in view of the approaching war, she would simply die of hunger, and that no one would publish her. Then, to my great joy, she read her funeral hymn to Czechoslovakia: 'Two hundred years of captivity, twenty years of freedom.' Subsequently, Il.Is. (Fondaminsky) told me that he had asked her if she would give this poem to *Cont. Annals* for publication, but that, having already taken her fatal decision, she was probably afraid of appearing in the émigré press.
>
> Also in the room was her son, who, uninhibited by a visitor, not only did not turn off, but did not even turn down the radio...At this point we bid farewell...I now recall involuntarily Pasternak's words, which he said to Tsvetayeva in a whisper during the celebrations in honour of the Soviet writers in Paris: 'Marina, do not go to Russia, it is cold there, a solid draught.' This was the last time I saw her.[6]

Just before Christmas 1938 Yury Ivask came to Paris from Estonia. He wanted to visit the poet persecuted by everyone, with whom he had corresponded for so many years. On 19 December he went for the first time to the hotel Innova, and knocked at the first door on the fifth floor:

> A dark hall, many doors. Shouts, stench. I knock at random: 'Go to the devil, Monsieur! Efron is opposite.' I manage to reach Marina Ivanovna with difficulty: the whole floor is covered with utensils, and I knock over

a coffee-grinder. Her pale face. Greyish hair. The elongated beak of her nose. Strange bird-like movements: everything at right angles. Mur – ruddy, heavy, podgy . . . [7]

They spoke about Gronsky, Marina's poetry, the Zograf-Plaksina music school in Moscow, which Ivask had also attended. Marina made him lunch, then they went to a café and talked for five or six hours, as though they had known each other for years. At their next meeting, on 21 December, Marina told Ivask about her plan for returning to the Soviet Union, and she spoke of her fear about the fate of her manuscripts. Ivask had brought Marina a gift from Yelizaveta Mahler from Basle, a jar of preserves. ('Do you know, Mur ate all of it, leaving nothing for me and he did well to do so!' Marina told him on the last evening.) Ivask suggested that she turn over to Yelizaveta Mahler in Basle for safekeeping those manuscripts which she could not take with her to the Soviet Union. Fortunately for posterity, Marina Tsvetayeva agreed to follow this advice, and sent to Basle a part of her unpublished manuscripts; in this way, *Swans' Encampment*, *Perekop* and *The Tale about Sonechka* survived the war. Other works, such as the poem about the end of the Imperial Family, as well as probably many others, which were sent to the Archive of the Socialist International in Amsterdam, went up in flames, as Mark Slonim maintains, during the German attacks on Amsterdam. But at the beginning of 1939, who could predict in which corner of Europe one could hope to save manuscripts?

Yury Ivask saw Tsvetayeva for the last time on 22 December 1938.

On 14 March 1939 Hitler received at Obersalzberg the "leaders" of Slovakia, Tiso and Durčanský, who requested the "assistance" of the Reich against the 'unbearable Czech terror'. On the night of 15 March the German forces entered Bohemia and Moravia without meeting the slightest resistance or firing a single shot. The 'native land of all, who have no country' ceased to exist.

The days before the imminent catastrophe rushed onwards. For Marina this meant her departure for the USSR, and for the rest of the world, the beginning of the war.

After the occupation of Prague, Tsvetayeva's correspondence with Tesková was broken off. Only on 22 May did the first sign of life appear:

> Dear Anna Antonovna! I hope that you have now recovered sufficiently so that you can read my letter without difficulty. I will try to write clearly. During all the time which has passed I have written a great deal, already a whole little book, and I somehow cannot stop, and indeed it is a shame

to give up, there is still so much which remains of the good and the true. The poems are pouring like a real torrent, they accompany me everywhere, as did those little brooks once upon a time ... Knowing how much you love poetry, the whole time that I write, all the time that they write themselves, I think of you ...

Tesková sent a postcard in reply, and then Marina informed her:

Dear Anna Antonovna! We will probably also soon leave for the country, far away and for a very long time. For the moment I am only telling you. But wherever I am I will, for my whole life (what remains of it) long for you, without you, who are inseparable for me from my flow of poetry. An entire little volume would have been the result, but I cannot occupy myself with this now. I will put it off until the country. There, there are pine trees, the only thing I know about it ... I now have much work and many worries: I do not have the arms or legs; I want to take more to my country friends, but I do not have any money to spare, and it is necessary to run ... and at the same time I have to sort notebooks, and books, and letters ... The rest will be a long one; my friends live in total isolation, as on an island, which they do not leave, winter or summer. The young lady goes into the city to work, but there will be no point in me doing that ... [8]

Marina was completely preoccupied with her preparations for her departure: the last purchases, the sending of her manuscripts and the distribution of books. On 7 June she wrote to Anna Tesková a farewell letter:

Thank you for your encouragement, you understood me immediately [2 lines deleted] but there was no choice: one cannot abandon a man in trouble, I was born like this, and Mur will have no life nor future in a city like Paris. So – there we are.
    ... The paths, which have turned into streams at one time will reach even you: a stream is always itself! and no one can send it, besides a glacier, or the earth, or God ... But you will always recognise my voice. God, how agonizing it all is! Now, in the last heat of the moment, in a sheer fever of hands and head and weather, I have still not felt it all through, but I know what is awaiting me: I know myself! I will wring my own neck, looking back: at you, at your world, at our world. But know one thing; whenever you think of me, know that you are thinking *in response* ... You are the person who has fulfilled all my requests and who has surpassed all my (silent) demands for loyalty and remembrance. No one has loved me as you have. I remember everything and I am infinitely and eternally grateful for everything.

Marina's friends were staggered by the news of her decision to return to the USSR. They, as well, however, did not see any other way out for her. At the beginning of June, Slonim invited Marina and Mur to his home for the last time. After dinner they began to recall the times they spent together in Prague. Marina read 'The Bus'. They then spoke about the manuscripts, which Marina had to leave in the West, and about the possibility of her publishing anything in the USSR. At the last minute Mur, who was quietly yawning, suddenly started up:

'Really, mama, you never believe anything: everything will be perfect!' Marina then repeated what she had already said on more than one occasion: ' . . . it is best for the writer, where he is least of all prevented from writing, that is, from breathing.'

We sat until late. Hearing the stroke of twelve from the nearby bell-tower, M.I. rose and said with a sad smile: 'It is now midnight, but we do not need a car, as we are not in Všenory, and can reach Pasteur on foot.' Mur hurried her, she tarried. On the landing in front of my flat we embraced. I could not say a word because of the emotion I felt, and I silently watched how M.I. and her son entered the lift-cabin, and how, as it moved, their faces vanished beneath for ever.[9]

Tsvetayeva's last communication from the West is a postcard she sent to Tesková on the day of her departure:

12 June 1939, in the still standing train. Dear Anna Antonovna! (I am writing on the palm of my hand, hence the childish writing). The enormous station with green glass: a terrible green garden, and what doesn't grow in it! Before our departure Mur and I sat according to ancient custom, and made the sign of the cross under the empty place where the icon hung (it has been left in good hands, it lived with me from 1918 – well, at some time you have to part with everything: completely. This is a lesson, so that later it will not be terrible, and not even strange . . .) 17 years of life have come to an end. How happy I was then! And the happiest period of my life – remember this! – Mokropsy and Všenory, and my native mountain. It is strange – yesterday I ran into its hero on the street, whom I had not seen in years. He flew up to me from behind and without any explanation put his arm under Mur's and mine, and walked in the middle, as though nothing had happened. And then I also met – in the same miraculous way – the old mad poet* and his wife, at some friends' house, where he had *not been in a year*. It was if everyone sensed. I was continually meeting – everyone. (Now I hear, booming and terrible: Express de Vienne and I recall the towers and bridges which I will never see again.) They are shouting: En voiture, Madame! as if to me, removing me from all the former places of my life. Mur has stocked up (at this word the train started) on newspapers. – We are approaching Rouen, where at one time human gratitude burnt Jeanne d'Arc . . . We have passed Rouen – račte dále! [Czech: onwards] I will wait for news from all of you, give my warmest greetings to the whole family, I wish you all health, courage and a long life. I dream of a meeting in Mur's native land, which is more native to me than my own. I turn round at the sound of it, as if to my own name. Do you remember I had a friend, Sonechka, and everyone used to say to me 'Your Sonechka'. I am leaving wearing *your* necklace and the coat with *your* buttons, and with *your* buckle on the belt. Everything simple and which I have madly loved I will take with me to the grave, or I will burn together with it. Good-bye! It is no longer painful now, it is now already – fate. I embrace you and all of yours, each one separately and everyone

together. I love you and admire you. I believe in you as in myself.

M.

[The postcard bears the stamp: Le Havre-Gare, 16h30, 12.6.1939][10]

(* Balmont)

She was travelling to meet her fate, but she no longer considered herself to be among the living: she had suffered the first mortal blow that night at the Paris 'Sûreté', and the second with the German occupation of Prague. Everything else was only a confirmation of what Marina already knew. One of her last *Poems of Czechia* is a premonition of her own death, which occurred two years later:

Oh, eyes in tears!
Lament of wrath and love!
Oh Czech land in tears!
Spain in blood!

Oh, black mountain,
Darkening the whole world!
It is time, it is time, it is time
To return my ticket to the Creator.

I refuse to exist.
In a Bedlam of non-humans
I refuse to live.
With the wolves of the squares,

I refuse to howl.
With the sharks of the plains
I refuse to swim –
Downstream along the current of spines.

I do not need either the openings
Of the ears, or prophetic eyes.
To your insane world
There is only one answer – refusal.[11]

After Tsvetayeva's departure with her son from France, rumours circulated in Paris that Sergey Efron had been arrested and shot following his return to the Soviet Union. Zinaida Shakhovskaya tells of her efforts to let Marina know about this, in order to warn her. But the telegram, which it appears she sent to Warsaw, never reached Tsvetayeva. Shakhovskaya also tells how, at their last meeting, Marina said to her: 'There is nowhere for me to go, the emigration is pushing me out.'

Irina Odoyevtseva confirms these words:

Marina Tsvetayeva is our common sin, our common guilt. We all stand before her with an unpaid debt... The emigration really did "drive" her out, she, who needed love like air, with its complete indifference and coldness towards her. We did not know how to appreciate her, we did not love her, nor restrain her from her fatal return to Moscow. We did not only not stop her, but we even rather pushed her to take this disastrous step.[12]

But what would have happened if Marina had actually remained at that time in the West? Hitler's Germany had concluded its pact with Stalin's Russia, and exactly forty days after Tsvetayeva's departure the Second World War broke out. A fatal hour had struck for the "émigré sons" of Montparnasse as well. France summoned them to its army, and the majority of them went to defend the country which had given them refuge. They followed, in this regard, the example of the head of the 'Paris School' Adamovich, who during the first days of the war, volunteered for the French army at the age of forty-five. Many of these people perished. One frequenter of 'Russian Montparnasse' Boris Wildé, with his friend Anatoly Levitsky, began the French resistance movement, and even thought up its name 'la Résistance'. They were shot in Paris near the Musée de l'Homme. Among the Russians, however, there were also collaborators, and those who believed in the struggle against Bolshevism. The occupation of Paris meant the end of Russian Montparnasse.

The older Russian writers were affected by the catastrophe in different ways, and not all of them survived. Some of them perished because they collaborated with the Germans, others because they took part in the Resistance. Some like Balmont died in occupied Paris in destitution, while members of the Resistance, such as Shakhovskaya and Sosinsky, survived. A third group of people, like the Bunins and Bakhrakh, reached the "free zone" of France and managed to save themselves, while Slonim, Struve, Ivask and Nabokov made their way to America. Fondaminsky died in a gas chamber of the Third Reich, as did Khodasevich's second wife. Mother Maria was executed in Buchenwald in 1945, when Soviet gun-fire could already be heard. Fate was more merciful to Khodasevich: on 14 June 1939, two days after Marina Tsvetayeva's departure, he died in his own bed of cancer.

PART FOUR

The Soviet Union

With the sharks of the plains
I refuse to swim –
Downstream along the current of spines.

Poems to Czechia

Marina Tsvetayeva: Moscow, 1940

CHAPTER 28

Bolshevo – Golitsyno – Moscow

JUNE 1939 – JUNE 1941

On 18 June 1939 Marina and Mur arrived in Moscow. We can assume that they were met at the station by Alya and Yelizaveta Yakovlevna Efron. Only at this moment did Tsvetayeva learn of something that they had been keeping from her: on 2 September 1937, soon after Gorky's death, her sister Asya was arrested and sent into "internal" exile.

Sergey Yakovlevich and Alya were living in an NKVD *dacha* that formerly belonged to M.P. Tomsky. Here they found the Klepinin-Sezeman family, which had arrived before them and which lived in the other half of the house. According to the Soviet view of the matter the Reiss affair was a fiasco. Hence they knew that sooner or later they would be called to account for it. Sergey Yakovlevich fell ill and was in very low spirits. They lived in Bolshevo near Moscow.

Every day Alya went into Moscow where she worked at the editorial office of the newspaper *Revue de Moscou*. She was also carrying on an affair with a colleague on the editorial staff, the producer Samuil ('Mulya') Gurevich, from whom she was expecting a child.

In the extracts from Tsvetayeva's journal published in Paris, we can read the following:

> Arrival in Moscow on 18 June. To the *dacha* to meet with S. who is ill. Discomfort. Out to buy kerosene. S. buys apples. Gradual feeling of heart-ache. Agony over the telephone. The enigmatic Alya, her forced cheerfulness. I live without seeing anyone. Kittens. My favourite unaffectionate adolescent is a cat. (All of this is for my memory, and nothing else: Mur, even if he reads it, would not understand. And he will not read it, for he avoids such things. There are cakes and pineapples – but that does not make it easier.) Walks with Mulya. My solitude. Dishes, water and tears. The overtone, the undertone of all

this is horror. They promise a partition – days go by. And a school for
Mur – days go by. And the usual wooded landscape, the absence of any
rocks: of any stability. S.'s illness. Fear for his heartfelt terror. Snatches
of his life without me, I do not have time to listen: my hands are full of
various chores, I listen like a wound up spring. The cellar: a hundred
times a day. When can I write?

The little girl Shura. For the first time the feeling of a stranger's
kitchen. Mad heat, which I do not notice: streams of sweat and tears in
the washing-up basin. No one I can hold on to. I begin to understand
that S. is helpless, utterly, in every way... [1]

If Marina Tsvetayeva really did not know about Sergey's
activities in Paris, it was now impossible to ignore them. Dmitry
Sezeman writes:

Having escaped to the Soviet Union, Seryozha Efron, who now found
himself in a narrow domestic circle, never denied his participation in
what he called the 'Swiss story'. He even recalled it with good-
humoured satisfaction. But his daughter, Ariadna Sergeyevna, Alya, did
not cease to deny that her father was capable of participating in such
criminal enterprises. She concurred that while he was an émigré he
worked for the Soviet régime, but exclusively in the noble rôle of an
unselfish carrier and propagandist of its bright ideals. Till her very
death in 1975 she tried to convince others, and what was still more
difficult, herself, that Seryozha (as she called him) was a 'dreamer in a
winged helmet', who simply could not be touched by anything base, nor,
much less, criminal or bloody.[2]

Forty years later, Sezeman, who at the time was seventeen,
distinctly recalled the famous writer who had returned to Russia.
He relates how she would read her poetry by the large stove,
holding herself so straight that one immediately became aware of
her upbringing in an earlier, different era:

Such strength emanated from her, such a powerful spiritual will, that
even a foolish, self-assured young man could not remain entirely
indifferent. I especially remember those evenings in Bolshevo by the
fire... when M.I. read her poems.

Sezeman regrets that he took so little notice of the advice his
mother gave him at the time: 'Look at her, remember her, she is
truly a great human being, a great poet. She is not a poetess, but a
poet.'

Sezeman does hint, however, that it was not easy to live under
the same roof with her:

I do not know whether it needs to be said what an impossibly difficult
person M.I. was in "communal life", as one calls it. As she was a person
with very thin skin, she reacted excessively (in general, excessiveness
was the distinguishing feature of her behaviour and of her whole
personality) to everything, which, in her opinion, offended the integrity
of her spiritual existence, the only one which was important for her.[3]

The overtones and undertones were dark indeed: Marina
Tsvetayeva had left Soviet Russia when the economic situation was
improving and when cultural life was beginning to appear again;
she was not, then, prepared for the atmosphere of terror and fear
created by the purges under Stalin. Her old friends were frightened
of coming into contact with suspect repatriated émigrés. Yelena
Tager told Viktoria Schweitzer that one day Pasternak said to her
husband:

> Marina Ivanovna has arrived and wishes me to visit her. But I met
> Kaverin [and some other writer, whom Ye. Tager does not remember],
> and they told me that I must not go under any circumstances, that it is
> dangerous. I did not go.[4]

It is much to Pasternak's credit, that even though he was no hero,
he did see Tsvetayeva and actively helped her. It was Pasternak
who, at the very beginning, introduced her to the influential literary
functionary Viktor Goltsev, who commissioned her to translate
some of the works of the Georgian poet, Vazha Pshavela, and thus
gave her the opportunity of earning some money. Their relations,
however, were not what Marina had at one time dreamt they should
be. Pasternak now had a second family (only later did he meet his
'Lara'). Ivinskaya writes:

> Is it not strange that in fourteen years I never heard B.L. tell the exact
> story of his first meeting with Marina after she returned to Moscow on
> 18 June from emigration. He obviously avoided memories of this. But
> when I once said as a joke, and not without malice: 'You should have
> married Marina', he protested fiercely: 'Olyusha, we could never have
> spent our lives together, in Marina was the concentration of all female
> hysterias! I would not have been able to bear it.'[5]

Suddenly, disaster struck at the *dacha*; on 27 August, Alya was
arrested.

> I am tearing into a wound, into living flesh. In brief: Alya was arrested
> on the night of 27 August. Cheerful Alya behaved with bravado and
> made jokes. I have forgotten something: the last time I saw her happy
> was about four days ago at the agricultural exhibition, dressed as a
> *kolkhoznitsa* [collective worker], and wearing a red head-scarf, a gift
> from me. She was radiant. She left without saying goodbye! 'What Alya,
> are you not going to say goodbye to anyone?' She waved, in tears, over
> her shoulder! The commandant (an old man with good humour): 'It is
> better this way. Long farewells mean extra tears.'[6]

Ariadna Sergeyevna Efron was twenty-seven when she was
arrested. The order came from 'high up' and was signed by Beria.
She was charged with spying for the French secret service. The
examining magistrate, who carried out the investigation, was a

known sadist; during the interrogation Ariadna was beaten so badly that she lost her child. On 2 July 1940 she was sentenced to eight years in a camp, which meant, according to the usual judicial practise of the time, that she was not guilty and that there was no case against her, other than that the order had been given from 'high up'.[7]

Several weeks later, on 8 October, Sergey Yakovlevich was also arrested in Bolshevo, and on 6 November, the parents of Dmitry Sezeman. Sezeman adds:

> Later on my meetings with M.I. took place at the entrance to the Butyrki prison where she brought parcels for her husband...and I for my parents.[8]

Marina and Mur remained at liberty, but they had to leave the *dacha* in Bolshevo. They obtained a room in a house belonging to the Union of Writers in Golitsyno, near Moscow, where they spent the winter of 1939-40. Mur began to go to school again, but was often ill, while Marina 'sunk her teeth into translating, like a wolf'. Already in the autumn she began to prepare a collection of her poetry for publication. She went through her work systematically and re-wrote what she did not like. According to her plan the first poem in the volume was to have been: 'I used to write it out on schoolroom slates', written in 1920 and dedicated to her husband:

> On tree trunks, a hundred winters old,
> Over again: I love you, love you, love you...

Tsvetayeva herself did not believe that this volume would ever be published:

> I am almost certain that they will not accept it, I would be surprised if they did. Well, I have done my share and have shown complete good will (I have done as I was told). I know that the verses are good, and that someone needs them (perhaps, even like bread)...[9]

Several decades later this work did bear fruit: the volumes of selected works which Tsvetayeva's daughter had published in 1961 and 1965 are partly based on the manuscript of this collection.

Evidently Tsvetayeva's autobiographical piece dated 'Winter 1939-40' belongs also to this period.

> In the spring of 1911 I came to know Maks Voloshin...at whose house in the Crimea I met my future husband, Sergey Efron. I made the decision that I would *never* part from him, *whatever might happen*, and in 1912 I married him. In 1914 my husband, then a student at the University of Moscow, went to the front as an orderly. In 1917 he fought in the ranks of the White Army. How is it that he joined the White Army? After all, his ancestors were revolutionaries and his parents were members of the Land and Freedom movement. He

considered this to be the greatest mistake of his life ... He saw in it the truth and Russia's salvation. When he lost his faith, however, he turned away from it completely, without any doubts, and he never looked back. As a witness I can confirm that this man loved the Soviet Union and the idea of Communism more than his own life ... In 1937 I renewed my Soviet citizenship and in 1939 I returned with my fourteen-year-old son, in order to follow my husband and daughter. The reason for my return to my native country was the desire to give my son a homeland and a future. There was also another desire: to work at home. There was also my total isolation in the emigration, with which I no longer had any ties during my last years.[10]

In the 'Litfond' house other writers were staying, among whom Tsvetayeva began to make some friends. From the letters of this period, which have appeared in print, it seems that she found a common language with the writer Nikolay Yakovlevich Moskvin, and that she took a special liking to his young wife Tatyana Nikolayevna Kvanina. From one letter to Moskvin we can deduce that Marina must have run into trouble with the administration of the house: she had to pay twice as much as the other residents for meals for herself and Mur. She requested that one of their names, i.e. her own, be removed from the ration list. But Kvanina adds that her husband managed to help Marina in this matter.

Tatyana Kvanina also recalls the moment when Marina Tsvetayeva and Mur appeared for the first time at lunch in the Union of Writers' house:

> And then, when everyone was seated at table and was chatting, the door opened and ... no, she did not even enter, and it was not as though anyone had opened the door ... rather there arose in the doorway a slender woman covered in silver ornaments ... They sat down, and immediately the atmosphere changed in the dining-room. At this point the lackey-like picking of other peoples' bones ceased ... The level of conversation at the table was raised. Banality and gossip were impossible in Tsvetayeva's presence ...[11]

During this time the writer Viktor Ardov was also staying at the 'Litfond' house in Golitsyno. Tsvetayeva's personality had a great effect on him:

> ... She was devoured by poverty, desolation and nostalgia. All of this left its traces on the splendid face of the poetess. She did not lower her head. Her energy and striking temperament amazed us ... But the impression of the sufferings she had endured, as well as her sufferings of the present, expressed themselves distinctly in her voice and glances, in her movements and in those moments of reflection which overcame the poetess even during cheerful dinner-table conversation ... And Marina Ivanovna was often cheerful in our milieu, which she had entered by accident. She easily captured the attention of our little society at dinner, and after dinner, in the small drawing-room of the

house in Golitsyno. Her conversation was always interesting and rich in content. Does it need to be emphasised that her erudition, taste and rare talent compelled all of us to listen to her words with respectful attention?[12]

Ardov adds that, as a "returnee", Marina Tsvetayeva had to be especially careful, since there were present: 'volunteers, who desired, according to their own initiative, without directions from above, to reprove those people who had returned to the Mother land'.[13]

In Golitsyno Tsvetayeva made the acquaintance of still another writer, the literary scholar Yevgeny Borisovich Tager, which is shown by a letter of 22 January 1940:

My dear! Come without fail, although you will find that we do not have "your room" – but my walls (which are *non*-walls!) will be here ... Thank you for the first joy, here, the first trust, here, and the first belief in me – for many years ...[14]

Three short poems are dedicated to Tager, which were written in Golitsyno between 7 and 23 January, and which did not come to light until 1982.[15]

That Marina Tsvetayeva was, nevertheless, lonely and desperate during this winter, can be seen from the letters she wrote from Golitsyno to two women writers she had known earlier at the time of the Revolution. They were Vera Merkureva and Olga Mochalova.[16] Without entering into great detail about her life, Marina enquired how she might find a room in Moscow. In these letters she clearly expresses her joy and gratitude that both women remembered her, an act of great courage during the persecutions under Stalin. Slonim says that Yevgeny Lozman, who was none other than 'Lann' of 1921, was another of those friends who took care of Marina, and that Aleksey Kruchyonykh also was not afraid of meeting the "dangerous" former émigré. Finally Antokolsky remarks that he too met Tsvetayeva:

I saw her several times, grey, monosyllabic, and partly, perhaps, on her guard. Our conversation was businesslike, professional, banal, meagre. I heard her read the 'Poem of the Staircase' at one of my friend's.[17]

Formerly, it was necessary for scholars in the West to search like detectives for traces of the last two years of Marina Tsvetayeva's life in Russian newspapers and journals. Since 1985 this too has changed. With the appearance of Maria Belkina's book, and the many publications which followed, one can learn of every step which the poet took after her return home. In general terms, however, it had been known for a while what happened to her.

Marina and Mur remained in Golitsyno until the end of the school-year in June 1940. They spent the following months in Moscow, moving nomadically from one flat to another, unable to find a permanent place to live anywhere. For a few weeks they were given a room in the House of Writers on Herzen Street, then they stayed with Lilya Efron. The idea of finding a roof over her head became an obsession with Marina. She wrote in her notebook on 26 October 1940: 'It appears that in my life I have loved security most of all. It has departed from my life irrevocably.'

In the West people often ask if Marina Tsvetayeva wrote any poems after her return to the Soviet Union. Her letter to Vera Merkureva answers this question:

> I have written everything I had to write. Naturally, I could write more, but I can also live without it.

In the same letter she quotes a few lines of her own poetry and adds: 'These are old ones. However, they are all old. There are no new ones.'[18]

In the autumn of 1940 Tsvetayeva's depression grew. On 5 September she wrote in her journal:

> Everyone thinks that I am brave. I do not know anyone who is more easily frightened then myself. I am afraid of everything. Eyes, darkness, footsteps, but most of all, myself, my own head, this head which has served me so faithfully in my notebooks, and has killed me so much in life. No one sees, no one knows, that for a year already (approximately) my eyes have been searching for a hook, but there aren't any, because there is electricity everywhere. There aren't any "chandeliers". N.P. has brought me some folksongs in translation: My favourite thing! Oh, how I used to love all this! I have been trying on death for a year. Everything is ugly and terrible. To swallow something is revolting, to jump into water is against my nature, because of my inborn fear of it. I do not want to frighten anyone (posthumously), it seems to me that I am already – posthumously – afraid of myself. I do not want to die. I want not to be. This is nonsense. As long as I am needed – ... but Lord, how little I am, how little I can do! To love to the end is like gnawing something to the end. Bitter wormwood... So many lines have passed by! I have written none of them down. With this it is all over![19]

This statement should not be taken quite so literally. Among the drafts which Marina Tsvetayeva made for her translations, Yelena Korkina found some unfinished stanzas and two completed poems, which date from the winter of 1940-41. The last of the poems, about whose existence we know at the present, is: 'I have laid the table for six people'. It is dated 6 March 1941. An even better expression of how she felt at the time might be the following four-line poem of February 1941.

It is time to take off my amber beads,
It is time to find new words,
It is time to extinguish the lamp
Above the door.[20]

There is also another letter by Marina which belongs to the
winter of 1940-41. It is addressed to Yevgeny Somov:

Zhenya dear, thank you. Your letter is the first one I have received in 4
months, and this letter is the first I have written in 4 months, and
perhaps, all the same, it will give you some joy, by *demonstrating* to you –
in a way which goes beyond *you*, the exceptional character of your sign
of affection, which simply places you (in a non-existent rank!) in the first
place – a lonely place, the only place.

   I am now crushed, I do *not* exist any longer, I do not know if I ever will
again, but feelings aside, with my complete sense of justice, which
cannot bear that such a letter should remain without an answer, with my
view from the future, with the view of the whole future, with the lips of
those who *are to come*, I reply

                         Thank You!
                                   M.[21]

Marina had also written to Tatyana Kvanina on 17 November
1940:

Dear Tanya, waking up just now I said to you in my thoughts: if you
were next to me, if we lived next to each other, I would be happier by
half. This is the truth!...Tanya, what I need from a human being is
love. My love, and if such a miracle is possible, the love of
another...What I need from another person, Tanya, is that the other
person need me, my need (and if possible, necessity) on the part of this
person, do you understand, is beyond bounds...The joy of someone
else's presence, Tanya, is a terribly rare thing. With almost everyone I
am unutterably bored, and if I have a "good time", then it is parce que
j'y mets des frais, in order not to expire myself. But what loneliness you
feel when, having been together, you suddenly find yourself on the
street with the sound of your own voice (and laughter) in your ears,
without having carried away a single word...Indeed, what are they
doing to me? They call me to ask me to read my poems, without
understanding that every line of mine is love, that if I had stood my
whole life like that reading out my poems, there would not have been
any poems...

Kvanina did not understand her. She told her husband with
amazement about one of Tsvetayeva's postcards adding 'I still don't
really understand why she needs me!' In 1982 she wrote:

It is now clear to me (and to my greatest regret only now) that Marina
Ivanovna passionately needed to feel that there were people around her,
who were well-disposed to her, who valued her, and perhaps who simply
showed a human interest in her...But the fact is that her loneliness
became unbearably heavy for her...[22]

The volume of letters published in Paris contains the following from October 1940:

> Dear Comrade T. Your book is delightful ... I will soon invite you to visit me some evening to listen to some poems from my forthcoming book ... I must ask you not to show this letter to anyone, I live in isolation ...[23]

We must thank Viktoria Schweitzer for the information that this letter was meant for the poet Arseny Tarkovsky.

Viktor Ardov's wife, Nina Antonovna Olshevskaya had been friends with Anna Akhmatova for many years, and the first meeting between the two great women poets took place, with some help from Pasternak, in the Ardovs' flat a few days before the outbreak of war in 1941. A great deal has already been written about this encounter.[24] According to Ardov, both of them were very moved by this first meeting, when they were able to see each other alone. On the following day they met again at N.I. Khardzhiev's, and then 'wandered together through Moscow'. Marina presented Akhmatova with a brooch and copied out from memory some poems for her. Akhmatova, however, had never really been very fond of Tsvetayeva's poetry, while Tsvetayeva, for her part, wrote in her journal, after reading Akhmatova's latest volume: 'It is old, weak ... This book is an irreparably blank page – what a pity!'[25] She obviously did not know of Akhmatova's most recent work, and had no idea of how difficult it had been to publish this collection, *From Six Books*. When Lidia Chukovskaya read these lines in 1979 she wrote in her *Notes About Anna Akhmatova*:

> From year to year Akhmatova complained with more and more bitterness that the published collections of her poems gave the reader a false impression of her poetry, of her development ... How saddened she would have been if she had been convinced that not only ordinary Soviet citizens, from whom the authorities had deliberately kept her poetry, that not only Russian émigrés, who had not been able to learn of the heroic feats of her indomitable muse, but even Marina Tsvetayeva, who had returned to her native land and held in her hands *From Six Books, did not guess about the passages she had been forced to omit, and about the censor's deletions*! When she asked, what had Akhmatova been doing 'inside herself' between 1917 and 1940, how could she not also have asked herself: and has much of what Akhmatova has done ... been published? 'What a pity'![26]

On 11 April 1941 a letter from Alya arrived; this was a sign that at least she was alive. Her mother answered the next day:

> Dear Alya! Finally your first letter, of the fourth, in a blue envelope. I looked at it from 9 a.m. to 3 p.m. when Mur comes home from school. It lay on his dinner plate, and he saw it already in the doorway, and with a

Aleksey Kruchyonykh, Georgy (Mur) Efron (sitting).
Marina Tsvetayeva, Lidia Libedinskaya (standing). July 1941

satisfied and even smug 'A-ha!' threw himself on it. He did not give it to
me to read, but read it aloud, his and mine. But even before this reading
– from impatience – I sent you a postcard. This was yesterday, the 11th.
On the 10th I took something for papa, which they accepted. Alya, I am
very busy with your rations, I already have sugar and cocoa, I will now
take a stab at bacon and cheese...[27]

This means that as of 10 April 1941 they were still "accepting"
parcels for Sergey Efron, an indication that he too was alive.

For the longest time there were in the West, as well as in the
East, only conjectures and rumours about the fate of Efron. Even
after the beginning of *glasnost* researchers had no access to the
archives of the KGB. So much more valuable, then, is the résumé
of the facts about Efron's case provided by A. Vaksberg in
November 1990.

Sergey Efron was arrested in September 1939, two months
before the Klepinins. They were all taken to the notorious
Lefortovo prison, where they were tortured during the interrogation. They were charged with membership in the 'Eurasian'
movement and collaboration with the French secret service. Efron
was also charged with a particularly surprising crime: resistance to
the establishment of friendly relations between the USSR and
Germany. (At this time the Hitler-Stalin pact was exactly one year
old and war had not yet broken out on the eastern front.) Under
torture they all incriminated each other and they all signed their
confessions of guilt.

Their case did not come to trial until 6 July 1941. The co-
defendants were E.E. Litauer, N.V. Atanasov and Prince [*sic*] Pavel
Nikolayevich Tolstoy. They were all sentenced to death, including
S. Efron, even though German troops had invaded Russia two
weeks before and the war was well under way. The sentence against
Klepinin was carried out on 28 July and against Efron only on 16
October, when the Germans were positioned directly outside
Moscow and other prisoners were being evacuated.[28]

In 1969 the journal *Novy Mir* published a 'Letter to My
Daughter' in which Marina speaks of her work as a translator:

... No notebooks of any kind, no honoraria of any kind, no *need* of any
kind can force me to hand over a manuscript until the last full stop, and
the right moment for this last point is known only to God. To the God
of Poets. 'With God' or 'Grant it, oh Lord!' is how every piece of my
work begins, this is how every one of even my most pathetic translations
begins. This is not a prayer, if only because it is a *demand*. I never asked
for a rhyme 'from on high' (*that* is my affair!) I asked (demanded!) for
the strength to find it, the strength for this torment. And this was
granted to me, yielded to me.[29]

Marina had only Mur left, although internally he had already gone his own way long ago. In the same way, as was once the case with her own mother, Marina did not understand that her son was almost grown-up, that this spoiled, impudent boy had his own problems, that it was no easy matter for him to be able to find a place in the real world around him, which differed so drastically from his daydreams about his parents' native land. In 1975 there appeared in the journal *Rodina* an article with the heading 'Lines about a Son', dedicated to G.S. Efron. In the article were included some of Mur's caricatures, drawn in 1939, which show a great deal of talent, as well as excerpts from letters to his sister. One can see in them that the main event for him in Russia was the discovery of Tchaikovsky and Dostoyevsky. In the future he planned to devote himself entirely to music and to write a new book about Dostoyevsky.

> An extraordinary writer! One day something entirely different from what has already been said, and is said, must be written![30]

At the beginning of the summer of 1941 Tsvetayeva was given a room on the fifth floor of a new house at no.14, Pokrovsky Boulevard, where some people visited her. A brief note to A. Kochetkov, dated 10 June, was written here: 'I need to see you very much. I am very confused and unhappy.'

On Wednesday 18 June she and Mur went with Aleksey Kruchyonykh and the young writer Lidia Libedinskaya (*née* Tolstaya) to Kuskovo. Libedinskaya has left a description of this long day, 'filled with walks, arguments, conversation and poetry', which was passed in the gardens and rooms of the former Sheremetiev palace. In the Paris edition of Tsvetayeva's unpublished correspondence, a reproduction of a photograph taken on this day is included. It shows Tsvetayeva, Mur, Kruchyonykh and Libedinskaya, and bears the dedication:

> To dear Aleksey Yeliseyevich Kruchyonykh, with gratitude for the first beauty here. Kuskovo, the lake and island, the porcelain. On the second anniversary of my return.[31]

On the way back to Moscow the conversation turned to the subject of foreign languages. When Marina learnt that Lidia Libedinskaya did not speak French, she suggested she give her lessons. When they said good-bye she reminded her: 'Telephone on Monday, and we shall decide when our lessons will begin...'

Before this Monday, however, Sunday, 22 June 1941, was still to come, 'the fatal day, when the war began...'

CHAPTER 29

Outbreak of War – Death in Yelabuga

JUNE – AUGUST 1941

A great deal of literature has already been written about the German attack on the Soviet Union in June 1941, and the first battles on Russian soil. It is a well-known fact that the German army advanced without meeting much resistance and almost managed to reach Moscow. This is when the evacuation of the city began.

All of her immediate circle of acquaintances corroborate that Marina Tsvetayeva was very afraid of the Germans, more on Mur's account, than on her own. Olga Ivinskaya relates the following:

> Mur was a well-built boy and he was conscripted into a detachment which collected incendiary bombs from roof-tops during air-raids. At this time Marina was renting a tiny room at the top of a high-rise building at no.14, Pokrovsky Boulevard. At the same time Boris Leonidovich was also putting out incendiaries on the roof of the writers' house on Lavrushinsky Lane. Marina went to ask him his advice about how she could protect Mur. She had a project ready in her mind: to evacuate to a Tatar region, where the Union of Writers had moved. B.L., as though sensing disaster, persistently tried to persuade her not to do this, but he did not suggest an alternative, which was exactly what she was hoping for. At 'Goslitizdat', she told Z.P. Kulmanova about her trip to Pasternak, and added with bitterness: 'Boris could have invited me, even for a short time, to stay in his *dacha* at Peredelkino.' Years later B.L. told me that his inertia and the domestic circumstances at the large *dacha* did not allow him to do the one thing he wanted to do: to invite Marina . . . [1]

In this hopeless situation Marina swallowed her pride and turned to one of the influential people who had hitherto not taken any notice of her return to Russia, Ilya Ehrenburg, who describes their

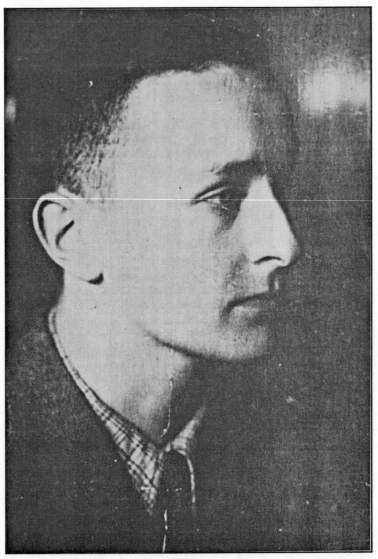

Georgy (Mur) Efron, 1940

first meeting after many years:

> She came to see me in August 1941; we met after many years and our meeting was not a success – which was my fault. It was in the morning and the military communiqué had already informed us that: 'our units have abandoned their positions . . . ' My thoughts were far away. Marina immediately felt this and gave the conversation a business-like air: she had come to seek advice about work, about translations. When she was leaving I said: 'Marina, we must see each other again, speak again . . . ' No, we never did see each other again. Tsvetayeva put an end to her life in Yelabuga where she had been evacuated.[2]

Various stories still circulate about Tsvetayeva's last days in Moscow. For example, Slonim heard the following from Paustovsky when he was in Rome in the autumn of 1965:

> Pasternak went to help her pack. He brought her a piece of rope to tie around her . . . suitcase, he praised its strength and joked that it would be strong enough for anything, you could even hang yourself with it. He later learnt that Tsvetayeva had hanged herself with this rope and for a long time he could not forgive himself for making what he called his "fatal joke".[3]

Lidia Libedinskaya saw Marina and Mur just before their departure from Moscow. This was a month after their trip to Kuskovo. Tsvetayeva had changed a great deal during this time; her eyes showed fear, and she clutched the hand of her son the whole time, although he did not move an inch from her. Earlier it had been suggested that Libedinskaya would leave with them as well, but for some reason nothing came of this. When they bid farewell, Marina embraced her and kissed her and said how much she regretted that she was staying behind in Moscow. Libedinskaya writes:

> It is now senseless (as well as too late) to look for the guilty. Everyone is guilty. I too am guilty. Presumptuous as this may sound, it sometimes seems to me that if I had gone to Yelabuga, perhaps Marina Ivanovna would still be alive. Of course, I could not have changed anything in her tragic fate, but I believe in the power of love to do good. And I loved Marina Ivanovna very much.[4]

About their journey by steamer, we only know that the children's writer, N. Saksonskaya, and her thirteen-year-old son, were travelling at the same time as Tsvetayeva.

At the beginning of the war there existed a category of people who could count on better food and living conditions once they had been evacuated from Moscow. To this category belonged members of the Union of Writers. For them and their families the city of Chistopol on the Kama River (in the Tatar Autonomous Soviet Republic) had been set aside. Among these writers were Aseyev,

Trenev, and Lidia Chukovskaya. Pasternak's wife and children also received permission to settle in Chistopol. As Marina Tsvetayeva was not a member of the Union, she had to travel further to the city of Yelabuga on the opposite bank of the Kama. Yelabuga was hopelessly overflowing with refugees from Russia proper, and the living conditions there were terrible. Their steamer moored at Yelabuga on 21 August 1941.

When Tsvetayeva and her son arrived in the crowded city they managed to find shelter in a five-walled hut at no.10, Voroshilov Street (today, no.20, Zhdanov Street). This belonged to Mikhail and Anastasia Brodelshchikov, who were kind, simple people. With them lived their six-year-old grandson. The room which Marina and Mur occupied was separated from the rest of the house by a wall which did not reach the ceiling. Everything they said could be overheard. Anastasia Brodelshchikova told how stormy conversations, which were carried on in a foreign language, would burst forth from their room. She basically understood that the son was reproaching his mother for having brought him to this place. His mother would then fall silent and smoked a great deal. By now Georgy was a grown-up and good-looking boy.

They had brought with them various possessions and provisions: table silver, some grain and 400 grammes of sugar. Arriving in Yelabuga Marina began to look for work, but found nothing. She tried to sell her silverware, but no one was interested. After a few days she went to Chistopol to see Aseyev, 'from where she returned depressed and in very low spirits'.

Sunday, 31 August was a *voskresnik* (a "voluntary" work day on Sunday) and the inhabitants of the city were supposed to help clear land for the new airport. In place of her husband, who preferred to go fishing with his grandson, Anastasia Brodelshchikova went to work, and took Mur, who substituted for his mother. Marina said that she wanted to stay at home and that they should not worry about her. The first to return home that evening was Anastasia Brodelshchikova. In the doorway she knocked against a chair and looking up she saw her lodger hanging in a noose. She called for a doctor and the police, who arrived two hours later. In Mur's presence the police made a thorough search of everything which she had left behind, to make sure nothing had been stolen in the meantime. During their search they found two letters, one of them addressed to Aseyev. The body of the dead woman was taken to the hospital and from there it was taken for burial. On the same evening Mur left the house and spent the night at N.

Saksonskaya's.

Milica Nikolić, who edited a selection of Tsvetayeva's works in
Serbian translation in 1972, quotes in her foreword the short
declaration made by the Brodelshchikovs, which was read at an
evening of Tsvetayeva's poetry held in Leningrad:

> In August 1941 M. Tsvetayeva came to us as an evacuee, and lived in
> my house. She brought with her two kilos of flour, grain, one kilo of
> sugar and a few silver spoons. She asked me if I knew of anyone who
> wanted to buy silver. I did not know of anyone. We often heard how
> mother and son spoke in a foreign language. It seemed the son often
> rebuked her for bringing him here, and for the fact that he did not have
> enough to eat and nothing to wear ... We did not know that she also had
> a daughter. She never spoke of her. And she never spoke about her
> husband. Once she said that she wanted to visit the writer Aseyev, who
> had also been evacuated near Yelabuga. She returned in a very
> depressed mood. On the following day she said that there was no way
> she could go with us to work (we had to help with the construction of the
> new airport); so I went alone with her son. In the evening I was the first
> to come home. I found her hanging by the wall. I immediately informed
> the police. They came and took away the body.
> We did not know that she was a writer. She did not tell us this. If we
> had known we would have gone to her funeral. Her son was also not
> present at her funeral. So no one knows where her grave is. After the
> war people came and looked for her grave, but they did not find it.
> She left behind only one letter to Aseyev. She asked him to look after
> her son. But he immediately went to the front. He was not yet sixteen.
> Later I learnt that he was killed.[5]

In 1966 Viktoria Schweitzer went to Yelabuga to find the places
where Tsvetayeva spent her last days. Her description of this trip is
included in the Paris edition of Tsvetayeva's unpublished correspondence.[6] She could not locate Tsvetayeva's grave, but she did
find the Brodelshchikovs, who were still alive. The old woman
repeated several times: 'They had a lot of goods ... she could have
held out longer ... she could have lasted until everything had been
eaten up ... '

When the first edition of this biography appeared in German in
1981 this was the extent of what was known about Tsvetayeva's last
days in Yelabuga. At that time it seemed as though we would not be
able to learn any more, as most of the people who had seen
Tsvetayeva then had died without leaving any further information.
During the Tsvetayeva symposium, however, which was held in
1982 in Lausanne, and which was attended by scholars from
around the world (with the exception of the Soviet Union)
Professor Efim Etkind found in his hotel room a letter from Lidia
Chukovskaya, which turned out to be a detailed account of her

meeting with Marina Tsvetayeva in Chistopol. In this letter she told
how on 4 September 1941, the day she heard the news of
Tsvetayeva's death, she wrote down everything she remembered
about their encounter in a notebook, which she locked away. It was
only in 1981, forty years after the events, that she opened this
notebook for the first time and decided to send the information it
contained to Lausanne. The basic content of her memoir is as
follows.[7]

Among the writers who had been evacuated, it became known
that Aseyev and Trenev, the representatives of 'Litfond', had
refused to give Tsvetayeva permission to reside in Chistopol. At
Chukovskaya's request, the writer Lev Moiseyevich Kvitko (who
was subsequently "repressed" and executed in 1952), testified on
Tsvetayeva's behalf before Aseyev. On 26 August Lidia Chukovskaya met Tsvetayeva, with whom she was not personally acquainted, on the street in Chistopol. Marina said to her: 'How glad
I am that you are here, ... I will move to Chistopol and we will
become friends.'

The next morning a young woman ran up to Chukovskaya and
asked if she were a member of the 'Litfond' Council, explaining:

'The 'Litfond' Council is meeting in the party offices. They have
summoned Tsvetayeva and are deciding whether they will grant her
permission to reside in Chistopol. She is in despair. Run there
quickly!'

In the corridor outside the party offices Chukovskaya found
Tsvetayeva who said to her: 'Don't go away, stay with me!', and
together they awaited the fatal decision. Lidia Chukovskaya was
then present when a woman writer came out and said to
Tsvetayeva: 'The matter has been decided in your favour. It was
not easy by any means, as Trenev was categorically against it;
Aseyev did not come, but sent a letter *for* it. In the end the council
resolved to come to a decision by a simple majority of votes, and the
majority was *for*.'

After this they went out together to look for a room for
Tsvetayeva. In the street Tsvetayeva asked Chukovskaya: 'Tell me
please, why do you think that life is still worth living? Don't you
understand that everything is finished?'

And in answer to Chukovskaya's question what exactly was
finished, Tsvetayeva said: 'Well, for example, Russia!'

They then spoke about life in Chistopol, and Lidia remarked
rather carelessly: 'I am glad about one thing, that Akhmatova is not
in Chistopol; she would certainly perish here ... She doesn't know

how to do anything, she doesn't know how to do absolutely anything...'

At this, Marina cried with a rabid voice: 'You think *I* do? Akhmatova could not live here, but according to you, I can?'

They dropped in on some friends of Lidia Chukovskaya's, the Schneiders, who were very glad to see Tsvetayeva. They gave her a meal, asked her to rest there for a while, and offered to help in any way possible. Marina began to read them her poem 'Homesickness...', then stopped in the middle of it, made her apologies, and promised to return in the evening to read them 'Poem of the Air' and other things. At the agreed time Lidia Chukovskaya also returned to the Schneiders, but Tsvetayeva was not there, and she never turned up.

The next day, 28 August, Chukovskaya heard that Tsvetayeva had gone back to Yelabuga for her son, so that, as she had said, they could look together for a room. A few days later, however, Chukovskaya was told in the post office that, 'M.I.'s son had arrived in the town, and had gone to Aseyev and said: "Mama has hanged herself"'.

At the end of her moving account Lidia Chukovskaya says that she has in her possession Tsvetayeva's letter to Aseyev. It reads: 'I request to be employed in the capacity of a dish-washer at the 'Litfond' canteen which is to be opened.'

On 4 September Georgy Efron removed his name from the police register in Yelabuga and boarded the steamer to Chistopol. He turned over his mother's last letter to Aseyev, who invited him to stay in his apartment. In a long letter to his aunt, Lilya Efron, Mur wrote: 'She spoke to me many times about her intention of killing herself, as the best decision she could make. I fully understand and excuse her.' He also wrote to his friend Sezeman: 'The most that I can say in this regard is that she acted correctly: she had sufficient grounds and this was the best way out of the situation, and I fully approve of her action.'[8]

Mur spent ten days in a 'Litfond' children's home in order to find a school in Chistopol. Aseyev then suggested that it would be better if he left for Moscow. Carrying with him his large baggage, which included the literary legacy of Marina Tsvetayeva, he arrived in Moscow with the greatest difficulties. He found accommodation in the room of his aunt's, for which he received a residence permit (*propiska*) on 11 October 1941. On 14 October, however, the evacuation of writers from Moscow to Tashkent began. He left the trunk containing his mother's writings with Lilya Efron and

travelled on to Tashkent. He remained there until 1943, suffering
from hunger and want, and was often ill. Once, when he was on the
verge of starvation, he even sold some of the possessions of his
landlady, for which he had to pay back a lot of money. He did,
however, complete his schooling. He was financially supported by
his aunt and Gurevich. In Tashkent he visited Anna Akhmatova
and the family of Aleksey Tolstoy. Here Mur was able, finally, not
only to establish contact with his sister, but also to find his aunt,
Anastasia Ivanovna, who was still in exile, somewhere in the vast
expanse of Russia. He wrote to her, sending his photograph, and
told her of his mother's death. Anastasia Ivanovna, who learnt of
Marina's death only in 1943 (and who was thus unable to see either
her sister or nephew again), has her own version of her sister's
death, which to a large degree appears plausible. After her return
from exile Anastasia met A.A. Sokolovsky, the son of N.
Saksonskaya, at whose house Mur spent the first night after his
mother's suicide. Anastasia has this to say about her conversation
with Sokolovsky:

> Mur repeated to him the words he had said to Marina in a fit of
> irritation in Yelabuga: 'Well, *one of us* is going to be *carried out* of here
> feet first! ... For the first time since 1943 when I learnt of her death, I
> saw her as she was during those days, at the moment of his careless,
> cruel, childish phrase, which roused her to the only action which was
> now possible, in order to save *him* from going 'feet first', to shield for the
> last time, with her own self, her son, whom she adored, the being to
> whom she had given life. Once things had gone this far, how could she
> not choose to leave? ... I repeat: the ruthlessly crude words of the
> sixteen-year-old Mur sounded like a death sentence to Marina's
> maternal instinct ... She left, so that *he* would not have to leave.[9]

After completing his schooling Mur went to Moscow in the
autumn of 1943, and on his nineteenth birthday, 1 February 1944,
he was conscripted into the Red Army. At that time his regiment
was fighting on the left bank of the Western Dvina, and Mur took
part in the offensive. In a letter to Ariadna Efron dated 17 June
1944 Mur says:

> Tomorrow I go into battle ... I am absolutely certain that my star will
> lead me unharmed out of the war, and that success will come without
> fail ...

On 7 July his regiment, no.437, was drawn into battle not far
from the small village of Druika in Latvia. They managed to win
back a height which had been occupied. Afterwards the wounded
were taken to the medical and sanitary battalion, no.183, which was
located four to five kilometres from Druika. In the battalion's

report for the day the following entry appears: 'The Red Army soldier Georgy Efron was taken into the charge of the Medical and Sanitary Battalion as one of the wounded. 7.7.44.' After this there is no further information about him.

Sometime later, in the environs of Druika the grave of an unidentified soldier, who had been killed in the summer of 1944 was found. We could suppose that this is the grave of Georgy Sergeyevich Efron, that "son" who was so happy to return with his mother to his native land, and for which, at the age of nineteen, he gave his life.[10]

The only member of the Efron family who had survived the catastrophe of these years was Ariadna Sergeyevna. But this does not mean that her fate, about which V. Lossky and M. Belkina have written extensively, was any easier.[11] Although a full portrayal of her life lies beyond the confines of this book, we can provide the following details. In 1947, two years after the end of the war, Alya had served her sentence and was released. As she could not live in Moscow, she moved to Ryazan where she shared a room with someone who had suffered a similar fate and his mother. On 2 February 1949 she was once again arrested. As before, she was convicted with the crime of spying for France and on 18 March she was condemned to 'lifelong exile in a remote region of the USSR'. In July she arrived in Turukhansk in the far north on the Yenisey river.[12] Her letters to Pasternak give a terrifying insight into her life in Turukhansk.[13] Pasternak supported her by sending money and parcels. In the beginning Gurevich did the same, however, in 1949 he was arrested as a "cosmopolitan" and in 1952 he was executed.

Ariadna Sergeyevna was rehabilitated only on 15 February 1955, two years after Stalin's death, and was allowed to return to Moscow. She stayed with her aunt Lilya Efron and her friend Zina, who had in their keeping the trunk containing her mother's manuscripts, letters and journals, which Mur had brought from Yelabuga and left with them. As one of the "aunts" slept on this trunk it was necessary, every time one wanted to open it, 'to destroy Zina's many-layered nest, and transfer her bed to that of the invalid Lilya, and lift the planks on which the mattress lay . . .'[14] In this way Tsvetayeva's archive was saved, and from this moment Ariadna began what was to become her new mission in life: the recognition of her mother by her native land. For Ariadna this was to include the publication of Tsvetayeva's unpublished work, as well as writing commentaries to her work, and various memoirs about her mother. The Western reader can only guess at how difficult this task must have been, which involved countless struggles with the censorship.

In the seventies Ariadna Efron's life became easier. She lived in Tarusa in a house which was built on some land that belonged at one time to 'Tante Tio'. She died here suddenly on 26 July 1975 from a heart attack.[15] She is buried in the cemetery of Tarusa on a height overlooking the Oka River, near the place where, at one time, her mother wished to be buried.

The last witness of Marina Tsvetayeva's youth, Anastasia Ivanovna, has survived her sister by more than forty-five years. She was arrested on three occasions; first after her trip to Italy, then in 1937, and finally in 1947. She was interned in various camps and was then sent into permanent exile in the vicinity of Novosibirsk. In 1958 she was rehabilitated. In the summer of 1960 she travelled to Yelabuga to look for her sister's grave, and as she could not find it she put up a cross which bore the inscription: 'On this side of the cemetery is buried Marina Ivanovna Tsvetayeva, 26 September (old style) 1892 – 31 August 1941'. A gravestone was later placed on this site.

Anastasia Ivanovna lives to this day (1991) in Moscow. She is a member of the Union of Writers and is still as active as in her youth. Her memoirs, which became bestsellers in Russia, describe in detail the Tsvetayev family milieu, her own childhood and youth, her relations with Marina, and the relations between the two sisters and their mother. We cannot underestimate the great service Anastasia Ivanovna has rendered in reviving her sister's image.

When the eighteen-year-old Marina Tsvetayeva met her future husband for the first time by the sea at Koktebel, she vowed that she would never leave him, wherever life might take them. She could not have known then how much courage it would take to fulfil this promise. She followed her husband through fire and water, and remained loyal to him to such an extent that it seemed as though even fate had pity on her: the couple whom life had separated at the end, were finally joined by death at almost the same time.

CHAPTER 30

After Tsvetayeva

The news of Tsvetayeva's death spread like lightning in the writers' colony in nearby Chistopol. Lidia Chukovskaya tells us how Anna Akhmatova, who had been evacuated by plane from Leningrad, now encircled by the German army, arrived in Chistopol during the second part of October 1941. She wanted to leave again, however, as quickly as possible because 'the shadow of Marina Tsvetayeva, who had killed herself a month and a half ago in the neighbouring town of Yelabuga, still hovered over the city...'[1]

It was autumn by the time news of the poet's death reached cold and hungry Moscow, which was now gripped by fear of the ever advancing front. Antokolsky writes:

> It was during the war. The frequent news of the deaths of many friends and relations crossed each other like beams of projectors in a night sky. These sad reports of losses, personal and general, losses of the famous and the nameless, of the bitterly mourned and the completely unmourned, stretched out like orphans their long, helpless fingers. But the sky remained black and starless, – full of new threats which for the most part came true. And the death of Marina was lost in this stormy winter gloom...[2]

A letter by Pasternak, dated '10 September in the morning', which he wrote to his wife in Chistopol, has also come down to us:

> Last night Fedin told me that supposedly Marina has taken her own life. I do not want to believe this. She is living somewhere near you, in Chistopol or Yelabuga. Please find out and write to me (telegrams take longer than letters). If this is true, then what a terrible thing has happened! Enquire after her boy, find out where he is and what state he is in. What guilt I bear, if this is so! After this how can we speak of "minor worries"! I will never be forgiven for this. Last year I stopped taking an interest in her. She was on a very high rung in intellectual society and among the connoisseurs she was in fashion, and my best

friends Garrik, Asmus, Kolya Vilyam, not to mention Aseyev, were part of this. Since it became very flattering to consider her to be a best friend, as well as for many other reasons, I withdrew from her and was not involved with her. Last year it seemed as though I had completely fogotten about her. And there you are! How terrible this is. I always knew in the depths of my soul that I was living for you and the children, but concern for everyone on earth is the duty of every human being, who is not a brute, and this is symbolised for me by Zhenya, Nina and Marina. Ah, why did I abandon this ideal![3]

It is amazing that even in the West, people soon learnt of Marina's death, despite the fact that they were on the other side of the front, and had their own troubles. Nina Berberova, who lived during the German occupation of France in a village not far from Paris, wrote in her journal in February 1942:

A rumour has spread that Tsvetayeva hanged herself in Moscow on 11 August. *Our Word* (*Nashe slovo*) or *The New Word* (*Novoye slovo*) published a vacuous illiterate notice about this. Re-reading recently her prose I came across a passage where she writes how from the back someone once mistook her for Yesenin. And now I can see them before me: hanging and swaying in nooses, both of them fair-haired. He is on the left, she on the right, but the hooks and ropes are identical, and they both have flaxen hair, cut in a bowl shape. They say that Efron has been shot. The son is for the party, and is probably in the war. How could you not hang yourself if your beloved Germany is dropping bombs on your beloved Moscow, your old friends are afraid of meeting you and you are hounded in the journals and have nothing to eat?[4]

After the war there appeared in Paris the sole issue of the *Russian Collection* (*Russky sbornik*), which it is now impossible to find anywhere. It carried the only obituary of Marina Tsvetayeva, which was written by Aleksandr Bakhrakh:

... Her life was prematurely cut short, and a remarkable person and a great Russian poet has departed from us, leaving for ever in the memory of those who knew her an image uneffaced by death. Before our eyes there still appears the aquiline nose, the high forehead, wreathed with puffs of cigarette smoke, and the arm encircled by silver bracelets, rummaging myopically in the "chaos" of papers, covered with her characteristic minute handwriting...[5]

After this a curtain of silence fell over Tsvetayeva, both in the East and in the West. In the Russian emigration poets and writers of another orientation set the tone, moreover their old centres of literary activity had been destroyed. Whoever survived the war fled to America and had to start all over again.

On 14 August 1941 Andrey Zhdanov delivered a speech in the Soviet Union in which he made his famous attack on Anna Akhmatova and Zoshchenko. On this day began the dark period of

'Zhdanovshchina' and the persecution of 'rootless cosmopolitans'.
It was perfectly clear that in such conditions it was impossible even
to mention the name of Marina Tsvetayeva in Russia. It could be
used, however, with success in publications destined for abroad, as
part of anti-Fascist propaganda. (Especially suitable in this regard
were parts of the *Poems to Czechia*.)

The first post-war volume of Tsvetayeva's work appeared in the
West in 1953, the year of Stalin's death. This was a selection of
prose, which was published by Marina's friend of many years in
Prague, Yekaterina Yeleneva, with a preface by Fyodor Stepun. In
spite of its imperfections and even mistakes, this collection was the
starting point for Tsvetayeva's revival in the West. In his foreword
Stepun drew the first significant literary portrait of the writer and
tried to evaluate objectively her work and its significance:

> The distinguishing feature of her poetry is the combination of a
> whirlwind inspiration with a conscious, almost calculated, artistry ... In
> her poetry can be equally felt both a belief in the primordial Word,
> which created the world, and an infinite love for poetic vocabulary, for
> ancient and modern words, for rhythms and metres, for the counter-
> point of vowels and consonants.[6]

Unfortunately space does not permit a detailed account of the
drastic changes which occurred in émigré Russian cultural life in
connection with the Second World War. The centres of Russian
intellectual life in the Balkans, the Baltic countries, Czechoslovakia
and the Far East completely disappeared. In Prague special agents
of the Red Army seized the Russian libraries and archives there
and sent them to the Soviet Union. The same thing happened with
many people as well. But other Russians who had settled here in
the twenties managed to flee from this part of Europe. Many of
them ended up in camps for displaced persons in Austria and
Germany. As early as 1946 Ye. Romanov and V. Zavalishin
founded the journal *Borders* (*Grani*) in one of these camps in
Germany.

After all the wartime and post-war upheavals, the rôle of
Germany for the Russian emigration changed a great deal. Of the
members of the older generation only Fyodor Stepun remained,
who became a professor at the University of Heidelberg. Later he
lived in Munich which has become the main Russian centre in
Germany, (without, however, rivaling the position of Berlin in the
twenties). In the 1950s and 1960s the journal *Bridges* (*Mosty*) was
published in Munich.

The German occupation of Paris during the war struck a terrible blow to the Russian colony there, from which it did not recover. After the war almost all the leading intellectual figures had either left, or were dead. The journal *The Messenger of the Russian Student Christian Movement* (*Vestnik R.S.Kh.D.*) (edited by Nikita Struve) and the only Russian language newspaper in Western Europe, *Russian Thought* (*Russkaya mysl'*) (for many years edited by Zinaida Shakhovskaya), continue to exist, but 'Russian Montparnasse' has disappeared for ever.

Those who could, sought refuge in the United States. As Nikolay Andreyev says this was 'the discovery of America', or more precisely, of New York, as a new literary centre.[7] Subsequently, other centres of Russian culture arose, especially in California. In distinction to the situation of the thirties in France, Russian writers and scholars were able to take up not only unskilled labour, but also influential positions in various universities. Mark Slonim, for example, taught in New York, while Yury Ivask found a place at the University of Massachusetts. Gleb Struve became a professor at the University of California and Vladimir Nabokov lectured at Cornell.

New York soon became the centre for Russian publishing. Already in 1942 Mark Aldanov and Mikhail Tsetlin founded there *The New Review* (*Novy zhurnal*), which continues the tradition of *Contemporary Annals*. From 1959 to 1986 its chief editor was Roman Gul.[8] In addition to the daily newspaper *The New Russian Word* (*Novoye russkoye slovo*), which was founded in 1910 and which is still in existence, there also appeared in New York the literary almanac *Experiments* (*Opyty*), which was published in the fifties by R.N. Grinberg and Yury Ivask. Finally we should mention the very valuable activity of the Chekhov Publishing House. With all these opportunities open to them, Tsvetayeva's friends and acquaintances began to publish their memoirs about her, and letters they had received from her, albeit with certain deletions. Tsvetayeva's letters to Ivask were published in *The Russian Literary Archive* (1956), those to Gul in *The New Review* (1959), to Steiger in *Experiments* (1960), to Bakhrakh in *Bridges* (1960), and to Fedotov in *The New Review* (1981). The first memoirs about Tsvetayeva appeared in *Experiments* in 1964. This was Yelena Izvolskaya's article 'Shadow on the Wall', which was followed by others, such as Nikolay Yelenev's 'Who was Marina Tsvetayeva?' (*Borders*, 1958). The most important memoir, however, was Mark Slonim's 'About Marina Tsvetayeva', published in *The New Review* (1970-71).

Little by little those works which Tsvetayeva herself had not been able to publish in journals before she left for Russia (and which remained in the West) began to appear in print. In 1957 Gleb Struve published *Swans' Encampment* in Munich, which was followed by a second, corrected, edition in 1971, together with the long poem *Perekop*. In the introduction to this volume Ivask wrote:

> Tsvetayeva's poetry is the poetry of praise and abuse. She praised many things and many people, and did this openly and loudly, without any attempt at concealment. Loud praise and loud abuse is the stuff of rhetoric, and rhetoric is supposedly "not a woman's business", but Tsvetayeva devoted herself to this business and was equal to this task... Rhetoric can be cold, and it can also be fiery. Tsvetayeva's rhetoric is of the fiery kind... [9]

In 1964 Mark Slonim published 'The History of a Dedication' in *Oxford Slavonic Papers*. In 1971 Günther Wyrtzens, professor at the University of Vienna, published a large volume of Tsvetayeva's "uncollected works" in Munich and in 1972 the Y.M.C.A. press in Paris brought out the extremely valuable volume *Unpublished Letters*, edited by Gleb Struve and Nikita Struve. In 1976 the same press published, although without indicating the editor, a volume entitled *Unpublished Works*, in which appeared for the first time the complete collection *Poems of Youth* (1913-1916), the play *The Stone Angel* (1919), and the full text of *The Tale about Sonechka* (1917).

It is also necessary to mention another significant aspect of the activities of Russian professors in America: their influence as teachers. Already two generations of American, French and Swiss Slavists have been educated by them in the spirit of Russian culture. One of Gleb Struve's students, Simon Karlinsky (who was born in Kharbin after the First World War and who is now a professor at the University of California) wrote his doctoral thesis about the life and work of Tsvetayeva. He later used this as the basis for a book which was published in 1966 and which remained the only biography of Tsvetayeva in either the West or East for fifteen years. This extremely important study not only facilitated, but actually made possible (at least in the West) all further research on Tsvetayeva, the present work included. It is a pleasure and duty to acknowledge this fact. [10]

One cannot say, however, that all the reminiscences of Tsvetayeva which have appeared in print over the years are positive or well-intentioned. Apparently several of Tsvetayeva's contemporaries had either kept too strong a recollection of the harsher, more disagreeable sides of her character, or were else unwilling to abandon their old prejudices. Thus, for example, Bunin writes in his memoirs:

... How many more of them were not normal! Tsvetayeva, with her
downpour of outrageous words and sounds which lasted a lifetime, and
who put an end to her life with a noose after her return to Soviet
Russia ... [11]

Or the opinion of Terapiano:

With those who disagreed with her, and naturally there were many of
these among the poets and writers, she quickly entered into an
argument, which she would carry on, harshly and arrogantly, offending
and wounding her opponents at every step ... In spite of such a
flowering of creativity Marina Tsvetayeva was one of the poets least
heard of during the entire course of her life in the emigration. She was
appreciated, and even extolled, by the rare connoisseurs of poetry and
by the most "qualified readers", at the time when the rest of her
audience, and, unfortunately, her patrons were turning away from her! [12]

Georgy Adamovich maintained his hostile views longer than
anyone else. He did not allow a single opportunity for arguing with
her to pass.

As far as I am concerned there can be no doubt about the fact that there
is no creative novelty in her rhythmic convulsions, that is, no grounds
for development. Tsvetayeva belongs to those who end an era, and only
the spirit of contradiction which possessed her, the spirit of every form
of "defiance" prevented her from admitting this, even to herself. [13]

Gradually these voices grew silent and there began to appear
more works expressing enthusiasm and understanding. In 1973, a
few weeks before his death, Adamovich wrote a poem which
sounded quite differently:

If only we could speak now, Marina!
While you were alive it did not happen, and now you are no more.
But I can still hear your swan-like voice,
As a herald of triumph and a herald of doom.
While you were alive it did not happen. I am not guilty.
Literature is an invitation to hell,
Which, I admit, I entered with joy,
And from which there is no return. [14]

In the Soviet Union the careful rehabilitation of the detested
"White Guard poetess" began in 1956 when Ilya Ehrenburg
published his novel *The Thaw* (which gave its name to the new era
in Soviet literature). In the same year the almanac *Literary Moscow*
(no.2) printed seven poems by Tsvetayeva. Among them were: 'For
my poems written down so soon ...', 'Attempt at Jealousy', and
'What can I do, a blind man, and a stepson' (from 'The Poets'
no.3). Ehrenburg wrote in the preface:

> It is still not the right time to speak of her difficult life; she is too close to us. But I would like to say, however, that Tsvetayeva was a person with a great conscience and that she lived her life purely and nobly. Always in need, she scorned the material goods of existence. She was inspired even on ordinary days, passionate both in her attachments and hatreds, and was extraordinarily sensitive ... [15]

The success of the period of the "thaw" was so great (especially with regard to Tsvetayeva) that official institutions were forced to back down and sound the retreat. On 16 May 1957, at the third plenum of the governing board of the Union of Writers Aleksandr Dymshits considered it necessary to make the following declaration:

> However, it is not correct to include certain works, which belong to the past, among the significant phenomena of our present life. The names of Khlebnikov, Tsvetayeva, Mandelstam are becoming well-known, but they are becoming popular in an incorrect manner, and under this influence young people are being carried away by them. What can we do with Akhmatova then? Indeed in comparison with Tsvetayeva she is immeasurably greater. Tsvetayeva is a minor phenomenon. In my opinion such an irresponsible attempt at the revision of the reputations of various poets will be harmful to a certain part of our young people ...

At the same plenum Aleksey Surkov expressed himself even more clearly:

> ... and are not these appeals, which have become more frequent of late, to send our young poets as apprentices to Marina Tsvetayeva and Boris Pasternak ... who by their lives and poetry displayed a detached attitude to everything which our people are doing and have done over the past forty years, echoes of that noise which is coming from our neighbours?* We have published the collected works of Bunin ... A volume by M. Tsvetayeva will soon be in print ... but we can hardly identify our editorial policy with recommending young people to learn from one or another of these masters ... [16]

This time Surkov kept his word, although with great delay. In 1961 a "small" volume of selected works by Tsvetayeva did appear. This was followed by a larger edition which was published in the Poet's Library series in 1965, with an introduction by Vladimir Orlov and with detailed notes by Ariadna Efron. This volume includes lyric poems, long poems, and dramatic works written between 1913 and 1939, many of which appeared in print for the first time.

At the beginning of the 1960s when the pressure on Russian cultural life had somewhat lifted, memoirs as well began to appear

* A reference to the Hungarian uprising of 1956.

in the Soviet Union. Abridged and filtered through the censorship, they are memoirs all the same. As before, the first of these was by Ilya Ehrenburg. In his book *People, Years, Life* he writes:

> I have met many poets in my life, and I know how dearly the artist pays for his passion for art, but it seems that I can recall no fate more tragic than Marina's. Everything in her life was unstable and illusory: her political ideas, her critical judgements, and her personal dramas – everything but her poetry.[17]

Now Pasternak as well could speak openly about Marina Tsvetayeva:

> Tsvetayeva was a woman with an active masculine soul, resolute, militant, indomitable. In her life and work she strove eagerly and almost rapaciously for perfection and precision, in pursuit of which she went very far and outstripped us all. Aside from the little of her work which is known she wrote a great quantity of things which we do not know, enormous, impetuous works, some in the style of Russian folk-tales, others based on motifs of universal historical legends and myths. Their publication will be a great triumph and a revelation for our national poetry and at one go our poetry will be enriched by this belated and unique gift. I think that the greatest reinterpretation and recognition await Tsvetayeva.[18]

When Pavel Antokolsky was asked to review one of Tsvetayeva's volumes in *Novy mir*, he took this as an occasion to render his due to his friend of many years past and to her work:

> She had a fate which was extraordinary to a high degree and a startling character. Behind both stand even wider categories: Marina Tsvetayeva's fate reflects our history and the first half of the century, whose very character revealed itself in her biography which came abruptly to a tragic end. The significance of her work, its living essence, inevitably and naturally defines itself through this correlation.[19]

But a still more important event now took place. Those people who had been living outside society for decades, as though already dead, began to return to normal everyday life. And these people began to speak up. Among the thousands of prisoners released during the Khrushchev era were Anastasia Tsvetayeva and Ariadna Efron, both of whom did their utmost to return Marina Tsvetayeva to her Russian readers. In 1969 Ariadna Efron succeeded in publishing in *Novy mir* an important selection of her mother's letters, and 1971 the same journal printed through her efforts the unfinished long poem 'Yegorushka'. Her own memoirs appeared in 1973 and 1975 in the journal *Zvezda*. For her part, Anastasia recounted her childhood with Marina for the first time in 1966 in *Novy mir* (no.1-2). Later these memoirs were published as a book in 1971. Two new editions came out in 1974 and 1984 and have been translated into many languages. Since then she has continued to write articles about her childhood and youth with Marina, about their mother and Russia before 1918. She died in 1993.

The first official evening dedicated to the poetry of Marina Tsvetayeva was held on 25 October 1962 in the House of Arts in Moscow. In his book Simon Karlinsky describes how a large crowd of enthusiasts stood by the doors hoping for returned tickets for the evening, to which 140 people had been invited. Anna Akhmatova and Lidia Chukovskaya spoke at great length about this evening, although neither of them was actually present.[20] In her account Chukovskaya quotes a stenograph made by Raisa Orlova of the evening's proceedings which passed into *samizdat* literature. To open the evening Ehrenburg told of his first acquaintance with Tsvetayeva's poetry, then Boris Slutsky and Yevgeny Tager spoke. Finally, members of the 'Studio of Young People of the Museum of Literature' read a selection of Tsvetayeva's poetry.

According to Chukovskaya, Akhmatova was not happy about the way the event was arranged:

> ... Marina's evening was badly organised. Ehrenburg came, bringing with him Slutsky and Tager. The audience somehow managed to listen to Slutsky, but Tager dragged on, and on, and on, and the auditorium gradually began to lead its own life. You know what that means? Everyone reverts to their own affairs. Some cough, others play ping-pong ... And this was Marina's return to Moscow, to *her* Moscow! ...[21]

No, as we now know this was not Marina's real return to Moscow. Since the 1960s Marina Tsvetayeva's poetry has found its own way to the hearts of a whole generation of Russian readers. In the beginning this meant *unofficial* events, such as poetry evenings and lectures organised by private persons, whose energy and enthusiasm deserve much admiration. More recently Tsvetayeva has begun to be recognised quasi-officially and the city of Moscow has decided to found a museum in her honour in the house on the former Borisoglebsky Lane (now Pisemsky Street) in which she once lived.

It should come as no surprise that the year 1985 proved to be a great turning point for Tsvetayeva admirers. Since then everything which had been worked on for many years and written 'for the desk drawer', and which was previously known to Russian readers only by hearsay or from foreign publications, has been published. They can now learn the truth about events in the life of the Efron family, which until recently had been supressed as they did not suit properly the hagiography of the great poet. With the appearance of

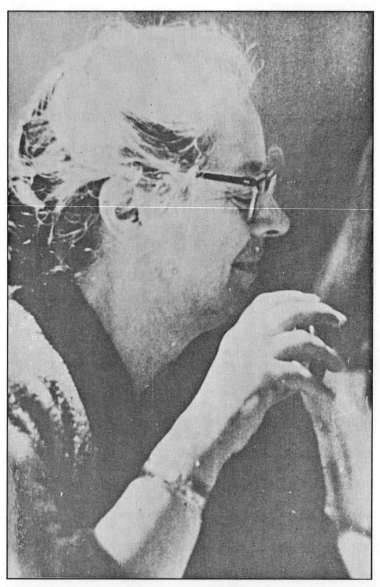

Ariadna Efron: early 1970s

Anastasia Tsvetayeva: Moscow, 1970

the third edition of Marina Tsvetayeva's poetry in the series 'The Poet's Library', edited by E. Korkina (1990), her complete poetic works are now available to the Russian reader.

Tatyana Kvanina tells of an incident which occurred during Tsvetayeva's stay at Golitsyno in 1940. One evening they were sitting on a bench in brilliant moonlight. All of a sudden Tsvetayeva said: 'It is good to be here.' 'Where?' asked Kvanina, who did not understand. 'In Russia!'[22]

If now, decades after her death, we reflect on the life and work of the great poet, we must admit she was right. In her person the two branches of Russian literature, within Russia and abroad, are reunited. Russian young people need Tsvetayeva's poetry in a way even she could not have dreamt of during her sad and ill-fated life. True, her return was tragic and she came back to Russia as a 'tolerated vestige'. Since then, however, she has become the 'welcome and expected guest' she had hoped to be. Marina Tsvetayeva has finally won the respect of the literary world at large and is loved in Russia.

Postscript

In September 1993, a few days before her 99th birthday, Anastasia Tsvetayeva died quietly in Moscow. She had done her utmost to return Marina Tsvetayeva to her Russian readers: her memoirs were published in three enlarged editions and are still a bestseller throughout the enormous country. And she lived long enough to see rectified her terrible accusation against her poor 16-year-old nephew that he had been in some way the cause of his mother's death. In October 1992, on the occasion of Tsvetayeva's 100th birthday, a little note appeared in the Moscow journal *Argumenty i fakty*:

> As to the testimony of a high-ranking employee of the Ministry of Security, who did not wish to reveal his identity, there exists in the archives a document in which it is stated that one KGB officer went to see Tsvetayeva literally on the eve before her death. The same person confirmed that the fact of this interview as well as its contents were deliberately held in a way that the poetess was left only one decision – suicide.

August 1994

NOTES

Part One

CHAPTER 1

1. Anastasia I. Cvetaeva, *Vospominanija*, (Moscow, 1971), p.23.
2. Marina Cvetaeva, 'Istorija odnogo posvjaščenija', in *Izbrannaja proza v 2 tomakh* (New York, 1979), I, p.349.
3. 'Babuške' (1914), in *Stikhotvorenija i poèmy v 5 tomakh* (New York, 1980 –), I, p.176.
4. M. Cvetaeva, letter to V. Rozanov, 8 April 1914, *Neizdannye pis'ma*, edited by Gleb Struve and Nikita Struve (Paris, 1972), p.27.
5. 'Pis'ma M. Cvetaevoj Ju. P. Ivasku', *Russkij literarturnyj arkhiv* (New York, 1956), p.217.
6. A.I. Cvetaeva, *Vospominanija*, op. cit, p.26.
7. M. Cvetaeva, *Neizd. pis'ma*, op. cit, p.27.
8. M. Cvetaeva, 'Mat' i muzyka', in *Izbr. proza*, op. cit, II, p.172.
9. A.I. Cvetaeva, *Vospominanija*, op. cit, p.7.
10. A. Cvetaeva, 'Korni i plody', *Zvezda*, 4 (1979), p.186.
11. Mark Slonim, 'O Marine Cvetaevoj', *Novyj žurnal*, 100 (1970), p.160
12. A.I. Cvetaeva, *Vospominanija*, op. cit, p.64.
13. M. Cvetaeva, 'Istorija odnogo posvjaščenija', op. cit, p.343.
14. M. Cvetaeva, 'Mat' i muzyka', op. cit, pp.187-88.
15. Ibid, pp.172-73.
16. M. Cvetaeva, 'Moj Puškin', in *Izbr. proza*, op. cit, II, p.268.
17. A.I. Cvetaeva, *Vospominanija*, op. cit, pp.65, 76, 93.
18. M. Cvetaeva, 'Svetovoj liven' ', in *Izbr. proza*, op. cit, I, p.135.
19. M. Cvetaeva, 'Dom u starogo Pimena', in *Izbr. proza*, op. cit, II, p.229.
20. M. Cvetajevová, 'Můj životopis', in *Hodina duše*, edited by J. Strobolová (Prague, 1971), p.9.
21. M. Cvetaeva, 'Moj Puškin', op. cit, pp.249-50.
22. M. Cvetaeva, 'Khlystovki', in *Izbr. proza*, op. cit, II, p.150.
23. 'Osen' v Taruse' (1909), in *Stikhotvorenija i poèmy*, op. cit, I, p.93.

CHAPTER 2

1. M. Cvetaeva, 'Moj Puškin', op. cit, p.261.
2. M. Cvetaeva, 'Istorija odnogo posvjaščenija', op. cit, p.343.
3. A.I. Cvetaeva, 'Iz prošlogo', *Novyj mir*, 1 (1966), p.107.
4. M. Cvetaeva, 'Moj Puškin', op. cit, p.275.
5. Ibid, p.279.
6. 'Na skalakh', 'On byl sineglazyj i ryžij', 'Bajard', in *Stikhotvorenija i poèmy*, op. cit, I, pp.15, 99, 84.
7. M. Cvetaeva, 'O Germanii', in *Izbr. proza*, op. cit, I, p.124.
8. M. Cvetaeva, *Neizd. pis'ma*, op. cit, p.402.
9. A.I. Cvetaeva, *Vospominanija*, op. cit, p.125ff.
10. Ibid, pp.131-32.
11. 'Naši carstva', in *Stikhotvorenija i poèmy*, op. cit, I, p.19.
12. A.I. Cvetaeva, *Vospominanija*, op. cit, p.197.
13. M. Cvetaeva, *Neizd. pis'ma*, op. cit, pp.402-03.
14. M. Cvetaeva, 'Bašnja v pljušče', in *Izbr. proza*, op. cit, II, pp.191-97.
15. See: Elisabeth K. Poretsky, *Our Own People* (London, 1969).

CHAPTER 3

1. See: A.I. Cvetaeva, *Vospominanija*, op. cit, p.205ff.
2. Simon Karlinsky, *Marina Cvetaeva: Her Life and Art* (Berkeley, Los Angeles, 1966), p.179.
3. 'Ne smejtes' vy nad junym pokolen'em', in A.I. Cvetaeva, *Vospominanija*, pp. 226-27.
4. Ibid, p.225.
5. M. Cvetaeva, 'Mat' i muzyka', op. cit, p.189f.
6. A.I. Cvetaeva, *Vospominanija*, op. cit, p.238-39.
7. Ibid, p.243.
8. 'Mame' (1909 or 1910), in *Stikhotvorenija i poèmy*, op. cit, I, p.21.
9. A.I. Cvetaeva, *Vospominanija*, op. cit, p.253.

CHAPTER 4

1. 'Stolovaja', in *Stikhotvorenija i poèmy*, op. cit, I, p.63.
2. Quoted by A.I. Cvetaeva, *Vospominanija*, op. cit, p.264-65.
3. Ibid.
4. 'Gordost' i robost' ' (20 September 1921), in *Stikhotvorenija i poèmy*, op. cit, II (1980), p.299.
5. 'V pjatnadcat' let', in *Stikhotvorenija i poèmy*, op. cit, I, p.95.
6. A.I. Cvetaeva, *Vospominanija*, op. cit, pp. 299-301. Tsvetayeva herself wrote to Rozanov: 'Between the ages of 14 and 16 I was obsessed by the idea of revolution, at sixteen I fell madly in love with Napoleon I and Napoleon II, for a whole year I lived without people, alone in my little room, in my vast world.' (8 April 1914). *Neizd. pis'ma*, op. cit, p.30.
7. A.I. Cvetaeva, *Vospominanija*, op. cit, p.344.
8. Ibid.

CHAPTER 5

1. See: *Otčet Moskovskago Publičnago i Rumjancevskago Muzeev za 1909 god* (Moscow, 1910).
2. A.I. Cvetaeva, *Vospominanija*, op. cit, p.316.
3. 'Čarodeju' (undated), in *Stikhotvorenija i poèmy*, op. cit, I, p.28.
4. A.I. Cvetaeva, *Vospominanija*, op.cit., p.317.
5. Letter to A.V. Bakhrakh, 27 September 1923, *Mosty*, 6 (1961), p.335
6. 'V Pariže' (June 1909), in *Stikhotvorenija i poèmy*, op. cit, I, p.52.
7. 'Molitva' (26 September 1909), in *Stikhotvorenija i poèmy*, op. cit, I, p.56.
8. M. Cvetaeva, *Neizd. pis'ma*, op. cit, p.18.
9. 'Novolun' e' (Tarusa, October 1909), in *Stikhotvorenija i poèmy*, op. cit, I, p.27.
10. *Otčet Moskovskago Publičnago i Rumjancevskago Muzeev za 1909 god*, op. cit. In his book *Between Two Revolutions* Andrey Bely describes in detail the 'Incident with Ellis'. This is his version: 'Now about Tsvetayev: he entertained a feeling of hatred for Ellis as he appeared almost every day in his house to preach Symbolism to his daughters, Marina and Asya. Their papa was horrified by the influence this "decadent" had on them, all the more so as they cultivated leftist tendencies for this confirmed Octobrist. At the time they called themselves anarchists. In the professor's opinion Ellis fed their tendencies, not to give a farthing for their papa. On another front the lady with whom their papa was in love was herself head over

heels in love with Ellis and so here as well the "decadent" stood in the father's way. He avenged his sense of injury in his capacity as director of the Rumyantsev Museum. And aside from everything else he wanted to clear himself in the eyes of the minister who hated him, so he demanded the strictest investigation with a view to indicting Ellis . . . ' (pp. 369-70).

11. 'Byvšemu čarodeju' (undated), in *Stikhotvorenija i poèmy*, op. cit, I, p.28
12. A.I. Cvetaeva, *Vospominanija*, op. cit, p.250.
13. 'Ošibka' (undated), in *Stikhotvorenija i poèmy*, op. cit, I, p.33.
14. 'Put' kresta', in *Stikhotvorenija i poèmy*, op cit, I, p.104.
15. A.I. Cvetaeva, *Vospominanija*, op. cit, p.365.
16. M. Cvetaeva, 'Pis'mo V. Ja. Brjusovu' (15 March 1910), *Novyj mir*, 1 (1966), p.186.
17. M. Cvetaeva, 'Geroj truda' in *Izbr. proza*, op. cit, I, p.186. About the relative truth of this essay see: A. Saakjanc, 'O pravde letopisi i pravde poeta', *Voprosy literatury*, 11 (1983), pp.208-14.
18. I.V. Cvetaeva, *Moskovskij Publičnyj i Rumjancevskij Muzei. Spornye voprosy. Opyt samozaščity I. Cvetaeva, byv. direktora sich muzeev* (Moscow-Dresden, 1910); I.V. Cvetaeva, *Delo byvšikh ministra Narodnogo prosveščenija A.N. Švarca i direktora Rumjancevskogo Muzeja I.V. Cvetaeva* (Leipzig, 1911).
19. M. Cvetaeva, 'Geroj truda', op. cit, p.186.
20. 'Ešče molitva', in *Stikhotvorenija i poèmy*, op. cit, I, p.71.

CHAPTER 6

1. See: Johannes von Guenther, *Ein Leben im Ostwind* (München, 1969), p.266f.
2. V. Ja. Brjusov, 'Novye sborniki stikhov', *Russkaja mysl'*, 2 (1911), p.233.
3. 'Nedoumen'e', in *Stikhotvorenija i poèmy*, op. cit, I. p.60; see also: A.I. Cvetaeva, *Vospominanija*, op. cit, pp.314-15.
4. 'V. Ja. Brjusovu', in *Stikhotvorenija i poèmy*, op. cit, I, p.120.
5. N.S. Gumilev, (Review), in *Sobranie sočinenij v 4 tomakh* (Washington D.C., 1962-68), IV, p.262.
6. Quoted by I. Kudrova, 'Pis'ma Mariny Cvetaevoj M. Vološinu', *Novyj mir*, 2 (1977), p.231.
7. 'Pis'ma Mariny Cvetaevoj M. Vološinu', *Novyj mir*, 2 (1977), p.236.
8. F.A. Stepun, *Byvšee i nesbyvšeesja* (New York, 1956), I, p.273.
9. M. Cvetaeva, 'Plennyj dukh', in *Izbr. proza*, op cit, II, p.90.
10. M. Cvetaeva, *Neizd. pis'ma*, op. cit, p.19.
11. M. Cvetaeva, 'Plennyj dukh', op. cit, p.90.
12. A.I. Cvetaeva, *Vospominanija*, op cit, p.388.

CHAPTER 7

1. M. Cvetaeva, 'Živoe o živom', in *Izbr. proza*, op. cit, II, p.58.
2. 'Pis'ma Mariny Cvetaevoj M. Vološinu' (18 April 1911), *Novyj mir*, 2 (1977), p.239.
3. Ju. Terapiano, *Vstreči* (New York, 1953), p.8.
4. M. Cvetaeva, 'Istorija odnogo posvjaščenija', op. cit, p.358.
5. M. Cvetaeva (Cvetajevová), 'Můj životopis', op. cit, p.10.
6. A.I. Cvetaeva, *Vospominanija*, op. cit, p.433.
7. Ibid, p.455.
8. 'Nerazlučnoj v dorogu', in *Stikhotvorenija i poèmy*, op. cit, I, p.129.
9. 'Pis'ma Mariny Cvetaevoj M. Vološinu' (28 October 1911), *Novyj mir*, 2 (1977), pp.241-43.

10. See: A.I. Cvetaeva, 'Vospominanija č. 2', *Moskva*, 3-5 (1981); 3, pp.116-60; 4, pp.117-60; 5, pp.112-59.
11. For details about places where Marina Tsvetayeva lived see: A.I. Cvetaeva, 'Marinin dom', *Zvezda*, 12 (1981), pp.142-57.
12. Yevgenia Gertsyk's memoirs were published in Paris in 1973 by the YMCA Press. As yet there is nothing known about the continuation of the memoirs, dedicated to the Tsvetayev sisters, which is mentioned in the book.
13. A.I. Cvetaeva, *Vospominanija*, op. cit, pp.391-92.
14. B. Zajcev, *Dalekoe* (Washington D.C., 1965), pp.130-34.
15. 'Pis'ma Mariny Cvetaevoj M. Vološinu' (19 November 1911), *Novyj mir*, 2 (1977), p.244.
16. 'Na radost' ' (undated), in *Stikhotvorenija i poèmy*, op. cit, I, p.127.
17. A.I. Cvetaeva, 'Vospominanija Č. 2', *Moskva*, 3 (1981), p.145.

Part Two

CHAPTER 8

1. Ariadna S. Èfron, *Stranicy vospominanij* (Paris, 1979), p.22f.
2. See: B. Zajcev, *Dalekoe*, op. cit, p.133; N. Elenev, 'Kem byla Marina Cvetaeva?', *Grani*, 39 (1958), p.145; M. Slonim, 'O Marine Cvetaevoj', *Novyj žurnal*, 100 (1970), p.160; Ariadna Èfron, op. cit. p.23.
3. Véronique Lossky, 'Marina Cvétaeva: Souvenirs de contemporains', *Marina Cvetaeva: Studien und Materialen, Wiener slawistischer Almanach*, Sonderband 3 (1981), p.213.
4. 'S.E.' (Koktebel', 3 June 1914), in *Stikhotvorenija i poèmy*, op. cit, I, p.166.
5. M. Cvetaeva, *Neizd. pis'ma*, op. cit, p.25.
6. Nikolay S. Gumilyov, 'Pis'ma o russkoj poèzii', in *Sobranie sočinenii*, op. cit, IV, p.293.
7. V. Ja. Brjusov, 'Segodnjašnij den' russkoj poèzii. 50 sbornikov stikhov', *Russkaja mysl'*, 7 (1912), p.233.
8. Quoted in: *Russkaja literatura konca XIX – načala XX veka (1908-17)* (Moscow, 1972), p.545.
9. M. Cvetaeva, 'Geroj truda', op. cit, p.188.
10. M. Cvetaeva, letter to Rozanov, 8 April 1914, *Neizd. pis'ma*, op. cit, p.30.
11. *Junošeskie stikhi*, in M. Cvetaeva, *Neizdannoe* (Paris, 1976), pp.3-92. Several of these poems were published between 1915 and 1917 in the Petersburg journal *Severnye zapiski*; a large selection of them were published in the 'Biblioteka poèta' edition *Izbr. proizvedenija* with commentaries by Ariadna Efron (Moscow, 1965), others appeared in *Tarusskie stranicy*, and in *Den' poèzii* (Moscow, 1968), with a preface by Viktoria Schweitzer.
12. See preface by V.P. Kupčenko, 'Pis'ma Mariny Cvetaevoj M. Vološinu', *Ežegodnik rukopisnogo otdela Puškinskogo doma* (1975) p.151f.
13. 'Moim stikham napisannym tak rano' (May 1913), in *Stikhotvorenija i poèmy*, op. cit, I, p.140.
14. See A. Cvetaeva, 'Glavy iz knigi', *Daugava*, 7 (1980), pp.58-72.
15. M. Cvetaeva, letter to Rozanov, 7 March 1914, *Neizd. pis'ma*, op. cit, pp.23-24.
16. Quoted by V.P. Kupčenko in preface to 'Pis'ma Mariny Cvetaevoj M. Vološinu', op. cit, pp.154-55.

CHAPTER 9

1. 'Vojna, vojna' (Moscow, 16 July 1914), in *Stikhotvorenija i poèmy*, op. cit, I, p.174.
2. A.I. Cvetaeva, 'Marinin dom', *Zvezda*, 12 (1981), pp.142-57.
3. See: S. Poljakova, *Zakatnye ony dni: Cvetaeva i Parnok* (Ann Arbor, 1983); Sofija Parnok, *Sobranie stikhotvorenij* (Ann Arbor, 1979); S. Karlinsky, *Marina Tsvetaeva* (Cambridge, 1985), p.51; S. Poljakova, 'Poèzija i pravda v cikle stikhotvorenij Cvetaevoj "Podruga" ', *Marina Cvetaeva: Studien und Materialen, Wiener slawistischer Almanach*, Sonderband 3 (1981), pp.113-21.
4. See N. Elenev, 'Kem byla Marina Cvetaeva?', *Grani*, 39 (1958), pp.141-47.
5. Grand-Duc Nicolas Mikhailovitch, *La fin du tsarisme: Lettres in édites à Frédéric Masson 1914-1918*, (Paris, 1968), pp. 76-81.
6. 'Germanii' (Moscow, 1 December 1914), in *Stikhotvorenija i poèmy*, op. cit, I, p.175.
7. 'Ja znaju pravdu' (3 October 1915), in *Stikhotvorenija i poèmy*, op. cit, I, p.194.

CHAPTER 10

1. All of these poems were later published either in *Izbrannye proizvedenija* (1965), or in *Nesobrannye proizvedenija* (1971).
2. F.A. Stepun, *Byvšee i nesbyvšeesja*, op. cit.
3. See Georgy Ivanov's letter to Gleb Struve, *Mosty*, 13/14 (1968), p.394. It is possible that Marina Tsvetayeva confused him with Georgy Adamovich, because in a letter to Olga Kolbasina-Chernova of 17 October 1924 (about a review of her work) she says: 'I know the person who wrote it, a certain Adamovich. He was a pupil of Gumilyov, he wrote poetic still-lifes; a Petersburgian who hated Moscow . . . '*Neizd. pis'ma*, op. cit, p.73.
4. 'M.A. Kuzminu', in *Stikhotvorenija i poèmy*, op. cit, II (1982), p.111.
5. 'Nezdešnij večer' in *Izbr. proza*, op. cit, II, p.136.
6. 'Iz ruk moikh – nerukotvornyj grad' (31 March 1916), in *Stikhotvorenija i poèmy*, op. cit, I, p.215.
7. Osip Mandelštam, 'V raznogolisice devičeskogo khora', in *Sobranie sočinenij* (Washington D.C., 1967-81), I.
8. M. Cvetaeva, letters to A. Bakhrakh, 25 May and 25 July 1923, *Mosty*, 5 (1960), pp.313, 316.
9. Nadežda Mandelštam, *Vtoraja kniga* (Paris), p.520.
10. M. Cvetaeva, 'Istorija odnogo posvjaščenija', op. cit, p.346. This text was published for the first time twenty years after Tsvetayeva's death by Mark Slonim in *Oxford Slavonic Papers*, 11 (1964).
11. See O. Mandelštam, *Sobranie sočinenij*, op. cit, I, p.433.
12. N. Mandelštam, op. cit, pp.522-23.
13. S. Karlinsky, *Marina Tsvetaeva* (1985), p.64.
14. See A. Saakjanc, *Marina Cvetaeva: stranicy žizni i tvorčestva 1910-1922 (Moscow, 1986), p.109f.*
15. 'Ruki dany mne' (2 July 1916), in *Stikhotvorenija i poèmy*, op. cit, I, p.237.
16. Charles de Chambrun, *Lettres à Marie, Pétrograd 1914-1917* (Paris, 1941), p.29.

CHAPTER 11

1. This set of poems was published for the first time in M. Cvetaeva, *Neizdannoe* (Paris, 1976). The first selection from this collection was published in the edition *Versty: Stikhi 1917-1921* (Kostry: Moscow, 1922) in an edition of 1,000 copies, and was reprinted twice in Berlin in 1922. The 'Don Juan' cycle appeared in an incomplete version for the first time in *Vestnik R.S.Kh.D.*, 100 (1971), pp.217-23.

2. *Lebedinyj stan* could not be published in its entirety during Tsvetayeva's lifetime. In 1922 P.B. Struve published some poems from it in *Russkaya mysl'*. The first complete edition based on the manuscript which is kept in the archive of the library of the University of Basle, was published, thanks to the efforts of Gleb Struve, in 1957. A second edition, also prepared by Gleb Struve, and accompanied by *Perekop* was published in 1971 in Paris by the YMCA Press.

3. 'Pis'ma M. Cvetaevoj Ju. P. Ivasku' (25 January 1937), Russkij literaturnyj arkhiv, op. cit p.231.

4. 'Nad cerkovkoj golubye oblaka' (2 March 1917), in *Stikhotvorenija i poèmy*, op. cit, II (1982), p.60.

5. See F. Stepun, *Byvšee i nesbyvšeesja*, op. cit.

6. 'Nadobno smelo priznat'sja, Lira' (1 August 1918), in *Stikhotvorenija i poèmy*, op. cit, II (1982), p.75.

7. 'Za Otroka – za Golubja – za Syna' (4 April 1917), ibid, p.61.

8. 'Čto že! koli kinut žrebij' (13 May 1917), ibid, p.201.

9. M. Cvetaeva, *Izbr. proizvedenija*, op. cit, p.737 (note).

10. 'I kto-to, upav na kartu' (21 May 1917, Pentecost Sunday), in *Stikhotvorenija i poèmy*, op. cit, II (1982), p.63.

11. 'Pis'ma M. Cvetaevoj Vološinu', *Ežegodnik rukopisnogo otdela Puškinskogo doma*, op. cit, pp.177-79.

12. See A.I. Cvetaeva, 'Vospominanija č. 2', *Moskva*, 4 (1981), p.137.

13. M. Cvetaeva, 'Oktjabr' v vagone', in *Izbr. proza*, op. cit, I, p.21.

14. M. Cvetaeva, 'Živoe o živom', op. cit, p.75.

CHAPTER 12

1. F.A. Stepun, *Byvšee i nesbyvšeesja*, op. cit, II, p.202.

2. Grand-Duc Nicolas Mikhailovitch, *La fin du tsarisme*, op. cit, p.282.

3. 'Moskve' – (9 December 1917), in *Stikhotvorenija i poèmy*, op. cit, II (1982), p.144.

4. I. Èrenburg, *Ljudi, gody, žizn'* (Moscow, 1961), p.370.

5. A Èfron, 'Stranicy bylogo', *Zvezda*, 6 (1975), p.152.

6. A. Èfron, 'Stranicy vospominanij', *Zvezda*, 3 (1973), p.166.

7. Letter to Roman Gul', 17 February 1923, *Novyj žurnal*, 58 (1959), p.175.

8. These are, in chronological order: 'Oktjabr' v vagone' (October-November 1917); 'O ljubvi' 1917 (written in 1918-1919); 'Vol'nyj proezd', September 1918; 'Moi služby', 11 November 1918 – 7 July 1919; 'Iz dnevnika (Smert' Stakhoviča)', February-March 1919; 'O Germanii', 1919; 'Otryvki iz knigi *Zemnye primety'*, *1919;* 'O blagodarnosti', July 1919; 'Čerdačnoe', 1919-1920: All of these can be found in *Izbr. proza*, op. cit, I. Of the memoirs written later about this period see 'Povest' o Sonečke' and 'Geroj truda'.

9. M. Cvetaeva, 'Povest' o Sonečke', *Neizdannoe*, op. cit, p.209.

10. P. Antokolskij, 'Kniga Mariny Cvetaevoj', *Novy mir*, 4 (1966), pp.212-24.

11. These plays are: Metel' (1918); *Červonnyj valet* (1918); *Fortuna*; *Kamennyj angel*; *Priključenie* and *Feniks* (all written in 1919). As of 1965 Ariadna Efron believed that the plays *Kamennyj angel* (*The Stone Angel*) and *Červonnyj valet* (*The Knave of Hearts*) had disappeared without a trace. Since then they have both been published. The first is included in *Neizdannoe*, op. cit, pp.135-201; and the second turned up in the estate of the producer N.F. Baliev, who emigrated in 1919, and was published for the first time in *Novyj žurnal*, 115 (1974), pp.20-40.
12. See M. Cvetaeva, 'Smert' Stakhoviča', in *Izbr. proza*, op. cit, I, p.72f.
13. 'Stikhi k Sonečke', in *Stikhotvorenija i poèmy*, op. cit, II (1982), p.252-58.
14. 'Don I' (11 March 1918), ibid, p.68.
15. M. Cvetaeva, 'Čerdačnoe', in *Izbr. proza*, op. cit, I, p.82.
16. M. Cvetaeva, 'Moi služby', in *Izbr. proza*, op. cit, I, pp.50-71.

CHAPTER 13

1. Ariadna Èfron, 'Ne stydis' strana Rossija', *Wiener slawistisches Jahrbuch*, 20 (1974), p.180. Although this poem has been erroneously attributed to Marina Tsvetayeva, A. Saakyants has established that it was written by the little Alya.
2. Konstantin Bal'mont, *Gde moj dom?* (Prague, 1924).
3. K. Bal'mont, 'Marina Cvetaeva', *Sovremennye zapiski*, 7 (1921), p.92.
4. A. Bakhrakh, 'Pis'ma M. Cvetaeva', *Mosty*, 5 (1960) p.317.
5. È. Mindlin, *Neobyknovennye sobesedniki* (Moscow, 1968), pp.55-56.
6. See *Otkliki na vojnu i revoljuciju* (Petrograd, 1918) and V. Majakovskij, *Polnoe sobranie sočinenij* (Moscow, 1959), XII, p.391.
7. M. Cvetaeva, 'Moi služby', op. cit, p.70.
8. 'Geroj truda', op. cit, p.204.
9. I. Èrenburg, *Portrety russkikh poètov* (Berlin, 1922; reprint München, 1972), p.150.
10. I. Èrenburg, *Ljudi, gody, žizn'*, op. cit, II, p.371-72.
11. M. Cvetaeva, letter to V. Zvjaginceva, 7 February 1920, *Russian Literature*, 4 (1981), p.335. For more details see V. Schweitzer in the same journal.
12. M. Cvetaeva, letter to A.I. Cvetaeva, 17 December 1920, *Neizd. pis'ma*, op. cit, p.42.
13. M. Cvetaeva, letter to V. Zvjaginceva, 9 February 1920, *Russian Literature*, 4 (1981), p.335.
14. A.S. Èfron, *Stranicy vospominanij*, op. cit, p.35.
15. A. Saakjanc, *Marina Cvetaeva: Stranicy žizni i tvorčestva 1910-1922*, op. cit, p.227f.
16. 'Kto sozdan iz kamnja' (20 May 1920), in *Stikhotvorenija i poèmy*, op. cit, II (1982), p.286.
17. 'Pisala ja na aspidnoj doske' (18 May 1920), ibid, p.283.
18. *Car'-devica* (Moscow, 1 July to 4 September [old style] 1920), in *Stikhotvorenija i poèmy*, op. cit, IV (1983), pp.9-90; 'Egoruška' (Moscow, 1920-21), ibid, pp.341-58; 'Na krasnom kone' (13-17 January 1921), ibid, pp.155-60; 'Pereuločki' (Moscow, April 1922), *Stikhotvorenija i poèmy*, op. cit, II (1982), pp.174-83. Simon Karlinsky provides a synopsis and detailed discussion of *Car-devica*, 'Egoruška', 'Na krasnom kone' and 'Pereuločki', in his *Marina Tsvetaeva* (1985), pp.100-03.
19. D.S. Mirsky, *Geschichte der russischen Literatur* (München, 1964), p.446.

20. M. Cvetaeva, 'Pis'ma Evgeniju Lannu' (6 December 1920 to 10 September 1921), *Wiener slawistischer Almanach*, Sonderband III, (1981), pp.161-94.
21. 'Pis'ma M. Cvetaevoj Vološinu', *Ežegodnik rukopsinogo otdela Puškinskogo doma*, op. cit, p.179.
22. M. Cvetaeva, letter to A.I. Cvetaeva, 17 December 1920, *Neizd. pis'ma*, op. cit, p.42.
23. 'Plač Jaroslavny' (23-31 December 1920), in *Stikhotvorenija i poèmy*, op. cit, II (1982), p.90.
24. Ju. P. Ivask, 'Poèzija staroj èmigracij', in *Russkaja literatura v èmigracii* (Pittsburgh, 1972), p.51.

CHAPTER 14

1. Louise Weiss, *Mémoires d'une européenne* (Paris, 1970), II, pp.105-07.
2. I. Èrenburg, *Ljudi, gody, žizn'*, op. cit, II, p.552.
3. 'Na krasnom kone', in *Stikhotvorenija i poèmy*, op. cit, IV (1983), pp.155-60.
4. M. Cvetaeva, 'Pis'ma Evgeniju Lannu' (19 January 1921), *Wiener slawistischer Almanach*, Sonderband III, p.179.
5. A. Saakjanc, *Marina Cvetaeva: stranicy žizni i tvorčestva*, op. cit, p.268.
6. A.I. Cvetaeva, 'Vospominanija č. 2', *Moskva*, 4 (1981), p.138f.
7. Ju. P. Ivask, 'Blagorodnaja Cvetaeva', preface to M. Cvetaeva, *Lebedinyj stan. Perekop* (Paris), 1971, p.30.
8. See È Mindlin, *Neobyknovennye sobesedniki*, op. cit, p.42-76.
9. A. Bakhrakh, 'Pis'ma M. Cvetaevoj' (10 January 1924), *Mosty*, 6 (1961), p.339.
10. 'Pis'ma M. Cvetaevoj Ju. P. Ivasku' (4 June 1934), *Russkij literaturnyj arkhiv*, op. cit, p.220.
11. Sergej Volkonskij, *Byt i bytie* (Berlin, 1924; reprint, Paris, 1979).
12. M. Cvetaeva, *Remeslo* (Berlin, Moscow: Gelikon, 1923); reprint in M. Cvetaeva, *Nesobrannye proizvedenija* (München, 1971), pp.115-278.
13. 'Bašennyj boj' ('May'), in *Stikhotvorenija i poèmy*, op. cit, II (1982), p.105.
14. 'Pis'ma M. Cvetaevoj k Borisu Pasternaku' (29 July 1922), *Neizd. pis'ma*, op. cit, p.267.
15. 'Blagaja vest' ', in *Stikhotvorenija i poèmy*, op. cit, II (1982), p.119.
16. 'Pis'ma M. Cvetaevoj k A. Akhmatovoj' (31 August [old style] 1921), *Neizd. pis'ma*, op. cit, p.57.
17. 'Pis'ma M. Cvetaevoj M. Vološinu' (7 November 1921), *Ežegodnik rukopisnogo otdela Puškinskogo doma*, op. cit, p.181.
18. 'Pis'ma M. Cvetaevoj k R. Gulju' (9 February 1923), *Novyj žurnal*, 58 (1959), pp.169-187.
19. 'Sugroby' (10 February to 5 March 1923); 'Pereuločki' (April 1922), in *Stikhotvorenija i poèmy*, op. cit, II (1982), pp.160-83.
20. 'Pis'ma M. Cvetaevoj Ju. P. Ivasku' (11 November 1935 and 25 January 1937), *Russkij literaturnyj arkhiv*, op. cit, pp.227, 230.
21. N. Mandel'štam, *Vtoraja kniga*, op. cit, pp.515-18.

Part Three

1. 'Moe ubežišče ot dikikh ord' (5 August 1918), in *Stikhotvorenija i poèmy*, op. cit, II (1982), p.231.

CHAPTER 15

1. R.C. Williams, *Culture in Exile, Russian Emigrés in Germany 1881-1941* (Ithaca, London, 1972). See also I. Èrenburg, *Ljudi, gody, žizn'*, II, ch.3; A. Bakhrakh, 'Pis'ma Mariny Cvetaevoj', *Mosty*, 5 (1960) and his article 'Po pamjati, po zapiskam: Andrej Belyj', *Kontinent*, 3 (1975), pp.288-321.

2. The most important journals were: *Èpopeja*, which was edited almost entirely by Andrey Bely; *Beseda*, edited by Maksim Gorky; *Novaja russkaja kniga*, on which Roman Gul' and Ehrenburg worked. Ehrenburg also helped El Lisitsky publish the arts journal *Vešč'*.

3. A. Bakhrakh, 'Pis'ma M. Cvetaevoj', *Mosty*, 5 (1960), p.300.

4. The following volumes by Tsvetayeva were published in Berlin: *Razluka* (Gelikon, 1922); *Stikhi k Bloku* (Ogon'ki, 1922); *Car'-devica* (Èpokha, 1922); *Remeslo* (Gelikon, 1923); *Psikheja* (Gržebin, 1923).

5. See E. Kannak, 'Vospominanija o Gelikone', *Russkaja mysl'*, 17 January 1974.

6. A. Èfron, *Stranicy vospominanij*, op. cit, pp.91-92

7. See Serena Vitale, introduction to *Le notte fiorentine* (Milano, 1983) and the Russian translation by R. Rodina, 'Florentijskie noči', *Novyj mir*, 8 (1985), pp.155-70.

8. I. Èrenburg, *Ljudi, gody, žizn'*, op. cit, p.373.

9. M. Cvetaeva, letter to A. Bakhrakh, 20 July 1923, *Mosty*, 5 (1960), p.311.

10. M. Cvetaeva, letter to Ivask, 4 April 1933, *Russkij lit. arkhiv*, op. cit, p.209.

11. M. Cvetaeva, letter to Bakhrakh, 20 July 1923, op. cit, p.311.

12. *Russkij Berlin 1921-1923* (Paris, 1983), pp.33-37.

13. M. Cvetaeva, *Russica: Sbornik* (New York, 1981), pp.347-49.

14. M. Cvetaeva, 'Plennyj dukh', in *Izbr. proza*, op. cit, II, p.97.

15. M. Slonim, 'O Marine Cvetaevoj', *Novyj žurnal*, 100 (1970), p.156.

16. M. Cvetaeva, letters to Leonid Pasternak and Boris Pasternak, both 29 June 1922, *Neizd. pis'ma*, op. cit, pp.251, 266.

17. M. Cvetaeva, 'Svetovoj liven' ', in *Izbr. proza*, op. cit, I, p.135.

18. A Èfron, *Stranicy vospominanij*, op. cit, p.108.

19. 'Berlinu' (10 July 1922), in *Stikhotvorenija i poèmy*, III (1983), p.21.

CHAPTER 16

1. After Kondakov's death in 1925 his students founded the Kondakov Institute in his memory. It lasted until the end of the war and had a very high reputation among scholars.

2. See N. Zernov, *The Russian Religious Renaissance of the 20th Century* (London, 1963).

3. N. Elenev, 'Kem byla Marina Cvetaeva?', *Grani*, 39 (1958), p.147.

4. A. Bakhrakh, 'Pis'ma M. Cvetaevoj' (20 July 1923), *Mosty*, 5 (1960), p.312.

5. M. Cvetaeva, letter to Pasternak, 19 November 1922, *Neizd. pis'ma*, op. cit, p.274.

6. A Èfron, *Stranicy vospominanij*, op. cit, p.27.

7. 'Rassvet na rel'sakh' (20 October 1922), in *Stikhotvorenija i poèmy*, III (1983), p.43.

8. A. Èfron, 'Stranicy bylogo', *Zvezda*, 6 (1975), p.137.

9. L. Čirikova, 'Pis'ma M. Cvetaevoj', *Novyj žurnal*, 124 (1976), pp.140-51.

10. M. Cvetaeva, letter to R. Gul', *Novyj žurnal*, 58 (1959), p.180.

11. N. Elenev, 'Kem byla M. Cvetaeva', *Grani*, 39 (1958), pp.141-47.

12. See Slonim's article 'O M. Cvetaevoj'. Slonim gives a somewhat later date for Tsvetayeva's first visit to the editorial offices of *Volja Rossii*, but Tsvetayeva's poem 'Khvala bogatym', which was written immediately after this event, is dated '30 September 1922'.

13. M. Cvetaeva, letter of 2/15 November 1922, *Pis'ma k Anne Teskovoj* (Prague, 1969), p.26. The cycle *Derev'ja (Trees)* in *Stikhotvorenija i poèmy*, III (1983), pp.29-35, was written between 5 September 1922 and 9 May 1923.

14. F. Kubka, 'Smutná romance o Marine Cvetajevové', *Hlasy od východu* (Prague, 1960), pp.17-20.

15. 'Sedye volosy' (27 September 1922), in *Stikhotvorenija i poèmy*, op. cit, III (1983), p.38.

16. M. Cvetaeva, letter to R. Gul', 1 December 1922, *Novyj žurnal*, 58 (1959), p.170.

17. O.E. Kolbasina-Černova, 'O Marine Cvetaevoj', *Mosty*, 15 (1970), pp.311-17.

18. Quoted from the catalogue of publishing house Epokha, *Beseda*, 1 (1922).

19. M. Cvetaeva, letter to R. Gul', 21 December 1922, *Novyj žurnal*, 58 (1959), p.172.

20. M. Cvetaeva, letter to Pasternak, 19 November 1922, *Neizd. pis'ma*, op. cit, p.273.

21. M. Cvetaeva, letter to Pasternak, 9 March 1923, *Neizd. pis'ma*, op. cit, p.283.

22. 'Provoda' (17 March to 11 April 1923) (Tsvetayeva wrote to Gul' on 28 March 1923: 'I am drowning in poems, I do not have enough hands for all of them...') 'Poètry' (8 to 23 April 1923), in *Stikhotvorenija i poèmy*, op. cit, III (1983), pp.57-63.

23. 'Poet, No. 3' (22 April 1923, Prague), in *Stikhotvorenija i poèmy*, op. cit, III (1983), p.68.

24. M. Cvetaeva, letter to R. Gul', 5 March 1923, *Novyj žurnal*, 58 (1959), pp.176-77.

25. To this day Tsvetayeva's book *Zemnye primety* has not been published in its entirety. Various excerpts from it appeared in 1924 and 1925 in different émigré newspapers, which were reprinted in *Izbr. proza*, op. cit, I, pp.106-22. Extracts from Ariadna Efron's journal are included in her *Stranicy vospominanija*, op. cit. The missing passages were finally published by A. Mnukhin under the title 'Zemnye primety. Vypiska iz prežnej zapisnoj knižki, veroj i pravdoj služivšej mne s 1 junja 1918 po 4 fevralja 1919g.' in *Russkaja mysl'*, nos.3896-3901 (1991).

26. V. Lur'e, *Novaja russkaja kniga*, 3/4 (1923), p.14.

27. 'Pis'mo kritiku' (rough draft), *Novyj mir*, 4 (1969), pp.191-92. This and the following letters are published in *Mosty*, 5 (1960), pp.299-318; 6 (1961), pp.319-46. The letters referred to below were finally published in *Novyj žurnal*, 180 (1990), pp.214-53; 181 (1991), pp.98-138.

28. 'Pis'mo' (30 August 1923), in *Stikhotvorenija i poèmy*, op. cit, III (1983), p.91.

29. M. Cvetaeva, letter to Bakhrakh, 28 August 1923, *Mosty*, 6 (1961), p.320.

CHAPTER 17

1. M. Cvetaeva, letter to Bakhrakh, 10 September 1923, *Mosty*, 6 (1961), pp.330, 331, 332.

2. A. Èfron, *Stranicy vospominanij*, op. cit, p.151. As late as 1988 A. Brossart revealed in his book *Agents de Moscou*, that Rodzevich was in fact the head of the GPU espionage centre for France and Spain and was S. Efron's "commanding officer".

3. I. Kudrova, 'Dom na gore', *Zvezda*, 8 (1987), pp.156-77. In her article Kudrova quotes from a letter (undated) which Efron wrote to Maksimilian Voloshin: 'That of which I speak requires of me definite actions and behaviour, and it is at this point that I lose my self-possession. My own weakness, as well as M.'s complete helplessness and blindness, my pity for her, the feeling of a hopeless impasse into which she has driven herself, my inability to help her definitely and decisively and the impossibility of finding a good solution – have all lead to a stalemate. It has turned out that every possible solution could result in disaster. M. is a creature of her passions: to an even greater extent than previously, that is, before my departure. To throw herself into her hurricane has become for her a necessity, the atmosphere of her life. Whoever the instigator of this hurricane might be is now unimportant. Someone is thought up and the hurricane has begun. If the insignificance and limitedness of the instigator of the hurricane are soon revealed, M. abandons herself to a hurricane of despair. A state which facilitates the appearance of a new instigator.'

4. 'Pražskij rycar' (27 September 1923), in *Stikhotvorenija i poèmy*, op. cit, III (1983), p.100. On the same day Tsvetayeva wrote to Bakhrakh: 'I have a friend in Paris [sic], a stone knight, who looks very much like me. He stands on the bridge and watches over the river and everything in it: vows, rings, waves, bodies. He is almost 500 years old and he is still very young: a boy in stone. When you think of me, imagine us together!' (Yelenev mentions that this small statue of the legendary knight Brunswick under the Charles Bridge is the work of Ludwig Schimek and dates from 1884.)

5. 'Ty menja ljubivšij fal'š'ju' (12 December 1923), in *Stikhotvorenija i poèmy*, op. cit, III (1983), p.133.

6. *Poèma gory* (1 January to 1 February 1924), in *Stikhotvorenija i poèmy*, op. cit, IV (1983), pp.161-67. *Poèma konca* (1 February to 8 June 1924), in *Stikhotvorenija i poèmy*, op. cit, IV (1983), pp.168-87.

7. M. Slonim: 'Both lyrical and intensely emotional pieces of love and separation, with tragic overtones...' ('Notes on Tsvetayeva', *The Russian Review*, 31 (1972), p.119. S. Karlinsky: ' "Poèma konca" is one of Cvetaeva's finest accomplishments. This poem and "Poèma gory"... show us the poet at the peak of her originality and poetic stature.' (*Marina Cvetaeva* (1966) op. cit, p.214).

8. M. Cvetaeva, letter to Pasternak, 26 May 1926, *Neizd. pis'ma*, op. cit, p.298.

9. N. Berberova, *Kursiv moj* (München, 1972), pp.241-42: 'Behind the window an early November evening. Since three o'clock we have been sitting under artificial light in a room of the Beranek hotel in Prague: Tsvetayeva, Efron, Khodasevich and myself... We have been sitting for long hours, drinking tea which I make on a small spirit stove and eating ham, cheese and rolls spread out on paper. Everything which Tsvetayeva has to say I find interesting: she displays for me a combination of wisdom and caprice, I drink up her conversation, but in her, in this conversation there is almost always something which is alien to me, a great streak of excitement, curiosity, intelligence, which cuts through me...'

10. Vladimir Nabokov, *Drugie berega* (New York, 1954), p.243.
11. See Olga Chernov-Andreyev, *Cold Spring in Russia* (Ann Arbor, 1979).
12. O. Kolbasina-Černova, 'O Marine Cvetaevoj', *Mosty*, 15 (1970), pp.311-17.
13. M. Cvetaeva, letter to O. Černova, 11 November 1924, *Neizd. pis'ma*, op. cit, p.78.
14. The first play was published under the title *Tezej*, for the first time in *Versty*, 2 (1927). In *Izbr. proizvedenija*, op. cit, it appears as *Ariadna*. (See notes to this edition, pp.784-88.) On 2 February 1924 Tsvetayeva wrote to Olga Chernova: 'I have finished my great composition: Theseus (Ariadna) – part one. A dramatic piece, perhaps even a tragedy. (I will never be able to make up my mind about such a subtitle, for I am a woman, and a woman cannot write a tragedy).'
15. M. Cvetaeva, 'Pis'ma k O.E. Černovoj-Kolbasinoj i ee dočeri Ariadne', (11 and 27 December 1924), *Neizd. pis'ma*, op. cit, pp.100, 104.
16. M. Cvetaeva, *Pis'ma k Anne Teskovoj* (Prague, 1969). Before her death Anna Tesková (1872-1954) gave these letters to a Russian writer who lived in Prague, Vadim Morkovin (d. 1973). Thanks to him and Z. Mathauser the greater part of these letters was published in 1969, albeit with certain abridgements.
17. M. Slonim, 'O Marine Cvetaevoj', (Part I), *Novyj žurnal*, 100 (1970), pp.155-79; (Part II), *Novyj žurnal*, 103, (1971), pp.143-76.
18. 'Popytka revnosti' (19 November 1924), in *Stikhotvorenija i poèmy*, op. cit, III (1983), p.111.
19. M. Slonim, op. cit, (Part I), p.176.

CHAPTER 18

1. M. Cvetaeva, letter of 10 February 1925, *Pis'ma k A. Teskovoj*, op. cit, p.28.
2. M. Cvetaeva, letter to O. Černova, 29 February 1925, *Neizd. pis'ma*, op. cit, pp.139-40.
3. 'Russkoj rži ot menja poklon' (Prague, 7 May 1925) in *Stikhotvorenija i poèmy*, op. cit, III (1983), p.126.
4. The complete text of *Krysolov* was printed in *Volja Rossii* in 1925-26. In the Moscow edition of *Izbr. proizvedenija* there is an abridged text, from which the anti-Bolshevik passages have been removed. (See the notes in this edition pp.769-73 and S. Karlinsky's book (1966), pp.230-31.) The most complete editions are the bilingual Russian-German: 'Krysolov: Der Rattenfänger', translated by Marie-Luise Bott; *Wiener slawistischer Almanach*, Sonderband VII (1982); and *Stikhotvorenija i poèmy*, op. cit, IV (1983), pp.186-246.
5. About Kondakov's death see M. Cvetaeva, letter to O. Černova, 19 February 1925, *Neizd. pis'ma*, op. cit, p.137.
6. M. Cvetaeva, 'Geroj truda', *Izbr. proza*, I, pp.176-220.
7. M. Cvetaeva, letter of 9 September 1925, *Pis'ma k A. Teskovoj*, op. cit, p.32.
8. See *Letopis' žizni i tvorčestva M. Gor'kogo* (Moscow, 1959), III, p.436.
9. Thus, for example, Mayakovsky wrote in 1928: 'If a "Komsomolka" comes with the almost firm intention of taking out a book by, say, Tsvetayeva, tell her, blowing the dust off the grey cover: "Comrade, if you are interested in Gypsy lyrics may I suggest Selvinsky instead. The same

theme, but much better done! At least he is a man!" ' V. Majakovsky, *Polnoe sobranie sočinenij* (1955-61), XII, p.79.

10. M. Cvetaeva, 'Vozroždenščina', *Izbr. proza*, op cit, II, pp.307-09. See also I. Kudrova, 'Polgoda v Pariže', *Wiener slawistischer Almanach*, Sonderband III, pp.142-43.
11. M. Cvetaeva, 'Otvet na anketu žurnala *Svoimi putjami*', *Izbr. proza*, op. cit, II, p.305.
12. M. Cvetaeva, letter to R. Gul', 9 February 1923, *Novyj žurnal*, 58 (1959), p.173.
13. M. Cvetaeva, letter to R.M. Rilke, 6 July 1926, *Zeitschrift für slavische Philologie*, 41 (1980), H.1, p.164.
14. M. Cvetaeva, letter to O. Černova, 14 August 1925, *Neizd. pis'ma*, op. cit, p.189.
15. M. Cvetaeva, letters of 1 and 6 October 1925, *Pis'ma k A. Teskovoj* op. cit, pp.34, 36.
16. M. Slonim, 'O Marine Cvetaevoj', *Novyj žurnal*, 100 (1970), p.179.
17. M. Cvetaeva, letter of 1 October 1925, *Pis'ma k A. Teskovoj*, op. cit, p.33.
18. M. Cvetaeva, letter of 20 October 1925, ibid, p.54.

CHAPTER 19

1. See the following: Gleb Struve, *Russkaja literatura v izgnanii* (New York, 1956); Nikolaj Andreev, 'Ob osobennostjakh i osnovnykh ètapakh razvitija russkoj literatury v èmigracii', in *Russkaja literatura v èmigracii* (Pittsburgh, 1972), pp. 15-38; Ju. Terapiano, *Vstreči*, op. cit; N. Berberova, *Kursiv moj*, op. cit; Zinaida Šakhovskaja, *Otraženija* (Paris, 1975); and I. Kudrova, 'Polgoda v Pariže', *Wiener slawistischer Almanach*, Sonderband III, pp.129-59.
2. *Sovremennye zapiski*, 9 (1921).
3. Z. Šakhovskaja, *Otraženija*, op. cit, p.43.
4. See Ju. Terapiano, *Vstreči*.
5. M. Cvetaeva, letter of 7 December 1925, *Pis'ma k A. Teskovoj*, op. cit, pp.39-40.
6. 'Tiše, khvala!' (26 January 1926), in *Stikhotvorenija i poèmy*, III (1983), p.135.
7. Only two issues of *Blagonamerenny* appeared: 1/2, 3/4 (1926). These two issues contained the following works by Tsvetayeva: 'O blagodarnosti: iz dnevnika 1919 g.' ('On Gratitude: From a Journal of 1919'); the poem 'Starinnoe blagogovenie', dedicated to D.A. Shakhovskoy and the essay 'Poèt o kritike'.
8. K. Kuprina, *Kuprin, moj otec* (Moscow, 1971), p.161.
9. A. Bakhrakh, 'Marina Cvetaeva v Pariže', *Russkaja mysl'*, no.3287 (20 December 1979).
10. Letter to D.A. Šakhovskoj, 15 November 1925, *Neizd. pis'ma*, p.346.
11. G. Adamovič, *Odinočestvo i svoboda* (New York, 1955), pp.154-57.
12. G. Adamovič, *Kommentarii* (Washington, 1967), pp.171-72.
13. A. Bakhrakh, 'M. Cvetaeva v Pariže', op. cit.
14. Gleb Struve, 'Ob Adamoviče-kritike', *Grani*, 34/35 (1957), pp.365-69.
15. Valentin Andreev, 'Vstreča s Akhmatovoj', *Russkaja mysl'*, 12 December 1970.
16. For further details see I. Kudrova, 'Polgoda v Pariže', op. cit, pp.129-59.
17. See Z. N. Gippius, *Pis'ma k Berberovoj i Khodaseviču* (Ann Arbor, 1978).

18. M. Cvetaeva, letter of 8 June 1926, *Pis'ma k A. Teskovoj*, op. cit, pp.38-40.
19. M. Cvetaeva, letter of 26 July 1926, *Pis'ma k A. Teskovoj*, op. cit, p.42.
    D.A. Shakhovskoy, whose religious name was Ioann (John), was first a
    monastic priest, and then Russian Orthodox Archbishop of San Fran-
    cisco. Before the end of the Second World War he was the priest at the
    Russian church in Berlin (Nachodstrasse). His literary pseudonym was
    'Strannik' (i.e. pilgrim). His *Biografija junosti* (*Biography of My Youth*)
    contains correspondence with various writers which illuminates the milieu
    around *Blagonamerennyj* (pp.167-418). This volume also includes letters
    by Shakhovskoy to Tsvetayeva and her last letter to him (the 21st), which
    is not included in *Neizd. pis'ma* (pp.403-04).

CHAPTER 20

1. The Pasternak-Tsvetayeva-Rilke correspondence of 1926 has appeared
   over the years in various journals and in separate editions. For the original
   German texts of the letters between Pasternak and Rilke, and between
   Tsvetayeva and Rilke see: Rilke, Zwetajewa, Pasternak, *Briefwechsel*,
   edited by Yevgeny Pasternak, Yelena Pasternak, and Konstantin M.
   Azadovsky, with translations from the Russian by Heddy Pross-Werth
   (Frankfurt am Main, 1983). For a complete English translation of this
   correspondence see: Pasternak, Tsvetayeva, Rilke, *Letters: Summer 1926*,
   edited by Yevgeny Pasternak, Yelena Pasternak, and Konstantin M.
   Azadovsky, translated by Margaret Wettlin and Walter Arndt (London,
   1986). For selections from this correspondence in the original Russian
   see: 'Iz perepiski Ril'ke, Cvetaevoj i Pasternaka v 1926 godu', *Voprosy
   literatury*, 4 (1978), pp.233-80. Pasternak's letter to Rilke of 12 April 1926
   can be found in *Briefwechsel*, op. cit, pp.75-78 and in *Letters*, op. cit, pp.53-
   56.
2. R.M. Rilke, letters to M. Cvetaeva, 3 May 1926, *Briefwechsel*, op. cit,
   p.103; *Letters*, op. cit, pp.79-80.
3. B. Pasternak, letter to M. Cvetaeva, 20 April 1926, 'Iz perepiski Ril'ke,
   Cvetaevoj i Pasternaka', op. cit, pp.240-41; *Letters*, op. cit, p.69.
4. B. Pasternak, letter to M. Cvetaeva, 19 May 1926, 'Iz perepiski Ril'ke
   Cvetaevoj i Pasternaka', op. cit, p.254; *Letters*, op. cit, p.103.
5. B. Pasternak, letter to M. Cvetaeva, 23 May 1926, 'Iz perepiski Ril'ke,
   Cvetaevoj i Pasternaka', op. cit, p.259; *Letters*, op. cit, p.114.
6. M. Cvetaeva, letter to Pasternak, 23 May 1926, 'Iz perepiski Ril'ke,
   Cvetaevoj i Pasternaka', op. cit, p.262; *Letters*, op. cit, p.120.
7. M. Cvetaeva, letter to Pasternak, 25 May 1926, 'Iz perepiski Ril'ke,
   Cvetaevoj i Pasternaka', op. cit, p.263; *Letters*, op. cit, pp.120-21.
8. M. Cvetaeva, letter to Rilke, 3 June 1926, *Briefwechsel*, op. cit, p.157;
   Letters, op. cit, p.128.
9. M. Cvetaeva, letter to Rilke, 14 June 1926, *Briefwechsel*, op. cit, p.173;
   Letters, op. cit, pp.141-42.
10. R.M. Rilke, letter to M. Cvetaeva, 8 June 1926, *Briefwechsel*, op. cit, p.158;
    Letters, p.129.
11. R.M. Rilke, 'Elegie für Marina Zwetajewa-Efron', *Briefwechsel*, op. cit,
    pp.159-60; *Letters*, pp.130-31.
12. M. Cvetaeva, letter of 2 January 1937, *Pis'ma k A. Teskovoj*, op. cit, p.148.
13. M. Cvetaeva, letter to Rilke, 2 August 1926, *Briefwechsel*, op. cit, p.231;
    Letters, op. cit, p.195-96.

14. M. Cvetaeva, letter to Rilke, 14 August 1926, *Briefwechsel*, op. cit, pp.234-36; *Letters*, op. cit, pp.198-99.
15. This phrase is quoted by Tsvetayeva in her letter to Pasternak of 31 December 1926. It is actually a "paraphrase" of Rilke's words in his last letter to her of 19 August 1926: 'Nicht bis in den Winter!'
16. M. Cvetaeva, letter to Rilke, 7 November 1926, *Briefwechsel*, op. cit, p.241, *Letters*, p.204.
17. M. Cvetaeva, letter to Pasternak, 10 July 1926, *Neizd. pis'ma*, op. cit, pp.310-14; *Letters*, op. cit, pp.176-79.
18. M. Cvetaeva, letter of 20 March 1931, *Pis'ma k A. Teskovoj*, op. cit, p.90.
19. M. Cvetaeva, letter to Pasternak, 9 February 1927, *Neizd, pis'ma*, op. cit, pp.322-23.
20. 'Lestnica'. The unabridged text was published for the first time in M. Cvetaeva, *Stikhotvorenija i poèmy* (Biblioteka poèta, 3rd edition, 1990), pp.555-68.
21. M. Cvetaeva, letter of 24 September 1926, *Pis'ma k A. Teskovoj*, op. cit, p.43.
22. M. Slonim, 'O Marine Cvetaevoj', *Novyj žurnal*, 103 (1971), p.145.
23. M. Cvetaeva, letter to Pasternak, 31 December 1926, *Neizd. pis'ma*, op. cit, p.316; *Letters*, op. cit, p.207.
24. 'Novogodnee' (Bellevue, 2 February 1927), in *Stikhotvorenija i poèmy*, op. cit, IV (1983), p.273; See also: Iosif Brodsky, 'Ob odnom stikhotvorenii' in M. Cvetaeva, *Stikhotvorenija i poèmy*, op. cit, I, pp.(39)-(80).
25. M. Cvetaeva, letter to E. Černosvitova, undated, (c. 15 January 1927), *Novyj mir*, 4 (1969), p.199; *Letters*, op. cit, p.214.

CHAPTER 21

1. A. Èfron, 'Pis'ma M. Cvetaevoj', *Novyj mir*, 4 (1969), p.185.
2. '9 pisem M. Cvetaevoj k L. Šestovu', *Vestnik R.Kh.D.*, 129 (1979), pp.124-30.
3. M. Cvetaeva, letter of 3 January 1928, *Pis'ma k A. Teskovoj*, op. cit, p.58.
4. E. Izvol'skaja, 'Ten' na stenakh', *Opyty*, 3 (1854), p.153.
5. E. Izvol'skaja, 'Poèt obrečennosti', *Vozdušnye puti*, 3 (1963), pp.157-58.
6. M. Cvetaeva, letter of 12 December 1927, *Pis'ma k A. Teskovoj*, op. cit, pp.55-57.
7. M. Cvetaeva, letter of 'the third day of Easter', 1927, *Pis'ma k A. Teskovoj*, op. cit, pp.51.
8. M. Cvetaeva, letter of 20 October 1927, *Pis'ma k A. Teskovoj*, op. cit, pp.54-55.
9. E. Izvol'skaja, 'Ten' na stenakh', op. cit, p.156.
10. M. Cvetaeva, letter to Pasternak, July 1927, *Novyj mir*, 4 (1969), p.196.
11. V.S. Varšavskij, *Nezamečennoe pokolenie* (New York, 1956).
12. A.I. Cvetaeva, *Vospominanija*, op. cit, I, p.503.
13. A.I. Cvetaeva, 'Iz prošlogo', *Novyj mir*, 1 (1966), p.102.
14. 'Gor'kij i sovetskie pisateli', *Literaturnoe nasledstvo*, T.70 (1963), pp.300-02.
15. M. Cvetaeva, letter of 12 December 1927, *Pis'ma k A. Teskovoj*, op. cit, p.57.
16. M. Slonim, 'O Marine Cvetaevoj', *Novyj žurnal*, 100 (1970), p.163.
17. P. Antokol'skij, 'Kniga M. Cvetaevoj', *Novyj mir*, 4 (1966), p.217.

18. See Tsvetayeva's leter to Ivask, 8 March 1935. The correspondence between Tsvetayeva and Gronsky has not been published yet.
19. M. Cvetaeva, letters of 9 September 1928 and 2 December 1934, *Pis'ma k A. Teskovoj*, op. cit, pp.65 and 117.
20. Gronsky's poem 'Belladonna' was published for the first time in *Vozdušnye puti*, 5 (1967), pp.215-25 along with Tsvetayeva's 'Posmertnyj podarok' (pp.203-14), the article which *Poslednie novosti* refused to print. (It is reprinted in *Izbr. proza*, op. cit, II, pp.122-30). In Tsvetayeva's lifetime it was published in a shortened version (in a Serbian translation) as 'Pesnik alpinist', *Ruski arhiv*, Belgrad, 32/33 (1935).
21. M. Cvetaeva, 'Razgovor s geniem' (Meudon, 4 June 1928), in *Stikhotvorenija i poèmy*, op. cit, III (1983), p.138; the poem 'Najada' (Pontaillac, 1 August 1928) also dates from the same time, in *Stikhotvorenija i poèmy*, op. cit, III, p.139.
22. Epigraph to *Perekop*, *Stikhotvorenija i poèmy*, op. cit, IV (1983), p.290.
23. M. Cvetaeva, letter of 18 November 1928, *Pis'ma k A. Teskovoj*, op. cit, p.68.
24. Ibid, see commentary to letter no.47, p.194.
25. V. Majakovskij, *Polnoe sobranie sočinenij*, op. cit, XII, p.391.

CHAPTER 22
1. For further details see, for example, R. Gul', 'Ja unes Rossiju', *Novyj žurnal*, 136 (1979), pp.105-09, and his book of the same name published in three volumes.
2. M. Cvetaeva, letter of 19 February 1929, *Pis'ma k A. Teskovoj*, op. cit, p.72.
3. M. Cvetaeva, letter of 7 April 1929, ibid, p.75.
4. M. Cvetaeva, 'Natalja Gončarova: žizn' i tvorčestvo', *Volja Rossii*, 5/6, 7, 8/9 (1929); and *Izbr. proza*, op. cit, I, 283-340.
5. M. Cvetaeva, 'Neskol'ko pisem R.M. Ril'ke', *Volja Rossii*, 2 (1929) and in *Izbr. proza*, op. cit, I, pp.268-73.
6. M. Cvetaeva, *Lebedinyj stan – Perekop* (Paris, 1971), pp.125, 135. First publication of *Perekop: Vozdušnye puti*, 5 (1967).
7. Mark Slonim recalls: 'At the beginning of 1929 M.I. finished her *Perekop* and gave this "White Guardist poem", as she ironically called it, to me to read. At the next opportunity she asked me whether it was worth offering it to *Freedom of Russia*. I said that if no other journal accepted it, we could publish it, as we had never rejected anything by her, but, to be frank, we would do this without any particular enthusiasm. It would be up to her to decide. "In other words you would do this out of friendship and condescension, not out of conviction," M.I. remarked, looking to the side ... After a moment of reflection she added: "well, never mind, I will put it aside". As I later learnt Sergey Yakovlevich advised her not to rush ahead with *Perekop*, and it turned out she listened to him, which was a rare event. She later wrote to Tesková about our discussion: "Even *Freedom of Russia* has refused, gently, of course, without offence; it merely deflected, rather than refused." As for me I did consider *Perekop* to be a poor work.' *Novyj žurnal*, 103 (1971), p.155.
8. M. Cvetaeva, letters of 30 September and 26 October 1929, *Pis'ma k A. Teskovoj*, op. cit, pp.56-57, 79-80.
9. M. Cvetaeva, letter to V. Bunina, 10 April 1930, *Neizd. pis'ma*, op. cit, p.407.

10. See the commentary to letter no.60, *Pis'ma k A. Teskovoj*, op. cit, pp.195-96.
11. 'Majakovskomu' (Savoie, August 1930), in *Stikhotvorenija i poèmy*, op. cit, III (1983), pp.142-48. For the background and description of these poems see S. Karlinsky, *Marina Tsvetayeva*, op. cit, (1985), p.202.
12. M. Cvetaeva, letter of 17 October 1930, *Pis'ma k A. Teskovoj*, op. cit, p.84.
13. M. Cvetaeva, letter to Charles Vildrac, *Novyj mir*, 4 (1969), pp.203-05.
14. E. Izvol'skaja, 'Poèt obrečennosti', *Vozdušnye puti*, 3 (1963), p.158.
15. Ibid.
16. M. Cvetaeva, letter of 17 October 1930, *Pis'ma k A. Teskovoj*, op. cit, p.85.

CHAPTER 23

1. See V. Varšavskij, *Nezamečennoe pokolenie*, op. cit.
2. See Zinaida Šakhovskaja, 'Marina Cvetaeva', *Novyj žurnal*, 87 (1969), pp.130-35, and Šakhovskaja, *Otraženija* (Paris, 1975), pp.160-68.
3. M. Cvetaeva, letter to Ju. Ivask, 4 April 1933, *Russkij lit. arkhiv*, op. cit, p.212. Tsvetayeva is alluding here to the assassination in May 1931 of the president of France by a Russian émigré, for which he was subsequently executed.
4. 'Naša sovest' – ne vaša sovest' ' ('Stikhi k synu', no.2, January 1932), in *Stikhotvorenija i poèmy*, op. cit, III (1983), pp.161-63.
5. M. Cvetaeva, 'O novoj russkoj detskoj knige', in *Izbr. proza*, op. cit, II, pp.573-78.
6. M. Cvetaeva, letter of 25 February 1931, *Pis'ma k A. Teskovoj*, op. cit, p.89.
7. 'Sibir' ' (Meudon, 1930), in *Stikhotvorenija i poèmy*, op. cit, IV (1983), p.328.
8. M. Cvetaeva, letter of 25 February 1931, *Pis'ma k A. Teskovoj*, op. cit, pp.87-88.
9. M. Cvetaeva, letter of 20 March 1931, ibid, pp.90-91.
10. For more about Salomea Nikolayevna Andronikova-Halpern (1888-1982) see G.P. Struve, 'Pamjati S.N. Gal'pern', *Russkaja mysl'*, 1 July 1982. Tsvetayeva's leters to Andronikova-Halpern, who had also been a friend of Akhmatova and Mandelstam, have not yet been published. The originals of these letters are kept at TSGALI.
11. M. Cvetaeva, letter of 31 August 1931, *Pis'ma k A. Teskovoj*, op. cit, p.92.
12. N. Elenev, 'Kem byla Marina Cvetaeva', *Grani*, 39 (1959), pp.158-59.
13. Tsvetayeva wrote to Tesková: 'I have three Pushkins. There are the "Poems to Pushkin", which I cannot imagine anyone having the *courage* to read, aside from myself. They are terribly sharp, terribly free, having nothing in common with the canonised Pushkin, and having everything in common with the anti-canonical. They are *dangerous* poems. I have taken them, for conscience's sake, to *Contemporary Annals*, but I have no doubt that they will not accept them; they *cannot* accept them. They are *inherently* revolutionary, revolutionary in a manner which those, the ones in Russia, would not even have dreamt of... This is the vengeance of one poet for another. For had N[icholas] I not kept Pushkin on a lead – that is, as close to himself as possible – had he let him go abroad – had he turned him loose to the four corners of the earth – Pushkin would not have been killed by d'Anthès, so he [the Emperor] is the inner murderer.' (Letter of 26

January 1937, *Pis'ma k A. Teskovoj*, op. cit, p.149.) 'Stikhi k Puškinu' were published for the first time in *Sovremennye zapiski*, 63/64 (1937) and are in *Stikhotvorenija i poèmy*, op. cit, III, pp.148-54.

14. 'Oda pešemu khodu' (Meudon, 26 August 1931), in *Stikhotvorenija i poèmy*, op. cit, III (1983), p.157. This poem should have been published in *Sovremennye zapiski* in 1934, but it was returned with the comment that it was incomprehensible for the average reader. It was first published in Moscow in 1961.

'Dom' (6 September 1931) in *Stikhotvorenija i poèmy*, op. cit, III (1983), p.159.

15. See M. Cvetaeva, 'Pis'ma k V. Rudnevu', *Novyj žurnal*, 133 (1978), pp.191-207.

16. M. Cvetaeva, 'Iskusstvo pri svete sovesti', in *Izbr. proza*, op. cit, I, pp.381-406; 'Poèt i vremja' (Meudon, January 1932), in *Izbr. proza*, op. cit, I, pp.367-80.

17. See M. Cvetaeva, 'Pis'ma k G.P. Fedotovu' *Novyj žurnal*, 63 (1961), pp.162-72 and M. Cvetaeva, 'Èpos i lirika sovremennoj Rossii: Majakovskij i Pasternak', in *Izbr. proza*, op. cit, II, pp.7-26.

18. 'Živoe o živom' (Clamart, 27 February 1933), in *Izbr. proza*, op. cit, II, pp.27-79. The cycle of poems 'Ici-haut' (28 October 1932) is also dedicated to Voloshin, in *Stikhotvorenija i poèmy*, op. cit, III (1983), pp.165-68. For a discussion of the publication of 'Živoe o živom', see V. Krejd, 'Marina Cvetaeva i *Sovremennye zapiski*', *Novyj žurnal*, 178 (1990), pp.258-69.

19. M. Cvetaeva, *Mon frère féminin – Lettre à l'Amazone* (Paris, 1979).

20. See Mark Višnjak, *Sovremennye zapiski* (Bloomington, 1957) and a similar article in *Russkaja literatura v èmigracii* (Pittsburgh, 1972).

21. M. Cvetaeva, 'Pis'ma k Fedotovu', *Novyj žurnal*, 63 (1961), pp.170, 172.

22. M. Cvetaeva, letter of 7 March 1933, *Pis'ma k A. Teskovoj*, op. cit, p.104.

23. M. Cvetaeva, *Le notte fiorentine – Lettera all'Amazzone*, a cura di S.Vitále (Milano, 1981); M. Cvetaeva, 'Florentijskie noči', edited by A. Saakjanc, *Novyj mir*, 7 (1985), pp.155-70.

24. M. Cvetaeva, letter of 16 October 1932, *Pis'ma k A. Teskovoj*, op. cit, p.101.

25. F. Kubka, *Hlasy od východu* (Prague, 1960).

26. M. Cvetaeva, letter to V. Bunina, 25 August 1933, *Neizd. pis'ma*, op. cit, p.424.

27. 'Tridcataja godovščina' ('Stol' no.2) (July 1933), in *Stikhotvorenija i poèmy*, op. cit, III (1983), p.171.

CHAPTER 24

1. V. Muromceva, 'U starogo Pimena', in M. Cvetaeva, *Neizd. pis'ma*, appendix I, pp.531-41. Published for the first time in the newspaper *Rossija i slavjanstvo* (Paris), 14 February 1931.

2. M. Cvetaeva, 'Dom u starogo Pimena', (Clamart, August-October 1933), first publication: *Sovremennye zapiski*, 54 (1934), pp.212-56; reprinted in *Neizd. pis'ma*, op. cit, appendix II, pp.542-99 and *Izbr. proza*, op. cit, II, pp.215-46.

3. 'Khlystovki' ('Women of the Flagellant Sect'), Paris, May 1934; 'Čort' ('The Devil'), 1935; 'Skazka materi' ('The Mother's Tale'), 1934; 'Mat' i muzyka' ('My Mother and Music'), 1935; 'Bašnja v pljušče' ('The Tower in Ivy'), 1933; 'Ženikh' ('The Fiancé'), September 1933.

4. M. Cvetaeva, letter to Ivask, 3 April 1934, *Russkij lit. arkhiv*, op. cit, p.214.
5. 'Pis'ma M.I. Cvetaevoj k Ju. P. Ivasku', *Russkij lit. arkhiv*, op. cit, pp.207-37.
6. M. Cvetaeva, letter to Ivask, 4 April 1933, ibid, p.213.
7. About the relations between Tsvetayeva and Khodasevich, see S. Karlinsky, 'Pis'ma M. Cvetaevoj k V. Khodaseviču', *Novyj žurnal*, 89 (1967), pp.102-09. For information about Khodasevich see N. Berberova, *Kursiv moj*, op. cit.
8. M. Cvetaeva, letter to Khodasevich, 19 July 1933, *Novyj žurnal*, 89 (1967), p.111.
9. M. Cvetaeva, letter to Khodasevich, May 1934, *Novyj mir*, 6 (1969), p.207.
10. M. Cvetaeva, letter to V. Bunina, 7 May 1935, *Neizd. pis'ma*, op. cit, pp.490-91.
11. M. Cvetaeva, letter of 24 November 1933, *Pis'ma k A. Teskovoj*, op. cit, p.106.
12. M. Cvetaeva, French translation of Pushkin, included in M. Tsvetaieva, *Tentative de jalousie & autres poèmes*, traduit et présenté par Eve Malleret (Paris, 1986).
13. M. Cvetaeva, 'Plennyj dukh: moja vstreča s Andreem Belym', in *Izbr. proza*, op. cit, II, pp.80-121.
14. Until recently these three works were known only in their Serbian translation in *Ruski arhiv*: 'Pesnici sa istorijom i pesnici bez istorije' (Clamart, 1 July 1933), *Ruski arhiv*, 26/27 (1934), pp.104-42; 'Pesnik alpinist' (Clamart, 1934), *Ruski arhiv*, 32/33 (1935), pp.62-88; 'Reč o Baljmontu', (24 April 1936), *Ruski arhiv*, 38/39 (1936), pp.58-67. Aside from the essay about Gronsky (see Ch. 21, note 20), the other two have been translated into Russian: 'Poèty s istoriej i poèty bez istorii', in M. Cvetaeva, *Sočinenija v 2 tomakh* (Moscow, 1980), II, pp.424-57; 'Slovo o Bal'monte', in *Izbr. proza*, op. cit, II, pp.329-37.
15. M. Cvetaeva, 'Dva lesnykh carja' ('Two Forest Kings'), *Izbr. proza*, op. cit, II, pp.314-18; 'Khlystovki' ibid, pp.145-50; 'Otec i ego muzej' ('My Father and his Museum'), ibid, pp.198-209; 'Čort', ibid, pp.151-66; 'Mat' i muzyka', ibid, pp.66-95; 'Kitaec' ('The Chinaman'), ibid, I, pp.415-20; 'Skazka materi', ibid, II, pp.167-71.
16. 'Est' sčastlivcy i sčastlivicy' (January 1933), from 'Pamjati Gronskomu', in *Stikhotvorenija i poèmy*, op. cit, III (1983), pp.181-83.
17. See Chapter 21, note 20.
18. M. Cvetaeva, letter to V. Bunina, 24 August 1935, *Neizd. pis'ma*, op. cit, p.424.
19. M. Slonim, 'O Marine Cvetaevoj' (part two), *Novyj žurnal*, 103 (1971), p.169.
20. A. Vaksberg, 'Pravda o "platnom agente" ', *Literaturnaja gazeta*, 21 Nov. 1990.

CHAPTER 25

1. B. Pasternak 'Avtobiografičeskij očerk', in *Sočinenija* (Ann Arbor, 1961), II, pp.46-47.
2. M. Slonim, 'O Marine Cvetaevoj', *Novyj žurnal*, 100 (1970), p.168.
3. M. Cvetaeva, letter of 15 February 1936, *Pis'ma k A. Teskovoj*, op. cit, pp.134-35.
4. O. Ivinskaja, *V plenu vremeni* (Paris, 1978), p.140.

5. M. Cvetaeva, letter of 12 July 1935, *Pis'ma k A. Teskovoj*, op. cit, p.127.
6. M. Cvetaeva, letter to V. Bunina, 28 August 1936, *Neizd. pis'ma*, op. cit, pp.502-03.
7. 'Pevica', in *Al'manakh Poèzija*, 30 (1981), pp.134-39.
8. M. Cvetaeva, letters of 15 February and 29 March 1936, *Pis'ma k A. Teskovoj*, op. cit, pp.137-38.
9. M. Slonim, 'O.M. Cvetaevoj', *Novyj žurnal*, 103 (1971), pp.167-68. During the Marina Tsvetayeva symposium held in Lausanne in 1982 one of the speakers present declared that he had not been able to find any record of this poem having been deposited in the International Socialist Archive in Amsterdam. It is possible then that this manuscript has survived somewhere. In the 1990 'Biblioteka poèta' edition of Tsvetayeva's poetry are published all the fragments which could be found in Tsvetayeva's notebooks at TSGALI (pp.669-72).
10. M. Cvetaeva, 'Otec i ego muzej' (1933). The second part, 'Otkrytie muzeja' ('The Opening of the Museum') was published for the first time in *Vstreči*, 2 (1934); the first part 'Lavrovyj venok' ('The Laurel Wreath') appeared for the first time in *Prostor*, 10 (1965). They are published together in *Izbr. proza*, op. cit, II, pp.198-209, and in Cvetaeva, *Sočinenija* (Moscow, 1980), II, pp.7-27. The French version has not been found.
11. M. Cvetaeva, letter of 7 June 1936, *Pis'ma k A. Teskovoj*, op. cit, p.140.
12. Z. Šakhovskaja, *Otraženija*, op. cit, p.162.
13. 'Avtobus', in *Stikhotvorenija i poèmy*, op. cit, IV (1983), pp.333-38. Tsvetayeva wrote in her notebook at that time: 'It is difficult to write about enthusiasm, love and trust, when there is neither the first, nor the second, nor third, and when there is cold and rain to boot (June 1936). But perhaps this is how they are created: enthusiasm, love, trust, and good weather to boot?' (In *Izbr. proizv.* (Moscow, 1965), p.778.
14. See K. Vil'čkovskij, 'Perepiska M. Cvetaevoj s Anatoliem Štejgerom', *Opyty*, 5 (1955), pp.40-45. The letters to Steiger are in the following issues of *Opyty:* 5 (1955), pp.45-67; 7 (1956), pp.8-18; 8 (1956), pp.21-25; One letter, apparently the last, (from the end of September 1936), was published in *Novyj mir*, 4 (1969).
15. 'Nakonec-to vstretila' ('Stikhi sirote' no.6, 11 September 1936), in *Stikhotvorenija i poèmy*, op. cit, III (1983), p.195.
16. M. Cvetaeva, letter of 16 September 1936, *Pis'ma k A. Teskovoj*, op. cit, p.143.
17. 'Perepiska M. Cvetaevoj s Anatoliem Štejgerom', *Novyj mir*, 4 (1969), pp.209-10.
18. M. Cvetaeva, letter to Ivask, 25 January 1937, *Russkij lit. arkhiv*, op. cit, p.231.
19. Dmitry Sezeman, Klepinin's stepson, recalls: 'In our kitchen there was already much less talk about universal *sobornost'* [the collective principle] and about the destined rôle of Communism for the realisation of the Russian Idea; but to make up for this they talked eagerly a lot about Troskyites, about their intrigues and their undoubted ties with the Gestapo. One could only be amazed at how my mother, Nina Nikolay-evna, the former officers Klepinin and Efron, and the former deacon Aleksey Eisner competently discussed the irreconcilable contradictions between the Leninist Third International and the Troskyite Fourth International ... ' (From D. Sezeman, 'Na bolševskoj dače, *Literaturnaja gazeta*, 21 November 1990.)

20. V. Serge, M. Wullens, A. Rosmer, *L'Assassinat politique et l'URSS: Crime à Lausanne (La mort d'Ignace Reiss)* (Paris, 1939).
21. K. Khenkin, 'Ispanskij bloknot', *Kontinent*, 16 (1978), pp.265-88.

CHAPTER 26

1. M. Cvetaeva, 'Puškin i Pugačev' in *Izbr. proza*, op. cit, II, pp.280-302.
2. M. Cvetaeva, letter of 26 January 1937, *Pis'ma k A. Teskovoj*, op. cit, p.150; letter to V. Bunina, 11 February 1937, *Neizd. pis'ma*, op. cit, p.509.
3. See Ch. 23, note 13.
4. See V. Serge, et al, *L'Assassinat politique et l'URSS*, op. cit, and E. Poretsky, *Our Own People* (London, 1969).
5. M. Cvetaeva, letter of 2 May 1937, *Pis'ma k A. Teskovoj*, op. cit, p.151.
6. M. Cvetaeva, letter to Khodasevič, 13 March 1937, *Novyj žurnal*, 89 (1967), p.113.
7. See E. Poretsky, *Our Own People*, op. cit; V. Serge, et al, *L'Assassinat politique*, op. cit; and W. Krivitsky, *Agent de Staline* (Paris, 1940). See also A. Brossart, *Agents de Moscou* (Paris, 1988) and V. Chentalinski, *La parole ressuscitée. Dans les archives littéraires du KGB* (Paris, 1993).
8. E. Izvol'skaja, 'Poèt obrečennosti' *Vozdušnye puti*, 3 (1963), p.158.
9. Z. Šakhovskaja, *Otraženija*, op. cit, p.165.
10. V. Lossky, *Marina Tsvétayeva: Un itinéraire poétique*, (Malakoff, 1987), pp.372-74.
11. M. Slonim, 'O Marine Cvetaevoj', *Novyj žurnal*, 103 (1971), pp.171-72.
12. N. Berberova, *Kursiv moj*, op. cit, p.490.
13. M. Cvetaeva, letter of 7 February 1938, *Pis'ma k A. Teskovoj*, op. cit, p.158.

CHAPTER 27

1. M. Cvetaeva, letter of 23 May 1938, *Pis'ma k A. Teskovoj*, op. cit, pp.158-59.
2. 'Gory – turam poprišče' ('Stikhi k Čekhii: Sentjabr' ', no.2, between 12 and 19 November 1938), in *Stikhotvorenija i poèmy*, op. cit, III (1983), p.199.
3. M. Cvetaeva, letter of 26 December 1938, *Pis'ma k A. Teskovoj*, op. cit, p.177.
4. I. Odoevceva, 'Nesostojavšajasja vstreča', *Russkaja mysl'*, no.3148 (21 April 1977).
5. M. Cvetaeva, letter of 24 November 1938, *Pis'ma k A. Teskovoj*, op. cit, pp.167-68.
6. E.M. Fedotova, 'Pis'ma M. Cvetaevoj k Fedotovu', *Novyj žurnal*, 63 (1961), p.163.
7. Ju Ivask, 'Blagorodnaja Cvetaeva' in M. Cvetaeva, *Lebedinyj stan – Perekop*, op. cit, p.29.
8. M. Cvetaeva, letter of 31 May 1939, *Pis'ma k A. Teskovoj*, op. cit, p.182.
9. M. Slonim, 'O.M. Cvetaevoj', *Novyj žurnal*, 103 (1971), pp.173-74.
10. M. Cvetaeva, letter of 12 June 1939 (the last), *Pis'ma k A. Teskovoj*, op. cit, pp.184-85.
11. 'O slezy na glazakh' ('Stikhi k Čekhii: Mart', no.8, 15 March – 11 May 1939), in *Stikhotvorenija i poèmy*, op. cit, III (1983), p.208.
12. I. Odoevceva, 'M. Cvetaeva: *Neizdannoe*' (review), *Russkaja mysl'*, no.3115 (2 September 1976).

Part Four

CHAPTER 28

1. M. Cvetaeva, 'Iz zapisnoj knižki', *Neizd. pis'ma*, op. cit, p.629.
2. D. Sezeman, 'Na bolševskoj dače', *Literaturnaja gazeta*, 21 November 1990.
3. D. Sezeman, 'M. Cvetaeva v Moskve', *Vestnik R.Kh.D.*, 128 (1979), pp.177-79.
4. V. Schweitzer, 'Vozvraščenie domoj', op. cit, p.189.
5. O. Ivinskaja, *V plenu vremeni*, op. cit, p.182.
6. M. Cvetaeva, *Neizd. pis'ma*, op. cit, p.630; correction to this text in M. Cvetaeva, *Stikhotvorenija i poèmy*, op. cit, III.
7. See A. Vaksberg, 'Pravda o "platnom agente" ', *Literaturnaja gazeta*, 21 November 1990.
8. D. Sezeman, 'M. Cvetaeva v Moskve', op. cit.
9. M. Cvetaeva, *Neizd. pis'ma*, op. cit, p.633.
10. M. Cvetajevová, *Hodina duše*, op. cit, pp.9-10.
11. T. Kvanina, 'Pis'ma', *Vestnik R.Kh.D.*, 128 (1979), pp.180-88.
12. V. Ardov, 'Vstreča A. Akhmatovoj s M. Cvetaevoj', *Grani*, 76 (1970), pp.110-14.
13. See also M. Šaginjan, 'Moskva malen'kaja', *Novyj mir*, 1 (1977), pp.84-133, for an account of her meeting with Tsvetayeva in Golitsyno at this time.
14. *Tallinn*, 2 (1986), pp.9-10.
15. M. Cvetaeva, 'Stikhi 1940-41', *Neva*, 4 (1982), p.197.
16. M. Cvetaeva, *Neizd. pis'ma*, pp.608-17.
17. P. Antokol'skij, 'Kniga M. Cvetaevoj', *Novyj mir*, 4 (1966), p.223; and Antokol'skij, *Sočinenija*, IV, p.73.
18. M. Cvetaeva, *Neizd. pis'ma*, p.613.
19. Ibid, p.630.
20. M. Cvetaeva, 'Stikhi 1940-41', *Neva*, 4 (1982), pp.197-98. Six poems are included in the 1990 'Biblioteka poèta' edition, *Stikhotvorenija i poèmy*, pp.469-72.
21. M. Cvetaeva, *Neizd. pis'ma*, op. cit, pp.617-18.
22. T. Kvanina, 'Tak bylo', *Oktjabr'*, 9 (1982), pp.198-99; and also in *Vestnik R.Kh.D.*, 128 (1979), pp.184-86.
23. M. Cvetaeva, *Neizd. pis'ma*, p.632.
24. V. Ardov, op. cit, see also: N. Il'ina, 'Akhmatova v poslednie gody ee žizni', *Oktjabr'*, 2 (1977), pp.126-27; L. Čukovskaja, *Zapiski ob A. Akhmatovoj* (Paris, 1976, 1980), II, pp.373-74; A. Èfron, 'Svjatoe remeslo poèta', *Lit. obozrenie*, 12 (1981), pp.98-100.
25. M. Cvetaeva, *Neizd. pis'ma*, op. cit, pp.631-32.
26. L. Čukovskaja, *Zapiski ob Anne Akhmatovoj*, op. cit, II (1980), p.534.
27. M. Cvetaeva, *Neizd. pis'ma*, op. cit, pp.618-20.
28. See A. Vaksberg, op. cit.
29. M. Cvetaeva, 'Pis'mo dočeri', *Novyj mir*, 4 (1969), pp.213-14.
30. S. Vikent'ev, 'Stroki o syne', *Rodina*, 3 (1975).
31. M. Cvetaeva, *Neizd. pis'ma*, op. cit, pp.605-06.

CHAPTER 29

1. O. Ivinskaja, *V plenu vremeni*, op. cit, pp.179-80.
2. I. Èrenburg, *Ljudi, gody, žizn'*, op. cit, II, p.378.
3. M. Slonim, 'Beseda s Paustovskim', *Novoe russkoe slovo*, 10 March 1974.
4. M. Korjakov, 'Listki iz bloknota', *Novoe russkoe slovo*, 4 July 1965.
5. Milica Nikolić, 'Odgovori Marine Cvetajeve', *M. Cvetajeva: Zemaljska obeležja* (Belgrad, 1973), pp.19-20.
6. V.V. (= V. Schweitzer), 'Poezdka v Elabugu', *Neizd. pis'ma*, op. cit, pp.639-47.
7. L. Čukovskaja, 'Predsmertie', *Vremja i my*, 66 (1982), pp.202-31.
8. M. Belkina, Skreščenie sudeb (Moscow, 1988), pp.288-89.
9. A.I. Cvetaeva, 'Vospominanija č. 2', *Moskva*, 5 (1981), p.146.
10. See S. Vikent'ev (S.V. Gribanov), 'Stroki o syne', *Rodina*, 3 (1975) and A. Èfron, *Pis'ma iz ssylki* (Paris, 1982).
11. V. Lossky, 'Marina Cvetaeva: Souvenirs de contemporains', *Wiener slawistischer Almanach*, Sonderband III, pp.213-59; Lossky, *Marina Tsvétaeva: Un itinéraire poétique* (1987); Lossky, *Marina Cvetaeva v žizni* (1989); M. Belkina, op. cit, pp.337-448.
12. See A. Vaksberg, op. cit.
13. A. Èfron, *Pis'ma iz ssylki* (Paris, 1982).
14. A. Èfron 'Iz vospominanij o E.G. Kazakeviče' (1963), in *Vospominanija o E. Kazakeviče* (Moscow, 1979), pp.241-59.
15. V. Lossky, 'Marina Cvétaeva: Souvenirs de contemporains', *Wiener slawistischer Almanach*, Sonderband III, pp.213-59.
16. 'Končina A.S. Èfron', *Russkaja mysl'*, 28 August 1975.

CHAPTER 30

1. L. Čukovskaja, 'Iz knigi 'Zapiski ob Anne Akhmatovoj' ', *Pamjati A.A. Akhmatovoj* (Paris, 1974), p.48.
2. P. Antokol'skij, 'Kniga Mariny Cvetaevoj', *Novyj mir*, 4 (1966), p.223.
3. B. Pasternak, 'Iz pisem k žene', *Vestnik R.S.Kh.D.*, 106 (1972), pp.222-23.
4. N. Berberova, *Kursiv moj*, op. cit, p.490.
5. A. Bakhrakh, 'Zvukovoj liven' ', *Russkij sbornik*, 1 (1946), p.183.
6. F. Stepun, (Introduction), M. Cvetaeva, *Proza* (New York, 1953).
7. N. Andreev, 'Ob osobennostjakh i osnovnykh ètapakh razvitija russkoj literatury za rubežom', in *Russkaja literatura v èmigracii*, op. cit, p.28.
8. See: G. Struve, *Russkaja literatura v izgnanii*, op. cit; N. Poltorackij (editor), *Russkaja literatura v èmigracii*, op. cit; R. Gul', ' "Novomu žurnalu" 40 let', *Russkaja mysl'*, no.3444 (23 December 1982).
9. Ju. Ivask, 'Blagorodnaja Cvetaeva', M. Cvetaeva, *Lebedinyj stan*, op. cit, p.15.
10. S. Karlinsky, *Marina Cvetaeva: Her Life and Art* (1966), op. cit.
11. I. Bunin, *Vospominanija* (Paris, 1950), p.43.
12. Ju. Terapiano, 'Samoubijstvo i ljubov' ", *Russkaja mysl'*, 11 July 1964.
13. G. Adamovič, 'Nevozmožnost' poèzii', *Opyty*, 9 (1958), p.45.
14. G. Adamovič, 'Pamjati M. Cvetaevoj', *Novyj žurnal*, 102 (1971).
15. I. Èrenburg, 'Poèzija M. Cvetaevoj', *Literaturnaja Moskva*, 11 (1956), pp.707-15.
16. *Literaturnaja gazeta*, 22 May 1957.
17. I. Èrenburg, *Ljudi, gody, žizn'*, II.

18. B. Pasternak, 'Tri teni' in *Sočinenija*, op. cit, II, pp.45-48.
19. P. Antokol'skij, 'Kniga M. Cvetaevoj', *Novyj mir*, 4 (1966), p.213. In Antokolsky's collected works (Moscow, 1973, IV), this paragraph is deleted.
20. See L. Čukovskaja, *Zapiski ob A. Akhmatovoj*, op. cit, II, pp.466, 618.
21. Ibid, p.466.
22. T. Kvanina, 'Tak bylo', *Oktjabr'*, 9 (1982), p.210.

BIBLIOGRAPHY

Abbreviations

Izbr. proizv. = *Izbrannye proizvedenija* (Moscow: Sov. pisatel', 1965)
Nesobr. = *Nesobrannye proizvedenija* (München: Fink, 1971)
NM = *Novyj mir*
NP = *Neizdannye pis'ma* (Paris: YMCA-Press, 1972)
Proza I, II = *Izbrannaja proza v 2 tomakh* (New York: Russica, 1979)
Soč. 80 = *Sočinenija v 2 tomakh* (Moscow: Khudož. literatura, 1980)
Stikh. I-V = *Stikhotvorenija i poèmy v 5 tomakh* (New York: Russica, 1980-)
Stikh. 1990 = *Stikhotvorenija i poèmy*, 'Biblioteka poèta', third edition (Leningrad: Sovetskij pisatel', 1990).
Neizd. = *Neizdannoe* (Paris: YMCA-Press, 1976)
Sovr. zap. = *Sovremennye zapiski*
A.T. = *Pis'ma k Anne Teskovoj* (Prague, 1969)
T = *Teatr*, sost. i kommentarii A. Saakjanc (Moscow: Iskusstvo, 1988).

Bibliographies

Gladkova, T.L., L.A. Mnukhin, *Marina Cvetaeva: Bibliografija/Bibliographie des oeuvres de Marina Tsvetayeva*, introduction de Véronique Lossky (Paris: Institut d'Études slaves, 1982).
Mnukhin, L.A., 'M.I. Cvetaeva: Bibliografičeskij ukazatel' literatury o žizni i dejatel'nosti (1910-1928)', *Wiener slawistischer Almanach*, Sonderband III (1981), pp.273-380.
Mnukhin, L.A., 'M.I. Cvetaeva: Bibliografičeskij ukazatel' literatury žizni i dejatel'nosti (1910-1941; 1942-62)', *Wiener slawistischer Almanach*, Sonderband 23 (1989).

Chronological List of Works by Tsvetayeva

Večernij al'bom: stikhi (*Evening Album: Poems*), 1908-1910 (Moscow: Tip. Mamontova, 1910; reprint, Paris: Lev, 1980), *Stikh.*, I, pp.3-72.
'Volšebstvo v stikhakh Brjusova' ('Magic in the Poetry of Bryusov'), 1910, edited by Anna Saakjanc, *Den' poèzii*, 1979, pp. 32-4.
Volšebnyj fonar': 2 kniga stikhov (*The Magic Lantern: Second Volume of Poetry*), 1910-1911 (Moscow: Ole-Lukoje, 1912; reprint, Ann Arbor, 1970 and Paris, 1979); *Stikh.*, I, pp.75-134.
Iz dvukh knig (*From Two Books*) (Moscow: Ole Lukoje, 1913); *Nesobr.*, pp.9-64.
'Alja: zapiski o moej pervoj dočeri' ('Alya: Notes about My First Daughter'), Feodosija, 26 December 1913, *Vestnik R.Kh.D.*, 135 (1981), pp.181-92.
Junošeskie stikhi (*Poems of Youth*), 1913, *Neizd.*, pp.3-92; *Stikh.*, I, pp.137-74.
Versty I (*Milestones I*), 1916 (Moscow: Gos. izdatel'stvo, 1922; reprint, Ann Arbor: Ardis, 1972); *Stikh.*, I, pp.201-48.
'Stikhotvorenija' ('Poems'), 1915-1918, *Neizd.*, pp.95-133.
Versty II (*Milestones II*), 1917-1921 (Moscow: Kostry, 1921 and 2nd ed, 1922; reprint, Letchworth: Prideaux Press, 1979).

'Oktjabr' v vagone: zapiski tekh dnej' ('October in a Railway Carriage: Notes of those Days'), October-November 1917, *Volja Rossii*, 11/12 (1927); *Nesobr.*, pp.667-77; *Proza*, I, pp.21-28.

Metel': dramatičeskie sceny v stikhakh (*The Snowstorm: Dramatic Scenes in Verse*), 16-25 December 1918, *Izbr. proizv.*, pp.561-77; (reprint, Letchworth: Prideaux Press, 1978); T, pp.41-54.

Červonnyj valet (*The Knave of Hearts*), 1918, *Novyj žurnal*, 115 (1974), pp.20-40; T, pp.25-40.

Priključenie (*The Adventure*), 25 December 1918-28 January 1919, *Volja Rossii*, 18-19 (1923); *Izbr. proizv.*, pp.578-625; (reprint, Letchworth: Prideaux Press, 1978); T, pp.131-66.

'O ljubvi: Iz dnevnika' ('On Love: From a Journal'), 1917 and Moscow 1918-1919, *Dni*, 25 December 1925; *Proza*, I, pp.90-100.

'Vol'nyj proezd' ('Free Passage'), Moscow, September 1918, *Sovr. zap.*, 21 (1924), pp.247-78; *Proza*, I, pp.29-49.

'Moi služby: vospominanija' ('My Services: Memoirs'), 11 November 1918 – 7 July 1919, *Sovr. zap.*, 26 (1925); *Proza*, I, pp. 50-71.

Kamennyj angel: p'esa v 6 kartinakh v stikhakh (*The Stone Angel: A Play in Verse in Six Acts*), 1919, T, pp.93-129.

'Iz dnevnika: smert' Stakhoviča' ('From a Journal: The Death of Stakhovich'), Moscow, February-March 1919, *Poslednie novosti*, 21 January 1926; *Proza*, I, pp.72-81.

'Iz dnevnika' ('From a Journal'), Moscow, 1918-1919, *Stikh.* II, pp.325-32.

Feniks: p'esa v 3 kartinakh v stikhakh (*The Phoenix: A Play in Verse in Three Acts*), 'Kartina 3: Konec Kazanovy' ('Act Three: The End of Casanova'), July-August 1919, *Volja Rossii*, 8/9 (1924); *Sovrem. dramaturgija* (Moscow, 1983), III, pp.183-213, postface by A. Efron and A. Saakjanc, pp.145-67; T, pp.167-232.

Fortuna: p'esa v 5 kart. v stikhakh (*Fortune: A Play in Verse in Five Acts*), 1919, *Sovr. zap.*, 4 (1923), pp.145-67; T, pp.54-91.

'O blagodarnosti: Iz dnevnika' ('On Gratitude: From a Journal'), Moscow, July 1919, *Blagonamerennyj*, 1 (1926); *Proza*, I, pp.101-105.

'Otryvki iz knigi *Zemnye primety*' ('Extracts from the Book *Omens of the Earth*'), Moscow, 1919, *Volja Rossii*, 1/2 (1924); *Proza*, I, pp.106-22.

'O Germanii: vyderžki iz dnevnika' ('On Germany: Extracts from a Journal'), 1919, *Dni*, 25 December 1925; *Nesobr.*, pp.469-79; *Proza*, I, pp.123-31.

'Čerdačnoe: iz moskovskikh zapisej' ('In the Attic: From Notes Made in Moscow'), 1919-1920, *Dni*, 25 December 1924; *Proza*, I, pp.82-89.

Car'-devica: poèma-skazka (*The Tsar-Maiden: A Poetic Tale*) 14 July-17 September 1920, Moscow (Berlin: Epokha, 1922); *Izbr. proizv.*, no.382; (reprint, Letchworth: Prideaux Press, 1971).

Stikhi k Bloku (*Poems to Blok*), 1916-1921, (Berlin: Ogon'ki, 1922; reprint, Letchworth: Prideaux Press, 1978); *Stikh.*, II, pp.47-59; *Soč. 80*, I, pp.72-81.

Lebedinyj stan (*Swans' Encampment*), poems 1921, edited by G.P. Struve with an introduction by Yury Ivask (München, 1957; 2nd edition, Paris: YMCA-Press, 1971); *Stikh.*, II, pp.59-91.

'Egoruška' ('Yegorushka'), 1920-1921, extracts published by A.S. Efron in *NM*, 10 (1971), pp.119-131; *Stikh.*, IV, pp.341-58.

'Na krasnom kone' ('On the Red Horse'), 13 July 1921, in *Razluka*, pp.19-38; *Izbr. proizv.*, no.383; *Stikh.*, IV, pp.155-60.

Razluka (Separation), May-17 June 1921 (Berlin: Gelikon, 1922); *Nesobr.*, pp.139-48.

Remeslo (The Craft), April 1921-April 1922, (Berlin-Moscow: Gelikon 1923); *Nesobr.*, pp.115-278 (reprint, Paris: Lev, 1978); *Stikh.*, II, pp.95-172.

'Avtobiografija' ('Autobiography'), 1922, *Vozdušnye puti*, 5 (1967), p.295.

'Pereuločki' ('Byways'), Moscow, April 1922, in *Remeslo*; *Nesobr.*, pp.259-72; *Stikh.*, II, pp.174-83; *Soč. 80*, I, pp.355-66.

Psikheja: romantika (Psyche: Romantic Verse) (Berlin: Gržebin, 1923; reprint, Paris: Lev, 1979); *Stikh.*, II, pp.29-44.

'Svetovoj liven' ' ('A Cloudburst of Light'), *Epopeja*, 2 (1922), pp.10-33; (London, Iskander, 1969); *Proza*, I, pp.135-48.

Molodec: skazka (The Swain: A Tale), Prague, Christmas Eve, 1922 (Prague: Plamja, 1924); *Nesobr.*, pp. 279-382 (reprint, Letchworth: Prideaux Press, 1971).

'*Kedr*: apologija' ('*The Cedar*: An Apologia'), Prague, January 1923, *Zapiski nabljudatelja*, 1924; *Proza*, I, pp.149-70.

Poèma gory (Poem of the Mountain), 1 January-1 February 1924, Prague, the mountain, *Versty*, 1 (1926); *Izbr. proizv.*, no.38; *Soč. 80*, 1, pp.366-73; *Stikh.*, IV, pp.161-67.

Poèma konca (Poem of the End), Prague, 1 February 1924-Jiloviště 8 June 1924, *Kovčeg*, Prague; *Izbr. proizv.*, no.385; *Soč. 80*, I, pp.374-95; *Stikh.*, IV, pp.168-87.

Ariadna: tragedija (Ariadna: A Tragedy), Spring 1923-October 1924, Prague; first published under the title *Tezej (Theseus)*, *Versty*, 2 (1927); *Izbr. proizv.*, no.391 (reprint, Letchworth: Prideaux Press: 1978); T, pp.235-89.

Krysolov: liričeskaja satira (The Pied Piper: A Lyrical Satire), Prague, March-November 1925, *Volja Rossii*, 4-8 (1925), 1 (1926); abridged text in *Izbr. proizv.*, no.386; Cantos 1 and 2, in *NM*, 3 (1965) (reprint, Letchworth: Prideaux Press, 1978); complete text with a German translation by M.L. Bott, *Wiener slawistischer Almanach*, Sonderband VII (1982); *Stikh.*, IV, pp.188-246.

'Bal'montu: k 30-letiju poètičeskogo truda' ('To Balmont: On the Thirtieth Anniversary of his Work as a Poet'), Prague, 25 April 1925, *Svoimi putjami*, 5 (1925); *Proza*, I, pp.171-75.

'Geroj truda' ('A Hero of Labour'), Summer 1925, *Volja Rossii*, 9-11 (1925); *Proza*, I, pp.176-220.

'Rodina ne est' uslovnost' territorii' ('One's Native Land is not an Accident of Territory'), 1925, *Svoimi putjami*, 8/9 (1925); *Proza*, I, pp.305-06; *Ogonek*, July 1982, pp.18-19.

'Vozroždenščina', Prague, 8 October 1925, *Dni*, 16 October 1926; *Proza*, II, pp.307-09.

Posle Rossii: stikhi (After Russia: Poems), 1922-1925. (Paris, 1925; reprint, Paris: YMCA-Press, 1976); *Stikh.*, III, pp.11-126.

'Poèt o kritike' ('A poet about Criticism'), Paris, beginning of 1926, *Blagonamerennyj*, 3/4 (1926); *Proza*, I, pp.221-41.

'Cvetnik: *Zveno* za 1925 god., 'Literaturnye besedy' G. Adamoviča' ('A Flower Bed: *Zveno* during 1925, the Literary Conversations of G. Adamovich'), *Blagonamerennyj*, 2 (1926); *Proza*, I, pp.242-50.

'S morja' ('From the Sea'), Saint-Gilles-sur-Vie, May 1926, *Versty*, 3 (1928); *Nesobr.*, pp.531-37.

'Popytka komnaty' ('Attempt at a Room'), Saint-Gilles-sur-Vie, 6 June 1926,

Volja Rossii, 2 (1928); *Nesobr.*, pp.538-45.

'Lestnica' ('The Staircase'), July 1926, *Volja Rossii*, 11 (1926); under the title 'Poèma lestincy' in *Izbr. proizv.*, no.387; *Soč. 80*, I, pp.396-409.

Novogodnee (New Year Letter), Bellevue, 7 February 1927, *Versty*, 3 (1928); *Nesobr.*, pp.480-85; *Stikh.*, I, pp.263-67.

'Tvoja smert' ' ('Your Death'), Bellevue, 27 February 1927, *Volja Rossii*, 5/6 (1927); *Nesobr.*, pp.487-511; *Proza*, I, pp.251-67.

Poèma vozdukha: dni Lindberga (Poem of the Air: The Days of Lindbergh), Meudon, 1927, *Volja Rossii*, 1 (1930); *Nesobr.*, pp.552-62; *Stikh.*, IV, pp.278-86.

Fedra: tragedija (Tezej č. 2) (Phaedra: A Tragedy (Theseus, Part II)), 1926-1927, *Sovr. zap.*, no.36-37 (1928); *Nesobr.*, pp.383-460; *Soč. 80*, I, pp.423-82; T, pp.291-341.

'Krasnyj byček' ('The Red Bull'), Meudon, April 1928, *Volja Rossii*, 12 (1928); *Nesobr.*, pp.547-50.

Perekop: poèma, 1 August 1928-5 February 1929, edited by G.P. Struve, *Vozdušnye puti*, 5 (1967), pp. 7-56; (2nd ed., Paris, 1971).

'Neskol'ko pisem R.M. Ril'ke' ('Some Letters of R.M. Rilke'), Meudon, February 1929, *Volja Rossii*, 2 (1929); *Nesobr.*, pp.513-20; *Proza*, I, pp.268-73.

'Natal'ja Gončarova: žizn' i tvorčestvo' ('Natalia Goncharova: Her Life and Work'), 1929, *Volja Rossii*, 5/6-8/9 (1929); *Proza*, I, pp.283-340.

'Majakovskomu' ('To Mayakovsky'), Savoie, August 1930, *Volja Rossii*, 2 (1930); *Den' poèzii*, (1967), p.231; *Nesobr.*, pp.564-71.

'Sibir' ' ('Siberia'), Meudon, 1930, *Volja Rossii*, 3/4 (1931); *Nesobr.*, pp.573-78; *Soč. 80*, I, pp.410-14.

'O novoj russkoj detskoj knige' ('About the New Russian Children's Book'), February 1931, *Volja Rossii*, 5/6 (1931); *Proza*, II, pp.310-13.

'Istorija odnogo posvjaščenija' ('The History of a Dedication'); Meudon, April-May 1931, *Oxford Slavonic Papers*, 11 (1964), pp.114-36; *Proza*, I, pp.341-66; *Soč. 80*, II, p.159-89.

Stikhi k Puškinu (Poems to Pushkin), July 1931, *Sovr. zap.*, 63 (1937); *Izbr. proizv.*, no.324-329; *Stikh.*, III, pp.148-55; *Soč. 80*.

Iskusstvo pri svete sovesti (Art in the Light of Conscience), 1931-1932, *Sovr. zap.*, 50-51 (1932); *Proza*, I, pp.381-406.

'Poèt i vremja' ('The Poet and Time'), Meudon 1932, *Volja Rossii*, 1-3 (1932); *Nesobr.*, pp. 617-36; *Proza*, I, pp. 367-80.

'Živoe o živom' ('A Living Word about a Living Man'), Summer 1932, *Sovr. zap.*, 52-53 (1933); *Proza*, II, pp.27-79; *Soč. 80*, II, pp.190-254.

'Ici-haut' (original title in French), cycle of poems dedicated to Voloshin, 1932, *Vstreči*, 4/5 (1934); *Nesobr.*, pp.579-81.

'Èpos i lirika sovremennoj Rossii: Vlad. Majakovskij i Boris Pasternak' ('The Epic and Lyric in Contemporary Russia: Mayakovsky and Pasternak'), Clamart, December 1932, *Novyj grad*, 6/7 (1933); *Izbr. proizv.*, pp.638-66; *Proza*, II, pp.7-26; *Soč. 80*, II, pp.399-423.

'Neuf lettres (avec une dixième retenue et une onzième reçue) et Postface', 1933, in M. Cvetaeva, *Le notte fiorentine* (Milan, 1983, and Paris: Clémence Hiver, 1986). The original text is in French, for a Russian translation see, 'Florentijskie noči', *Novyj mir*, 5 (1985), pp.155-70.

'Bašnja v pljušče' ('The Tower in Ivy'), 1933, *Posled. novosti*, 16 July 1933; *Nesobr.*, pp.462-68; *Proza*, II, pp.191-97; *Soč. 80*, II, pp.28-37.

'Otkrytie muzeja' ('The Opening of the Museum'), 1933, *Vstreči*, 2 (1934); *Prostor*, 10 (1965); *Proza*, II, pp.198-209; *Soč. 80*, II, pp.7-24.

'Pesnici sa istorijom i pesnici bez istorije' ('Poets with History and Poets without History'), Clamart, 1 July 1933, *Ruski arhiv* (Beograd), 54 (1934); for the Russian translation by O. Kutasova see: 'Poèty s istoriej i poèty bez istorii', *Soč. 80*, II, pp.424-57.

'Dom u starogo Pimena' ('The House by Old Pimen'), Clamart, August-October 1933, *Sovr. zap.*, 54 (1934); *Proza*, II, pp.215-40; *Soč. 80*, II, pp.38-76.

'Ženikh' ('The Fiancé'), September 1933, *Zvezda*, 10 (1970); *Proza*, II, pp.210-14.

'Dva lesnykh carja' ('Two Forest Kings'), November 1934, *Čisla*, 10 (1934); *Nesobr.*, pp.521-27; *Proza*, II, pp.314-18; *Soč. 80*, II, pp.458-64.

'Plennyj dukh: moja vstreča s Andreem Belym' ('A Captive Spirit: My Meeting with Andrey Bely'), 8 January to the beginning of March 1934, *Sovr. zap.*, 55 (1934); *Proza*, II, pp.80-121; *Soč. 80*, II, pp.255-313.

'Avtobus' ('The Bus'), April 1934–June 1936, *Izbr. proizv.*, no.388; *Soč. 80*, I, pp.415-20.

'Strakhovka žizni' ('Life Insurance'), June 1934, *Posled. novosti*, 3 August 1934; *Avrora*, 6 (1978), pp.56-57; *Proza*, II, pp.409-14; *Soč. 80*, II, pp.77-84.

'Khlystovki' ('Women of the Flagellant Sect'), Paris, May 1934, *Vstreči*, 6 (1934); *Proza*, II, pp. 145-50; reprint under the title 'Kirillovny' in *Tarusskie stranicy* (Kaluga, 1961), pp.252-54; *Soč. 80*, II, pp.77-84.

Mon frère féminin: Lettre à l'Amazone (original in French), 1933, edited with notes by Ghislaine Limont (Paris: Mercure de France, 1979).

'Histoire de chevaux: Un fait authentique', the original French text has not been published, but is available in a Russian translation by B. Kazanskij: 'Slučaj s lošad'mi: podlinnyj fakt', *Proza*, II, pp.325-28.

'Skazka materi' ('Mother's Tale'), 1934, *Posled. novosti*, 17 February 1935; *Proza*, II, pp.167-71; *Soč. 80*, II, pp.120-26.

'Kitaec' ('The Chinaman'), 1934, *Posled. novosti*, 24 October 1934; *Proza*, I, pp.415-20.

'Pesnik alpinist' ('The Alpinist Poet'), Clamart, Christmas 1934, *Ruski arhiv*, 32/33 (1935); Russian translation under the title: 'Posmertnyj podarok' ('The Posthumous Gift'), *Voždušnye puti*, 5 (1967), pp.203-14; *Proza*, II, pp.122-30.

'Nadgrobnoe: pamjati Gronskomu' ('Funeral Oration: To the Memory of Gronsky'), 3 January 8 February 1935, *Sovr. zap.*, 58 (1935); *Izbr. proizv.*, no.348-352; *Soč. 80*, I, pp.324-28.

'Pevica' ('The Singer'), 1935, published by E. Korkina, *Al'manakh poèzija*, 1981, pp.134-39; *Stikh.*, IV.

'Čort' ('The Devil'), Vanves, 19 June 1935, *Sovr. zap.*, 57 (1935), pp.172-90; *Soč. 80*, II, pp.94-119; edited by Robin Kemball, with corrections and additions, *Russkij al'manakh*, (Paris, 1981), pp.21-38.

'O knige N.P. Gronskogo *Stikhi i poèmy*' ('About N.P. Gronsky's Book *Lyric Verses and Poems*'), 1936, *Sovr. zap.*, 61 (1936), *Proza*, II, pp.319-21.

'Reč o Baljmontu: povodom 50-god. knjiž. delatnosti' ('A Speech about Balmont on the Fiftieth Anniversary of his Literary Career'), *Ruski arhiv*, 38/39 (1936); Russian translations (as 'Slovo o Bal'monte'): *Literaturnaja*

Gruzija, 7 (1977); by V. Blinov, *Proza*, II pp.329-37; by O. Kutasova, *Soč. 80*, II, pp.314-24.

'Mundir' ' ('The Uniform'), 1936, the original French text has not been published, but is available in a Russian translation by Ariadna Èfron, *Zvezda*, 10 (1970); *Proza*, II, pp.342-44; *Soč. 80*, II, pp.22-25.

'Lavrovyj venok' ('The Laurel Wreath'), 1936, the original French text has not been published, but is available in a Russian translation by Ariadna Èfron, *Zvezda*, 10 (1970); *Proza*, II pp.345-46; *Soč. 80*, II, pp.25-27. In 1936 this had been grouped with 'Otkrytie muzeja' under the title 'Otec i ego muzej' ('My Father and his Museum').

'Šarlottenburg' ('Charlottenburg'), 1936 (the original French text has not been published), *Proza*, II, pp.338-341; *Soč. 80*, II, pp.18-24.

'Nezdešnij večer' ('An Otherworldly Evening'), March-May 1936, *Sovr. zap.*, 61 (1936); *Proza*, II, pp.131-41.

Stikhi sirote (Poems to an Orphan), 16 August – 20 October 1936, *Sovr. zap.*, 66 (1938); *Izbr. proizv.*, pp.358-64; *Soč. 80.*, I, pp.333-36; *Stikh.*, III, pp.192-96.

'Moj Puškin' ('My Pushkin'), 1936, *Sovr. zap.*, 64 (1937); *Proza*, II, pp.249-79; *Soč. 80*, II, pp.327-67.

'Puškin i Pugačev' ('Pushkin and Pugachov'), Vanves, 1937, *Russkie zapiski*, 2 (1937); *Proza*, II, pp.280-302; *Soč. 80*, II, pp.368-96.

Povest' o Sonečke (The Tale about Sonechka), Lacanau-Océan, summer 1937, part one, *Russkie zapiski*, 3 (1938); parts one and two, *Neizd.*, pp.205-362; part one, *NM*, 3 (1976), part two, *NM*, 12 (1979).

'Pis'mo detjam' ('Letter to the Children'), winter 1937-1938, *NM*, 4 (1969), pp.210-11.

Stikhi k Čekhii (Poems to Czechia), part one: September 1938, part two: March 1939, *Izbr. proizv.*, pp.367-81; *Soč. 80*, I, pp.338-52; *Stikh.*, IV.

'Můj životopis' ('My Autobiography'), winter 1939-1940, in J. Strobolová, *Hodina duše*, pp.9-10 (in Czech). Only in 1992 it became clear that the so-called "autobiography" published in Czech is part of C's letter to L. Berija, of 23.12.1939 (publ. by M. Fejnberg and Ju. Kljukin in *Lit. gazeta*, 2.9.1992).

'Iz zapisnoj knižki' ('From a Notebook'), 23 April 1939-24 October 1940, *NP*, pp.627-34.

'Stikhi 1940-1941' ('Poems: 1940-1941'), 7 January 1940–6 March 1941, published by E. Korkina, *Neva*, 4 (1982), pp.197-98; *Stikh. 1990*, pp.469-72.

Selected Works in English

Pasternak, Tsvetayeva, Rilke: *Letters: Summer 1926*, edited by Yevgeny Pasternak, Yelena Pasternak and Konstantin M. Azadovsky, translated by Margaret Wettlin and Walter Arndt (London: Jonathan Cape, 1986).

Tsvetayeva, Marina: *Art in the Light of Conscience*, translated by Angela Livingstone (London: Bristol Classical Press, 1991).

Tsvetayeva, Marina Ivanovna: *A Captive Spirit: Selected Prose*, with a new introduction by Susan Sontag, edited and translated by J. Marin King (London: Virago, 1983).

Tsvetayeva, Marina Ivanovna: *The Demesne of the Swans/Lebedinyj stan*, a bilingual edition, including the definitive version of the Russian text, established by the editor, with an introduction, notes, commentaries and translated for the first time into English by Robin Kemball (Ann Arbor: Ardis, 1980).

Tsvetayeva, Marina: *Selected Poems*, translated by Elaine Feinstein, with a foreword by Max Hayward (Oxford: Oxford University Press, 1971 & 1981; London: Hutchinson, 1986).

Tsvetayeva, Marina Ivanovna: *Selected Poems*, translated by David McDuff (Newcastle upon Tyne: Bloodaxe Books, 1987; second edition 1991).

Letters of Marina Tsvetayeva

Collections:

Cvetaeva, Marina, *Pis'ma*, edited and annotated by A.S. Èfron, commentary by A.A. Saakjanc, *NM*, 4 (1969), pp.185-214.

Cvetaeva, Marina, *Neizdannye pis'ma*, edited by G. and N. Struve (Paris: YMCA-Press, 1972).

Correspondence from Marina Tsvetayeva to:

Adamovič, G.V.: 31.3.1933 in *NP*, pp.385-90.

Akhmatova, Anna: 26.4.1921–12.11.1926 in *NP*, pp.53-61 and 377-378.

Aminado, Don: 31.5.1938 in *NM*, pp.211-213, and in Šakhovskaja, *Otraženija*.

Andronikova-Halpern, S.: 15.7.1926-1934, *Vestnik R.Kh.D.* 138 (1983), pp.167-89.

Andronikova-Halpern, S.: 12.8.1932, *Den' poèzii* (Moscow, 1980), p.139-40; 20.9.1930 and 18.5.1931, *Čast' reči*, 2/3, pp.38-45.

Bakhrakh, A.V.: 9.5.1923–29.5.1928, *Mosty*, 5 (1960), pp.303-18; 6 (1961), pp.319-46; *Novyj žurnal*, 180 (1990), pp.214-53; 181 (1991), pp.98-138.

Berg, Ariadna: 29.11.1934–12.6.1939, edited by N. Struve (Paris: YMCA, 1990).

Berija, L.P.: 23.12.1939, 14.6.1940 in: *Literaturnaja gazeta*, 2.9.1992, p.6.

Brjusov, V.Ja.: 15.3.1910 in *NM*, p.186.

Bulgakov, V.F. 1925-27. Ed. G. Vaněčková (Praga Muzej češskoj literatury, 1992).

Bunina, V.N.: 20.3.1928 to February 1937 in *NP*, pp.393-527.

Černosvitova, E.: c. 15.1.1927 in *NP*, pp.199-200.

Černova-Kolbasina, and Černova, A.: 1.7.1924–26.10.1925 in *NP*, pp.65-228; 4.1.1925–11.12.1926, *Wiener slavistisches Jahrbuch*, 22 (1976), pp.109-15.

Čirikova, L.E.: 4.8.1922–November 1926 (or 1925); *Novyj žurnal*, 124 (1976), pp.140-51.

Cvetaeva, A.I.: 17.12.1920–3.5.1928 in *NP*, pp.41-50; 381-84.

Èfron, A.S.: 12.4.1941 in *NP*, pp.618-21; February 1941 in *NM*, pp.213-14.

Èfron, E.Ja.: 12.6.1916, *Čast' reči*, 4/5 (1984), pp.420-25.

Èllis: (no date) 1909 and 12.12.1910 in *NP*, pp.9, 20. The second letter is also in A. Cvetaeva, *Vospominanija*, pp.342-43.

Fedotov, G.P.: 16.5.1932–24.5.1933, *Novyj žurnal*, 63 (1961), pp.162-72.

Gol'cev, V.V.: 2.2.1940–26.2.1940, *Vestnik R.Kh.D.*, 128 (1979), pp.189-91.

Gor'kij, A.M.: August 1927–October 1927 in *NM*, pp.200-01.
Gronskij, N.P.: August, September 1928 (extracts) in *NM*, pp.202-03.
Gul', R.B.: 12.11.1922–11.8.1924, *Novyj žurnal*, 58 (1959), pp.169-89; 165 (1986), pp.275-90.
Imamutdinov, Rafael: 16.8.1941, *Vestnik R.Kh.D.*, 147 (1986), p.162.
Ivask, Ju.P.: 4.4.1933–27.2.1937 in *Russkij literaturnyj arkhiv* (New York, 1956), pp.207-37; 27.2.1939 (end of the last letter), *Vestnik R.Kh.D.*, 128 (1979), pp.175-76.
Jaščenko, A.S. 26.6 and 6.7.1922 in *Russkij Berlin: 1921-1923*, p.156-58.
Jurkevič, P.I.: (Moscow) 21.7.1916, *Tallin*, 2 (1986), jpp.97-98.
Kantor, M.L.: 25.2.1934 in *NP*, pp.391-92.
Khodasevič, V.F.: 12.7.1933–13.3.1937, publication and commentary by S. Karlinsky, *Novyj žurnal*, 89 (1967), pp.102-14; 15.4.1934 to May 1934 in *NM*, pp.205-07.
Kočetkov, A.S.: 10.6.1941 in *NP*, p.621.
Kuprina, E.M.: 21.1.1926 in Kuprina, K.A., *Kuprin, moj otec* (Moscow, 1971), p.161.
Kuznecova, M.I.: 16.3.1921 in *NP*, pp.49-50.
Kvanina, T.N.: 17.11.1940–25.5.1941 *Vestnik R.Kh.D.*, 128 (1979), pp.184-88; and *Oktjabr'*, 9 (1982), pp.195-201.
Litford: 26.8.1941 in *Stikh.* III (facsimile), p.416.
Lomonosova, R.N.: 20.4.1928–29.12.1931 in *Minuvšee: istoričeskij al'manakh*, (Paris), 8 (1989), pp.208-73.
Majakovskij, V.V.: 3.12.1928 in Katanjan, V., *Majakovskij* (Moscow, 1961), pp.375-76.
Merkur'eva, V.A.: 20.2.1940–31.8.1940 in *NP*, pp.605-14.
Močalova, O.A.: 20.5.–31.5.1940 in *NP*, pp.614-17.
Moskvin, N.Ja.: 22.3.–28.3.1940 *Vestnik R.Kh.D.*, 128 (1979), pp.180-84.
Nikitina, E.F.: 22.1.1922 in *NP*, pp.51-52.
Pasternak, B.L.: 29.6.1922–9.2.1927 in *NP*, pp.263-337; 11.2.1923–October 1935 in *NM*, pp.194-98; 10.2.1923, *Vestnik R.Kh.D.*, 128 (1979), pp.169-74; 'Perepiska Ril'ke, Cvetaevoj i Pasternaka v 1926 godu', *Voprosy literatury*, 4 (1978), pp.233-80; R.M. Rilke, M. Zwetajewa, B. Pasternak, *Briefwechsel*, edited by Je. and H. Pasternak and K.M. Azadovskij, with translations by H. Pross-Werth (Frankfurt: Insel, 1983); English edition; Pasternak, Tsvetayeva, Rilke, *Letters: Summer 1926*, translated by M. Wettlin and Walter Arndt (London: Jonathan Cape, 1986); *Perepiska Borisa Pasternaka* (Moscow, 1990), pp.298-408.
Pasternak, L.O.: 29.7.1922–20.3.1928 in *NP*, pp.249-62 and in *NM*, p.202.
Reznikov, D.G.: 1926, *Vestnik R.Kh.D.*, 138 (1983), pp.191-94.
Rilke, R.M.: 9.5.–7.11.1926, *Zeitschrift für Slavische Philologie*, 41-I (1980), p.146-73; R.M. Rilke, M. Zwetajewa, B. Pasternak, *Briefwechsel/Letters: Summer 1926*, etc., see details under Pasternak, B.L.
Rozanov, V.V.: 7.3.–18.4.1914 in *NP*, pp.21-39; the second letter is in *NM*, pp.186-89.
Šaginjan, M.: 28.3.1940, *Oktjabr'*, 3 (1986), p.199.
Šakhovskaja, Z.A.: 18.5.–21.9.1936, *Novyj žurnal*, 87 (1967), pp.135-41; and in Šakhovskaja, *Otraženija*, pp.169-75.
Šakhovskoj, D.A.: 6.10.1925–18.5.1926 in *NP*, pp.339-76; the last letter, 1.6.1926 is in Šakhovskoj, *Biografija junosti*, pp.417-18.
Šestov, L.I.: 25.1.1926–31.7.1927, *Vestnik R.Kh.D.*, 129 (1979), pp.124-30.

Sieber-Rilke, Ruth: 24.1.1932, *Russkaja mysl'*, 28.6.1991.
Somov, E.: the end of 1940/beginning of 1941 in *NP*, pp.617-18.
Sosinskij, V.B.: 14.7.1926–16.6.1938 in *NP*, pp.229-48; 11.5.1926, *Vestnik R.Kh.D.*, 114 (1974), pp.207-14.
Steiger, A.S.: 29.7.–17.8.1936, *Opyty*, 5 (1955), pp.45-67; 7 (1955), pp.8-18; 8 (1955), pp.21-5; 1.9.1936 in *NM*, pp.208-10.
Struve, G.P.: 30.6.1923–29.11.1925, *Mosty*, 13/14 (1968), pp.395-98.
Tager, E.B.: (Golicyno) 22.1.1940, *Tallinn* 2 (1986), pp.99-100.
Tèffi, N.A.: October 1932 in *NM*, p.205.
Tesková, Anna: 2/15.1.1922–12.6.1939, *Pis'ma k Anne Teskovoj* (Prague: Academia, 1969).
Tikhonov, N.S.: 6.7.1935, *Čast' reči*, 4/5 (1984), pp.244-46.
Tolstoj, A.N.: (Berlin) 3.6.1922 in *Russica* (1981), pp.347-49.
Tukalevskaja, N.N., June 1939, *Vestnik R.Kh.D.*, 135 (1981), pp.193-95.
Vildrac, Charles: 1930 in *NM*, pp.203-05.
Vološin, M.A.: 23.12.1910–10.1.1912 in *NM*, 2 (1977), pp.231-46, edited by Irma Kudrova; 23.12.1910–10.5.1923, *Ežegodnik rukopisnogo otdela Puškinskogo Doma* (1975), pp.151-85, edited by V.R. Kupčenko.
Wunderly-Volkart, Nanny and Ruth Sieber-Rilke, 2.4.1930–23.9.1993, in: *R.M. Rilke u. M. Zwetajewa: Ein Gespräch in Briefen*, pp.161-92.
Zvjaginceva, V.K.: 18.9.1919–20.10.1920, *Russian Literature*, IX-IV (15.5.1981), pp.323-56.

Secondary Sources

Note: A more extensive bibliography of secondary sources can be found in the French edition of this book, *Marina Tsvetaieva: Mythe et réalité* (Montricher, Suisse: Les Editions Noir sur Blanc, 1988), pp.442-59.

Adamovič, Georgij Viktorovič, *Kommentarii* (Washington: V. Kamkin, 1967).
Adamovič, G.V., *Odinočestvo i svoboda* (New York, 1955).
Adamovič, G.V., 'Pamjati Mariny Cvetaevoj', *Novyj žurnal*, 102 (1971).
Andreev, Nikolaj Efremovič, 'Ob osobennostjakh i osnovnykh ètapakh razvitija literatury za rubežom', in *Russkaja literatura v èmigracii*, (Pittsburgh, 1972), pp.15-38.
Andronikova-Halpern, Salomea, 'Iz pisem k G.P. Struve 1965-1968', *Vestnik R.Kh.D.*, 138 (1983), pp.164-67.
Antokol'skij, Pavel, 'Kniga Mariny Cvetaevoj', *NM*, 4 (1966), pp.213-24.
Antologija (Moscow: Musaget, 1911).
Ardov, Viktor Efimovič, 'Vstreča Anny Akhmatovoj s Marinoj Cvetaevoj', *Grani*, 76 (1970), pp.110-14.
Bakhrakh, Aleksandr Vasil'evič, 'Marina Cvetaeva i ee doč' ', *Russkaja mysl'*, no.3263, 5.7.1979.
Bakhrakh, A.V., 'Marina Cvetaeva v Pariže', *Russkaja mysl'*, no.3287, 20.12.1979.
Bakhrakh, A.V., 'Pis'ma Mariny Cvetaevoj', *Mosty*, 5 (1960), pp.299-304; 6 (1961), pp.319-41.
Bakhrakh, A.V., 'Zvukovoj liven' ', in *Russkij sbornik* (Paris, 1946), pp.183-86.
Bal'mont, Konstantin D., 'Marina Cvetaeva', *Sovr. zap.*, 7 (1921), p.92.
Bal'mont, K.D., *Gde moj dom? Očerki 1920-1923* (Prague, 1924).
Belkina, Marija, *Skreščenie sudeb* (Moscow: Kniga, 1988).

Belyj, Andrej, *Meždu dvukh revolucij* (Chicago: Russian Language Specialities, 1966).

Belyj, Andrej, *Vospominanija o A.A. Bloke* (Moscow-Berlin, 1922-23; reprint, München: Fink, 1969).

Berberova, Nina, *Kursiv moj* (München: Fink, 1972).

Bott, Marie-Louise, 'Krysolov: Der Rattenfänger', mit einem Glossar von G. Wytrzens, *Wiener slawistischer Almanach*, Sonderband VII (1982).

Brjusov, Valerij Jakovlevič, 'Novye sborniki stikhov', *Russkaja mysl'*, 2 (1911), pp.227-35.

Brjusov, V.Ja., 'Segodnjašnij den' russkoj poèzii; 50 sbornikov stikhov 1911-1912', *Russkaja mysl'*, 7 (1912).

Brodskij, Iosif, 'Ob odnom stikhotvorenii (vmesto predislovija)', in Marina Cvetaeva, *Stikhotvorenija i poèmy v 5 tomakh*, I, pp, (39) – (80).

Brook-Shepherd, Gordon, *The Storm Petrels* (London: Collins, 1977).

Brossat, Alain, *Agents de Moscou* (Paris: Gallimard, 1988).

Bunin, Ivan Alekseevič, *Vospominanija* (Paris, 1950).

Černova-Kolbasina, Ol'ga Eliseevna, 'O Marine Cvetaevoj', *Mosty*, 15 (1970), pp.311-17.

Chambrun, Charles de, *Lettres à Marie: Pétersbourg-Petrograd 1914-1918* (Paris: Plon, 1941).

Chernov-Andreyev, Olga, *Cold Spring in Russia* (Ann Arbor: Ardis, 1979).

Čirikova, L.E., Čirikova, V.E., 'Pis'ma Mariny Cvetaevoj', *Novyj žurnal*, 124 (1976), pp.140-43.

Čukovskaja, Lidija Korneevna, 'Iz knigi *Zapiski ob Anne Akhmatovoj*', in *Pamjati Akhmatovoj* (Paris: YMCA-Press, 1974).

Čukovskaja, L.K., 'Predsmertie', *Vremja i my*, 66 (1982), pp.202-31.

Čukovskaja, L.K., *Zapiski ob Anne Akhmatovoj*, v. I-II (Paris: YMCA-Press, 1976, 1980).

Cvetaeva, Anastasija Ivanovna, 'Glavy iz knigi', *Daugava* (Riga), 7 (1980), pp.58-72.

Cvetaeva, A.I., 'Iz prošlogo', *NM*, 1 (1966), pp.79-183; 2, pp.98-128.

Cvetaeva, A.I., 'Iz vospominanij', *Zvezda*, 2 (1985), pp.169-74.

Cvetaeva, A.I., 'Korni i plody: po povodu stat'i I. Kudrovoj 'List'ja i korni' ', *Zvezda*, 4 (1979), pp.186-93.

Cvetaeva, A.I., 'Marinin dom', *Zvezda*, 12 (1981), pp.142-57.

Cvetaeva, A.I., *Vospominanija* (Moscow: Sov. pisatel', 1971; 2nd ed., 1974; 3rd ed., 1984).

Cvetaeva, A.I., 'Vospominanija č. 2', *Moskva*, 3 (1981), pp.116-60; 4, pp.117-60; 5, pp.112-59.

Marina Cvetaeva: Studien und Materialien (*Wiener slawistischer Almanach*, Sonderband II, 1981).

Cvetaeva, Valerija Ivanovna, 'Takim ja pomnju otca svoego', *Sovetskij muzej*, 5 (103) (1988), pp.61-72.

Den' poèzii (Moscow, 1962-1980).

Èfron, A.S. 'Iz vospominanij o E.G. Kazakeviče' (1963), in *Vospominanija o E. Kazakeviče* (Moscow, 1979).

Èfron, A.S. and Anna Saakjnac, 'Marina Cvetaeva: perevodčik', *Don*, 2 (1966).

Èfron, A.S., *Pis'ma iz ssylki* (Paris: YMCA-Press, 1982).

Èfron, A.S., 'Pis'ma Mariny Cvetaevoj', *NM*, 4 (1966), p.185.

Èfron, A.S., 'Samofrakijskaja pobeda', *Lit. Armenija*, 8 (1967), pp.80-84.

Èfron, A.S., 'Stranicy bylogo', *Zvezda*, 6 (1975), pp.148-49.

Èfron, A.S., 'Stranicy vospominanij', *Zvezda*, 3 (1973), pp.154-80; extracts in *Vestnik R.Kh.D.*, 116 (1975), pp.179-84.

Èfron, A.S. *Stranicy vospominanij* (Paris: Lev, 1979).

Èfron, A.S., 'Ustnye rasskazy', *Zvezda*, 7 (1988), pp.41-45.

'Končina A.S. Èfron', *Russkaja mysl'*, 28.5.1975.

Elenev, Nikolaj, 'Kem byla Marina Cvetaeva?', *Grani*, 39 (1958), pp.141-59.

Enišerlov, V., 'Esli duša rodilas' krylatoj', *Ogonek*, October 1982, pp.18-19.

Èrenburg, Ilja Grigor'evič, *Ljudi, gody, žizn'* (Moscow: Sov. pisatel', 1961), v. II, pp.369-80.

Èrenburg, I.G., 'Poèzija Mariny Cvetaevoj', in *Literaturnaja Moskva*, v. II, (1956), pp.709-15.

Èrenburg, I.G., *Portrety russkikh poètov* (Berlin: Argonavty, 1922; reprint, München, 1972).

Études de lettres, Faculté des lettres de l'Université de Lausanne, Ser. III, t. 10, 1977.

Fedotova, E.N., 'Pis'ma Mariny Cvetaevoj k Fedotovu', *Novyj žurnal*, 63 (1961), pp.162-64.

Feinstein, Elaine, *A Captive Lion: The Life of Marina Tsvetayeva* (London: Hutchinson, 1987).

Feinstein, Elaine: *Marina Tsvetayeva*, Lives of Modern Women (London: Penguin Books, 1989).

Flejšman, L., Kh'juz (Hughes), R., Raevskaja-Kh'juz, O., *Russkij Berlin 1921-23: Po materialam arkhiva B.I. Nikolaevskogo* (Paris: YMCA-Press, 1983).

Foster, Ludmilla A., *Bibliography of Russian Émigré Literature 1918-68*, v. I-II (Boston, Mass.: Hall, 1970).

Gercyk, Evgenija, *Vospominanija* (Paris: YMCA-Press, 1973).

Gibson, Aleksey, *Russian Poetry and Criticism in Paris from 1920 to 1940* (The Hague: Leuxenhoff, 1990).

Gippius, Zinaida Nikolaevna, *Pis'ma k Berberovoj i Khodaseviču*, edited by Erika Freiberger Sheikholeslami (Ann Arbor: Ardis, 1978).

Gordon, Nina, 'O Marina Cvetaevoj', *Voprosy literatury*, 12 (1988), pp.176-187.

Gor'kij i sovetskie pisateli: neizdannaja perepiska (Moscow, 1963).

Guenther, Johannes von, *Ein Leben im Ostwind* (München: Biederstein, 1969).

Gul', Roman, *Ja unes Rossiju: apologija èmigracii*, part I, *Rossija v Germanii* (New York, 1981); part II, *Rossija vo Francii* (New York, 1984).

Gumilev, Nikolaj Stepanovič, 'Stat'i i zametki o russkoj poèzii', in *Sobranie sočinenij v 4 tomakh* (Washington, 1968), IV, pp.293-94.

Il'ina, Natal'ja, 'Anna Akhmatova v poslednie gody ee žizni', *Oktjabr'*, 2 (1977), pp.107-34.

Istorija Gos. ordena Lenina Biblioteki SSSR im. V.I. Lenina za 100 let 1862-1962 (Moscow: Izd. biblioteki, 1962).

Ivanov, Georgij Vladimirovič, 'Kitajskie teni', *Poslednie novosti*, 22.2.1930 (Depositum Marina Cvetaeva, Basle).

Ivask, Jurij P., 'Blagorodnaja Cvetaeva', in Cvetaeva, *Lebedinyj stan* (Paris: YMCA-Press, 1971), pp.15-34.

Ivask, Ju. P., 'Pis'ma M.I. Cvetaevoj', in *Russkij literaturnyj arkhiv* (New York: 1956), pp.207-08.

Ivask, Ju.P., 'Proščanie s Marinoj Cvetaevoj: Roždestvo 1938', *Russkaja mysl'*, no.3225, 12.10.1978.

Ivinskaja, Ol'ga, *V plenu vremeni: gody s B. Pasternakom* (Paris: Fayard, 1978).

350 BIBLIOGRAPHY

Izvol'skaja, Elena, 'Poèt obrečennosti', *Vozdušnye puti*, 3 (1963), pp.150-60.
Izvol'skaja, E.A., 'Ten' na stenakh: o Cvetaevoj', *Opyty*, 3 (1954), pp.153-59.
Kagan, Ju.M., *I.V. Cvetaev* (Moscow, 1987).
Kannak, Evgenija, 'Vospominanija o "Gelikone" ', *Russkaja mysl'*, 17.1.1974.
Karlinsky, Simon, *Cvetaeva: Her Life and Art* (Berkeley, Los Angeles: University of California Press, 1966).
Karlinsky, S., *Marina Tsvetayeva: The Woman, her World and her Poetry* (Cambridge University Press, 1985).
Karlinsky, S., 'Pis'ma M. Cvetaevoj k V. Khodaseviču', *Novyj žurnal*, 89 (1967), pp.102-09.
Karlinsky, S., 'Tsvetayeva's Turn', *London Review of Books*, 12.11.1987.
Kemball, Robin, 'La poétique de Tsvetayeva: son audace, – et son innocence', in *Etudes de lettres*, Univ. de Lausanne, III, t. 10 (1977), pp.38-43.
Khenkin, Kirill, 'Ispanskij bloknot', *Kontinent*, 16 (1978), pp.265-88.
Khodasevič, Vladislav Felicianovič, 'Marina Cvetaeva "Molodec": zametki o stikhakh', *Čast' reči*, 4/5 (1984), pp.44-49.
Korjakov, Mikhail, 'Listki iz bloknota: Marina Cvetaeva v Moskve', *Novoe russkoe slovo*, 4.7.1965.
Kovalevskij, P.E., *Zarubežnaja Rossija* (Paris: Librarie des Cinq Continents, 1971).
Kovčeg: sbornik russkikh pisatelej v Čekhoslovakii, pod red. Val. Bulgakova, S.V. Zavadskogo, Mariny Cvetaevoj (Prague: Legiographie, 1926).
Kozlova, L., 'Foto, kotorykh togda ne bylo', *Neva*, 9 (1987), pp.184-88.
Krajnyj, Anton (pseudonym of Z. Gippius), 'Stikhi, um i glupost' ', *Poslednie novosti*, 22.7.1926 (Depositum M. Cvetaeva, Basle).
Krejd, V., 'Marina Cvetaeva i *Sovremennye zapiski*', *Novyj žurnal*, 178 (1990), pp.257-69.
Krivitsky, W.G., *Agent de Staline* (Paris: Coopération, 1940).
Kubka, František, 'Smutná romance o Marině Cvětajevové', in *Hlasy od východu* (Prague: Čs. spisovatel, 1960), p.14-25.
Kudrova, Irma, 'Dom na gore: M.C., 1923 god', *Zvezda*, 8 (1987), pp.156-77.
Kudrova, I., 'Pis'ma M.C. k Maksimilianu Vološinu', *NM*, 2 (1977), pp.231-36.
Kudrova, I., 'Polgoda v Pariže: k biografii M. Cvetaevoj', *Wiener slawistischer Almanach*, Sonderband III, pp.129-59.
Kudrova, I., 'Poslednie gody čužbiny: Vanv-Pariž 1937-1938', *Novyj mir*, 3 (1989), pp. 213-228.
Kudrova, Irma, *Versty, dali: Marina Cvetaeva, 1922-1939* (Moscow: Sov. Rossija, 1991).
Kupčenko, V.P., 'M.C., pis'ma k M.A. Vološinu', *Ežegodnik rukopisnogo otdela Puškinskogo Doma* (1975), pp.151-57.
Kupčenko, V.P., *Ostrov Koktebel'* (Moscow, 1981).
Kuprina, Ksenija A., *Kuprin – moj otec* (Moscow: Sov. Rossija, 1971).
Kvanina, Tatjana, 'Tak bylo', *Oktjabr'* 9 (1982), pp.195-201.
Lampl, Horst, 'Briefe Marina Cvetaevas an Ol'ga Kolbasina-Černova', *Wiener slavistisches Jahrbuch*, 22 (1976), pp.109-16.
50 let Gosudarstvennomu Muzeju izobrazitel'nykh iskusstv im. A.S. Puškina (Moscow, 1962).
Letopis' žizni i tvorčestva M. Gor'kogo, v. III, (Moscow: AN, 1959).
Literaturnaja Moskva: lit.-khudožestvennyj sbornik Moskovskikh pisatelej, II (1956).

BIBLIOGRAPHY 351

Losskaja, V. (Lossky, V.), *Marina Cvetaeva v žizni* (Tenafly N.J., 1989).
Lossky, Veronique, 'M. Cvetaeva: Souvenirs de contemporains', *Wiener slawistischer Almanach*, Sonderband III, (1981), pp.213-59.
Lossky, V., *Marina Tsvétaeva: Un itinéraire poétique* (Malakoff: Solin, 1987).
Lur'e, Vera, 'M. Cvetaeva: *Remeslo*' (review), *Novaja russkaja kniga*, 3/4 (1923), pp.14-15.
Majakovskij, V.V., *Polnoe sobranie sočinenij*, v. XII (Moscow, 1959).
Mandel'štam, Nadežda Jakovlevna, *Vospominanija* (New York: Izd. im. Čekhova, 1970).
Mandel'štam, N.Ja., *Vtoraja kniga* (Paris: YMCA-Press, 1972).
Mandel'štam, Osip E., *Sobranie sočinenij v 3 t.*, second edition, v. I, (Washington, 1967).
Marina Tsvetaeva: trudy 1-go meždunarodnogo simpozinma (Lausanne, 30, VI.-3. VII. 1982) pod red. R. Kemballa v Sotrudničestve s E.G. Ètkindom i L.M. Gellerom (Bern: Peter Lang, 1991).
Mindlin, Emilij L., *Neobyknovennye sobesedniki* (Moscow: Sov. pisatel', 1968).
Mirskij, Dmitrij S., *Geschichte der russischen Literatur* (München: Piper, 1964).
Mnukhin, L.A., 'Svjatoe remeslo poèta: pis'ma i vospominanija A. Èfron o materi', *Literaturnoe obozrenie*, 12 (1982), pp.89-103.
Morkovin, Vadim, ed., *Marina Cvetaeva: pis'ma k A. Teskovoj* (Prague: Academia, 1969).
Muromceva (Bunina), V.N., 'U starogo Pimena', in *NP*, pp.531-41.
Nicolas Mikhailovitch, Grand Duc, *La Fin du tsarisme; Lettres inédites à Frédéric Masson 1914-18*, publ. par la Bibliothèque Slave de Paris (Paris: Payot, 1968).
Nikolić, Milica, 'Odgovori Marine Cvetajeve', in M.C., *Zemaljska obeležja* (Belgrad, 1973), pp.7-51.
Odoevceva, Irina, 'Nesostojavšajasja vstreča', *Russkaja mysl'*, no.3148, 21.4.1977.
Otčet Moskovskago Publičnago i Rumjancovskago muzeev za 1909 god (Moscow, 1910).
Pamjati A.A. Akhmatovoj (Paris: YMCA-Press, 1974).
Parnok, Sofija Jakovlevna, *Sobranie stikhotvorenij*, edited by S. Poljakova (Ann Arbor: Ardis, 1979).
Pasternak, Boris Leonidovič, *Sočinenija*, v. II (Ann Arbor: Ardis, 1961); see 'Avtobiografičeskij očerk, Tri teni', pp.45-48; 'Okhrannaja gramota', pp.203-93; 'Posmertnoe pis'mo R.M. Ril'ke', pp.343-45.
Pasternak, B.L., 'Brief an Rilke, 12.4.1926', in M.C., *Nesobr. proizvedenija* (München: 1971), pp.681-83.
Pjatidesjatiletie Rumjancovskago Muzeja v Moskve 1862-1912 (Moscow, 1913).
'Poezdka v Elabugu', in M.C., *NP*, pp.639-47, see: Schweitzer, V.
Poljakova, Sofija, 'Poèzija i pravda v cikle stikhotvorenij Cvetaevoj "Podruga" ', *Wiener slawistischer Almanach*, Sonderband III, pp.113-21.
Poljakova, S., *Zakatnye ony dni: Cvetaeva i Parnok* (Ann Arbor: Ardis, 1982).
Poretsky, Elisabeth, K., *Our Own People: A Memoir of 'Ignace Reiss' and his Friends* (Oxford: Oxford University Press, 1969).
Rakusa, Ilma; F. Ingold, 'M.I. Cvetaeva im Briefwechsel mit R.M. Rilke', *Zeitschrift für slavische Philologie*, 41 (1980) no.1, pp.127-73.
Razumovsky, Maria, *Marina Cvetaeva: mif i dejstvitel'nost'* (London: Overseas Publications Interchange, 1983).
Razumovsky, M., *Marina Zwetajewa: Mythos und Wahrheit* (Vienna: Age

d'Homme/Karolinger, 1981); second edition, *Marina Zwetajewa: Eine Biographie* (Frankfurt: Suhrkamp, 1989 and 1994).

Razumovsky, M., *Marina Tsvetaieva: Mythe et réalité*, traduit du russe par Alexandra Pletnioff-Boutin (Montricher/Suisse/: Les Editions Noir sur Blanc, 1988).

Reznikova, Natalja Viktorovna, 'Pamjati Mariny Ivanovny Cvetaevoj' *Vestnik R.Kh.D.*, 135 (1981), pp.159-63.

Rilke, Rainer Maria, *Sämtliche Werke*, v. II (Wiesbaden: Insel, 1955).

Rilke, R.M., M. Zwetajewa, B. Pasternak, *Briefwechsel*, edited by Yevgeny Pasternak, Yelena Pasternak and K. Azadovsky, translations from the Russian by H. Pross-Werth (Frankfurt: Insel, 1983).

Rilke, R.M. 'Iz perepiski Ril'ke, Cvetaevoj i Pasternaka v 1926 g.', edited by K. Azadovskij and E. Pasternak, *Voprosy literatury*, 4 (1978), pp.233-80.

Russkaja literatura v èmigracii; sbornik statej pod red. N. Poltorackogo (Pittsburgh: 1972).

Russkij literaturnyj arkhiv, pod red. M. Karpoviča i Dm. Čiževskogo (New York: 1956).

Russkij sbornik, v. I (Paris, 1946).

Saakjanc, Anna Aleksandrovna, 'O pravde "letopisi" i pravde poèta', *Voprosy literatury*, 11 (1983), p.208-15.

Saakjanc, A.A., *Marina Cvetaeva: stranicy žizni i tvorčestva 1910-1922* (Moscow: Sov. pisatel', 1986).

Saakjanc, A.A., 'Stranicy žizni: beseda o tvorčestve Mariny Cvetaevoj', *Knižnoe obozrenie*, no.34, 22.8.1986.

Šaginjan, Marietta S., 'Čelovek i vremja, č. 5: Moskva-malen'kaja', *NM*, 1 (1977), pp.79-134.

Šaginjan, M.S., 'Samaja nastojaščaja poèzija' (1911), *Voprosy literatury*, 12 (1983), pp.203-09

Šakhovskaja Zinaida Alekseevna, 'Marina Cvetaeva', *Novyj žurnal*, 87 (1967), pp.130-35; the same in Šakhovskaja, Z., *Otraženija* (Paris: YMCA-Press, 1975), pp.160-75.

Šakhovskoj, Ioann, Arkhiepiskop, *Biografija junosti* (Paris: YMCA-Press, 1977).

(Schweitzer, Viktoria), 'Poezdka v Elabugu', in M.C. *Neizdannye pis'ma*, (Paris: YMCA-Press, 1972), pp.639-47.

Schweitzer, V., *Byt i bytie Mariny Cvetaevoj* (Fontenay-aux-Roses: Sintaksis, 1988 and Moscow: Interprint, 1992).

Schweitzer, V., 'Svoimi putjami: biograf. očerk', *Stikh. I*, pp.(7)-(38).

Schweitzer, V., 'Vozvraščenie domoj', *Sintaksis*, 11 (1983), pp.188-204.

Serge, Victor; Maurice Wullens; Alfred Rosmer, *L'Assassinat politique et l'URSS: Crime à Lausanne en marge des procès de Moscou (La mort d'Ignace Reiss)* (Paris: Tisné, 1939).

Sezeman, D., 'M. Cvetaeva v Moskve (Po ličnym vospominanijam)', *Vestnik R.Kh.D.*, 128 (1979), p.177-79.

Sezeman, Dmitrij, 'Na bol'ševskoj dače', *Literaturnaja gazeta*, 27.11.1990.

Slonim, Mark L'vovič, 'Beseda s Paustovskim', *Novoe russkoe slovo*, 10.3.1974.

Slonim, M.L., 'O Marine Cvetaevoj: iz vospominanij', *Novyj žurnal*, 100 (1970), pp.155-79; 103 (1971), pp.143-76.

Slonim, M.L., ' "The History of a Dedication": Marina Tsvetayeva's Reminiscences of Osip Mandelstam', *Oxford Slavonic Papers* 11 (1964), p.112-13.

BIBLIOGRAPHY 353

Slonim, M.L., 'Notes on Tsvetayeva', *The Russian Review*, 31 (1972), no.2, pp.117-25.

Stepun, Fedor A., *Byvšee i nesbyvšeesja* (New York: Izd, im Čekhova, 1956), v. I.

Stroblová, Jana, *Marina Cvetajevová: Hodina duše*, (Prague: Čs. spisovatel, 1971).

Struve, Gleb Petrovič (editor), M. Cvetaeva, *Lebedinyj stan* (München, 1957); 2nd ed., *Lebedinyj stan, Perekop* (Paris: YMCA-Press, 1972).

Struve, G.P., 'Ob Adamoviče – kritike', *Grani*, 34/35 (1957), pp.365-69.

Struve, G.P., *Russkaja literatura v izgnanii* (New York: Izd. im Čikhova, 1956).

Struve, G.P. and Nikita Struve (editors), M. Cvetaeva, *Neizdannye pis'ma* (Paris: YMCA-Press, 1972).

Tarusskie stranicy: lit. khudožestvennyj illjustrirovannyj sbornik (Kaluga, 1961).

Terapiano, Jurij, *Vstreči* (New York: Izd. im Čekhova, 1953).

Vaksberg, Arkadij, 'Pravda o platnom agente', *Literaturnaja gazeta*, 21.11.1990.

Varšavskij, Vladimir, *Nezamečennoe pokolenie* (New York: Izd. im. Čekhova, 1956).

Vikent'ev, S., 'Stroki o syne', *Rodina*, 3 (1975), p.28-29.

Vil'čkovskij, Kiril, 'Perepiska Mariny Cvetaevoj s Anatoliem Štejgerom', *Opyty*, 5 (1955), pp.40-45.

Višnjak, Mark V., *'Sovremennye zapiski'*, (Bloomington, 1957).

Volkonskij, Sergej (Prince), *Byt i bytie* (Berlin, 1924; reprint, Paris, 1978).

Volosov, V.M.; I.M. Kudrova, 'Pis'ma M.S. Evgeniju Lannu', *Wiener slawistischer Almanach*, Sonderband III, pp.162-94.

Vospominanija o E. Kazakeviče (Moscow: Sov. Pisatel', 1979).

Weidlé, Vladimir, 'Cvetaeva – do Elabugi', in *O poètakh i poèzii* (Paris: YMCA-Press, 1973), pp.65-73.

Weiss, Louise, *Mémoires d'une européenne*, v. II (Paris: Payot, 1970).

Williams, Robert C., *Culture in Exile: Russian Émigrés in Germany 1881-1941* (Ithaca: Cornell Univ. Press, 1972).

Zajcev, Boris K., *Dalekoe* (Washington: Inter-Language Literature Association, 1965).

Žernakova-Nikolaeva, Aleksandra, 'Cvetaevskij dom', *Russkaja mysl'*, 23.3.1963 and 26.3.1963.

Neue Zürcher Zeitung, September 1937–February 1938.

Additions to Secondary Sources, 1994

Bolševo. Lit. almanakh. 2 (Moscow: Pisatel, 1992).

Chentalinski, Vitali, *La parole ressuscitée. Dans les archives littéraires du K.G.B.* (Paris: Laffont, 1993).

Kudrova, I., 'Tret'ja versija. Ešče raz o poslednikh dnjakh M.C', *NM* 2 (1994), pp.205-29.

Marina Cvetaeva. Stat'i i teksty (*Wiener slawist. Almanach*, Sonderbd. 32, 1992).

Marina Cvetaeva. Poet i vremja. Vystavka k 100-letiju so dnja roždenija (Moscow: Galart 1992).

Mierau, Fritz, *Russen in Berlin, 1918-33* (Berlin: Quarriga, 1988).

Vospominanija o Marine Cvetaevoj. Ed. L.A. Mnukhin i L.M. Turčinskij (Moscow: Sov. pisatel', 1992).

Zubova, L.V., 'Pis'ma Sergeja Efrona Evgeniju Nezdel'skomu', Abo/Turku 1994 (*Russica Aboensia*. 1).

INDEX AND NOTES ON PERSONS
MENTIONED IN THE TEXT

have achieved popular success in French and English translations. 172, 210, 266, 302; *notes* 327; *bibl.* 348, 349.

Berdjaev (Berdyayev), Nikolaj Aleksandrovič (1874-1948): Philosopher and religious thinker. Exiled from the USSR in 1922. Lived in Paris. Has had a certain influence on Western thought. 70, 110, 135, 137, 153, 187, 210, 232, 233, 266.

Berg, Ariadna Emil'evna. (*née* Wolters) (1899-1979). *bibl.* 345.

Bessarabov, Boris Ivanovič (1903?-1970): Soviet agronomist. 126, 131.

Blok, Aleksandr Aleksandrovič (1880-1921): Famous Petersburg Symbolist poet. 56, 95, 110, 111, 125, 135, 143, 242; *bibl.* 340.

Brjusov (Bryusov), Valerij Jakovlevič (1873-1924): Poet and leader of the Symbolist movement in Moscow. Editor of the journal *Vesy*. From 1920 member of the Communist Party, and literary bureaucrat. 15, 44, 46, 52-3, 56-8, 70-1, 78-80, 110, 121, 181; *bibl.* 339, 345, 348.

Bulgakov, Sergej Nikolaevič (Father Sergy) (1870-1944): Philosopher and Christian thinker. Ordained a priest in Moscow in 1918. Lived in Prague, Berlin and Paris. Professor of Orthodox theology. 110, 137, 149, 153, 179, 187, 232, 241.

Bulgakov, Valentin Fedorovič (1886-1966): Last secretary of Lev Tolstoy. Emigrated to Prague. Returned to the USSR in 1949. 174; *bibl.* 350.

Bunin, Ivan Alekseevič (1870-1953): Prose writer. Emigrated to France. Awarded the Nobel Prize for Literature in 1933. 171, 187, 192, 210, 214, 226, 241, 275, 305-6, 307; *bibl.* 348.

Bunina, Vera Nikolaevna (*née* Muromceva) (1881-1961): Wife of I.A. Bunin. 214, 221, 235, 237-8, 241, 244, 248, 258, 275; *notes* 332, 335; *bibl.* 345, 351.

Čabrov-Podgaeckij (Chabrov-Podgayetsky), Aleksej Aleksandrovič (1888-1935?): Actor of the Vakhtangov Theatre. Emigrated to the West after 1922. Entered a Catholic monastic order in the thirties. 142.

Čackina (Chatskina), Sofija Isaakovna: Until 1917 editor of the journal *Severnye zapiski*. 90-1.

Černov (Chernov), Viktor Mikhajlovič (1876-1952): Leader of the Social Revolutionary party. Minister for Agriculture under the Provisional Government. Emigrated to the United States in 1920. 172.

Černova-Kolbasina, Ol'ga Eliseevna (1886-1964): Married first to V.M. Černov. Lived in Prague and Paris. Returned to the USSR in 1964 and died three months later in Moscow. 160, 173-3, 174, 176-7, 179, 181, 183, 188, 193-4; *notes* 326, 327; *bibl.* 345, 348, 350.

Černova-Sosinskaja, Ariadna Viktorovna (1909-1978): Daughter of the above. Returned to the USSR in 1964. 172, 173 (*ill.*), 174, 193-4; *bibl.* 345.

Černyj (Chorny), Saša (real name: Aleksandr Mikhajlovič Glikberg) (1880-1932): Poet. Emigrated to Berlin, later to Paris. 147.

Cetlin (Tsetlin), Mikhail Osipovič (Pseudonym: Amari) (1882-1946): Muscovite poet. Emigrated to Paris. Founded the journal *Novyj žurnal* in New York. 112, 304.

Chambrun, Charles Comte de (1875-1952): First secretary of the French Embassy in Petrograd, later Ambassador of France. 99, 101, 109; *bibl.* 348.

Chernov-Andreyev, Olga: Daughter of C. Kolbasina. 174, 194.

Čirikov (Chirikov), Evgenij Nikolaevič (1864-1932): Prose writer. Emigrated to Prague. 155.

Čukovskaja (Chukovskaya), Lidija Korneevna (*b.* 1907): Woman of letters. Friend of Akhmatova. 287, 294, 295, 301, 309; *bibl.* 348.

358INDEX & NOTES

Halpern-Andronikova: see Andronikova-Halpern.
Hippius: see Gippius.
Holliday, Sofija Evgen'evna (Sonechka) (1896-1935): Actress of the Vakh-tangov Theatre in Moscow. 114-15, 258-9, 273; notes 320; bibl. 344.
Ilovajskij (Ilovaisky), Dmitrij Ivanovič (1832-1919): Historian. 9, 18, 117, 214, 237.
Ivanov, Georgij Vladimirovič (1894-1958): Poet of the Petersburg School. Emigrated to France. Important representative of the Paris School of Russian poetry. 91, 94, 221, 223, 269; bibl. 349.
Ivanov, Vjačeslav Ivanovič (1866-1949): Symbolist poet in Petersburg and Moscow. From 1924 lived in Italy. 56, 90, 112.
Ivask, Jurij Pavlovič (Prof. George Ivask) (1896-1986): Poet and literary critic. After the war, professor at the University of Massachusetts. 12, 53, 73, 81, 132, 136, 145, 226, 238-9, 255, 270-1, 275, 304-5; notes 320, 330, 333; bibl. 340, 346, 349.
Ivinskaja, Ol'ga Vsevolodovna (b. 1912): Translator and memoirist. 247-8, 281, 291; bibl. 349.
Izvol'skaja, Elena Aleksandrovna (Helen Iswolsky) (1897-1975): Woman of letters. Emigrated to Paris and Rome. After the war lived in the United States. 206-7, 209-10, 222-3, 229, 265-6, 304; bibl. 350.
Jakobson, Roman Osipovič (1896-1982): Linguist. Co-founder of the Prague Linguistic Circle. Emigrated to the United States, from 1949 to 1967 professor at Harvard University. 151.
Jašvil (Yashvil), Princess Natal'ja Grigor'evna (1861-1939): Translator. Emigrated to Prague. Director of the Kondakov Institute. 151.
Kandaurov, K.B. (1865-1930): Painter of M. Vološin's circle. 84.
Kannak, Evgenija Osipovna (1903-87): Woman of letters. Emigrated to Germany. After 1933 lived in France. 143; bibl. 350.
Kannegiesser, Leonid Ioakimovič (d. 1919): Petersburg poet. Executed after his assassination attempt on Urickij. 91.
Kantor, Mikhail L'vovič (1884-1970): Editor of the newspaper Zveno in Paris. bibl. 346.
Kerenskij (Kerensky), Aleksandr Fedorovič (1881-1970): President of the Council of the Provisional Government in 1917. From 1940 lived in the United States. 104-5.
Khodasevič (Khodasevich), Vladislav Felicianovič (1886-1939): Muscovite poet. Emigrated to Paris. Influential literary critic of the newspaper Vozroždenie. 63, 71, 145, 158, 172, 181, 194, 210-11, 233, 239-40, 242, 258, 266, 275; notes 333; bibl. 346, 349, 350.
Kočetkov (Kochetkov), Aleksandr Sergeevič (1900-53): Poet and translator in Moscow. 290; bibl. 346.
Kogan, Petr Semenovič (1872-1932): Historian. People's Commissar after the Revolution. 136.
Kolbasina-Černova: see Černova-Kolbasina.
Kondakov, Nikodim Pavlovič (1884-1925): Famous Byzantinist. From 1919 professor at the University of Prague. 104, 151, 178, 180.
Kručenykh (Kruchonykh), Aleksej Eliseevič (1886-1968): Muscovite poet and theoritician of Futurism. 284, 288 (ill.), 290.
Kubka, František (1894-1969): Czech writer, lived in Prague. 159, 235; bibl. 350.
Kuprin, Aleksandr Ivanovič (1870-1938): Prose writer. Emigrated to Paris.

[Indexed by Timothy H. Penton]